World of the Buddha

World of the Buddha

An Introduction to Buddhist Literature

Edited with Introduction and Commentaries by
LUCIEN STRYK

GROVE PRESS, INC.
NEW YORK

First Evergreen Edition 1982
First Printing 1982
ISBN: 0-394-17974-9
Library of Congress Catalog Card Number: 81-48543

Library of Congress Cataloging in Publication Data

Main entry under title:

World of the Buddha.

    (Grove Press Eastern philosophy and literature series)
       Reprint. Originally published: 1st ed. Garden City, N.Y.:
       Doubleday, 1968.
    1. Buddhist literature. I. Stryk, Lucien.
    II. Series.
[BQ1012.W67 1982]   294.3′8   81-48543
ISBN 0-394-17974-9 (pbk.)   AACR2

Manufactured in the United States of America

GROVE PRESS, INC., 196 West Houston Street, New York, N.Y. 10014

Grove Press Eastern Philosophy and Literature Series
Edited by Hannelore Rosset

Grateful acknowledgment is made to the following for copyrighted material:

CASSELL AND COMPANY LTD.
Excerpts from *The Living Thoughts of Gotama The Buddha*, by Ananda K. Coomaraswamy and I. B. Horner. Reprinted by permission of the publisher and I. B. Horner.

THE CLARENDON PRESS
Excerpts from *Sacred Books of the East*, edited by F. Max Muller. Vol. X *The Dhammapada*, translated by F. Max Muller, Vol. XXXI *The Saddharma-Pundarika*, translated by H. Kern, Vol. XLIX *The Buddha-Karita of Asvaghosha*, translated by E. B. Cowell. *A Record of the Buddhist Religion*, by I-Tsing, translated by J. Takakusu. Reprinted by permission of the publisher.

COLUMBIA UNIVERSITY PRESS
Excerpts from Sources of *Chinese Tradition, Sources of Indian Tradition, Sources of Japanese Tradition*, by William Theodore De Bary and others. Reprinted by permission of the publisher.

CONSTABLE PUBLISHERS
"The Going Forth" from *Early Buddhism*, by T. W. Rhys Davids. Reprinted by permission of the publisher.

DOUBLEDAY & COMPANY, INC.
Excerpts from *Zen: Poems, Prayers, Sermons, Anecdotes, Interviews*, by Lucien Stryk and Takashi Ikemoto. Reprinted by permission of the publisher.

E. P. DUTTON & CO., INC.
Excerpts from *A Buddhist Bible*, by Dwight Goddard. Copyright 1938 by E. P. Dutton & Co., Inc. Reprinted by permission of the publisher.

HARPER & ROW, PUBLISHERS & GEORGE G. HARRAP & COMPANY LIMITED
Excerpts from *Buddha and the Gospel of Buddhism*, by Ananda K. Coomaraswamy. Reprinted by permission of the publishers.

C. F. HORNE
Excerpts from "Khaggavisana Sutta" in *The Sacred Books and Early Literature of The East*, Vol. X, edited by Charles F. Horne. Reprinted by permission.

THE HUDSON REVIEW
The text of *Sin Xai*, translated by Ronald Perry. Reprinted by permission from *The Hudson Review*, Vol. XX, Number 1 (Spring 1967). Copyright © 1967 by *The Hudson Review, Inc.*

THE OPEN COURT PUBLISHING COMPANY
Excerpts from *Acvaghosa's Discourse on the Awakening of Faith in the Mahayana*, by Daisetz Teitaro Suzuki. Reprinted by permission of the publisher.

OXFORD UNIVERSITY PRESS
Excerpts from *The Tibetan Book of the Great Liberation,* edited by W. Y. Evans-Wentz. *The Hevajra Tantra,* by D. L. Snellgrove. Reprinted by permission of the publisher.

PALI TEXT SOCIETY
Excerpts from *Minor Anthologies of the Pali Canon,* Part II, by F. L. Woodward. "Tevigga Sutta" in *Sacred Books of the Buddhists,* Vol. II, translated by T. W. Rhys Davids. Reprinted by permission of the publisher.

G. P. PUTNAM'S SONS
Excerpts from *Buddhism,* by T. W. Rhys Davids. Reprinted by permission of the publisher.

THE RONALD PRESS COMPANY
Excerpts from *The Path of Buddha: Buddhism Interpreted by Buddhists,* edited by Kenneth W. Morgan. Copyright © 1956 by The Ronald Press Company, New York. Reprinted by permission of the publisher.

ROUTLEDGE & KEGAN PAUL LTD. AND BARNES & NOBLE, INC.
Excerpts from *The History of Buddhist Thought,* by Edward Thomas. Reprinted by permission of the publishers.

SCHOKEN BOOKS INC. AND LUZAC & COMPANY LTD.
Excerpts from *Outlines of Mahayana Buddhism,* by Daisetz Teitaro Suzuki. Reprinted by permission of the publisher.

THE SIXTIES PRESS
"This Slowly Drifting Cloud Is Pitiful," by Dogen, translated by Lucien Stryk, in *The Sixties #10.* Reprinted by permission of the publisher.

WESLEYAN UNIVERSITY PRESS
Excerpts from "From the Mahāvastu" in *The Life of The Buddha,* by A. Foucher. Reprinted by permission of the publisher.

YALE UNIVERSITY PRESS
Excerpts from *Buddhist Parables,* by E. W. Burlingame. Reprinted by permission of the publisher.

The editor is indebted to the Asian Literature Program of the Asia Society for a grant which made possible the inclusion of some of the material in this book.

To the memory of Takashi Ikemoto

1906-1980

LUCIEN STRYK studied literature and philosophy at Indiana University, the Sorbonne, and London University, and held graduate grants in Asian thought at Yale and the University of Chicago. He has published eight books of verse, including *Selected Poems*, a book of essays, *Encounter with Zen: Writings on Poetry and Zen*, and, with the late Takashi Ikemoto, translated, among other volumes, *Zen Poems of China and Japan: the Crane's Bill; Zen: Poems, Prayers, Sermons, Anecdotes, Interviews; The Penguin Book of Zen Poetry;* and two collections of the Zen poems of Shinkichi Takahashi, *Afterimages* and *Triumph of the Sparrow*. Among awards he has received for poetry and translation was The Island and Continents Translation Award, and he has held a National Translation Center Grant and a National Endowment for the Arts Poetry Fellowship. Two spoken records of his work have been issued by Folkways Records, *Zen Poems* and *Selected Poems*. He has given poetry readings and lectures throughout the United States and England, and has held a Fulbright Travel/Research Grant and two visiting lectureships in Japan. He teaches Asian literature and poetry at Northern Illinois University.

FOREWORD

There is nothing more personal than an anthology, however one would wish otherwise, and *World of the Buddha*, which draws upon a literature twenty-five hundred years old and sacred to one-third of the world's population, is no exception. I have selected for it texts which, in their English versions, have been of importance to me but which at the same time, I am emboldened to add, have been considered by generations as among the most remarkable in Buddhist literature. This collection, no less imperfect than any of its type, differs in at least one respect from others known to me: it offers fuller versions of some of the most significant works, the *Questions of Milinda* for example, thus, hopefully, preserving the dramatic development of what is essentially a literature of philosophical confrontation.

The book's plan is basically chronological and relatively simple. It begins with a few Jātakas, tales concerning the Buddha's previous states of existence, followed by an account of the life itself. Then come sermons, parables, and numerous discourses, long and short, most involving the Buddha, some his disciples, from both canonical and non-canonical Pāli literature of the Theravada school (the one exception, a selection from the Sanskrit poem and Buddha biography, the *Buddha-Karita*, is placed at the front of the volume for obvious reasons). The second half of the book—more or less—is devoted to the literature of Mahayana Buddhism, in translations from the Sanskrit, Tibetan, Chinese, Japanese, and, the exception there, Lao.

As the book is meant mainly for the newcomer to Bud-

dhism, a scholarly apparatus is not provided, though the
brief commentaries found throughout are designed to be of
help. Diacritical marks and transliterations, on the assumption that words are best left in the form the translators wanted
them, have not been tampered with. Thus in one selection
the Pāli word for doctrine or religious law, "Dhamma," is
employed, in another its Sanskrit form, "Dharma," and so on.
The alert reader should not find the differences between
such variants confusing.

In dividing the book, roughly, between Theravada (Hinayana or Lesser Vehicle) and Mahayana (Great Vehicle)
texts, I have attempted to suggest something of the balance
which, in the Buddhist world, actually exists. The differences
between the schools are treated elsewhere, in the Introduction, and explained in many of the selections, yet it is possible
to see Mahayana as a natural outgrowth of Theravada. There
are of course parallels to be found in the development of a
number of religions, and, schisms and heresies notwithstand-
ing, Buddhism's growth has been consistently strong and comparatively pure.

I am greatly indebted to P. V. Bapat's comprehensive and
authoritative volume *2500 Years of Buddhism* (Publications
Division, Ministry of Information and Broadcasting, Delhi,
India, 1959), not only for much information on Buddhist
literature and history used throughout the book but for the
table of the Tripitaka found at the end of the Foreword.
Other texts which have been of great value, for facts and
suggestive ideas, are Edward J. Thomas's *The History of Buddhist Thought* (Routledge & Kegan Paul, London, 1933),
Christmas Humphreys' *A Buddhist Students' Manual* (The
Buddhist Society, London, 1956), Ananda Coomaraswamy's
Buddha and the Gospel of Buddhism (University Books Inc.,
New York, 1964) and Sir Charles Eliot's *Hinduism and Buddhism*, Volumes I and II (Routledge & Kegan Paul, London,
1921).

Henry Clarke Warren, on whose *Buddhism in Translations*
(Harvard University Press, Cambridge, 1896) I have drawn

heavily in putting together this reader, had this to say about
the differences between Pāli and Sanskrit Buddhist literature:

> After long bothering my head over Sanskrit, I found
> much more satisfaction when I took up the study of
> Pāli. For Sanskrit literature is a chaos; Pāli, a cosmos.
> In Sanskrit every fresh work or author seemed a new
> problem; and as trustworthy Hindu chronology and
> recorded history are almost nil, and as there are many
> systems of philosophy, orthodox as well as unorthodox, the
> necessary data for the solution of the problem were usually
> lacking. Such data, I mean, as who the author was, when
> he lived and wrote, what were the current beliefs and con-
> ceptions of his day, and what his own position was in
> respect to them; such data, in short, as are necessary in
> order to know what to think of an author, and fully to un-
> derstand what he says. Now the subject-matter of Pāli
> literature is nearly always the same, namely, the definite
> system of religion propounded by The Buddha. . . .
> There is, in a general way and in respect of subject-matter,
> considerable unity in Pāli literature.

In spite of the fact that since these words were written much
work has been done, notably by Dr. D. T. Suzuki, to sys-
tematize and make available to English-speaking readers the
chief works of Sanskrit literature, it is nevertheless true that
Buddhists generally think of the Pāli Canon as containing the
larger part of their scripture. Whether, on the other hand,
Pāli literature is clearer in intention and design is still very
much a matter of faith. Certainly Mahayanists are less inclined to think so.

The Pāli Canon is usually referred to as the Tripitaka, or
Three Baskets, and is divided into as many sections, or
Pitakas: Vinaya, which means discipline; Sutta, which means
thread; and Abhidhamma, which means pre-eminent doctrine. There is another division of Pāli scriptures in nine
angas (members): Suttas; Geyya (mixed verse and prose);
Gâthâ (verse); Udâna (impassioned utterance); Veyyâkarana
(explanation); Itivuttaka (sayings beginning with the phrase

"Thus said the Buddha"); Jātaka (stories of former births); Abbhutadhamma (stories of wonders); and Vedalla (questions and answers). Yet the division according to Pitakas is by far the more commonly accepted as authentic. The precise manner in which the Pitakas are broken down into collections, or Nikāyas, would take a great deal of space to describe, but it is to be hoped that the table of the Tripitaka provided will be of some help to the reader anxious to keep his bearings as he reads through the Pāli selections, all identified as such, in the first part of the volume.

Henry Clarke Warren, in the paragraph quoted above, spoke of Pāli literature as a cosmos, but he was an Orientalist who spent his best years in charting it, and his was a labor of love. To one who is not an Orientalist, even the Tripitaka, which gives Pāli literature whatever design it possesses, is a most difficult canon of scriptural writings to read through without confusion. With that in mind, it might prove useful to give some idea at least of what the Tripitaka is. This much we know for certain: it does contain the main scriptures or essential documents of Buddhist literature, though strictly speaking they are the sacred writings of only one Hinayana school, the Theravadins, those of the others being preserved in Sanskrit and Chinese.

The Tripitaka, or Pāli Canon, was not written down until long after the Buddha's death. Though writing was widely practiced in his lifetime, the lack of suitable writing materials made the composition of lengthy works impossible, but there was another reason for its not being recorded: in the tradition of the age the Buddha's disciples were expected to remember his sayings. Like the other Indian teachers of his time, the Buddha taught through dialogue, using set phrases, or sutras, on which he enlarged in a number of ways to suit the occasion. These sutras, rather like catchwords, were meant to be easily remembered, which in part explains their graphic quality and brevity.

Not long after the Buddha's death his sayings were collected by his disciples into the Nikāyas, which probably reached their final form some fifty years later. For a few generations the Nikāyas were handed down by word of mouth, though it is probable that written notes and commentaries were used. The Nikāyas are not books in the ordinary sense. Rather they are compilations of usually short passages the arrangement of which is meant to help in the task of memorization. The suttana, for example, is a group of sutras on a similar theme, yet even a suttana is rarely over a dozen pages long. The first of the Nikāyas is a collection of the longest suttanas, thus it is called the Dīghanikāya, or Collection of Long Ones, while that which follows it in the canon, the Majjhima-nikāya, is the Collection of Suttanas of Medium Length. Such arbitrary arrangement by length rather than theme had obvious disadvantages, which is doubtless why the two Nikāyas added later, the Samyutta and the Anguttara, were put together more systematically into episodes and in order of subjects. The sayings and verses of the Buddha's disciples were compiled in a supplementary Nikāya, the Khuddaka, to which additions were being made as late as the third century B.C. The five Nikāyas form the major portion, and at least to the layman the most important part, of the Tripitaka, the Sutta-pitaka.

The other two parts of the Tripitaka, the Vinaya-pitaka and the Abhidhamma-pitaka, are more easily described. The Vinaya gives the rules of discipline for monks, and is contained in two chief sections followed by a minor work, five books in all. The first book, the Sutta-vibhanga, contains the Pātimokkha, given in part and described in Chapter XII of this volume. Each rule of the Vinaya is followed by a commentary explaining its every word, an account, often lengthy, of the incident which led to the creation of the rule, and special cases and exceptions. The Khandhaka has both a Great Series (Mahāvagga) and a Small Series (Cullavagga) of rules, while the Parivāra is a supplement containing summaries and classifications of the rules. There are rules covering the admission to the Order of Monks (Sangha), the taking of food and medicine, the use of leather for shoes, dress, and furniture, relations with the opposite sex, etc. Every aspect of the monk's life, in and out of the monastery, is touched on by the Vinaya, and prescribed punishments for offences are grave. There is little doubt that the Vinaya is responsible for making the Sangha the longest lived of all religious orders, as active today, particularly in Southeast Asia, as it was over two thousand years ago.

The seven books making up the Abhidhamma-pitaka, which offer a more elaborate and more classified exposition of the doctrine as it is set out in the Nikāyas, were added to the canonical books, though the tradition is that the works were thought out by the Buddha in the fourth week after his enlightenment. The Abhidhamma is the most difficult to read—and to the layman the least interesting—of the Pitakas. The first book, the Dhamma-sangani, or Enumeration of Dharmas, concerns mental elements or processes, the second, the Vibhanga, or Distinction or Determination, is a further examination of the same subjects, and so on.

Regarding Pāli, the language of the Tripitaka, Sir Charles Eliot, in Volume I of the book mentioned above, has this to say:

> Pali . . . is regarded by Buddhist tradition as the language spoken by the Master. In the time of Asoka the dialect of Magadha must have been understood over the greater part of India, like Hindustani in modern times, but in some details of grammar and phonetics Pali differs from Mâgadhî Prakrit and seems to have been influenced by Sanskrit and by western dialects. Being a literary rather than a popular language it was probably a mixed form of speech and it has been conjectured that it was elaborated in Avanti or in Gândhâra where was the great Buddhist University of Takshaśîlâ. Subsequently it died out as a literary language in India but in Ceylon, Burma, Siam, and Camboja it became the vehicle of a considerable religious and scholastic literature. . . . It is probable that the Buddha used not Pali in the strict sense but the spoken language of Magadha, and that this dialect did not differ from Pali more than Scotch or Yorkshire from standard English. . . .

In addition to canonical Pāli literature, there are important non-canonical works such as the *Milindapañha,* Buddhaghosa's *Vissudhi Magga,* and the verse chronicles of Ceylon history *Dīpavamsa* and *Mahāvamsa,* all either represented or described in the text of this volume.

Pāli Buddhist literature, whether canonical or not, is associated with the Theravada school, while Sanskrit Buddhist literature is associated with the Mahayana school. Though there is no complete canon of books preserved in the latter, the Sarvāstivada school possessed the Āgamas, which corresponded to the Pāli Nikāyas, and seven books of its own Abhidhamma, while the Mūla-sarvāstivada sect had a Vinaya-pitaka. Sanskrit Buddhist classics like the *Mahāvastu, Lalitavistara,* Asvaghosha's *Buddha-Karita,* and *Mahāyāna-sraddha-utpadda* are either represented in the volume or discussed in commentaries. The *Jātakamālā* (Garland of Birth Stories), a popular work by Asvaghosha's follower, Āryasūra, was not only praised by the Chinese traveler I-Tsing but provided the versions of the Jātakas used by the painters of the walls of the world-famous Ajantā caves. The vast Mahayana sutra literature is both represented and described in the volume, as is the work of the three greatest philosophers of the school—Nāgārjuna, Asanga, and Vasubandhu—and that of Shāntideva, perhaps the most eminent of late Mahayana poet-philosophers of India.

For a description of Mahayana Sanskrit, the language in which all the above are written, we turn once again to Sir Charles Eliot's *Hinduism and Buddhism* (Volume II):

> The Mahayana scriptures are composed in Sanskrit . . . but it is only rarely—for instance in the works of Asvaghosha —that Buddhist Sanskrit conforms to the rules of the classical language. Usually the words deviate from this standard both in form and meaning and often suggest that the text as we have it is a sanskritized version of an older work in some popular dialect, brought into partial conformity with literary usage. . . . Sanskrit did not become a sacred language for the Mahayanists like Latin for Roman Catholics. It is rather Pali which has assumed this

position among the Hinayanists, for Burmese and Sinhalese translations of the Pitakas acquired no authority. But in the north (the region of Mahayana) the principle that every man might read the Buddha's word in his own vernacular was usually respected: and the populations of Central Asia, the Chinese, the Tibetans, and the Mongols, translated the scriptures into their own languages without attaching any superstitious importance to the original words, unless they were Dhâranîs or spells.

In Tibet there exist more than forty-five hundred translations of Indian Buddhist texts, which are divided into two groups, the Kanjur and the Tanjur, the larger of the two. The former is made up of seven parts—Vinaya, Prajña-pāramitā, Buddhavatamsaka, Ratnakūta, Sutra, Nirvana, and Tantra—while the latter has two parts, Tantra and Sutra. Tibetan translations were made, mainly in the ninth and eleventh centuries, from the literature esteemed by the medieval Buddhism of Bengal. Part at least of the Tibetan Canon has been translated into Mongol.

In China, in addition to native works like those of I-Tsing and Hui-neng, which are represented, there are around sixteen hundred translations from Indian texts, classified in Bunyiu Nanjio's *Catalogue* into four divisions—Sutra-pitaka, Vinaya-pitaka, Abhidharma-pitaka, and Miscellaneous. *Hobo-girin,* a later catalogue, mentions well over two thousand translations. This huge collection was made and revised by order of various Emperors, and the imperial imprimatur is the only standard of canonicity.

In Japan, apart from writings like those of the Zen masters, there are three complete translations of the Chinese Tripit-aka, including twenty-five supplementary volumes in the Taisho edition. As in the case of most Japanese Buddhist texts, those of Korea are simply special editions of the Chinese Canon and do not represent an independent tradi-tion. This is equally true of texts discovered in Central Asia, where translations have been made into Uigur, Sogdian, Ku-chanese, and other languages. Throughout Southeast Asia,

Pāli and, more rarely, Sanskrit Buddhist texts have been translated into native tongues, though whenever possible the works are read in the original.

Finally, it is to be hoped that readers finding certain selections of particular interest will trace them to their sources, given in the Acknowledgments, where they can be read in a more scholarly context, often with notes, etc. In order to keep the volume to a manageable length, and in the interest of consistency, it has, regrettably, been impossible to present such material. Good glossaries and bibliographies are provided by a number of the books drawn upon, including those mentioned above, a fine single source for both being Christmas Humphreys' *A Buddhist Students' Manual.*

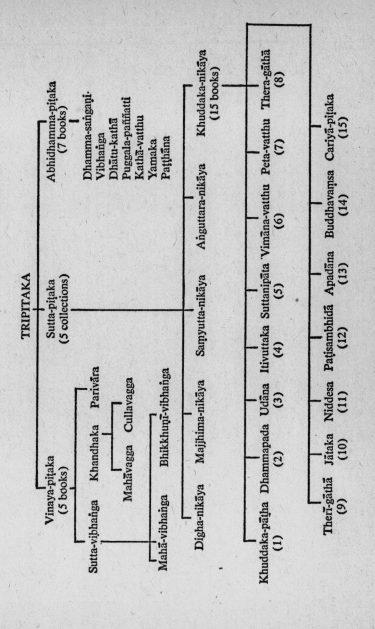

TRIPITAKA

Vinaya-piṭaka (5 books)
- Sutta-vibhaṅga
  - Mahā-vibhaṅga
  - Bhikkhuṇī-vibhaṅga
- Khandhaka
  - Mahāvagga
  - Cullavagga
- Parivāra

Sutta-piṭaka (5 collections)
- Digha-nikāya
- Majjhima-nikāya
- Saṃyutta-nikāya
- Aṅguttara-nikāya
- Khuddaka-nikāya (15 books)
  - Khuddaka-pāṭha (1)
  - Dhammapada (2)
  - Udāna (3)
  - Itivuttaka (4)
  - Suttanipāta (5)
  - Vimāna-vatthu (6)
  - Peta-vatthu (7)
  - Thera-gāthā (8)
  - Therī-gāthā (9)
  - Jātaka (10)
  - Niddesa (11)
  - Paṭisambhidā (12)
  - Apadāna (13)
  - Buddhavaṃsa (14)
  - Cariyā-piṭaka (15)

Abhidhamma-piṭaka (7 books)
- Dhamma-saṅgaṇi
- Vibhaṅga
- Dhātu-kathā
- Puggala-paññatti
- Kathā-vatthu
- Yamaka
- Paṭṭhāna

CONTENTS

Contents

Contents

Herb-Shop of the Buddha
Ambrosia-Shop of the Buddha
Jewel-Shop of the Buddha
Jewel of Morality
Jewel of Concentration
Jewel of Wisdom
Jewel of Deliverance
Jewel of Insight Through Knowledge of
    Deliverance
Jewel of the Analytical Powers
Jewel of the Prerequisites of
    Enlightenment
General Shop of the Buddha

The Pure Practices

Contents

Contents

INTRODUCTION

A MEASURE OF THE BUDDHA'S ACHIEVEMENT

In order to appreciate the magnitude of the Buddha's achievement it is necessary to try to imagine what life was like in early India, particularly in towns of the Ganges Valley like Kapilavastu, eighty miles north of Benares, where he was born about 560 B.C. Every year the river flooded the valley, destroying overnight crops wrung from a harsh earth; yearly, too, the monsoons came, spawning famine and drought and spreading their leavings—dysentery, cholera and countless other ills; weakening men for the predatory beasts, particularly tigers and snakes. Meanwhile the Brahmanas, Hindu priests, chanted the Vedic hymns and offered fire sacrifices to Brahma, in one of his many forms, yet nothing they did could improve the conditions of the common man.

From earliest times Hindu society was stratified to such a degree, caste so firmly established in the economy, that to rise against it, as the Buddha in his own way certainly did, questioning even the wayward nature of asceticism, was to arouse anger. The Brahmanas, creators and perpetuators of a social order highly favorable to themselves, must have thought him a dangerous lunatic. Of caste the Buddha said, "A man does not become a Brahmana by his family or by birth. In whom there is truth and righteousness, he is blessed, he is a Brahmana." Nor did the Buddha accept the existing belief that because of their caste some were naturally unworthy of salvation: "My doctrine makes no distinction between high and low, rich and poor; it is like the sky, it has room for all; like water it washes all alike." And, worst of heresies, the Buddha went so far as to deny the existence of Brahma himself: "Is there a single one of the Brahmanas . . . who has ever seen Brahma face to face? Does it not follow, then, that it is foolish talk to point the way to a state of union with that which we have not seen?" The gods, to the Buddha, were creatures with very human attributes, as much in need of salvation as men.

Perhaps the Buddha's greatest spiritual accomplishment was the doctrine of the Middle Way, which he discovered only after renouncing the harsh practices of the forest dwellers, among whom he lived as an ascetic for some time. And yet, despite his doubts about existing religious practices, and his strong sense of mission, he did not think of himself as the creator of a new religion. Rather—and in this he was like Jesus Christ—he felt the need to purify the religion of his day. He took for granted the truth of Hindu conceptions such as Karma (causality), while insisting that they be examined in relation to their psychological sources. It must have been evident to him that the Brahmanas, whether consciously or not, used a number of means to preserve the status quo, especially caste, which seemed almost designed to prove their superiority over the three other *varnas—*

Kshatriyas (warriors), *Vaisyas* (traders and farmers), *Su-dras* (serfs)—whom they considered to be little more than at-tendants upon themselves. It was not difficult for the Brahma-nas to keep the lower groups in line, and they were actually able to convince the Sudras—so powerful was their hold—that their lot was miserable because in past lives they had accumu-lated a store of bad Karma. These lowest of the low were good enough to sweep roads and cart dung, but not worthy of entering a temple in the hope of purification. The Buddha described the caste arguments of the Brahmanas as casuis-tical as well as cruel, and he declared that all men lived within reach of Nirvana.

The sixth century B.C. has been called the most remark-able in the spiritual history of mankind, producing in addi-tion to the Buddha, Mahavira, Lao-Tze, Confucius, Zara-thustra and Parmenides. The main events of the Buddha's life are well known: the miraculous birth and precocious childhood, the princely upbringing, his marriage and the birth of his son, the fatal encounters with the old man, the sick man, the corpse and the religious ascetic, which made him aware of suffering and convinced him that his mission was to seek liberation for himself and others; his renunciation and the six years spent in studying doctrines and undergoing yogic austerities, the giving up of ascetic practices for nor-mal life, the seven weeks spent in the shade of the Bodhi tree until, finally, one night toward dawn, enlightenment came; then his sermons and missionary travels, which lasted forty-five years, during which he affected the lives of thou-sands, high and low; and, at the age of eighty his parinirvana, extinction itself.

Such is the simple, dramatic outline of his life and mis-sion, yet as in the case of all great religious leaders the literature inspired by the Buddha's story is as various as those who have told it in the last twenty-five hundred years. To the first of his followers and the tradition associated with Theravada Buddhism and figures like the great Emperor Ashoka, the Buddha was a man, not a God; a teacher, not a savior. To those who, a few hundred years later, formed the

Mahayana school, he was a savior and often a God, one concerned with man's sorrows above all else. To this day the former tradition prevails in parts of India, Ceylon, Burma, Cambodia, and Thailand; the latter in Tibet, Mongolia, Vietnam, Korea, China, and Japan.

THE THERAVADA AND MAHAYANA SCHOOLS

Exactly how and when the Mahayana school came into being is one of the mysteries of world religion, yet most Buddhist historians seem fairly certain that of great importance to its inception was the Fourth Council of monks convened by King Kanishka, a convert to Buddhism, around A.D. 100. Whatever the purpose of the council, which has never been recognized by the Theravada, it represents an epoch-making event in the story of Buddhism in that it established Sanskrit as the language of the scriptures. Certainly the proceedings of the council resulted in a new atmosphere which, not long after, made it possible for figures like the metaphysician Nāgārjuna, thought to be the founder of Mahayana, to work in a spirit of free inquiry.

The simplest description of the differences between the schools is that of the Chinese traveler I-Tsing (635–713), who saw both, impartially, as living realities in India: "Those who worship Bodhisattvas (enlightened beings) and read Mahayana Sutras are called Mahayanists, while those who do not do this are called Hinayanists (Theravadins)." Sir Charles Eliot, in his *Hinduism and Buddhism* (Volume II), enlarges on I-Tsing's definition by listing conveniently seven lines of thought or practice found in Mahayana:

1. A belief in Bodhisattvas and in the power of human beings to become Bodhisattvas.

2. A code of altruistic ethics which teaches that everyone must do good in the interest of the whole world and make over to others any merit he may acquire by his virtues. The aim of the religious life is to become a Bodhisattva, not to become an Arhat.

3. A doctrine that Buddhas are supernatural beings, distributed through infinite space and time, and innumerable. In the language of later theology a Buddha has three bodies and still later there is a group of five Buddhas.

4. Various systems of idealist metaphysics, which tend to regard the Buddha essence or Nirvana much as Brahman is regarded in the Vedanta.

5. A canon composed in Sanskrit and apparently later than the Pali Canon.

6. Habitual worship of images and elaboration of ritual. There is a dangerous tendency to rely on formulae and charms.

7. A special doctrine of salvation by faith in a Buddha, usually Amitâbha, and invocation of his name. Mahayanism can exist without this doctrine but it is tolerated by most sects and considered essential by some.

Though it was during the reign of the third century B.C. Theravadin, King Ashoka, that Buddhism began to spread from India to other parts of Asia, there is little question that its greatest expansion, particularly in East Asia, was inspired by the altruistic Bodhisattva ideals of Mahayana, which was as a school less monastic, more outgoing, warmer in charity, and more disposed to evolution and development than Theravada. As a result of this new spirit, Buddhism began to be felt as a force in the secular history and art of China around the second century A.D. A few centuries later, largely due to China's great influence, it reached, with like impact, Korea and Japan.

THE NOBLE TRUTHS

To bring about a change in the way man views himself in the world is the highest purpose of religion and philosophy, and if today many are turning to Buddhism as the doctrine best able to help them achieve such transformations, it is not because other systems of belief have failed in their purpose but because, simply, they have been unable to coexist with those views of reality offered by science and humanistic disciplines, such as psychology, conditioned if not created by the empirical approach. That is claiming much, but many of the most penetrating thinkers of our time, from Jung to Toynbee, have for one reason or another been strongly attracted by Buddhism. In any case, it is with the greatest sense of relief apparently that some Occidentals have discovered a doctrine which, while dispensing with ritualistic trappings and other hindrances to intelligent appraisal, offers answers both profoundly spiritual and fully rational. The Buddha stated his views in the clearest possible manner according to the capacity for understanding of his listeners, sometimes through the use of analogies and parables, sometimes straightforwardly, as when he claimed that man's subjection to Samsara (time, life-and-death consciousness) is due to *avidyā* (ignorance) leading to *āsava* (illusion, depraved craving), from which state he must rise to *vidyā* (enlightenment). From the moment of his own awakening to his death, he attempted to show men how to transform themselves, proclaiming the Four Noble Truths, the Noble Eightfold Path and the Middle Way.

The Middle Way was meant to help men find peace with themselves and the world, whose Four Noble Truths were that there is *Dukkha* (suffering), that its origin is *Samudaya* (thirst, desire), that men can bring about its cessation, *Nirodha*, through the attainment of Nirvana, and that the only way to achieve Nirvana is to follow the *Magga* (the Noble Eightfold Path): Right Views, or acceptance of the Buddha's teaching; Right Thought, or aspirations leading to purity and charity; Right Speech; Right Conduct; Right Livelihood; Right Effort, or avoidance of lapses into frailty; Right Mindfulness, or constant awareness of the truth of the doctrine; and Right Concentration, or spiritual exercises leading to an awakening.

KARMA AND SAMSARA

The Buddha's doctrines were centered in two basic Hindu conceptions, Karma and Samsara. The Hindus believed that the universe is inhabited by numberless souls in various degrees of elevation, each passing through many births and deaths in a variety of bodily forms. Each instant of existence experienced by the soul, in each incarnation, is directly the result of action performed in a former birth, and in its turn affecting future experience. In short, each soul is made up of an endless chain of sorrow, and the only escape possible is spiritual insight and union with the supreme being, Brahma. As is well known, the Buddha formulated the doctrine of *anatta* (no-soul), rejecting not only the idea of self but of God as well. He felt that by denying them he could rid humanity of its moral and intellectual weakness, caused in part by an insistence on individuation and its accompanying dualisms. One of the most strongly held views in the Buddha's time was that, "Whatsoever happiness or pain or neutral feeling the person experiences, all that is due to the creation of a Supreme Deity." In the *Anguttara-nikāya*, a book of the Pāli Canon, his comment on this fatalistic view is quoted:

So, then, owing to the creation of a Supreme Deity men will become murderers, thieves, unchaste, liars, slanderers, abusive, babblers, covetous, malicious, and perverse in views. Thus for those who fall back on the creation of a God as the essential reason, there is neither the desire to do, nor the effort to do, nor necessity to do this deed or abstain from that deed.

Though much has been written about Karma (Pāli: Kamma) and the principle of no-soul, they are still poorly understood, the chief reason being that few have gone for clarification to Buddhist literature itself, the *Questions of Milinda*, for example, preferring, as is unfortunately the custom in the West, to consult expositions of the subjects which, for the most part, are ponderously tricked out with psychological jargon. Avoiding such an approach, and using one of the best known analogies and inventing an extremely effective one of his own, Ananda Coomaraswamy, in his *Buddha and the Gospel of Buddhism,* discusses Karma and no-soul:

Many are the similes employed by Gautama to show that no *thing* transmigrates from one life to another. The ending of one life and the beginning of another, indeed, hardly differ in kind from the change that takes place when a boy becomes a man—that also is a transmigration, a wandering, a new becoming. Among the similes most often used we find that of the flame especially convenient. Life is a flame, and transmigration . . . is the transmitting of the flame from one combustible aggregate to another; just that, and nothing more. If we light one candle from another, the communicated flame is one and the same, in the sense of an observed continuity, but the candle is not the same. Or, again, we could not offer a better illustration, if a modern instance be permitted, than that of a series of billiard balls in close contact: if another ball is rolled against the last stationary ball, the moving ball will stop dead, and the foremost stationary ball will move on. Here precisely is Buddhist transmigration: the first moving ball does not pass over, it remains behind, it dies; but it is undeniably the *movement of that ball*, its momentum, its *kamma*, and not any newly created movement, which is reborn in the foremost ball. Buddhist reincarnation is the endless transmission of such an impulse through an endless series of forms; Buddhist salvation is the coming to understand that the forms . . . are compound structures subject to decay, and that nothing is transmitted but an impulse . . . dependent on the heaping up of the past. It is a man's character, and not himself, that goes on.

In order to explain, in the light of his doctrine, the nature of being, the Buddha hit upon the important formula of "Origination in a Sequential Series" (Pāli: *Patichchasamuppāda*), which is made up of the following: Ignorance caused by Karma, the false belief in self; Conformations issuing from ignorance, the potentialities of love, hatred and similar attachments which are the results of actions in a former existence and inspire to future actions; Consciousness of finite beings, resulting in "Name and Form" (Pāli and Sanskrit: *nāma-rūpa*), the conception of a world of particulars; Six sense organs, from such a conception, which make contact with these particulars, leading to sensations of feeling and desire which, in turn, lead to the attraction of individual life and its attachments; Being (Pāli and Sanskrit: *Bhava*), or finite existence and the passing of consciousness through its stages of birth, sorrow, death. Then, as the result of the old Karma and reinforced by that newly acquired, the process begins again.

In other words the Buddha reasoned that the individual is merely a combination of name and form, the former including all the subjective phenomena of thought, feeling and the above-mentioned conformations, all of which are called "aggregations" (Pāli: *khandhas*); the latter standing for the four elements of physical nature (earth, water, fire, air) and their products, a fifth khandha. It is Karma which unites the five khandhas into an apparent individual, and represents the link preserving the identity of a being through the countless changes undergone in its progress through Samsara. Buddhism's purpose is to destroy Karma, which can be accomplished only by voyaging the Eightfold Path to salvation either in the present or, as the result of perfections, in the future.

NEITHER PESSIMIST NOR OPTIMIST

Because of such doctrines it is quite naturally assumed by Westerners that Buddhism is pessimistic, but to consider it as such is to simplify grossly and infer, at the same time, that even in the face of incontrovertible evidence that they live in a fool's paradise, men prefer their illusions. Buddhism is neither pessimistic nor optimistic, it is realistic, dealing objectively with the human experience. What the Buddha meant by Dukkha was not suffering alone but impermanence and imperfection, and he was very far from denying the possibility of happiness, spiritual and material. He simply maintained that it could not last, and that to believe otherwise was to court disappointment. Yet there was a form of happiness that could endure, and it came with the knowledge and acceptance of the universal essence, manifesting itself as the *Tri-kāya* (Three Divine Bodies): *Dharmakaya*, or Essential Body, which is primordial, formless, and eternal; *Sambhogakaya,* or Reflected Body, wherein dwell the Buddhas and the Bodhisattvas while embodied in superhuman form; and *Nirmanakaya,* or Incarnated Body, in which exist the earth-bound Buddhas.

It is the first of these, Dharmakaya, which is considered to be the Buddha-nature and noumenal source of the cosmic whole, the One Mind which, when grasped, leads to the perception of the undifferentiated nature of Samsara and Nirvana. Though Samsara and Nirvana form an inseparable entity, the Buddha himself declared that Nirvana is a state of transcendence over "that which is become, born, made and formed." Thus it is realized as the result of the stripping down of appearances, the penetration of their reality. As has been seen, the concept of Samsara, in which the law of Karma operates, is based on the belief that nothing is permanent, not even death, which must turn to new life. The Buddha was no fatalist. He maintained that man can work out his future, conquer time, but only at the cost of great sacrifice and the rooting out of self.

In his "Psychological Commentary" on *The Tibetan Book of the Great Liberation* (ed. by W. Y. Evans-Wentz, Oxford University Press, 1954), Dr. Jung writes:

> The fact that the East can dispose so easily of the ego seems to point to a mind that is not to be identified with our "mind." Certainly the ego does not play the same role in Eastern thought as it does with us. It seems as if the Eastern mind were less egocentric, as if its contents were more loosely connected with the subject, and as if greater stress were laid on mental states which include a depotentiated ego. It also seems as if Hathayoga were chiefly useful as a means for extinguishing the ego by fettering its unruly impulses. There is no doubt that the higher forms of *yoga,* in so far as they strive to reach *samādhi,* seek a mental condition in which the ego is practically dissolved. Consciousness in our sense of the word is rated a definitely inferior condition, the state of *avidyā* (ignorance), whereas what we call the "dark background of consciousness" is understood to be a "higher"

consciousness. Thus our concept of the "collective unconscious" would be the European equivalent of *buddhi*, the
enlightened mind.

There have been many attempts in the West to describe
philosophically and morally the "collective unconscious," yet
it is one thing to claim that all men share in something, another to behave as if one really believed that they do. As the
Buddhist scholar and translator Edward Conze, discussing the
Western interest in the philosophy, has said, "Although one
may originally be attracted by its remoteness, one can appreciate the real value of Buddhism only when one judges it by
the result it produces in one's own life from day to day."

The failure in such terms of much Western philosophy,
even the most progressive, is due largely to its being too easily
acquired, calling for very little discipline and sacrifice on
the part of its adherents. If one reads Plato and approves of
his view of the world, one is automatically a Platonist, if one
"understands" the phenomenologists and appreciates the
imaginative writings of Jean-Paul Sartre one can call oneself
an Existentialist, and so on. Of course there are Occidentals
who accept, as if converts, a rather spurious neo-Buddhism
which, as one commentator claimed, "Plays amongst living
religions the part of Esperanto amidst the natural languages."
Yet when one takes into account the varying capacities of
men, one finds it possible to tolerate almost anything, even the
apparent need for escapism satisfied by a strange doctrine.
By and large Western response to Buddhism is based on the
most human of needs, that of self-understanding, and the
philosophy's value is judged by the result it produces.

THE QUEST FOR PEACE

Regarding Western religious practice, it would appear that
in order to "belong" to a church very little effort is required
and less questioning countenanced. To become a Buddhist
the Emperor Ashoka knew that he must renounce all that he
had hitherto believed and lived by, including warfare. His

Thirteenth Rock Edict, which refers to his decimation of the Kalingas, suggests how complete was the transformation brought about in him through his conversion:

> When the king, Beloved of the Gods and of Gracious Mien, had been consecrated eight years Kalinga was conquered, 150,000 people were deported, 100,000 killed and many times that number died. But after the conquest of Kalinga, the Beloved of the Gods began to follow Righteousness (Dharma). . . . Now (he) regrets the conquest of Kalinga, for when an independent country is conquered people are killed, they die, or are deported, and that (he) finds very painful and grievous. . . . For all beings the Beloved of the Gods desires security, self-control, calm of mind, and gentleness. (He) considers that the greatest victory is the victory of Righteousness.

Echoing Ashoka, the contemporary Japanese Zen master Tanzan Yasuda, in an interview dealing in part with warfare, had this to say: "In a sense Buddhism is the only religion capable of helping the world achieve peace. Its fundamental teaching is that all things are Buddhas—not men alone but all things, sentient and non-sentient. And not merely the earth, but the other planets as well. Universal peace will be realized when men all over the world bow to the preciousness and sacredness of everything." According to Buddhism, then, there is no justification whatsoever, least of all political expediency, to think of another human being as an enemy.

In the essay from which I have already quoted, Dr. Jung describes the Western religious attitude:

> In its religious attitude, too, the West is extraverted. Nowadays it is gratuitously offensive to say that Christianity implies hostility, or even indifference, to the world and the flesh. On the contrary, the good Christian is a jovial citizen, an enterprising business man, an excellent soldier, the very best in every profession there is. Worldly goods are often interpreted as special rewards for Christian behavior, and in the Lord's Prayer the adjective . . . *supersubstantialis*, referring to bread, has long since been omitted, for the real bread obviously makes so very much

more sense! It is only logical that extraversion, when carried to such lengths, cannot credit man with a psyche which contains anything not imported into it from the outside, either by human teaching or divine grace. From this point of view it is downright blasphemy to assert that man has it in him to accomplish his own redemption. Nothing in our religion encourages the idea of the self-liberating power of the mind.

Yet today it is precisely that which is being attempted by many in the West, if not through the study of Eastern philosophy, particularly Zen Buddhism and Yoga, then with the aid of the so-called consciousness-expanding drugs such as LSD, which as one chiefly responsible for the interest in them has explained, make of the body a virtual laboratory if not temple, the last refuge of the freedom-seeking man. Now no one seriously involved in the study of Buddhism can witness such short cuts to nowhere as less than pathetic, but equally appalling are the conditions forcing men to grope in such directions.

To many modern life is simply unbearable, and there are things happening, or threatening to, which make of our time a perilous absurdity. Man's choices have been so severely curtailed, his involvement in decisions of life-or-death magnitude so limited, that he often finds himself lacking totally in purpose. Paradoxically, Western man's strong response to Buddhism may very well be the result of his being forced by circumstances to accept one of its major premises, that human experience is not individualistic. Those things which have made of life, for some, a veritable hell, have at the same time thrown its richest possibilities into relief, the chief being the sense of man's oneness with others.

If the writings of authors like Hesse and Salinger are popular with the young, it is because they too seem to offer alternatives to what is clearly no longer acceptable. When they think back to their own school years, it must seem incredible to the parents of today's students that they have chosen as models, even heroes, figures like Siddhartha of Hesse's story of the same name, or the suddenly enlightened coed, Franny, of Salinger's. Siddhartha, another of the Buddha's titles, meaning "he whose aim is accomplished," is made to say things by Hesse which in this age are well-nigh blasphemous: "Wisdom is not communicable. The wisdom which a wise man tries to communicate always sounds foolish," and "The world is not imperfect or slowly evolving along a long path to perfection. No, it is perfect at every moment."

If formerly it was customary to cite philosophers like Bergson when questioning some of the findings of science, today one is as likely to hear quoted an authority like the thirteenth-century Japanese Zen master Dogen, who in his great work *Shobogenzo* (The Correct-Law Eye Treasury), a collection of ninety-five essays dealing with Zen dialectics, said of time that it is man's experience of it which gives it form and duration—it is otherwise nonexistent. Everywhere one turns one observes doubt concerning thought structures of the past, a questioning of the very nature of our response to the physical world, our measuring, codifying, categorizing, the neat formulae and pat answers. If once it was natural to look out and name the day and the hour, experiencing Wednesday as something different from Sunday, we now realize that these equivalent periods of time have no consciousness of the roles we have given them. The solipsistic fairyland and pathetic fallacy men have made of the world is being shattered, partly as a result of the interest in Oriental philosophy.

BUDDHISM AND MODERN SCIENCE

Indeed, as has already been suggested, and as Maurice Percheron points out (*Buddha and Buddhism,* Harper and Brothers, New York, 1957), modern science fully supports the earliest findings of Buddhism:

And so we see physics joining Buddhism in its theory of universal flux, of the lack of substance inherent in matter, of impermanence, of fundamental error attaching to the testimony of the senses and consequently of doubt over the validity of the mind's speculations. We also see modern psychology concerned only with an essentially labile psyche: a fluid personality governed by temporary conjunctions escaping all control, and depending more or less on circumstances, acts and thoughts either barely acknowledged or not acknowledged at all. What else did the Buddha understand two thousand five hundred years ago but this?—that man has a certain vision of the universe through the medium of his senses; that he has another if he disengages himself from his sensory impressions; and yet another if he goes beyond perception of the laws that rule the balances of the universe and outside the causal sphere, to reach the domain of the unconditioned, which is as unthinkable for the intellect as is the identity of matter with magnetic fields and energic forces of attraction or repulsion. If we accept atomic physics as true . . . it is perfectly legitimate to accept the idea of vacuity, a state of unconditionedness outside phenomenal perceptions of time and space.

If Occidentals have been able to find in Buddhism parallels to their own thought and ideas sufficiently novel to make of it a source of insight and discovery, they have by and large proved themselves insensitive to its spiritual content. Many books of a generally pragmatic nature have been produced in recent years, showing the usefulness of Buddhism, especially Zen, to the development of new approaches to psychotherapy, literature, architecture, sports, even organized religion, yet for the most part their authors view the philosophy as technique and discipline, or one which perhaps more than any other offers concrete evidence, particularly in the arts, of its vitality. There is no gainsaying that aspect of Buddhism, and its gifts to the West have been substantial, yet Buddhists are often made uncomfortably aware of what they sense to be an exclusively utilitarian involvement in their doctrine. They would prefer, without proselytizing, to make Westerners conscious of Buddhism as religion, or at least as keenly melioristic philosophy.

The Occident's difficulty in accepting Buddhism's spiritual role is due in part to certain historical misconceptions. Even those familiar with its literature do not distinguish properly between the Theravada and Mahayana, assuming their differences, some of which have already been discussed, to be similar to those between, say, the Catholic and Protestant churches. The fact is that in comparison, and in the things that most matter, the differences between the schools are, if not considerable, certainly of great importance. As has been seen, Mahayana not only elevated the Buddha from noble teacher to virtual God, but even created something very close to a pantheon, in which the Bodhisattvas (enlightened beings) had their just place.

The Bodhisattva, unlike his Theravada counterpart the Arhat, who is concerned mainly with self-salvation, voluntarily renounces the bliss of Nirvana, though fully qualified for it, so as to remain among the still unenlightened and work for their salvation. He is reverenced, even worshiped, for his ardor and compassion. Small wonder, then, that Mahayanists consider "Hinayanists" to be selfish. Their views on such matters led the Mahayanists to an acceptance—often reluctant—of myth and superstition associated with popular worship, resulting in the formation of, among others, the Japanese Pure Land Sect, which promises its followers a heaven as delectable in every way as the Christian or Muslim, and the Nembutsu cults, which consider the invocation of the Buddha Amida's name, and his praise, in this formula, *Namu Amida Butsu* (Honor to the Buddha Amida), as sufficient, if sincerely repeated, to assure salvation. Yet, balancing this tendency and of much more importance to Mahayana is the metaphysical speculation the most gifted of its followers have always engaged in, on subjects which in Theravada literature the Buddha refused to take seriously and the like of which has rarely been witnessed elsewhere. The differences between the schools are dealt with openly throughout Buddhist literature, and in the Lotus Sutra the Buddha is quoted as claiming that he had first taught the Theravada doctrine because men were not yet ready for the more advanced ideas of the Mahayana.

THE TEN STAGES OF ENLIGHTENMENT

So far as the West is concerned, it is perhaps in Mahayana literature that Buddhism's spiritual message is most clearly heard, and it is as exalting as that of any comparable doctrine. As much as anything else in the literature, the *Dacabhûmî* (Ten Stages of Bodhisattvahood), as given in the Avatamsaka Sutra, suggests the purity and zeal of Mahayana faith. As they fully represent salvational Buddhism and define the ideal Buddhist, in what follows, a paraphrasing of Dr. Suzuki's account of them in his *Outlines of Mahayana Buddhism,* an attempt is made to relate the Ten Stages, briefly, to the philosophy as a whole.

Pramuditâ (Joy), the first stage of Bodhisattvahood, is the result of turning from what Mahayanists see as the nihilistic contemplation of Nirvana practiced by Hinayanists, and is inspired by the realization that self-salvation is not enough, that there are others walking about in ignorance who must be made to recognize the error of their ways. It is only when men are made aware of suffering that the greatest joy possible to them, sacrifice for others, can be achieved. Once this stage is reached it is natural for the enlightened man to teach and exhort, to go among the people, without discrimination, bearing his gifts.

Vimulâ (Purity) is attained through the spiritual insight gained at the first stage. Now that he is selfless, the enlightened one is without anger or malice. No longer can he conceive of taking the life of a living creature, no longer does he covet what belongs to others. His speech is direct and considerate, though never flattering. Now he is not only possessed of a sense of mission, he is morally qualified to carry it out.

Prabhâkari (Brightness) characterizes the intellectual condition of the awakened man, and is the result of newly acquired insight into the nature of things. He now understands that all is impure, impermanent, subject to sorrow and without soul, and recognizes at the same time that the real nature of things is neither created nor subject to death. All share in the selfsame essence, which is above time and space. It is only the unenlightened man, consumed with worry over the passing of grasped things, who adds to his store of Karma and is certain to suffer for it in future states. Yet it is precisely such a man that the Bodhisattva is sworn to save, his plight which fills him with spiritual energy. The following prayer by the Japanese Zen master Daichi expresses the feeling of this stage:

> My one desire is to dedicate this body born of my parents to the vow-ocean of Buddha, Law and Order. May I in all bodily actions be fully in accord with the holy rules, cherishing Buddha's Law throughout the rounds of birth and death until my reincarnation as a Buddha. May I never grow tired of saving all that is sentient wherever I happen to be. May I ever be masterful, whether in the forest of spears, the mountain of swords, the boiling cal- dron, or the heap of burning coals, always bearing the Treasure of the Correct-Law Eye. May Buddha, Law and Order testify to my faith! May Buddhas and patriarchs safeguard me!

And here is a similar prayer by the Zen master Bassui:

> May I, with clear *Marga* (truth) -eye, inherit the wis- dom of Buddhas and patriarchs and, training superior be- ings, pitying those in error, conduct men and devas along the road to enlightenment. If any be so unlucky as to fall into the three hells—fire, blood, swords—I will suffer for him. Should the torment last a hundred million *kalpas* (aeons), I will not retreat.

Arcismati (Burning) refers to the manner in which the enlightened man consumes all elements of evil and illusion in the purifying crucible of his new insight. It is at this stage that he practices strenuously the thirty-seven *Bodhipâksikas* (Virtues Conducive to Enlightenment), among the seven categories of which are the "Four Contemplations": on the impurity of the body, the evils of sensuality, the passing away of worldly interests, and the soul-less quality of things.

Sudurjayâ (Invincibility) is reached by the awakened man when, armed with the Virtues, he breaks the hold of all evil passions. Feeling intense love for humanity, inheriting the wisdom of past Buddhas, he is fearless in his quest for even greater truth, which in its highest form is perceived by him as an essence manifesting itself in a world of particulars. He also sees that absolute and relative knowledge are one and the same, and that the quality of particularity appears only when subjectivity is disturbed.

Abhimukhî (Revealing Oneself) is entered upon when the enlightened man reflects on the essence of all Dharmas (doctrines), which are of a piece. Perceiving their truth, he feels compassion for those still straying in Samsara and meditates on Karma, which brings about and is at the same time brought about by the hunger for individuation. His insight makes it possible for him to see beyond what is created and destroyed.

Dûrangamâ (Going Far Away) is the stage in which the awakened one attains *Upâyajñâ*, the knowledge which enables him to find whatever expediency is necessary to the work of salvation. Though he realizes that the Buddhas are no different from himself, he does not cease to do them homage, though he thinks constantly on the nature of the absolute, he does not abandon merit-accumulation, though no longer troubled by worldly thoughts, he does not disdain secular affairs. He knows that life is illusion, yet he toils on in the world of particulars and submits to the workings of Karma. He knows that the language of the Buddhas is beyond normal comprehension, yet he uses many devices to make it intelligible to the people. All of which suggests that while he lives on the highest plane of spirituality, he does not withdraw, preferring to engage himself in Samsara for the benefit of mankind.

Acalâ (Immovability) is the state attained by the Bodhisattva when he acquires the very highest knowledge, which is that everything in the world partakes of Suchness (Sanskrit: *Tathatā*). This knowledge, unconscious, intuitive, is the opposite to that derived by logic. Suchness is the term used by Mahayanists for the absolute and unconditioned quality of life, and in a sense is the positive expression of Voidness (Sanskrit: *Sūnyatā*), for it is to be found in all separate things and is neither different from nor divided by them. As it is not distinct from anything, it cannot be named the One as distinct from the Many, and nothing concerning it can be affirmed or denied, for these are modes of expression which by excluding suggest opposition. Nāgārjuna, the greatest Mahayana metaphysician and founder of the Madhyamika school, was the first to teach the doctrines of Suchness and Voidness. Possessing such knowledge, the awakened man enters a stage where all is immediately brilliant and his actions are spontaneous, innocent, even playful. He wills and it is done, he is nature itself.

Sâdhumatî (Good Intelligence) is the stage reached by the enlightened man when already sentient beings benefit by his works, and he is led to the Dharma of the deepest mystery, the penetration of which requires the four aspects of comprehensive knowledge: the self-essence of all beings, their individual attributes, their indestructibility and their eternal order.

Dharmameghâ (Clouds of Dharma), the last stage of Bodhisattvahood, is attained when the enlightened man has practiced all the virtues of purity, has accumulated all that constitutes transcendent power, is fortified with intelligence men see as genius, practices universally the principle of compassion, and has followed with vigor the path of the Buddhas. His every thought now reaches the realm of eternal tranquility, for he has the knowledge of all things and has arrived at the summit of all activities. He is the personification of love, sympathy and the Good Law, and the least of his actions results in benefit to mankind.

In the Dacabhûmî we see detailed not only those qualities gained, step by step, by the Bodhisattva but the specific ideals of Mahayana throughout the Buddhist world it dominates. The first step in the pilgrimage to the Mahayana was the idealization of the Buddha, the second the positive view of Nirvana, and the last, and perhaps most important, the salvational mission of the Bodhisattvas, founded on the conviction that at the heart of the Eternal there is a love which surpasses all human understanding. The Mahayana brought about great changes in Buddhism, but the philosophy's major goals remained the same, and so did its chief assumptions regarding the world and man's journey through it. Without *Kshanti* (patience), *Karuna* (compassion), and *Prajna* (wisdom) it would be a chaos, and man could never liberate himself from Samsara.

"The West will never be 'Buddhist,'" Christmas Humphreys, who is in a position to speculate, has said (*Buddhism*, Penguin Books, 1957), "and only the most unthinking zealot would strive to make it so." He goes on:

> The Western mind will never be content with second-hand clothing, and all that Western Buddhists have the right to do is to proclaim the Dhamma to all who have "ears to hear," and to suggest why, and in principle how, it should be applied. It may be that from the mingling streams of the Pali Canon, the compassionate splendour of the Mahayana and the astringent force of Zen will come a Navayama, a new "vehicle" of salvation.

But is there need for a Navayama? In his syncretistic approach to Buddhism, however noble its aim, does the Occidental betray the very characteristic which places its greatest truth beyond his reach? If the most cherished of Buddhism's gifts to the West is the pointing out of the path to self-discovery, its most valuable lesson is that as the consequence of that discovery the self is lost. With that in mind, why should not the West be Buddhist? Why should Westerners resist, merely because it is "second-hand clothing," a doctrine which can lead to the vision of a realm which knows neither East nor West? The Buddha, who spoke the first and must have the last word concerning the doctrine, never stated it more simply or movingly than while staying at Kosambī in the Sisu Grove:

> The Buddha gathered up a handful of sisu leaves and addressed the monks: "Which do you think are the more

numerous, monks, this small handful of leaves or those in the whole grove?"

"Very few in number are the leaves you have taken up. Much more in number are those in the whole grove."

"Even so, monks, much more in number are those things I have discovered but not revealed. And why, monks, have I not revealed them? Because they are not concerned with profit, they do not conduce to the holy life, nor to aversion, to detachment, to cessation, to tranquility, to comprehension, to wisdom, to Nirvana. That is why I have not revealed them.

"And what is it, monks, that I have revealed?

"Why, that this is suffering, this the arising of suffering, this the ceasing of suffering, this the practice leading to the cessation of suffering.

"And why did I reveal this alone?

"Because, monks, this is concerned with profit and is the beginning of the holy life; this conduces to aversion, detachment, cessation, tranquility, comprehension, wisdom, Nirvana. Therefore have I revealed it."

LUCIEN STRYK

Chapter I
JĀTAKA TALES

The tales which follow are from the *Jātaka Book*, a work of mixed verse and prose relating the 550 states of existence, as animal or human, of the Buddha prior to his final birth as Gautama. The *Jātaka Book* was originally in verse alone, to which the reciter, in the oral tradition of the time, added explanation. It is thought by Buddhists to be a compilation of the highest significance for social and literary history, and is the basis, for example, of the traditional Buddhist literature of Southeast Asia. The chief elements of the Jātaka are the introductory episode and the identification of characters, and its main purpose is clearly to edify. The stories were not completed before the fifth century, and they belong as much to Indian as specifically Buddhist literature, few having their origin in the latter. What makes them important to Buddhism is the fact that the Buddha is distinguished in part by his ability to remember in detail all of his previous lives and the manner in which they reveal his gradual perfection. The tales vary considerably in subject and literary value, which is attributable to the composite authorship of the collection, and those given here are altogether typical in their dramatic structure and in the morals they draw.

THE ASS IN THE LION'S SKIN

"Nay, this is not a lion's roar." This also was related by The Teacher concerning Kokālika: and it was while dwelling in Jetavana monastery. Kokālika, at the time, was desirous of intoning a doctrinal recitation before the congregation of

1

the priests. When The Teacher heard this, he related the following tale:—

Once upon a time, when Brahmadatta was reigning at Benares, the Future Buddha, having been born in a farmer's family, and now come of age, was making his living by husbandry. Now at that time, a certain peddler went about selling his wares, which he carried on the back of an ass. And at every place he came to, he would unload the ass, and dressing him up in the skin of a lion, let him loose in some field of rice or barley. And the field-watchers did not dare approach, as they thought it was a lion. Now one day the peddler took up his abode at the gate of a village, and while his breakfast was cooking, he dressed up the ass in the lion's skin, and let him loose in a field of barley. The field-watchers did not dare approach, as they thought it was a lion, but went home and announced the news. Then all the inhabitants of the village took up arms, and blowing conch-shells, and beating drums, went to the field and shouted, so that the ass became afraid for his life, and brayed. Then the Future Buddha knew it was an ass, and pronounced the first stanza:

> "Nay, this is not a lion's roar,
> Nor tiger, panther, gives its vent;
> But dressed up in a lion's skin,
> It is a wretched ass that brays."

And also the inhabitants of the village knew it was an ass, and beat him until his bones broke, and took the lion's skin away with them. Then came the peddler, and seeing that his ass had come to grief, he pronounced the second stanza:

> "Long might the ass have lived to eat
> The green and tender barley grain,
> Accoutred in the lion's skin,
> But that he brayed, and ruined all."

And while he was thus speaking, the ass died, whereupon the peddler left him and went his way.

2

The Teacher, having given this doctrinal instruction, identified the characters in the Birth-Story:

"At that time the ass was Kokālika, but the wise farmer was I myself."

QUAIL, CROW, FLY, FROG, AND ELEPHANTS

Hearing that the monks of Kosambi were quarreling, the Exalted One went to them and said: "Enough, monks! No quarreling! No brawling! No contending! No wrangling!" Then he said: "Monks, quarrels, brawls, contentions, wrangles,—all these are unprofitable. For because of a quarrel even a tiny quail brought about the destruction of a noble elephant."

In times past, when Brahmadatta ruled at Benares, the Future Buddha was reborn as an elephant. He grew up to be a fine big animal, acquired a retinue of eighty thousand elephants, and becoming the leader of a herd, made his home in the Himālaya region. At that time a tiny female quail laid her eggs in the elephants' stamping-ground. When the eggs were hatched, the fledglings broke the shells and came out. Before their wings had grown and while they were yet unable to fly, the Great Being came to that spot with his retinue of eighty thousand elephants in search of food.

When the tiny quail saw him, she thought: "This elephant-king will crush my fledglings and kill them. Well, I will ask of him righteous protection for the defense of my little ones." So folding her wings and standing before him, she uttered the first stanza:

> I salute you, elephant of sixty years,
> Forest-ranger, glorious leader of a herd;
> With my wings I do you homage.
> I am weak: do not kill my little ones.

Said the Great Being: "Do not worry, tiny quail; I will protect your little ones." And he stood over the fledglings, and the eighty thousand elephants passed by. Then he addressed the tiny quail: "Behind us comes a single solitary elephant; he will not obey our command. If you ask him also when he comes, you may obtain safety for your little ones." So saying, he went his way.

The tiny quail went forth to meet the solitary elephant, did homage to him with her wings, and uttered the second stanza:

> I salute you, solitary elephant,
> Forest-ranger, pasturing on mountain and on hill;
> With my wings I do you homage.
> I am weak: do not kill my little ones.

The solitary elephant, hearing her words, uttered the third stanza:

> I will kill your little ones, tiny quail.
> What can you do to me? You are a weakling.
> Even a hundred thousand like you
> Could I crush with my left foot.

And so saying, he pulverized her little ones with his foot, washed them away with a torrent of urine, and went his way trumpeting. The tiny quail perched on the branch of a tree and thought: "Just now you go your way trumpeting. In only a few days you will see what I can do! You do not understand that the mind is stronger than the body. Ah, but I will make you understand!" And threatening him, she uttered the fourth stanza:

> For not always does strength avail;
> For strength is the destruction of a fool.
> Elephant-king, I will do you harm,
> You who killed my little ones since I was weak.

Thus spoke the tiny quail. For a few days she ministered to a crow. The crow was pleased and said: "What can I do for you?" Said the tiny quail: "Master, there is only one thing I want done. I expect you to peck out the eyes of that solitary elephant." "Very well," assented the crow. The tiny quail then ministered to a green fly. The fly also said: "What can I do for you?" Said the tiny quail: "When this crow has put out the eyes of the solitary elephant, I wish you would drop a nit on them." "Very well," assented the fly also. The tiny quail then ministered to a frog. Said the frog: "What can I do?" Said the tiny quail: "When this solitary elephant has gone blind and seeks water to drink, then please squat on the mountain-top and croak; and when he has climbed to the top of the mountain, then please hop down and croak at the bottom. This is all I expect of you." The frog also, hearing her words, assented, saying, "Very well."

Now one day the crow pecked out both of the elephant's eyes, and the fly let a nit drop on them. The elephant, eaten up by maggots, maddened with pain, overcome with thirst, wandered about seeking water to drink. At that moment the frog, squatting on the mountain-top, let out a croak. The elephant thought: "There must be water there;" and climbed the mountain. Then the frog hopped down, and squatting at the bottom, let out a croak. The elephant thought: "There must be water there." And going to the brink of the precipice, he tumbled and fell to the foot of the mountain, and met destruction.

When the tiny quail realized that he was dead, she cried out: "I have seen the back of my enemy!" And pleased and delighted, she strutted over his shoulders, and passed away according to her deeds.

Behold the quail, the crow, the fly, the frog!
They slew the elephant! Behold the hatred of the haters!

THE HARE-MARK IN THE MOON

"Some red-fish have I, seven in all." This was related by The Teacher while dwelling in Jetavana monastery; and it

5

was concerning a donation of all the requisites to the congregation of the priests.

It seems that a householder of Sāvatthi prepared a donation of all the requisites for The Buddha and for the Order. At the door of his house he had a pavilion built and gotten ready, and having invited The Buddha and the congregation of the priests, he made them sit down on costly seats which had been spread for them in the pavilion, and gave them an excellent repast of savory dishes. Then he invited them again for the next day, and again for the next, until he had invited them seven times. And on the seventh day he made the donation of all the requisites to The Buddha and to five hundred priests.

At the end of the breakfast The Teacher returned thanks and said,

"Layman, it is fitting that you thus manifest a hearty zeal; for this alms-giving was also the custom of the wise of old time. For the wise of old time surrendered their own lives to chance suppliants, and gave their own flesh to be eaten."

Then, at the request of the householder, he related the by-gone occurrence:

Once upon a time, when Brahmadatta was ruling at Benares, the Future Buddha was born as a hare, and dwelt in a wood. Now on one side of this wood was a mountain, on another a river, and on another a border village. And there were three other animals that were his comrades—a monkey, a jackal, and an otter. These four wise creatures dwelt together, catching their prey each in his own hunting ground, and at night resorting together. And the wise hare would exhort the other three, and teach them the Doctrine, saying, "Give alms, keep the precepts, and observe fast-days." Then the three would approve of his admonition, and go each to his own lair in the thicket, and spend the night.

Time was going by in this manner, when one day the Future Buddha looked up into the sky and saw the moon, and perceived that the next day would be fast-day. Then said he to the others,

"To-morrow is fast-day. Do you three keep the precepts and observe the day; and as alms given while keeping the precepts bring great reward, if any suppliants present themselves, give them to eat of your own food."

"Very well," said they, and passed the night in their lairs.

On the next day the otter started out early, and went to the banks of the Ganges to hunt for prey. Now a fisherman had caught seven red-fish and strung them on a vine, and buried them in the sand on the banks of the Ganges, and had then gone on down-stream catching fish as he went. The otter smelt the fishy odor, and scraping away the sand, perceived the fish and drew them out. Then he called out three times, "Does any one own these?" and when he saw no owner, he bit hold of the vine with his teeth, and drew them to his lair in the thicket. There he lay down, remembering that he was keeping the precepts, and thinking, "I will eat these at the proper time."

And the jackal also went out to hunt for prey, and found in the hut of a field-watcher two spits of meat, and one iguana, and a jar of sour cream. Then he called out three times, "Does any one own these?" and when he saw no owner, he placed the cord that served as a handle for the jar of sour cream about his neck, took hold of the spits of meat and of the iguana with his teeth, and brought them home, and placed them in his lair in the thicket. Then he lay down, remembering that he was keeping the precepts, and thinking, "I will eat these at the proper time."

And the monkey also, entering the forest, fetched home a bunch of mangoes, and placed them in his lair in the thicket. Then he lay down, remembering that he was keeping the precepts, and thinking, "I will eat these at the proper time."

The Future Buddha, however, remained in his thicket, thinking, "At the proper time I will go out and eat dabba-grass." Then he thought,

"If any suppliants come, they will not want to eat grass, and I have no sesamum, rice, or other such food. If any suppliant comes, I will give him of my own flesh."

Such fieriness of zeal in keeping the precepts caused the marble throne of Sakka to grow hot. Then, looking carefully, Sakka discovered the cause, and proposed to himself to try the hare. And disguised as a Brahman, he went first to the lair of the otter.

"Brahman, why stand you there?" said the otter.

Said he, "Pandit, if I could but get something to eat, I would keep fast-day vows, and perform the duties of a monk."

"Very well," said the otter; "I will give you food." And he addressed him with the first stanza:

> "Some red-fish have I, seven in all,
> Found stranded on the river bank.
> All these, O Brahman, are my own;
> Come eat, and dwell within this wood."

"I will return a little later," said the Brahman; "let the matter rest until to-morrow."

Then he went to the jackal. And the latter also asking, "Why stand you there?" the Brahman answered the same as before.

"Very well," said the jackal; "I will give you some food." And he addressed him with the second stanza:

> "A watchman guards the field close by,
> His supper have I ta'en away;
> Two spits of meat, iguana one,
> One dish of butter clarified.
> All these, O Brahman, are my own;
> Come eat, and dwell within this wood."

"I will return a little later," said the Brahman; "let the matter rest until to-morrow."

Then he went to the monkey. And the latter also asking, "Why stand you there?" the Brahman answered the same as before.

"Very well," said the monkey; "I will give you some food." And he addressed him with the third stanza:

8

"Ripe mangoes, water clear and cold,
And cool and pleasant woodland shade—
All these, O Brahman, are my own;
Come eat, and dwell within this wood."

"I will return a little later," said the Brahman; "let the matter rest until to-morrow."

Then he went to the wise hare. And he also asking, "Why stand you there?" the Brahman answered the same as before.

The Future Buddha was delighted. "Brahman," said he, "you have done well in coming to me for food. To-day I will give alms such as I never gave before; and you will not have broken the precepts by destroying life. Go, my friend, and gather wood, and when you have made a bed of coals, come and tell me. I will sacrifice my life by jumping into the bed of live coals. And as soon as my body is cooked, do you eat of my flesh, and perform the duties of a monk." And he addressed him with the fourth stanza:

"The hare no seed of sesamum
Doth own, nor beans, nor winnowed rice.
But soon my flesh this fire shall roast;
Then eat, and dwell within this wood."

When Sakka heard this speech, he made a heap of live coals by his superhuman power, and came and told the Future Buddha. The latter rose from his couch of dabba-grass, and went to the spot. And saying, "If there are any insects in my fur, I must not let them die," he shook himself three times. Then throwing his whole body into the jaws of his liberality, he jumped into the bed of coals, as delighted in mind as a royal flamingo when he alights in a cluster of lotuses. The fire, however, was unable to make hot so much as a hair-pore of the Future Buddha's body. He felt as if he had entered the abode of cold above the clouds.

Then, addressing Sakka, he said,

"Brahman, the fire you have made is exceeding cold, and is not able to make hot so much as a hair-pore of my body. What does it mean?"

9

"Pandit, I am no Brahman; I am Sakka, come to try you."

"Sakka, your efforts are useless; for if all beings who dwell in the world were to try me in respect of my liberality, they would not discover in me any unwillingness to give." Thus the Future Buddha thundered.

"Wise hare," said then Sakka, "let your virtue be proclaimed to the end of this world-cycle." And taking a mountain, he squeezed it, and with the juice drew the outline of a hare in the disk of the moon. Then in that wood, and in that thicket, he placed the Future Buddha on some tender dabba-grass, and taking leave of him, departed to his own celestial abode.

And these four wise creatures lived happily and harmoniously, and kept the precepts, and observed fast-days, and passed away according to their deeds.

When The Teacher had given this instruction, he expounded the truths, and identified the characters of the Birth-Story: [At the close of the exposition of the truths, the householder who had given all the requisites became established in the fruit of conversion.]

"In that existence the otter was Ānanda, the jackal was Moggallāna, the monkey was Sāriputta, while the wise hare was I myself."

Chapter II
LIFE OF THE BUDDHA

Asvaghosha, poet and Mahayana philosopher, was a first-century contemporary of King Kanishka, an Indo-Scythian ruler and convert to Buddhism who was instrumental in spreading Mahayana Buddhism in India and Afghanistan. As Sanskrit poet, Asvaghosha was the chief forerunner of Kālī-dāsa, and his masterwork the *Buddha-Karita* (Course of the Buddha), the first part of which follows, concerns the Buddha's life up to the time of his enlightenment. The poem is the earliest example of a Kâvya, or "artificial epic," and it depicts the life, with great restraint, in twenty-eight cantos, of which only seventeen are preserved in Sanskrit and only the first thirteen are regarded as authentic. The Chinese pilgrim I-Tsing, who is represented in this volume, wrote of the poet's literary style, "He is read far and wide throughout the five Indies and the lands of the southern seas. He clothes in but few words many thoughts and ideas, which so rejoice the reader's heart that he never wearies of the poem. Very profitable also it is to read the poem, for here the noble doctrines are set forth with convenient brevity." The selection from the *Buddha-Karita* is followed by a translation, from Pāli sources, including the introduction to the *Jātaka Book*, of the phases of the Buddha's life. The whole of the life is not given, yet it is to be hoped that its spirit is suggested by the translations.

FROM *THE BUDDHA-KARITA* OF ASVAGHOSHA

BOOK I

1. That Arhat is here saluted, who has no counterpart,
—who, as bestowing the supreme happiness, surpasses (Brahman) the Creator,—who, as driving away darkness, vanquishes the sun,—and, as dispelling all burning heat, surpasses the beautiful moon.

2. There was a city, the dwelling-place of the great saint Kapila, having its sides surrounded by the beauty of a lofty broad table-land as by a line of clouds, and itself, with its high-soaring palaces, immersed in the sky.

3. By its pure and lofty system of government it, as it were, stole the splendour of the clouds of Mount Kailâsa, and while it bore the clouds which came to it through a mistake, it fulfilled the imagination which had led them thither.

4. In that city, shining with the splendour of gems, darkness like poverty could find no place; prosperity shone resplendently, as with a smile, from the joy of dwelling with such surpassingly excellent citizens.

5. With its festive arbours, its arched gateways and pinnacles, it was radiant with jewels in every dwelling; and unable to find any other rival in the world, it could only feel emulation with its own houses.

6. There the sun, even although he had retired, was unable to scorn the moon-like faces of its women which put the lotuses to shame, and as if from the access of passion, hurried towards the western ocean to enter the (cooling) water.

7. 'Yonder Indra has been utterly annihilated by the people when they saw the glories acquired by the Sâkyas,'—uttering this scoff, the city strove by its banners with gay-fluttering streamers to wipe away every mark of his existence.

8. After mocking the water-lilies even at night by the

12

moonbeams which rest on its silver pavilions,—by day it assumed the brightness of the lotuses through the sunbeams falling on its golden palaces.

9. A king, by name Suddhodana, of the kindred of the sun, anointed to stand at the head of earth's monarchs,—ruling over the city, adorned it, as a bee-inmate a full-blown lotus.

10. The very best of kings with his train ever near him, —intent on liberality yet devoid of pride; a sovereign, yet with an ever equal eye thrown on all,—of gentle nature and yet with wide-reaching majesty.

11. Falling smitten by his arm in the arena of battle, the lordly elephants of his enemies bowed prostrate with their heads pouring forth quantities of pearls as if they were offering handfuls of flowers in homage.

12. Having dispersed his enemies by his pre-eminent majesty as the sun disperses the gloom of an eclipse, he illuminated his people on every side, showing them the paths which they were to follow.

13. Duty, wealth, and pleasure under his guidance assumed mutually each other's object, but not the outward dress; yet as if they still vied together they shone all the brighter in the glorious career of their triumphant success.

14. He, the monarch of the Sâkyas, of native pre-eminence, but whose actual pre-eminence was brought about by his numberless councillors of exalted wisdom, shone forth all the more gloriously, like the moon amidst the stars shining with a light like its own.

15. To him there was a queen, named Mâyâ, as if free from all deceit (mâyâ)—an effulgence proceeding from his effulgence, like the splendour of the sun when it is free from all the influence of darkness,—a chief queen in the united assembly of all queens.

16. Like a mother to her subjects, intent on their welfare, —devoted to all worthy of reverence like devotion itself,— shining on her lord's family like the goddess of prosperity,— she was the most eminent of goddesses to the whole world.

17. Verily the life of women is always darkness, yet when

it encountered her, it shone brilliantly; thus the night does not retain its gloom, when it meets with the radiant crescent of the moon.

18. 'This people, being hard to be roused to wonder in their souls, cannot be influenced by me if I come to them as beyond their senses,'—so saying, Duty abandoned her own subtile nature and made her form visible.

19. Then falling from the host of beings in the Tushita heaven, and illumining the three worlds, the most excellent of Bodhisattvas suddenly entered at a thought into her womb, like the Nâga-king entering the cave of Nandâ.

20. Assuming the form of a huge elephant white like Himâlaya, armed with six tusks, with his face perfumed with flowing ichor, he entered the womb of the queen of king Suddhodana, to destroy the evils of the world.

21. The guardians of the world hastened from heaven to mount watch over the world's one true ruler; thus the moonbeams, though they shine everywhere, are especially bright on Mount Kailâsa.

22. Mâyâ also, holding him in her womb, like a line of clouds holding a lightning-flash, relieved the people around her from the sufferings of poverty by raining showers of gifts.

23. Then one day by the king's permission the queen, having a great longing in her mind, went with the inmates of the gynaeceum into the garden Lumbinî.

24. As the queen supported herself by a bough which hung laden with a weight of flowers, the Bodhisattva suddenly came forth, cleaving open her womb.

25. At that time the constellation Pushya was auspicious, and from the side of the queen, who was purified by her vow, her son was born for the welfare of the world, without pain and without illness.

26. Like the sun bursting from a cloud in the morning, —so he too, when he was born from his mother's womb, made the world bright like gold, bursting forth with his rays which dispelled the darkness.

27. As soon as he was born the thousand-eyed (Indra) well-pleased took him gently, bright like a golden pillar; and

two pure streams of water fell down from heaven upon his head with piles of Mandâra flowers.

28. Carried about by the chief suras, and delighting them with the rays that streamed from his body, he surpassed in beauty the new moon as it rests on a mass of evening clouds.

29. As was Aurva's birth from the thigh, and Prithu's from the hand, and Mândhâtri's, who was like Indra himself, from the forehead, and Kakshîvat's from the upper end of the arm,—thus too was his birth (miraculous).

30. Having thus in due time issued from the womb, he shone as if he had come down from heaven, he who had not been born in the natural way,—he who was born full of wisdom, not foolish,—as if his mind had been purified by countless aeons of contemplation.

31. With glory, fortitude, and beauty he shone like the young sun descended upon the earth; when he was gazed at, though of such surpassing brightness, he attracted all eyes like the moon.

32. With the radiant splendour of his limbs he extinguished like the sun the splendour of the lamps; with his beautiful hue as of precious gold he illuminated all the quarters of space.

33. Unflurried, with the lotus-sign in high relief, far-striding, set down with a stamp,—seven such firm footsteps did he then take,—he who was like the constellation of the seven rishis.

34. 'I am born for supreme knowledge, for the welfare of the world,—thus this is my last birth,"—thus did he of lion gait, gazing at the four quarters, utter a voice full of auspicious meaning.

35. Two streams of water bursting from heaven, bright as the moon's rays, having the power of heat and cold, fell down upon that peerless one's benign head to give refreshment to his body.

36. His body lay on a bed with a royal canopy and a frame shining with gold, and supported by feet of lapis lazuli, and in his honour the yaksha-lords stood round guarding him with golden lotuses in their hands.

37. The gods in homage to the son of Mâyâ, with their heads bowed at his majesty, held up a white umbrella in the sky and muttered the highest blessings on his supreme wisdom.

38. The great dragons in their great thirst for the Law, —they who had had the privilege of waiting on the past Buddhas,—gazing with eyes of intent devotion, fanned him and strewed Mandâra flowers over him.

39. Gladdened through the influence of the birth of the Tathâgata, the gods of pure natures and inhabiting pure abodes were filled with joy, though all passion was extinguished, for the sake of the world drowned in sorrow.

40. When he was born, the earth, though fastened down by (Himâlaya) the monarch of mountains, shook like a ship tossed by the wind; and from a cloudless sky there fell a shower full of lotuses and water-lilies, and perfumed with sandalwood.

41. Pleasant breezes blew soft to the touch, dropping down heavenly garments; the very sun, though still the same, shone with augmented light, and fire gleamed, unstirred, with a gentle lustre.

42. In the north-eastern part of the dwelling a well of pure water appeared of its own accord, wherein the inhabit-ants of the gynaeceum, filled with wonder, performed their rites as in a sacred bathing-place.

43. Through the troops of heavenly visitants, who came seeking religious merit, the pool itself received strength to behold Buddha, and by means of its trees bearing flowers and perfumes it eagerly offered him worship.

44. The flowering trees at once produced their blossoms, while their fragrance was borne aloft in all directions by the wind, accompanied by the songs of bewildered female bees, while the air was inhaled and absorbed by the many snakes (gathering near).

45. Sometimes there resounded on both sides songs mingled with musical instruments and tabours, and lutes also, drums, tambourines, and the rest,—from women adorned with dancing bracelets.

46. 'That royal law which neither Bhrigu nor Aṅgiras ever

made, those two great seers the founders of families, their two sons Sukra and Vrihaspati left revealed at the end.

47. 'Yea, the son of Sarasvatî proclaimed that lost Veda which they had never seen in former ages,—Vyâsa rehearsed that in many forms, which Vasishtha helpless could not compile;

48. 'The voice of Vâlmîki uttered its poetry which the great seer Kyavana could not compose; and that medicine which Atri never invented the wise son of Atri proclaimed after him;

49. 'That Brahmanhood which Kusika never attained,—his son, O king, found out the means to gain it; (so) Sagara made a bound for the ocean, which even the Ikshvâkus had not fixed before him.

50. 'Ganaka attained a power of instructing the twice-born in the rules of Yoga which none other had ever reached; and the famed feats of the grandson of Sûra (Krishna) Sûra and his peers were powerless to accomplish.

51. 'Therefore it is not age nor years which are the criterion; different persons win pre-eminence in the world at different places; those mighty exploits worthy of kings and sages, when left undone by the ancestors, have been done by the sons.'

52. The king, being thus consoled and congratulated by those well-trusted Brahmans, dismissed from his mind all unwelcome suspicion and rose to a still higher degree of joy;

53. And well-pleased he gave to those most excellent of the twice-born rich treasures with all due honour,—'May he become the ruler of the earth according to your words, and may he retire to the woods when he attains old age.'

54. Then having learned by signs and through the power of his penances this birth of him who was to destroy all birth, the great seer Asita in his thirst for the excellent Law came to the palace of the Sâkya king.

55. Him shining with the glory of sacred knowledge and ascetic observances, the king's own priest,—himself a special student among the students of sacred knowledge,—introduced into the royal palace with all due reverence and respect.

56. He entered into the precincts of the king's gynae-ceum, which was all astir with the joy arisen from the birth of the young prince,—grave from his consciousness of power, his pre-eminence in asceticism, and the weight of old age.

57. Then the king, having duly honoured the sage, who was seated in his seat, with water for the feet and an arghya offering, invited him (to speak) with all ceremonies of respect, as did Antideva in olden time to Vasishtha:

58. 'I am indeed fortunate, this my family is the object of high favour, that thou shouldst have come to visit me; be pleased to command what I should do, O benign one; I am thy disciple, be pleased to show thy confidence in me.'

59. The sage, being thus invited by the king, filled with intense feeling as was due, uttered his deep and solemn words, having his large eyes opened wide with wonder:

60. 'This is indeed worthy of thee, great-souled as thou art, fond of guests, liberal and a lover of duty,—that thy mind should be thus kind towards me, in full accordance with thy nature, family, wisdom, and age.

61. 'This is the true way in which those seer-kings of old, rejecting through duty all trivial riches, have ever flung them away as was right,—being poor in outward substance but rich in ascetic endurance.

62. 'But hear now the motive for my coming and rejoice thereat; a heavenly voice has been heard by me in the heavenly path, that thy son has been born for the sake of supreme knowledge.

63. 'Having heard that voice and applied my mind thereto, and having known its truth by signs, I am now come hither, with a longing to see the banner of the Sâkya race, as if it were Indra's banner being set up.'

64. Having heard this address of his, the king, with his steps bewildered with joy, took the prince, who lay on his nurse's side, and showed him to the holy ascetic.

65. Thus the great seer beheld the king's son with wonder,—his foot marked with a wheel, his fingers and toes webbed, with a circle of hair between his eyebrows, and signs of vigour like an elephant.

66. Having beheld him seated on his nurse's side, like the son of Agni (Skanda) seated on Devī's side, he stood with the tears hanging on the ends of his eyelashes, and sighing he looked up towards heaven.

67. But seeing Asita with his eyes thus filled with tears, the king was agitated through his love for his son, and with his hands clasped and his body bowed he thus asked him in a broken voice choked with weeping,

68. 'One whose beauty has little to distinguish it from that of a divine sage, and whose brilliant birth has been so wonderful, and for whom thou hast prophesied a transcendent future,—wherefore, on seeing him, do tears come to thee, O reverend one?

69. 'Is the prince, O holy man, destined to a long life? Surely he cannot be born for my sorrow. I have with difficulty obtained a handful of water, surely it is not death which comes to drink it.

70. 'Tell me, is the hoard of my fame free from destruction? Is this chief prize of my family secure? Shall I ever depart happily to another life,—I who keep one eye ever awake, even when my son is asleep?

71. 'Surely this young shoot of my family is not born barren, destined only to wither! Speak quickly, my lord, I cannot wait; thou well knowest the love of near kindred for a son.'

72. Knowing the king to be thus agitated through his fear of some impending evil, the sage thus addressed him: 'Let not thy mind, O monarch, be disturbed,—all that I have said is certainly true.

73. 'I have no feeling of fear as to his being subject to change, but I am distressed for mine own disappointment. It is my time to depart, and this child is now born,—he who knows that mystery hard to attain, the means of destroying birth.

74. 'Having forsaken his kingdom, indifferent to all worldly objects, and having attained the highest truth by strenuous efforts, he will shine forth as a sun of knowledge to destroy the darkness of illusion in the world.

75. 'He will deliver by the boat of knowledge the distressed world, borne helplessly along, from the ocean of misery which throws up sickness as its foam, tossing with the waves of old age, and rushing with the dreadful onflow of death.

76. 'The thirsty world of living beings will drink the flowing stream of his Law, bursting forth with the water of wisdom, enclosed by the banks of strong moral rules, delightfully cool with contemplation, and filled with religious vows as with ruddy geese.

77. 'He will proclaim the way of deliverance to those afflicted with sorrow, entangled in objects of sense, and lost in the forest-paths of worldly existence, as to travellers who have lost their way.

78. 'By the rain of the Law he will give gladness to the multitude who are consumed in this world with that fire of desire whose fuel is worldly objects, as a great cloud does with its showers at the end of the hot season.

79. 'He will break open for the escape of living beings that door whose bolt is desire and whose two leaves are ignorance and delusion,—with that excellent blow of the good Law which is so hard to find.

80. 'He, the king of the Law, when he has attained to supreme knowledge, will achieve the deliverance from its bonds of the world now overcome by misery, destitute of every refuge, and enveloped in its own chains of delusion.

81. 'Therefore make no sorrow for him,—that belongs rather, kind sire, to the pitiable world of human beings, who through illusion or the pleasures of desire or intoxication refuse to hear his perfect Law.

82. 'Therefore since I have fallen short of that excellence, though I have accomplished all the stages of contemplation, my life is only a failure; since I have not heard his Law, I count even dwelling in the highest heaven a misfortune.'

83. Having heard these words, the king with his queen and his friends abandoned sorrow and rejoiced; thinking, 'such is this son of mine,' he considered that his excellence was his own.

84. But he let his heart be influenced by the thought, 'he will travel by the noble path,'—he was not in truth averse to religion, yet still he saw alarm at the prospect of losing his child.

85. Then the sage Asita, having made known the real fate which awaited the prince to the king who was thus disturbed about his son, departed by the way of the wind as he had come, his figure watched reverentially in his flight.

86. Having taken his resolution and having seen the son of his younger sister, the saint, filled with compassion, enjoined him earnestly in all kinds of ways, as if he were his son, to listen to the sage's words and ponder over them.

87. The monarch also, being well-pleased at the birth of a son, having thrown off all those bonds called worldly objects, caused his son to go through the usual birth-ceremonies in a manner worthy of the family.

88. When ten days were fulfilled after his son's birth, with his thoughts kept under restraint, and filled with excessive joy, he offered for his son most elaborate sacrifices to the gods with muttered prayers, oblations, and all kinds of auspicious ceremonies.

89. And he himself gave to the brahmans for his son's welfare cows full of milk, with no traces of infirmity, golden-horned and with strong healthy calves, to the full number of a hundred thousand.

90. Then he, with his soul under strict restraint, having performed all kinds of ceremonies which rejoiced his heart, on a fortunate day, in an auspicious moment, gladly determined to enter his city.

91. Then the queen with her babe having worshipped the gods for good fortune, occupied a costly palanquin made of elephants' tusks, filled with all kinds of white flowers, and blazing with gems.

92. Having made his wife with her child enter first into the city, accompanied by the aged attendants, the king himself also advanced, saluted by the hosts of the citizens, as Indra entering heaven, saluted by the immortals.

93. The Sâkya king, having entered his palace, like Bhava

well-pleased at the birth of Kârttikeya, with his face full of joy, gave orders for lavish expenditure, showing all kinds of honour and liberality.

94. Thus at the good fortune of the birth of the king's son, that city surnamed after Kapila, with all the surrounding inhabitants, was full of gladness like the city of the lord of wealth, crowded with heavenly nymphs, at the birth of his son Nalakûvara.

BOOK II

1. From the time of the birth of that son of his, who, the true master of himself, was to end all birth and old age, the king increased day by day in wealth, elephants, horses, and friends as a river increases with its influx of waters.

2. Of different kinds of wealth and jewels, and of gold, wrought or unwrought, he found treasures of manifold variety, surpassing even the capacity of his desires.

3. Elephants from Himavat, raging with rut, whom not even princes of elephants like Padma could teach to go round in circles, came without any effort and waited on him.

4. His city was all astir with the crowds of horses, some adorned with various marks and decked with new golden trappings, others unadorned and with long flowing manes,— suitable alike in strength, gentleness, and costly ornaments.

5. And many fertile cows, with tall calves, gathered in his kingdom, well nourished and happy, gentle and without fierceness, and producing excellent milk.

6. His enemies became indifferent; indifference grew into friendship; his friends became specially united; were there two sides,—one passed into oblivion.

7. Heaven rained in his kingdom in due time and place, with the sound of gentle winds and clouds, and adorned with wreaths of lightning, and without any drawback of showers of stones or thunderbolts.

8. A fruitful crop sprang up according to season, even without the labour of ploughing; and the old plants grew more vigorous in juice and substance.

9. Even at that crisis which threatens danger to the body like the collision of battle, pregnant women brought forth in good health, in safety, and without sickness.

10. And whereas men do not willingly ask from others, even where a surety's property is available,—at that time even one possessed of slender means turned not his face away when solicited.

11. There was no ruin nor murder,—nay, there was not even one ungenerous to his kinsmen, no breaker of obligations, none untruthful nor injurious,—as in the days of Yayâti the son of Nahusha.

12. Those who sought religious merit performed sacred works and made gardens, temples, and hermitages, wells, cisterns, lakes, and groves, having beheld heaven as it were visible before their eyes.

13. The people, delivered from famine, fear, and sickness, dwelt happily as in heaven; and in mutual contentment husband transgressed not against wife, nor wife against husband.

14. None pursued love for mere sensual pleasure; none hoarded wealth for the sake of desires; none practised religious duties for the sake of gaining wealth; none injured living beings for the sake of religious duty.

15. On every side theft and its kindred vices disappeared; his own dominion was in peace and at rest from foreign interference; prosperity and plenty belonged to him, and the cities in his realm were (healthy) like the forests.

16. When that son was born it was in that monarch's kingdom as in the reign of Manu the son of the Sun,—gladness went everywhere and evil perished; right blazed abroad and sin was still.

17. Since at the birth of this son of the king such a universal accomplishment of all objects took place, the king in consequence caused the prince's name to be Sarvârthasiddha.

18. But the queen Mâyâ, having seen the great glory of her new-born son, like some Rishi of the gods, could not sustain the joy which it brought; and that she might not die she went to heaven.

19. Then the queen's sister, with an influence like a mother's, undistinguished from the real mother in her affection or tenderness, brought up as her own son the young prince who was like the offspring of the gods.

20. Then like the young sun on the eastern mountain or the fire when fanned by the wind, the prince gradually grew in all due perfection, like the moon in the fortnight of brightness.

21. Then they brought him as presents from the houses of his friends costly unguents of sandalwood, and strings of gems exactly like wreaths of plants, and little golden carriages yoked with deer;

22. Ornaments also suitable to his age, and elephants, deer, and horses made of gold, carriages and oxen decked with rich garments, and carts gay with silver and gold.

23. Thus indulged with all sorts of such objects to please the senses as were suitable to his years,—child as he was, he behaved not like a child in gravity, purity, wisdom, and dignity.

24. When he had passed the period of childhood and reached that of middle youth, the young prince learned in a few days the various sciences suitable to his race, which generally took many years to master.

25. But having heard before from the great seer Asita his destined future which was to embrace transcendental happiness, the anxious care of the king of the present Sâkya race turned the prince to sensual pleasures.

26. Then he sought for him from a family of unblemished moral excellence a bride possessed of beauty, modesty, and gentle bearing, of wide-spread glory, Yasodharâ by name, having a name well worthy of her, a very goddess of good fortune.

27. Then after that the prince, beloved of the king his father, he who was like Sanatkumâra, rejoiced in the society of that Sâkya princess as the thousand-eyed (Indra) rejoiced with his bride Sakî.

28. 'He might perchance see some inauspicious sight which could disturb his mind,'—thus reflecting the king had

a dwelling prepared for him apart from the busy press in the recesses of the palace.

29. Then he spent his time in those royal apartments, furnished with the delights proper for every season, gaily decorated like heavenly chariots upon the earth, and bright like the clouds of autumn, amidst the splendid musical concerts of singing-women.

30. With the softly-sounding tambourines beaten by the tips of the women's hands, and ornamented with golden rims, and with the dances which were like the dances of the heavenly nymphs, that palace shone like Mount Kailâsa.

31. There the women delighted him with their soft voices, their beautiful pearl-garlands, their playful intoxication, their sweet laughter, and their stolen glances concealed by their brows.

32. Borne in the arms of these women well-skilled in the ways of love, and reckless in the pursuit of pleasure, he fell from the roof of a pavilion and yet reached not the ground, like a holy sage stepping from a heavenly chariot.

THE GREAT RETIREMENT

Now on a certain day the Future Buddha wished to go to the park, and told his charioteer to make ready the chariot. Accordingly the man brought out a sumptuous and elegant chariot, and adorning it richly, he harnessed to it four state-horses of the Sindhava breed, as white as the petals of the white lotus, and announced to the Future Buddha that everything was ready. And the Future Buddha mounted the chariot, which was like to a palace of the gods, and proceeded towards the park.

"The time for the enlightenment of prince Siddhattha draweth nigh," thought the gods; "we must show him a sign:" and they changed one of their number into a decrepit old man, broken-toothed, gray-haired, crooked and bent of body, leaning on a staff, and trembling, and showed him to

the Future Buddha, but so that only he and the charioteer
saw him.

Then said the Future Buddha to the charioteer, in the
manner related in the Mahāpadāna,—

"Friend, pray, who is this man? Even his hair is not like
that of other men." And when he heard the answer, he said,
"Shame on birth, since to every one that is born old age must
come." And agitated in heart, he thereupon returned and
ascended his palace.

"Why has my son returned so quickly?" asked the king.

"Sire, he has seen an old man," was the reply; "and because he has seen an old man, he is about to retire from
the world."

"Do you want to kill me, that you say such things? Quickly
get ready some plays to be performed before my son. If we
can but get him to enjoying pleasure, he will cease to think
of retiring from the world." Then the king extended the guard
to half a league in each direction.

Again, on a certain day, as the Future Buddha was going
to the park, he saw a diseased man whom the gods had
fashioned; and having again made inquiry, he returned, agitated in heart, and ascended his palace.

And the king made the same inquiry and gave the same
orders as before; and again extending the guard, placed them
for three quarters of a league around.

And again on a certain day, as the Future Buddha was
going to the park, he saw a dead man whom the gods had
fashioned; and having again made inquiry, he returned, agitated in heart, and ascended his palace.

And the king made the same inquiry and gave the same
orders as before; and again extending the guard, placed them
for a league around.

And again on a certain day, as the Future Buddha was
going to the park, he saw a monk, carefully and decently clad,
whom the gods had fashioned; and he asked his charioteer,
"Pray, who is this man?"

Now although there was no Buddha in the world, and
the charioteer had no knowledge of either monks or their

good qualities, yet by the power of the gods he was inspired to say, "Sire, this is one who has retired from the world;" and he thereupon proceeded to sound the praises of retirement from the world. The thought of retiring from the world was a pleasing one to the Future Buddha, and this day he went on until he came to the park. The repeaters of the Dīgha, however, say that he went to the park after having seen all the Four Signs on one and the same day.

When he had disported himself there throughout the day, and had bathed in the royal pleasure-tank, he went at sunset and sat down on the royal resting-stone with the intention of adorning himself. Then gathered around him his attendants with diverse-colored cloths, many kinds and styles of ornaments, and with garlands, perfumes, and ointments. At that instant the throne on which Sakka was sitting grew hot. And Sakka, considering who it could be that was desirous of dislodging him, perceived that it was the time of the adornment of a Future Buddha. And addressing Vissakamma, he said,—

"My good Vissakamma, to-night, in the middle watch, prince Siddhattha will go forth on the Great Retirement, and this is his last adorning of himself. Go to the park, and adorn that eminent man with celestial ornaments."

"Very well," said Vissakamma, in assent; and came on the instant, by his superhuman power, into the presence of the Future Buddha. And assuming the guise of a barber, he took from the real barber the turban-cloth, and began to wind it round the Future Buddha's head; but as soon as the Future Buddha felt the touch of his hand, he knew that it was no man, but a god.

Now once round his head took up a thousand cloths, and the fold was like to a circlet of precious stones; the second time round took another thousand cloths, and so on, until ten times round had taken up ten thousand cloths. Now let no one think, "How was it possible to use so many cloths on one small head?" for the very largest of them all had only the size of a sāma-creeper blossom, and the others that of kutumbaka flowers. Thus the Future Buddha's head resembled a kuyyaka blossom twisted about with lotus filaments.

And having adorned himself with great richness,—while adepts in different kinds of tabors and tom-toms were showing their skill, and Brahmans with cries of victory and joy, and bards and poets with propitious words and shouts of praise saluted him,—he mounted his superbly decorated chariot.

At this juncture, Suddhodana the king, having heard that the mother of Rāhula had brought forth a son, sent a messenger, saying, "Announce the glad news to my son."

On hearing the message, the Future Buddha said, "An impediment [rāhula] has been born; a fetter has been born."

"What did my son say?" questioned the king; and when he had heard the answer, he said, "My grandson's name shall be prince Rāhula from this very day."

But the Future Buddha in his splendid chariot entered the city with a pomp and magnificence of glory that enraptured all minds. At the same moment Kisā Gotamī, a virgin of the warrior caste, ascended to the roof of her palace, and beheld the beauty and majesty of the Future Buddha, as he circumambulated the city; and in her pleasure and satisfaction at the sight, she burst forth into this song of joy:—

> "Full happy now that mother is,
> Full happy now that father is,
> Full happy now that woman is,
> Who owns this lord so glorious!"

On hearing this, the Future Buddha thought, "In beholding a handsome figure the heart of a mother attains Nirvana, the heart of a father attains Nirvana, the heart of a wife attains Nirvana. This is what she says. But wherein does Nirvana consist?" And to him, whose mind was already averse to passion, the answer came: "When the fire of lust is extinct, that is Nirvana; when the fires of hatred and infatuation are extinct, that is Nirvana; when pride, false belief, and all other passions and torments are extinct, that is Nirvana. She has taught me a good lesson. Certainly, Nirvana is what I am looking for. It behooves me this very day to quit the household life, and to retire from the world in quest of Nirvana. I will send this lady a teacher's fee." And loosening from his neck a pearl necklace worth a hundred thousand pieces of money, he sent it to Kisā Gotamī. And great was her satisfaction at this, for she thought, "Prince Siddhattha has fallen in love with me, and has sent me a present."

And the Future Buddha entered his palace in great splendor, and lay on his couch of state. And straightway richly dressed women, skilled in all manner of dance and song, and beautiful as celestial nymphs, gathered about him with all kinds of musical instruments, and with dance, song, and music they endeavored to please him. But the Future Buddha's aversion to passion did not allow him to take pleasure in the spectacle, and he fell into a brief slumber. And the women, exclaiming, "He for whose sake we should perform has fallen asleep. Of what use is it to weary ourselves any longer?" threw their various instruments on the ground, and lay down. And the lamps fed with sweet-smelling oil continued to burn. And the Future Buddha awoke, and seating himself cross-legged on his couch, perceived these women lying asleep, with their musical instruments scattered about them on the floor,—some with their bodies wet with trickling phlegm and spittle; some grinding their teeth, and muttering and talking in their sleep; some with their mouths open; and some with their dress fallen apart so as plainly to disclose their loathsome nakedness. This great alteration in their appearance still further increased his aversion for sensual pleasures. To him that magnificent apartment, as splendid as the palace of Sakka, began to seem like a cemetery filled with dead bodies impaled and left to rot; and the three modes of existence appeared like houses all ablaze. And breathing forth the solemn utterance, "How oppressive and stifling is it all!" his mind turned ardently to retiring from the world. "It behooves me to go forth on the Great Retirement this very day," said he; and he arose from his couch, and coming near the door, called out,—

"Who's there?"

"Master, it is I, Channa," replied the courtier who had been sleeping with his head on the threshold.

"I wish to go forth on the Great Retirement to-day. Saddle a horse for me."

"Yes, sire." And taking saddle and bridle with him, the courtier started for the stable. There, by the light of lamps fed with sweet-smelling oils, he perceived the mighty steed Kanthaka in his pleasant quarters, under a canopy of cloth beautified with a pattern of jasmine flowers. "This is the one for me to saddle to-day," thought he; and he saddled Kanthaka.

"He is drawing the girth very tight," thought Kanthaka, whilst he was being saddled; "it is not at all as on other days, when I am saddled for rides in the park and the like. It must be that to-day my master wishes to issue forth on the Great Retirement." And in his delight he neighed a loud neigh. And that neigh would have spread through the whole town, had not the gods stopped the sound, and suffered no one to hear it.

Now the Future Buddha, after he had sent Channa on his errand, thought to himself, "I will take just one look at my son;" and, rising from the couch on which he was sitting, he went to the suite of apartments occupied by the mother of Rāhula, and opened the door of her chamber. Within the chamber was burning a lamp fed with sweet-smelling oil, and the mother of Rāhula lay sleeping on a couch strewn deep with jasmine and other flowers, her hand resting on the head of her son. When the Future Buddha reached the threshold, he paused, and gazed at the two from where he stood.

"If I were to raise my wife's hand from off the child's head, and take him up, she would awake, and thus prevent my departure. I will first become a Buddha, and then come back and see my son." So saying, he descended from the palace.

Now that which is said in the Jātaka Commentary, "At that time Rāhula was seven days old," is not found in the other commentaries. Therefore the account above given is to be accepted.

When the Future Buddha had thus descended from the palace, he came near to his horse, and said,—

"My dear Kanthaka, save me now this one night; and then, when thanks to you I have become a Buddha, I will save the world of gods and men." And thereupon he vaulted upon Kanthaka's back.

Now Kanthaka was eighteen cubits long from his neck to his tail, and of corresponding height; he was strong and swift, and white all over like a polished conch-shell. If he neighed or stamped, the sound was so loud as to spread through the whole city; therefore the gods exerted their power, and muffled the sound of his neighing, so that no one heard it; and at every step he took they placed the palms of their hands under his feet.

The Future Buddha rode on the mighty back of the mighty steed, made Channa hold on by the tail, and so arrived at midnight at the great gate of the city.

Now the king, in order that the Future Buddha should not at any time go out of the city without his knowledge, had caused each of the two leaves of the gate to be made so heavy as to need a thousand men to move it. But the Future Buddha had a vigor and a strength that was equal, when reckoned in elephant-power, to the strength of ten thousand million elephants, and, reckoned in man-power, to the strength of a hundred thousand million men.

"If," thought he, "the gate does not open, I will straightway grip tight hold of Kanthaka with my thighs, and, seated as I am on Kanthaka's back, and with Channa holding on by the tail, I will leap up and carry them both with me over the wall, although its height be eighteen cubits."

"If," thought Channa, "the gate is not opened, I will place my master on my shoulder, and tucking Kanthaka under my arm by passing my right hand round him and under his belly, I will leap up and carry them both with me over the wall."

"If," thought Kanthaka, "the gate is not opened, with my master seated as he is on my back, and with Channa holding

31

on by my tail, I will leap up and carry them both with me over the wall."

Now if the gate had not opened, verily one or another of these three persons would have accomplished that whereof he thought; but the divinity that inhabited the gate opened it for them.

At this moment came Māra, with the intention of persuading the Future Buddha to turn back; and standing in the air, he said,—

"Sir, go not forth! For on the seventh day from now the wheel of empire will appear to you, and you shall rule over the four great continents and their two thousand attendant isles. Sir, turn back!"

"Who are you?"

"I am Vasavatti."

"Māra, I knew that the wheel of empire was on the point of appearing to me; but I do not wish for sovereignty. I am about to cause the ten thousand worlds to thunder with my becoming a Buddha."

"I shall catch you," thought Māra, "the very first time you have a lustful, malicious, or unkind thought." And, like an ever-present shadow, he followed after, ever on the watch for some slip.

Thus the Future Buddha, casting away with indifference a universal sovereignty already in his grasp,—spewing it out as if it were but phlegm,—departed from the city in great splendor on the full-moon day of the month Āsāḷhī, when the moon was in Libra. And when he had gone out from the city, he became desirous of looking back at it; but no sooner had the thought arisen in his mind, than the broad earth, seeming to fear lest the Great Being might neglect to perform the act of looking back, split and turned round like a potter's wheel. When the Future Buddha had stood a while facing the city and gazing upon it, and had indicated in that place the spot for the "Shrine of the Turning Back of Kanthaka," he turned Kanthaka in the direction in which he meant to go, and proceeded on his way in great honor and exceeding glory.

For they say the deities bore sixty thousand torches in front of him, and sixty thousand behind him, and sixty thousand on the right hand, and sixty thousand on the left hand. Other deities, standing on the rim of the world, bore torches past all numbering; and still other deities, as well as serpents and birds, accompanied him, and did him homage with heavenly perfumes, garlands, sandal-wood powder, and incense. And the sky was as full of coral flowers as it is of pouring water at the height of the rainy season. Celestial choruses were heard; and on every side bands of music played, some of eight instruments, and some of sixty,—sixty-eight hundred thousand instruments in all. It was as when the storm-clouds thunder on the sea, or when the ocean roars against the Yugandhara rocks.

Advancing in this glory, the Future Buddha in one night passed through three kingdoms, and at the end of thirty leagues he came to the river named Anomā.

But was this as far as the horse could go? Certainly not. For he was able to travel round the world from end to end, as it were round the rim of a wheel lying on its hub, and yet get back before breakfast and eat the food prepared for him. But on this occasion the fragrant garlands and other offerings which the gods and the serpents and the birds threw down upon him from the sky buried him up to his haunches; and as he was obliged to drag his body and cut his way through the tangled mass, he was greatly delayed. Hence it was that he went only thirty leagues.

And the Future Buddha, stopping on the river-bank, said to Channa,—

"What is the name of this river?"

"Sire, its name is Anomā [Illustrious]."

"And my retirement from the world shall also be called Anomā," replied the Future Buddha. Saying this, he gave the signal to his horse with his heel; and the horse sprang over the river, which had a breadth of eight usabhas, and landed on the opposite bank. And the Future Buddha, dismounting and standing on the sandy beach that stretched away like a sheet of silver, said to Channa,—

"My good Channa, take these ornaments and Kanthaka and go home. I am about to retire from the world."

"Sire, I also will retire from the world."

Three times the Future Buddha refused him, saying, "It is not for you to retire from the world. Go now!" and made him take the ornaments and Kanthaka.

Next he thought, "These locks of mine are not suited to a monk; but there is no one fit to cut the hair of a Future Buddha. Therefore I will cut them off myself with my sword." And grasping a simitar with his right hand, he seized his top-knot with his left hand, and cut it off, together with the diadem. His hair thus became two finger-breadths in length, and curling to the right, lay close to his head. As long as he lived it remained of that length, and the beard was proportionate. And never again did he have to cut either hair or beard.

Then the Future Buddha seized hold of his top-knot and diadem, and threw them into the air, saying,—

"If I am to become a Buddha, let them stay in the sky; but if not, let them fall to the ground."

The top-knot and jewelled turban mounted for a distance of a league into the air, and there came to a stop. And Sakka, the king of the gods, perceiving them with his divine eye, received them in an appropriate jewelled casket, and established it in the Heaven of the Thirty-three as the "Shrine of the Diadem."

"His hair he cut, so sweet with many pleasant scents,
This Chief of Men, and high impelled it towards the sky;
And there god Vāsava, the god with thousand eyes,
In golden casket caught it, bowing low his head."

Again the Future Buddha thought, "These garments of mine, made of Benares cloth, are not suited to a monk."

Now the Mahā-Brahma god, Ghaṭīkāra, who had been a friend of his in the time of the Buddha Kassapa, and whose affection for him had not grown old in the long interval since that Buddha, thought to himself,—

"To-day my friend has gone forth on the Great Retirement. I will bring him the requisites of a monk."

> "Robes, three in all, the bowl for alms,
> The razor, needle, and the belt,
> And water-strainer,—just these eight
> Are needed by th' ecstatic monk."

Taking the above eight requisites of a monk, he gave them to him.

When the Future Buddha had put on this most excellent vesture, the symbol of saintship and of retirement from the world, he dismissed Channa, saying,—

"Channa, go tell my father and my mother from me that I am well."

And Channa did obeisance to the Future Buddha; and keeping his right side towards him, he departed.

But Kanthaka, who had stood listening to the Future Buddha while he was conferring with Channa, was unable to bear his grief at the thought, "I shall never see my master any more." And as he passed out of sight, his heart burst, and he died, and was reborn in the Heaven of the Thirty-three as the god Kanthaka.

At first the grief of Channa had been but single; but now he was oppressed with a second sorrow in the death of Kanthaka, and came weeping and wailing to the city.

THE GREAT STRUGGLE AND THE ATTAINMENT OF BUDDHASHIP

Then the Future Buddha took his noonday rest on the banks of the river, in a grove of sal-trees in full bloom. And at nightfall, at the time the flowers droop on their stalks, he rose up, like a lion when he bestirs himself, and went towards the Bo-tree, along a road which the gods had decked, and which was eight usabhas wide.

The snakes, the fairies, the birds, and other classes of beings did him homage with celestial perfumes, flowers, and other offerings, and celestial choruses poured forth heavenly music; so that the ten thousand worlds were filled with these perfumes, garlands, and shouts of acclaim.

Just then there came from the opposite direction a grass-cutter named Sotthiya, and he was carrying grass. And when he saw the Great Being, that he was a holy man, he gave him eight handfuls of grass. The Future Buddha took the grass, and ascending the throne of wisdom, stood on the southern side and faced the north. Instantly the southern half of the world sank, until it seemed to touch the Avīci hell, while the northern half rose to the highest of the heavens.

"Methinks," said the Future Buddha, "this cannot be the place for the attainment of the supreme wisdom;" and walking round the tree with his right side towards it, he came to the western side and faced the east. Then the western half of the world sank, until it seemed to touch the Avīci hell, while the eastern half rose to the highest of the heavens. Wherever, indeed, he stood, the broad earth rose and fell, as though it had been a huge cart-wheel lying on its hub, and some one were treading on the rim.

"Methinks," said the Future Buddha, "this also cannot be the place for the attainment of supreme wisdom;" and walking round the tree with his right side towards it, he came to the northern side and faced the south. Then the northern half of the world sank, until it seemed to touch the Avīci hell, while the southern half rose to the highest of the heavens.

"Methinks," said the Future Buddha, "this also cannot be the place for the attainment of supreme wisdom;" and walking round the tree with his right side towards it, he came to the eastern side and faced the west. Now it is on the eastern side of their Bo-trees that all The Buddhas have sat cross-legged, and that side neither trembles nor quakes.

Then the Great Being, saying to himself, "This is the immovable spot on which all The Buddhas have planted themselves! This is the place for destroying passion's net!" took hold of his handful of grass by one end, and shook it out there. And straightway the blades of grass formed themselves into a seat fourteen cubits long, of such symmetry of shape as not even the most skilful painter or carver could design.

Then the Future Buddha turned his back to the trunk of the Bo-tree and faced the east. And making the mighty resolution, "Let my skin, and sinews, and bones become dry, and welcome! and let all the flesh and blood in my body dry up! but never from this seat will I stir, until I have attained the supreme and absolute wisdom!" he sat himself down cross-legged in an unconquerable position, from which not even the descent of a hundred thunder-bolts at once could have dislodged him.

At this point the god Māra, exclaiming, "Prince Siddhattha is desirous of passing beyond my control, but I will never allow it!" went and announced the news to his army, and sounding the Māra war-cry, drew out for battle. Now Māra's army extended in front of him for twelve leagues, and to the right and to the left for twelve leagues, and in the rear as far as to the confines of the world, and it was nine leagues high. And when it shouted, it made an earthquake-like roaring and rumbling over a space of a thousand leagues. And the god Māra, mounting his elephant, which was a hundred and fifty leagues high, and had the name "Girded-with-mountains," caused a thousand arms to appear on his body, and with these he grasped a variety of weapons. Also in the remainder of that army, no two persons carried the same weapon; and diverse also in their appearances and countenances, the host swept on like a flood to overwhelm the Great Being.

Now deities throughout the ten thousand worlds were busy singing the praises of the Great Being. Sakka, the king of the gods, was blowing the conch-shell Vijayuttara. (This conch, they say, was a hundred and twenty cubits long, and when once it had been filled with wind, it would sound for four months before it stopped.) The great black snake-king sang more than a hundred laudatory verses. And Mahā-Brahma stood holding aloft the white umbrella. But as Māra's army gradually drew near to the throne of wisdom, not one of these gods was able to stand his ground, but each fled straight before him. The black snake-king dived into the ground, and coming to the snake-abode, Mañjerika, which was five hundred leagues in extent, he covered his face with both hands and lay down. Sakka slung his conch-shell Vijayuttara over his back, and took up his position on the rim of the world. Mahā-Brahma left the white umbrella at the end of the world, and fled to his Brahma-abode. Not a single deity was able to stand his ground, and the Great Being was left sitting alone.

Then said Māra to his followers,—

"My friends, Siddhattha, the son of Suddhodana, is far greater than any other man, and we shall never be able to fight him in front. We will attack him from behind."

All the gods had now disappeared, and the Great Being looked around on three sides, and said to himself, "There is no one here." Then looking to the north, he perceived Māra's army coming on like a flood, and said,—

"Here is this multitude exerting all their strength and power against me alone. My mother and father are not here, nor my brother, nor any other relative. But I have these Ten Perfections, like old retainers long cherished at my board. It therefore behooves me to make the Ten Perfections my shield and my sword, and to strike a blow with them that shall destroy this strong array." And he remained sitting, and reflected on the Ten Perfections.

Thereupon the god Māra caused a whirlwind, thinking, "By this will I drive away Siddhattha." Straightway the east wind and all the other different winds began to blow; but although these winds could have torn their way through mountain-peaks half a league, or two leagues, or three leagues high, or have uprooted forest-shrubs and trees, or have reduced to powder and scattered in all directions, villages and towns, yet when they reached the Future Buddha, such was the energy of the Great Being's merit, they lost all power and were not able to cause so much as a fluttering of the edge of his priestly robe.

Then he caused a great rain-storm, saying, "With water will I overwhelm and drown him." And through his mighty power, clouds of a hundred strata, and clouds of a thousand strata arose, and also the other different kinds. And these rained down, until the earth became gullied by the torrents of water which fell, and until the floods had risen over the tops of every forest-tree. But on coming to the Great Being, this mighty inundation was not able to wet his priestly robes as much as a dew-drop would have done.

Then he caused a shower of rocks, in which immense mountain-peaks flew smoking and flaming through the sky. But on reaching the Future Buddha they became celestial bouquets of flowers.

Then he caused a shower of weapons, in which single-edged, and double-edged swords, spears, and arrows flew smoking and flaming through the sky. But on reaching the Future Buddha they became celestial flowers.

Then he caused a shower of live coals, in which live coals as red as kimsuka flowers flew through the sky. But they scattered themselves at the Future Buddha's feet as a shower of celestial flowers.

Then he caused a shower of hot ashes, in which ashes that glowed like fire flew through the sky. But they fell at the Future Buddha's feet as sandal-wood powder.

Then he caused a shower of sand, in which very fine sand flew smoking and flaming through the sky. But it fell at the Future Buddha's feet as celestial flowers.

Then he caused a shower of mud, in which mud flew smoking and flaming through the sky. But it fell at the Future Buddha's feet as celestial ointment.

Then he caused a darkness, thinking, "By this will I frighten Siddhattha, and drive him away." And the darkness became fourfold, and very dense. But on reaching the Future Buddha it disappeared like darkness before the light of the sun.

Māra, being thus unable with these nine storms of wind, rain, rocks, weapons, live coals, hot ashes, sand, mud, and darkness, to drive away the Future Buddha, gave command to his followers, "Look ye now! Why stand ye still? Seize, kill, drive away this prince!" And, arming himself with a discus, and seated upon the shoulders of the elephant "Girded-with-mountains," he drew near the Future Buddha, and said,—

"Siddhattha, arise from this seat! It does not belong to you, but to me."

When the Great Being heard this he said,—

"Māra, you have not fulfilled the Ten Perfections in any of their three grades; nor have you made the five great donations; nor have you striven for knowledge, nor for the welfare of the world, nor for enlightenment. This seat does not belong to you, but to me."

Unable to restrain his fury, the enraged Māra now hurled his discus. But the Great Being reflected on the Ten Perfections, and the discus changed into a canopy of flowers, and remained suspended over his head. Yet they say that this keen-edged discus, when at other times Māra hurled it in anger, would cut through solid stone pillars as if they had been the tips of bamboo shoots. But on this occasion it became a canopy of flowers. Then the followers of Māra began hurling immense mountain-crags, saying, "This will make him get up from his seat and flee." But the Great Being kept his thoughts on the Ten Perfections, and the crags also became wreaths of flowers, and then fell to the ground.

Now the gods meanwhile were standing on the rim of the world, and craning their necks to look, saying,—

"Ah, woe the day! The handsome form of prince Siddhattha will surely be destroyed! What will he do to save himself?"

Then the Great Being, after his assertion that the seat which Future Buddhas had always used on the day of their complete enlightenment belonged to him, continued, and said,—

"Māra, who is witness to your having given donations?"

Said Māra, "All these, as many as you see here, are my witnesses;" and he stretched out his hand in the direction of his army. And instantly from Māra's army came a roar, "I am his witness! I am his witness!" which was like to the roar of an earthquake.

Then said Māra to the Great Being,—

"Siddhattha, who is witness to your having given donations?"

"Your witnesses," replied the Great Being, "are animate

beings, and I have no animate witnesses present. However, not to mention the donations which I gave in other existences, the great seven-hundred-fold donation which I gave in my Vessantara existence shall now be testified to by the solid earth, inanimate though she be." And drawing forth his right hand from beneath his priestly robe, he stretched it out towards the mighty earth, and said, "Are you witness, or are you not, to my having given a great seven-hundred-fold donation in my Vessantara existence?"

And the mighty earth thundered, "I bear you witness!" with a hundred, a thousand, a hundred thousand roars, as if to overwhelm the army of Māra.

Now while the Great Being was thus calling to mind the donation he gave in his Vessantara existence, and saying to himself, "Siddhattha, that was a great and excellent donation which you gave," the hundred-and-fifty-league-high elephant "Girded-with-mountains" fell upon his knees before the Great Being. And the followers of Māra fled away in all directions. No two went the same way, but leaving their head-ornaments and their cloaks behind, they fled straight before them.

Then the hosts of the gods, when they saw the army of Māra flee, cried out, "Māra is defeated! Prince Siddhattha has conquered! Let us go celebrate the victory!" And the snakes egging on the snakes, the birds the birds, the deities the deities, and the Brahma-angels the Brahma-angels, they came with perfumes, garlands, and other offerings in their hands to the Great Being on the throne of wisdom. And as they came,—

"The victory now hath this illustrious Buddha won!
The Wicked One, the Slayer, hath defeated been!"
Thus round the throne of wisdom shouted joyously
The bands of snakes their songs of victory for the Sage;

"The victory now hath this illustrious Buddha won!
The Wicked One, the Slayer, hath defeated been!"
Thus round the throne of wisdom shouted joyously
The flocks of birds their songs of victory for the Sage;

"The victory now hath this illustrious Buddha won!
The Wicked One, the Slayer, hath defeated been!"
Thus round the throne of wisdom shouted joyously
The bands of gods their songs of victory for the Sage;

"The victory now hath this illustrious Buddha won!
The Wicked One, the Slayer, hath defeated been!"
Thus round the throne of wisdom shouted joyously
The Brahma-angels songs of victory for the Saint.

And the remaining deities, also, throughout the ten thousand worlds, made offerings of garlands, perfumes, and ointments, and in many a hymn extolled him.

It was before the sun had set that the Great Being thus vanquished the army of Māra. And then, while the Bo-tree in homage rained red, coral-like sprigs upon his priestly robes, he acquired in the first watch of the night the knowledge of previous existences; in the middle watch of the night, the divine eye; and in the last watch of the night, his intellect fathomed Dependent Origination.

Now while he was musing on the twelve terms of Dependent Origination, forwards and backwards, round and back again, the ten thousand worlds quaked twelve times, as far as to their ocean boundaries. And when the Great Being, at the dawning of the day, had thus made the ten thousand worlds thunder with his attainment of omniscience, all these worlds became most gloriously adorned. Flags and banners erected on the eastern rim of the world let their streamers fly to the western rim of the world; likewise those erected on the western rim of the world, to the eastern rim of the world; those erected on the northern rim of the world, to the southern rim of the world; and those erected on the southern rim of the world, to the northern rim of the world; while those erected on the level of the earth let theirs fly until they beat against the Brahma-world; and those of the Brahma-world let theirs hang down to the level of the earth. Throughout the ten thousand worlds the flowering trees bloomed; the fruit trees were weighted down by their burden of fruit; trunk-lotuses bloomed on the trunks of trees; branch-lotuses on the branches of trees; vine-lotuses on the vines; hanging-lotuses in the sky; and stalk-lotuses burst through the rocks and came up by sevens. The system of ten thousand worlds was like a bouquet of flowers sent whirling through the air, or like a thick carpet of flowers; in the intermundane spaces the eight-thousand-league-long hells, which not even the light of seven suns had formerly been able to illumine, were now flooded with radiance; the eighty-four-thousand-league-deep ocean became sweet to the taste; the rivers checked their flowing; the blind from birth received their sight; the deaf from birth their hearing; the cripples from birth the use of their limbs; and the bonds and fetters of captives broke and fell off.

When thus he had attained to omniscience, and was the centre of such unparalleled glory and homage, and so many prodigies were happening about him, he breathed forth that solemn utterance which has never been omitted by any of The Buddhas:

> "Through birth and rebirth's endless round,
> Seeking in vain, I hastened on,
> To find who framed this edifice.
> What misery!—birth incessantly!
>
> "O builder! I've discovered thee!
> This fabric thou shalt ne'er rebuild!
> Thy rafters all are broken now,
> And pointed roof demolished lies!
> This mind has demolition reached,
> And seen the last of all desire!"

The period of time, therefore, from the existence in the Tusita Heaven to this attainment of omniscience on the throne of wisdom, constitutes the Intermediate Epoch.

THE DEATH OF THE BUDDHA

Then The Blessed One addressed the venerable Ānanda:—

"It may be, Ānanda, that some of you will think, 'The word of The Teacher is a thing of the past; we have now no Teacher.' But that, Ānanda, is not the correct view. The Doctrine and Discipline, Ānanda, which I have taught and enjoined upon you is to be your teacher when I am gone. But whereas now, Ānanda, all the priests address each other with the title of 'brother,' not so must they address each other after I am gone. A senior priest, Ānanda, is to address a junior priest either by his given name, or by his family name, or by the title of 'brother;' a junior priest is to address a senior priest with the title 'reverend sir,' or 'venerable.' If the Order, Ānanda, wish to do so, after I am gone they may abrogate all the lesser and minor precepts. On Channa, Ānanda, after I am gone, the higher penalty is to be inflicted."

"Reverend Sir, what is this higher penalty?"

"Let Channa, Ānanda, say what he likes, he is not to be spoken to nor admonished nor instructed by the priests."

Then The Blessed One addressed the priests:—

"It may be, O priests, that some priest has a doubt or perplexity respecting either The Buddha or the Doctrine or the Order or the Path or the course of conduct. Ask any questions, O priests, and suffer not that afterwards ye feel remorse, saying, 'Our Teacher was present with us, but we failed to ask him all our questions.'"

When he had so spoken, the priests remained silent.

And a second time The Blessed One, and a third time The Blessed One addressed the priests:—

"It may be, O priests, that some priest has a doubt or perplexity respecting either The Buddha or the Doctrine or the Order or the Path or the course of conduct. Ask any question, O priests, and suffer not that afterwards ye feel re-

44

morse, saying, 'Our Teacher was present with us, but we failed to ask him all our questions.'"

And a third time the priests remained silent.

Then The Blessed One addressed the priests:—

"It may be, O priests, that it is out of respect to The Teacher that ye ask no questions. Then let each one speak to his friend."

And when he had thus spoken, the priests remained silent.

Then the venerable Ānanda spoke to The Blessed One as follows:—

"It is wonderful, Reverend Sir! It is marvellous, Reverend Sir! Reverend Sir, I have faith to believe that in this congregation of priests not a single priest has a doubt or perplexity respecting either The Buddha or the Doctrine or the Order or the Path or the course of conduct."

"With you, Ānanda, it is a matter of faith, when you say that; but with The Tathāgata, Ānanda, it is a matter of knowledge that in this congregation of priests not a single priest has a doubt or perplexity respecting either The Buddha or the Doctrine or the Order or the Path or the course of conduct. For of all these five hundred priests, Ānanda, the most backward one has become converted, and is not liable to pass into a lower state of existence, but is destined necessarily to attain supreme wisdom."

Then The Blessed One addressed the priests:—

"And now, O priests, I take my leave of you; all the constituents of being are transitory; work out your salvation with diligence."

And this was the last word of The Tathāgata.

Thereupon The Blessed One entered the first trance; and rising from the first trance, he entered the second trance; and rising from the second trance, he entered the third trance; and rising from the third trance, he entered the fourth trance; and rising from the fourth trance, he entered the realm of the infinity of space; and rising from the realm of the infinity of space, he entered the realm of the infinity of consciousness; and rising from the realm of the infinity of consciousness, he entered the realm of nothingness; and rising from the realm

of nothingness, he entered the realm of neither perception
nor yet non-perception; and rising from the realm of neither
perception nor yet non-perception, he arrived at the cessation of perception and sensation.

Thereupon the venerable Ānanda spoke to the venerable
Anuruddha as follows:—

"Reverend Anuruddha, The Blessed One has passed into
Nirvana."

"Nay, brother Ānanda, The Blessed One has not passed
into Nirvana; he has arrived at the cessation of perception and
sensation."

Thereupon The Blessed One rising from the cessation of
his perception and sensation, entered the realm of neither
perception nor yet non-perception; and rising from the realm
of neither perception nor yet non-perception, he entered
the realm of nothingness; and rising from the realm of nothingness, he entered the realm of the infinity of consciousness;
and rising from the realm of the infinity of consciousness, he
entered the realm of the infinity of space; and rising from
the realm of the infinity of space, he entered the fourth trance;
and rising from the fourth trance, he entered the third trance;
and rising from the third trance, he entered the second trance;
and rising from the second trance, he entered the first
trance; and rising from the first trance, he entered the second
trance; and rising from the second trance, he entered the
third trance; and rising from the third trance, he entered
the fourth trance; and rising from the fourth trance, immediately The Blessed One passed into Nirvana.

Chapter III
"THE GOING FORTH" AND TWO SERMONS

"The Going Forth," one of the oldest poems in Buddhist literature, is based on the Buddha's encounter with the King of Magadha, Bimbisâra, who even with promises of worldly glory was unable to tempt Gautama from his resolve to gain enlightenment. After his enlightenment the Buddha went to Benares, where in a deer park outside the city he delivered his first sermon to the five ascetics who had left him in despair when he had given up the practice of extreme austerities. With this sermon, which offers in highly condensed form the essence of Buddhist philosophy, Gautama set in motion the Wheel of Law by proclaiming the Four Noble Truths, the Noble Eightfold Path, and the Middle Way. The first sermon is followed by the Fire Sermon, which was the third in order and was given on the Gayā Scarp at Uruvelā as a protest against three Brahmanical ascetics, fire-worshippers, chief of whom was Uruvelā Kassapa. The Buddha by the use of his superhuman powers made it impossible for them to kindle the fire, and there was a great flood from which he saved the sacrificers. Thereupon he delivered the sermon, converting on the spot to the Order of Monks, Uruvelā Kassapa and his thousand followers.

"THE GOING FORTH"

1. I will praise going forth as the far-seeing One did, the Wanderer's life, such as when he had thought the matter out he deliberately chose.

2. 'Full of hindrances is this household life, the haunt of

47

passion. Free as the air is the homeless state.' Thus he considered, and went forth.

3. When he had gone forth he gave up wrong-doing in action, and evil speech he left behind; pure did he make his mode of livelihood.

4. To the king's town the Buddha went, to Giribbaja in Magadha. Full of outward signs of worth, he was collecting alms for food.

5. Him saw Bimbisâra standing on the upper terrace of his palace. On seeing that he had those signs, thus did he speak:—

6. 'Hearken to this man, Sirs, handsome is he, great and pure; guarded in conduct, he looks not more than a fathom's length before him.

7. 'With downcast eye and self-possessed is he, surely of no mean birth. Let the king's messengers hasten and find out: Where is the mendicant going?'

8. Thus sent, the messengers hurried after him, and asked themselves: 'Where is the Bhikshu going, where does he mean to stay?

9. 'Going on his round for alms regularly from house to house, guarded as to the door (of his senses), well restrained, quickly has he filled up his bowl, he the while calm and self-possessed.

10. 'His round for alms accomplished, the Sage has gone out from the town. He has gained the mountain Paṇḍava. There is it that he means to stay.'

11. No sooner had they seen him stop than the messengers in their turn stopped. One messenger alone returned, and to the king made speech:—

12. 'On the eastern slope of Mount Paṇḍava, that Bhikshu, O King, has taken his seat, like a tiger-king, like a lion in his mountain cave.'

13. When he heard his servant's word the warrior, in all haste, went forth in his state chariot to the mountain Paṇḍava.

14. Where the carriage-road ended, there alighting from

his car, on foot the prince went on till he came near; and
then he took his seat.

15. On sitting down the king, with courteous words, exchanged with him the greetings of a friend. Then he spake
thus:—

16. 'Young art thou and of tender years, a lad in his
first youth, fine is thy colour like a high-born noble's.

17. 'As the glory of the vanguard of the army, at the
head of a band of heroes I would give thee wealth. Do thou
accept this, and tell me thy lineage now that I ask it.'

18. 'Hard by Himâlaya's slopes, O King, there is a land of
wealth and power, the dwellers therein are of the Kosalas;

19. 'Descendants of the Sun by race, Sâkiyas they are by
birth. 'Tis from that clan I have gone forth, longing no more
for sensual delights.

20. 'Seeing the danger in them, looking on going forth
as bliss, I shall go on in the struggle, for in that my mind delights.'

THE SERMON AT BENARES

The five bhikshus saw their old teacher approach and
agreed among themselves not to salute him, nor to address
him as a master, but by his name only. "For," so they said,
"he has broken his vow and has abandoned holiness. He
is no bhikshu but Gautama, and Gautama has become a man
who lives in abundance and indulges in the pleasures of
worldliness."

But when the Blessed One approached in a dignified
manner, they involuntarily rose from their seats and greeted
him in spite of their resolution. Still they called him by his
name and addressed him as "friend."

When they had thus received the Blessed One, he said:
"Do not call the Tathâgata by his name nor address him
'friend,' for he is Buddha, the Holy One. Buddha looks
equally with a kind heart on all living beings and they there-

fore call him 'Father.' To disrespect a father is wrong; to despise him, is sin.

"The Tathâgata," Buddha continued, "does not seek salvation in austerities, but for that reason you must not think that he indulges in worldly pleasures, nor does he live in abundance. The Tathâgata has found the middle path.

"Neither abstinence from fish or flesh, nor going naked, nor shaving the head, nor wearing matted hair, nor dressing in a rough garment, nor covering oneself with dirt, nor sacrificing to Agni, will cleanse a man who is not free from delusions.

"Reading the Vêdas, making offerings to priests, or sacrifices to the gods, self-mortification by heat or cold, and many such penances performed for the sake of immortality, these do not cleanse the man who is not free from delusions.

"Anger, drunkenness, obstinacy, bigotry, deception, envy, self-praise, disparaging others, superciliousness, and evil intentions constitute uncleanness; not verily the eating of flesh.

"Let me teach you, O bhikshus, the middle path, which keeps aloof from both extremes. By suffering, the emaciated devotee produces confusion and sickly thoughts in his mind. Mortification is not conducive even to worldly knowledge; how much less to a triumph over the senses!

"He who fills his lamp with water will not dispel the darkness, and he who tries to light a fire with rotten wood will fail.

"Mortifications are painful, vain, and profitless. And how can any one be free from self by leading a wretched life if he does not succeed in quenching the fires of lust.

"All mortification is vain so long as self remains, so long as self continues to lust after either worldly or heavenly pleasures. But he in whom self has become extinct is free from lust; he will desire neither worldly nor heavenly pleasures, and the satisfaction of his natural wants will not defile him. Let him eat and drink according to the needs of the body.

"Water surrounds the lotus-flower, but does not wet its petals.

"On the other hand, sensuality of all kind is enervating. The sensual man is a slave of his passions, and pleasure-seeking is degrading and vulgar.

"But to satisfy the necessities of life is not evil. To keep the body in good health is a duty, for otherwise we shall not be able to trim the lamp of wisdom, and keep our mind strong and clear.

"This is the middle path, O bhikshus, that keeps aloof from both extremes."

And the Blessed One spoke kindly to his disciples, pitying them for their errors, and pointing out the uselessness of their endeavors, and the ice of ill-will that chilled their hearts melted away under the gentle warmth of the Master's persuasion.

Now the Blessed One set the wheel of the most excellent law a-rolling, and he began to preach to the five bhikshus, opening to them the gate of immortality, and showing them the bliss of Nirvâna.

And when the Blessed One began his sermon, a rapture thrilled through all the universes.

The dêvas left their heavenly abodes to listen to the sweetness of the truth; the saints that had parted from life crowded around the great teacher to receive the glad tidings; even the animals of the earth felt the bliss that rested upon the words of the Tathâgata: and all the creatures of the host of sentient beings, gods, men, and beasts, hearing the message of deliverance, received and understood it in their own language.

Buddha said:

"The spokes of the wheel are the rules of pure conduct; justice is the uniformity of their length; wisdom is the tire; modesty and thoughtfulness are the hub in which the immovable axle of truth is fixed.

"He who recognises the existence of suffering, its cause, its remedy, and its cessation has fathomed the four noble truths. He will walk in the right path.

"Right views will be the torch to light his way. Right

aims will be his guide. Right words will be his dwelling-place on the road. His gait will be straight, for it is right behavior. His refreshments will be the right way of earning his livelihood. Right efforts will be his steps: right thoughts his breath; and peace will follow in his footprints."

And the Blessed One explained the instability of the ego.

"Whatsoever is originated will be dissolved again. All worry about the self is vain; the ego is like a mirage, and all the tribulations that touch it will pass away. They will vanish like a nightmare when the sleeper awakes.

"He who has awakened is freed from fear; he has become Buddha; he knows the vanity of all his cares, his ambitions, and also of his pains.

"It easily happens that a man, when taking a bath, steps upon a wet rope and imagines that it is a snake. Horror will overcome him, and he will shake from fear, anticipating in his mind all the agonies caused by the serpent's venomous bite. What a relief does this man experience when he sees that the rope is no snake. The cause of his fright lies in his error, his ignorance, his illusion. If the true nature of the rope is recognised, his tranquillity of mind will come back to him; he will feel relieved; he will be joyful and happy.

"This is the state of mind of one who has recognised that there is no self, that the cause of all his troubles, cares, and vanities is a mirage, a shadow, a dream.

"Happy is he who has overcome all selfishness; happy is he who has attained peace; happy is he who has found the truth.

"The truth is noble and sweet; the truth can deliver you from evil. There is no saviour in the world except the truth.

"Have confidence in the truth, although you may not be able to comprehend it, although you may suppose its sweetness to be bitter, although you may shrink from it at first. Trust in the truth.

"The truth is best as it is. No one can alter it; neither can any one improve it. Have faith in the truth and live it.

"Errors lead astray; illusions beget miseries. They intoxicate like strong drinks; but they fade away soon and leave you sick and disgusted.

"Self is a fever; self is a transient vision, a dream; but truth is wholesome, truth is sublime, truth is everlasting. There is no immortality except in truth. For truth alone abideth forever."

And when the doctrine was propounded, the venerable Kaundinya, the oldest one among the five bhikshus, discerned the truth with his mental eye, and he said: "Truly, O Buddha, our Lord, thou hast found the truth."

And the dêvas and saints and all the good spirits of the departed generations that had listened to the sermon of the Tathâgata, joyfully received the doctrine and shouted: "Truly, the Blessed One has founded the kingdom of righteousness. The Blessed One has moved the earth; he has set the wheel of Truth rolling, which by no one in the universe, be he god or man, can ever be turned back. The kingdom of Truth will be preached upon earth; it will spread; and righteousness, good-will, and peace will reign among mankind."

THE FIRE-SERMON

Then The Blessed One, having dwelt in Uruvelā as long as he wished, proceeded on his wanderings in the direction of Gayā Head, accompanied by a great congregation of priests, a thousand in number, who had all of them aforetime been monks with matted hair. And there in Gayā, on Gayā Head, The Blessed One dwelt, together with the thousand priests.

And there The Blessed One addressed the priests:—

"All things, O priests, are on fire. And what, O priests, are all these things which are on fire?

"The eye, O priests, is on fire; forms are on fire; eye-consciousness is on fire; impressions received by the eye are on fire; and whatever sensation, pleasant, unpleasant, or indifferent, originates in dependence on impressions received by the eye, that also is on fire.

"And with what are these on fire?

"With the fire of passion, say I, with the fire of hatred, with the fire of infatuation; with birth, old age, death, sorrow, lamentation, misery, grief, and despair are they on fire.

"The ear is on fire; sounds are on fire; . . . the nose is on fire; odors are on fire; . . . the tongue is on fire; tastes are on fire; . . . the body is on fire; things tangible are on fire; . . . the mind is on fire; ideas are on fire; . . . mind-consciousness is on fire; impressions received by the mind are on fire; and whatever sensation, pleasant, unpleasant, or indifferent, originates in dependence on impressions received by the mind, that also is on fire.

"And with what are these on fire?

"With the fire of passion, say I, with the fire of hatred, with the fire of infatuation; with birth, old age, death, sorrow, lamentation, misery, grief, and despair are they on fire.

"Perceiving this, O priests, the learned and noble disciple conceives an aversion for the eye, conceives an aversion for forms, conceives an aversion for eye-consciousness, conceives an aversion for the impressions received by the eye; and whatever sensation, pleasant, unpleasant, or indifferent, originates in dependence on impressions received by the eye, for that also he conceives an aversion. Conceives an aversion for the ear, conceives an aversion for sounds, . . . conceives an aversion for the nose, conceives an aversion for odors, . . . conceives an aversion for the tongue, conceives an aversion for tastes, . . . conceives an aversion for the body, conceives an aversion for things tangible, . . . conceives an aversion for the mind, conceives an aversion for ideas, conceives an aversion for mind-consciousness, conceives an aversion for the impressions received by the mind; and whatever sensation, pleasant, unpleasant, or indifferent, originates in dependence on impressions received by the mind, for this also he conceives an aversion. And in conceiving this aversion, he becomes divested of passion, and by the absence of passion he becomes free, and when he is free he becomes aware that he is free; and he knows that rebirth is exhausted, that he has lived the holy life, that he has done what it behooved him to do, and that he is no more for this world."

Now while this exposition was being delivered, the minds of the thousand priests became free from attachment and delivered from the depravities.

Chapter IV
THE *DHAMMAPADA*

Of the *Dhammapada* (Path of the Buddha's Teaching), chapters of which follow, the Orientalist Hermann Oldenberg wrote, "For the elucidation of Buddhism nothing better could happen that, at the very outset of Buddhist studies, there should be presented to the student the *Dhammapada,* to which anyone who is determined to know Buddhism must over and over again return." The work is a first-century B.C. anthology, one of the fifteen books of the *Khuddaka-nikāya,* made up of ethical proverbs turned to poetry. It consists of 423 verses arranged according to topics into 26 chapters, and has achieved in many translations world-wide popularity, representing for Buddhism what the *Bhagavad Gītā* does for Hinduism and the *Tao-te Ching* for Taoism. As its versified form makes it relatively easy to commit to memory, it is learned by heart by young monks in the Buddhist countries of South Asia. The *Dhammapada* upholds good conduct, the life of meditation, and the practice of sound reason.

OLD AGE

How is there laughter, how is there joy, as this world is always burning? Do you not seek a light, ye who are surrounded by darkness?

Look at this dressed-up lump, covered with wounds, joined together, sickly, full of many schemes, but which has no strength, no hold!

This body is wasted, full of sickness, and frail; this heap of corruption breaks to pieces, life indeed ends in death.

After one has looked at those gray bones, thrown away like gourds in the autumn, what pleasure is there left in life!

After a stronghold has been made of the bones, it is covered with flesh and blood, and there dwell in it old age and death, pride and deceit.

The brilliant chariots of kings are destroyed, the body also approaches destruction, but the virtue of good people never approaches destruction—thus do the good say to the good.

A man who has learnt little, grows old like an ox; his flesh grows, but his knowledge does not grow.

Looking for the maker of this tabernacle, I have run through a course of many births, not finding him; and painful is birth again and again. But now, maker of the tabernacle, thou hast been seen; thou shalt not make up this tabernacle again. All thy rafters are broken, thy ridge-pole is sundered; the mind, approaching the Eternal (Visankhâra, Nirvâna), has attained to the extinction of all desires.

Men who have not observed proper discipline, and have not gained wealth in their youth, perish like old herons in a lake without fish.

Men who have not observed proper discipline, and have not gained wealth in their youth, lie, like broken bows, sighing after the past.

THE WORLD

Do not follow the evil law! Do not live on in thoughtlessness! Do not follow false doctrine! Be not a friend of the world.

Rouse thyself! do not be idle! Follow the law of virtue! The virtuous rest in bliss in this world and in the next.

Follow the law of virtue; do not follow that of sin. The virtuous rest in bliss in this world and in the next.

Look upon the world as you would on a bubble, look upon it as you would on a mirage: the king of death does not see him who thus looks down upon the world.

Come, look at this world, glittering like a royal chariot; the foolish are immersed in it, but the wise do not touch it.

He who formerly was reckless and afterwards became sober brightens up this world, like the moon when freed from clouds.

He whose evil deeds are covered by good deeds, brightens up this world, like the moon when freed from clouds.

This world is dark, few only can see here; a few only go to heaven, like birds escaped from the net.

The swans go on the path of the sun, they go miraculously through the ether; the wise are led out of this world, when they have conquered Mâra and his train.

If a man has transgressed the one law, and speaks lies, and scoffs at another world, there is no evil he will not do.

The uncharitable do not go to the world of the gods; fools only do not praise liberality; a wise man rejoices in liberality, and through it becomes blessed in the other world.

Better than sovereignty over the earth, better than going to heaven, better than lordship over all worlds, is the reward of Sotâpatti, the first step in holiness.

THE BUDDHA—THE AWAKENED

He whose conquest cannot be conquered again, into whose conquest no one in this world enters, by what track can you lead him, the Awakened, the Omniscient, the trackless?

He whom no desire with its snares and poisons can lead astray, by what track can you lead him, the Awakened, the Omniscient, the trackless?

Even the gods envy those who are awakened and not forgetful, who are given to meditation, who are wise, and who delight in the repose of retirement from the world.

Difficult to obtain is the conception of men, difficult is the life of mortals, difficult is the hearing of the True Law, difficult is the birth of the Awakened (the attainment of Buddhahood).

Not to commit any sin, to do good, and to purify one's mind, that is the teaching of all the Awakened.

The Awakened call patience the highest penance, long-suffering the highest Nirvàna; for he is not an anchorite (Pravragita) who strikes others, he is not an ascetic (Sramana) who insults others.

Not to blame, not to strike, to live restrained under the law, to be moderate in eating, to sleep and sit alone, and to dwell on the highest thoughts—this is the teaching of the Awakened.

There is no satisfying lusts, even by a shower of gold pieces; he who knows that lusts have a short taste and cause pain, he is wise; even in heavenly pleasures he finds no satisfaction, the disciple who is fully awakened delights only in the destruction of all desires.

Men, driven by fear, go to many a refuge, to mountains and forests, to groves and sacred trees.

But that is not a safe refuge, that is not the best refuge; a man is not delivered from all pains after having gone to that refuge.

He who takes refuge with Buddha, the Law, and the Church; he who, with clear understanding, sees the four holy truths: pain, the origin of pain, the destruction of pain, and the eightfold holy way that leads to the quieting of pain;—that is the safe refuge, that is the best refuge; having gone to that refuge, a man is delivered from all pain.

A supernatural person (a Buddha) is not easily found: he is not born everywhere. Wherever such a sage is born, that race prospers.

Happy is the arising of the Awakened, happy is the teaching of the True Law, happy is peace in the church, happy is the devotion of those who are at peace.

He who pays homage to those who deserve homage, whether the awakened (Buddha) or their disciples, those who have overcome the host of evils, and crossed the flood of sorrow, he who pays homage to such as have found deliverance and know no fear, his merit can never be measured by anyone.

THIRST

The thirst of a thoughtless man grows like a creeper; he runs from life to life, like a monkey seeking fruit in the forest.

Whomsoever this fierce poisonous thirst overcomes, in this world, his sufferings increase like the abounding Bîrana grass.

But from him who overcomes this fierce thirst, difficult to be conquered in this world, sufferings fall off, like water-drops from a lotus leaf.

This salutary word I tell you, "Do ye, as many as are here assembled, dig up the root of thirst, as he who wants the sweet-scented Usîra root must dig up the Bîrana grass, that Mâra, the tempter, may not crush you again and again, as the stream crushes the reeds."

As a tree, even though it has been cut down, is firm so long as its root is safe, and grows again, thus, unless the feeders of thirst are destroyed, this pain of life will return again and again.

He whose thirty-six streams are strongly flowing in the channels of pleasure, the waves—his desires which are set on passion—will carry away that misguided man.

The channels run everywhere, the creeper of passion stands sprouting; if you see the creeper springing up, cut its root by means of knowledge.

A creature's pleasures are extravagant and luxurious; given up to pleasure and deriving happiness, men undergo again and again birth and decay.

Beset with lust, men run about like a snared hare; held in fetters and bonds, they undergo pain for a long time, again and again.

Beset with lust, men run about like a snared hare; let therefore the mendicant drive out thirst, by striving after passionlessness for himself.

He who, having got rid of the forest of lust (after having

reached Nirvâna), gives himself over to forest-life (to lust), and who, when free from the forest (from lust), runs to the forest (to lust), look at that man! though free, he runs into bondage.

Wise people do not call that a strong fetter which is made of iron, wood, or hemp; passionately strong is the care for precious stones and rings, for sons and a wife.

That fetter wise people call strong which drags down, yields, but is difficult to undo; after having cut this at last, people leave the world, free from cares, and leaving the pleasures of love behind.

Those who are slaves to passions, run down the stream of desires, as a spider runs down the web which he has made himself; when they have cut this, at last, wise people go onwards, free from cares, leaving all pain behind.

Give up what is before, give up what is behind, give up what is between, when thou goest to the other shore of existence; if thy mind is altogether free, thou wilt not again enter into birth and decay.

If a man is tossed about by doubts, full of strong passions, and yearning only for what is delightful, his thirst will grow more and more, and he will indeed make his fetters strong.

If a man delights in quieting doubts, and, always reflecting, dwells on what is not delightful, he certainly will remove, nay, he will cut the fetter of Mâra.

He who has reached the consummation, who does not tremble, who is without thirst and without sin, he has broken all the thorns of life: this will be his last body.

He who is without thirst and without affection, who understands the words and their interpretation, who knows the order of letters (those which are before and which are after), he has received his last body, he is called the great sage, the great man.

"I have conquered all, I know all, in all conditions of life I am free from taint; I have left all, and through the destruction of thirst I am free; having learnt myself, whom should I indicate as my teacher?"

The gift of the law exceeds all gifts; the sweetness of the

law exceeds all sweetness; the delight in the law exceeds all delights; the extinction of thirst overcomes all pain.

Riches destroy the foolish, if they look not for the other shore; the foolish by his thirst for riches destroys himself, as if he were destroying others.

The fields are damaged by weeds, mankind is damaged by passion: therefore a gift bestowed on the passionless brings great reward.

The fields are damaged by weeds, mankind is damaged by hatred: therefore a gift bestowed on those who do not hate brings great reward.

The fields are damaged by weeds, mankind is damaged by vanity: therefore a gift bestowed on those who are free from vanity brings great reward.

The fields are damaged by weeds, mankind is damaged by lust: therefore a gift bestowed on those who are free from lust brings great reward.

THE BRÂHMANA

Stop the stream valiantly, drive away the desires, O Brâhmana! When you have understood the destruction of all that was made, you will understand that which was not made.

If the Brâhmana has reached the other shore in both laws, in restraint and contemplation, all bonds vanish from him who has obtained knowledge.

He for whom there is neither the hither nor the further shore, nor both, him, the fearless and unshackled, I call indeed a Brâhmana.

He who is thoughtful, blameless, settled, dutiful, without passions, and who has attained the highest end, him I call indeed a Brâhmana.

The sun is bright by day, the moon shines by night, the warrior is bright in his armor, the Brâhmana is bright in his meditation; but Buddha, the Awakened, is bright with splendor day and night.

Because a man is rid of evil, therefore he is called Brâh-

mana; because he walks quietly, therefore he is called Samana; because he has sent away his own impurities, therefore he is called Pravragita (Pabbagita, a pilgrim).

No one should attack a Brâhmana, but no Brâhmana, if
attacked, should let himself fly at his aggressor! Woe to him
who strikes a Brâhmana, more woe to him who flies at his
aggressor!

It advantages a Brâhmana not a little if he holds his mind
back from the pleasures of life; the more all wish to injure
has vanished, the more all pain will cease.

Him I call indeed a Brâhmana who does not offend by
body, word, or thought, and is controlled on these three
points.

He from whom he may learn the law, as taught by the
Well-awakened (Buddha), him let him worship assiduously,
as the Brâhmana worships the sacrificial fire.

A man does not become a Brâhmana by his plaited hair,
by his family, or by birth; in whom there is truth and righteousness, he is blessed, he is a Brâhmana.

What is the use of plaited hair, O fool! what of the raiment
of goat-skins? Within thee there is ravening, but the outside
thou makest clean.

The man who wears dirty raiments, who is emaciated and
covered with veins, who meditates alone in the forest, him I
call indeed a Brâhmana.

I do not call a man a Brâhmana because of his origin or
of his mother. He is indeed arrogant, and he is wealthy: but
the poor, who is free from all attachments, him I call indeed
a Brâhmana.

Him I call indeed a Brâhmana who, after cutting all fetters,
never trembles, is free from bonds and unshackled.

Him I call indeed a Brâhmana who, after cutting the strap
and the thong, the rope with all that pertains to it, has destroyed all obstacles, and is awakened.

Him I call indeed a Brâhmana who, though he has committed no offence, endures reproach, stripes, and bonds: who
has endurance for his force, and strength for his army.

Him I call indeed a Brâhmana who is free from anger,

dutiful, virtuous, without appetites, who is subdued, and has received his last body.

Him I call indeed a Brâhmana who does not cling to sensual pleasures, like water on a lotus leaf, like a mustard seed on the point of a needle.

Him I call indeed a Brâhmana who, even here, knows the end of his own suffering, has put down his burden, and is unshackled.

Him I call indeed a Brâhmana whose knowledge is deep, who possesses wisdom, who knows the right way and the wrong, and has attained the highest end.

Him I call indeed a Brâhmana who keeps aloof both from laymen and from mendicants, who frequents no houses, and has but few desires.

Him I call indeed a Brâhmana who without hurting any creatures, whether feeble or strong, does not kill nor cause slaughter.

Him I call indeed a Brâhmana who is tolerant with the intolerant, mild with the violent, and free from greed among the greedy.

Him I call indeed a Brâhmana from whom anger and hatred, pride and hypocrisy have dropped like a mustard seed from the point of a needle.

Him I call indeed a Brâhmana who utters true speech, instructive and free from harshness, so that he offend no one.

Him I call indeed a Brâhmana who takes nothing in the world that is not given him, be it long or short, small or large, good or bad.

Him I call indeed a Brâhmana who fosters no desires for this world or for the next, has no inclinations, and is unshackled.

Him I call indeed a Brâhmana who has no interests, and when he has understood the truth, does not say How, how? and who has reached the depth of the Immortal.

Him I call indeed a Brâhmana who in this world has risen above both ties, good and evil, who is free from grief, from sin, and from impurity.

Him I call indeed a Brâhmana who is bright like the moon,

pure, serene, undisturbed, and in whom all gayety is extinct.

Him I call indeed a Brâhmana who has traversed this miry road, the impassable world, difficult to pass, and its vanity, who has gone through, and reached the other shore, is thoughtful, steadfast, free from doubts, free from attachment, and content.

Him I call indeed a Brâhmana who in this world, having abandoned all desires, travels about without a home, and in whom all concupiscence is extinct.

Him I call indeed a Brâhmana who, having abandoned all longings, travels about without a home, and in whom all covetousness is extinct.

Him I call indeed a Brâhmana who, after leaving all bondage to men, has risen above all bondage to the gods, and is free from all and every bondage.

Him I call indeed a Brâhmana who has left what gives pleasure and what gives pain, who is cold, and free from all germs of renewed life: the hero who has conquered all the worlds.

Him I call indeed a Brâhmana who knows the destruction and the return of beings everywhere, who is free from bondage, welfaring (Sugata), and awakened (Buddha).

Him I call indeed a Brâhmana whose path the gods do not know, nor spirits (Gandharvas), nor men, whose passions are extinct, and who is an Arhat.

Him I call indeed a Brâhmana who calls nothing his own, whether it be before, behind, or between; who is poor, and free from the love of the world.

Him I call indeed a Brâhmana, the manly, the noble, the hero, the great sage, the conqueror, the indifferent, the accomplished, the awakened.

Him I call indeed a Brâhmana who knows his former abodes, who sees heaven and hell, has reached the end of births, is perfect in knowledge, a sage, and whose perfections are all perfect.

Chapter V
"IS THERE A LIFE AFTER DEATH?"

From the *Dīgha-nikāya*, the first of the *Sutta-pitaka*'s five collections, comes one of the "Long Discourses," a dialogue between the stubbornest of unbelievers and one of the Buddha's chief disciples, "Is There a Life After Death?" The *Pāyāsi-suttana*, as the work is known, is named after the Khattiya teacher and philosopher, as well as warrior, Pāyāsi, who advances to the sage Kumāra Kassapa the materialistic doctrine and heresy that there is no birth after death and no Karma. In order to convince Pāyāsi that he is perilously in error, Gautama's disciple relates thirteen parables, through the use of which he is able—slowly to be sure—to defeat the antagonist. While it may be true that his arguments are essentially those which have always been used when this momentous subject has been discussed, the sage's patience and inventiveness give to this work a distinction rarely attained in canonical writing.

PARABLES FROM THE LONG DISCOURSES ON THE SUBJECT: "IS THERE A LIFE AFTER DEATH?"

On a certain occasion Pāyāsi the Warrior said to Venerable Kumāra Kassapa: "I, my lord Kassapa, hold this doctrine, this view: 'There is no life after death; there are no living beings reborn without the intervention of parents; there is no fruition, no ripening, of good and evil deeds.'" "Warrior, I never encountered or heard such a view. For how can a man say such a thing as this: 'There is no life after death; there are no living beings reborn without the intervention of parents; there is no fruition, no ripening, of good and evil deeds'? Have you any reason for this view?" "My lord Kassapa, I have a reason for this view." "Warrior, what is it like?"

The wicked do not return to earth.

"Here, my lord Kassapa, I have friends and companions, kinsmen and relatives, who are murderers, thieves, fornicators and adulterers, liars, backbiters, calumniators, triflers, covetous, malevolent of spirit, holders of false views. Sometimes they fall sick, suffer pain, are in a bad way. When I feel certain that these men will not recover from that sickness, I go to them and speak thus: 'There are some monks and Brahmans who hold this doctrine, this view: "Men who are murderers, thieves, fornicators and adulterers, liars, backbiters, calumniators, triflers, covetous, malevolent of spirit, holders of false views,—such men, on dissolution of the body, after death, go to a state of punishment, to a state of pain, to a state of suffering, to hell." You, sirs, are such men. If the words of these reverend monks and Brahmans are true, you, sirs, on dissolution of the body, after death, will go to a state of punishment, to a state of pain, to a state of suffering, to hell. If, on dissolution of the body, after death, you should be reborn in a state of punishment, in a state of pain, in a state of suffering, in hell, pray return and say to me: "There is a life after death; there are living beings reborn without the intervention of parents; there is a fruition, a ripening, of good and evil deeds." ' Now my friends are trustworthy and reliable. If my friends saw anything and said they had seen it, such a thing would necessarily be true. 'Very well,' say they, giving me their word. But for all that, they never return and say it, nor do they send a messenger either. This, my lord Kassapa, is one reason why I hold the view: 'There is no life after death; there are no living beings reborn without the intervention of parents; there is no fruition, no ripening, of good and evil deeds.' "

"Well, Warrior, I will reply by asking you a question on the subject. You may answer it in any way you please. Warrior, what have you to say to the following?"

THE CONDEMNED CRIMINAL

Suppose your men were to capture a brigand, a criminal, and arraign him here before you, saying: "Here, lord, is a brigand, a criminal. Inflict upon him whatever punishment you desire." And you were to say: "Well, take this fellow, bind his arms tight behind his back with a stout rope, shave his head, and to the loud beating of a drum lead him about from street to street, from crossing to crossing, conduct him out of the South gate, and cut off his head in the place of execution south of the city." And they were to say: "Very well;" and in obedience to your command were to take that fellow, bind his arms tight behind his back with a stout rope, shave his head, and to the loud beating of a drum lead him about from street to street, from crossing to crossing, conduct him out of the South gate, and make him sit down in the place of execution south of the city. And suppose that brigand were to say to his executioners: "Let my lord-executioners wait,— in such-and-such a village or market-town I have friends and companions, kinsmen and relatives,—until I show myself to them and return." Would he obtain his request? Would not the executioners rather, even as he babbled, cut off his head?

"Quite right, my lord Kassapa."

"Suppose, Warrior, your friends reborn in hell say to the warders of hell: 'Let our lord-warders of hell wait until we go and say to Pāyāsi the Warrior: "There is a life after death; there are living beings reborn without the intervention of parents; there is a fruition, a ripening, of good and evil deeds."' Are they likely to obtain their request?"

But Pāyāsi the Warrior remained unconvinced. Said he:

The virtuous do not return to earth.

"Here, my lord Kassapa, I have friends and companions, kinsmen and relatives, who refrain from murder, theft, fornication and adultery, lying, backbiting, calumny, trifling, covetousness, malevolence of spirit, holders of orthodox views. Sometimes they fall sick, suffer pain, are in a bad way. When I feel certain that these men will not recover from that sickness, I go to them and speak thus: 'There are some monks and Brahmans who hold this doctrine, this view: "Men who refrain from murder, theft, fornication and adultery, lying, backbiting, calumny, trifling, covetousness, malevolence of spirit, holders of orthodox views,—such men, on dissolution of the body, after death, go to a state of bliss, to heaven." You, sirs, are such men. If the words of these reverend monks and Brahmans are true, you, sirs, on dissolution of the body, after death, will go to a state of bliss, to heaven. If, on dissolution of the body, after death, you should be reborn in a state of bliss, in heaven, pray return and say to me: "There is a life after death; there are living beings reborn without the intervention of parents; there is a fruition, a ripening, of good and evil deeds."' Now my friends are trustworthy and reliable. If my friends saw anything and said they had seen it, such a thing would necessarily be true. 'Very well,' say they, giving me their word. But for all that, they never return and say it, nor do they send a messenger either. This, my lord Kassapa, is another reason why I hold the view: 'There is no life after death; there are no living beings reborn without the intervention of parents; there is no fruition, no ripening, of good and evil deeds.'"

"Well, Warrior, I will compose a parable for you. Even by a parable does many a man of intelligence in this world comprehend the meaning of a statement."

THE MAN IN THE DUNG-PIT

Warrior, it is precisely as though a man were submerged in a dung-pit, head and all. And you were to order your men: "Now then, pull that man out of that dung-pit." And they were to say: "Very well;" and in obedience to your command were to pull that man out of that dung-pit. And you were to say to them: "Now then, scrape the dung from off the body of that man, and scrape it well." And they were to say: "Very well;" and in obedience to your command were to scrape the dung from off the body of that man, and were to scrape it well. And you were to say to them: "Now then, massage the body of that man three times with yellow clay, and massage it well." And they were to massage the body of that man three times with yellow clay, and were to massage it well. And you were to say to them: "Now then, anoint that man with oil and bathe him well three times with soft bath-powder." And they were to anoint that man with oil and to bathe him well three times with soft bath-powder. And you were to say to them: "Now then, dress that man's hair and beard." And they were to dress that man's hair and beard. And you were to say to them: "Now then, present that man with costly garlands and costly perfumes and costly garments." And they were to present that man with costly garlands and costly perfumes and costly garments. And you were to say to them: "Now then, escort that man into a palace and furnish him with the Five Pleasures of Sense." And they were to escort that man into a palace and to furnish him with the Five Pleasures of Sense.

What think you, Warrior? Would that man, well bathed, well anointed, with hair and beard dressed, decked with garlands and ornaments, dressed in clean garments, aloft in a splendid palace, supplied and provided with the Five Pleasures of Sense, ministered unto,—would that man desire to plunge once more into that dung-pit?

"No, indeed, my lord Kassapa." "Why not?" "A dung-pit, my lord Kassapa, is a filthy place; filthy in fact, and so regarded; foul-smelling in fact, and so regarded; disgusting in fact, and so regarded; repulsive in fact, and so regarded."

"Precisely so, Warrior, to the gods, human beings are filthy and so regarded, foul-smelling and so regarded, disgusting and so regarded, repulsive and so regarded. Indeed, Warrior, the stench of human beings drives the gods a hundred leagues away! How can you expect your virtuous friends, reborn in a state of bliss, in heaven, to return and say to you: 'There is a life after death; there are living beings reborn without the intervention of parents; there is a fruition, a ripening, of good and evil deeds'?"

The virtuous do not return to earth.

But Pāyāsi the Warrior, still unconvinced, repeated once more what he had said before regarding his virtuous friends, remarking that those of his friends who had refrained from murder, theft, fornication and adultery, lying, and occasions of heedlessness through the use of intoxicating liquor and spirits, and who therefore, according to the monks and Brahmans, must have been reborn in the heaven of the Thirty-three gods, had never returned to earth.

"Well, Warrior," said Venerable Kumāra Kassapa, "I will reply by asking you a question on the subject. You may answer it in any way you please. Warrior, what have you to say to the following?"

TIME IN HEAVEN

Warrior, a hundred of our years are equivalent to a night and a day in the heaven of the Thirty-three gods. Thirty of these nights make up a month, and twelve of these months make up a year. The term of life of the Thirty-three gods is a thousand of these celestial years. Your friends have indeed been reborn in the heaven of the Thirty-three gods. Now suppose the thought has occurred to them: "We are supplied and provided with the Five Pleasures of Sense. After we have been ministered to for two or three celestial nights and days, we will go and say such-and-such to Pāyāsi the Warrior." Have they, in fact, had time to do so?

How do we know that the gods exist?

"No, indeed, my lord Kassapa. The fact is, my lord Kassapa, we should be dead and gone long before they returned. But who told my lord Kassapa that the Thirty-three gods exist, or that they live as long as this? I, my lord Kassapa, do not believe that the Thirty-three gods exist, or that they live as long as this."

71

THE BLIND MAN

Warrior, it is precisely as though a blind man could not see black and white objects, could not see blue objects, could not see yellow objects, could not see red objects, could not see pink objects, could not see even and uneven, could not see the stars, could not see the moon and the sun. And that man were to say: "There are no black and white objects; there is no one who can see black and white objects. There are no blue objects; there is no one who can see blue objects. There are no yellow objects; there is no one who can see yellow objects. There are no red objects; there is no one who can see red objects. There are no pink objects; there is no one who can see pink objects. There is no even and uneven; there is no one who can see even and uneven. There are no stars; there is no one who can see the stars. Moon and sun do not exist; there is no one who can see the moon and the sun. I do not know them, I do not see them; therefore they do not exist." Warrior, would that man speak correctly were he to speak thus?

"No, indeed, my lord Kassapa. There *are* black and white objects; there are those who can see black and white objects. There *are* blue objects; there are those who can see blue objects. There *are* yellow objects; there are those who can see yellow objects. There *are* red objects; there are those who can see red objects. There *are* pink objects; there are those who can see pink objects. Even and uneven *do* exist; there are those who can see even and uneven. There *are* stars; there are those who can see the stars. Moon and sun *do* exist; there are those who can see the moon and the sun. 'I do not know them, I do not see them; therefore they do not exist!' No, indeed, my lord Kassapa! That man would not speak correctly were he to speak thus."

"Warrior, you are just like the blind man in the parable when you speak thus: 'But who told my lord Kassapa that the Thirty-three gods exist, or that they live as long as this? I, my lord Kassapa, do not believe that the Thirty-three gods exist, or that they live as long as this.'

"By no means, Warrior, can the next world be seen in the way you imagine it can,—with this Eye of Flesh. But, let me tell you, Warrior, there are monks and Brahmans who resort to forest-hermitages in the wilderness, remote lodgings where there is little sound, little noise; and there, living heedful, ardent, resolute, they clarify the Heavenly Eye; with the Heavenly Eye, transcending any mere human eye, clarified, they behold not only this world, but the next, and living beings reborn without the intervention of parents."

But Pāyāsi the Warrior remained unconvinced. Said he:

Why do not the virtuous commit suicide?

"Here, my lord Kassapa, I see monks and Brahmans observing the Precepts, doing good works, desiring to live, not desiring to die, desiring happiness, avoiding suffering. When, my lord Kassapa, I see them, the following thought occurs to me: 'If these reverend monks and Brahmans really knew, "Better than this would it be were we dead," immediately these reverend monks and Brahmans, observing the Precepts, doing good works, would either eat poison, or draw the sword, or kill themselves by hanging, or jump off a jumping-off place.' But since evidently these reverend monks and Brahmans do not know, "Better than this would it be were we dead," therefore these reverend monks and Brahmans, observing the Precepts, doing good works, desiring to live, not desiring to die, desiring happiness, avoiding suffering, do not kill themselves. This, my lord Kassapa, is another reason why I hold the view: 'There is no life after death; there are no living beings reborn without the intervention of parents; there is no fruition, no ripening, of good and evil deeds.'"

"Well, Warrior, I will compose a parable for you. Even by a parable does many a man of intelligence in this world comprehend the meaning of a statement."

THE WOMAN WITH CHILD

In olden times, Warrior, a certain Brahman had two wives. One had a son about ten or twelve years old; the other was with child, about to bring forth. Now that Brahman died. And that youth said this to his mother's fellow: "My lady, whatever money or grain or silver or gold there is, all this is mine. You have no part in this; turn over to me, my lady, the inheritance of my father." Upon this, that Brahman's wife said this to that youth: "Just wait, my dear, until I bring forth. If it is a boy, he also will have one portion; if it is a girl, she also will be yours to be enjoyed."

The second time also the youth said this to his mother's fellow: "My lady, whatever money or grain or silver or gold there is, all this is mine. You have no part in this; turn over to me, my lady, the inheritance of my father." The second time also that Brahman's wife said this to that youth: "Just wait, my dear, until I bring forth. If it is a boy, he also will have one portion; if it is a girl, she also will be yours to be enjoyed."

The third time also that youth said this to his mother's fellow: "My lady, whatever money or grain or silver or gold there is, all this is mine. You have no part in this; turn over to me, my lady, the inheritance of my father."

Thereupon that Brahman's wife took a sword, went into an inner room, and plunged the sword into her belly: "Until I know whether it is a boy or a girl!" She destroyed herself, her living child, and her property. She met destruction and ruin, like the foolish, short-sighted woman she was, seeking an inheritance otherwise than in the right way.

"Precisely so, Warrior, you, a foolish, short-sighted man, will meet destruction and ruin by seeking the next world otherwise than in the right way, just as that Brahman's wife, that foolish, short-sighted woman, also met destruction and ruin by seeking an inheritance otherwise than in the right way.

"No, indeed, Warrior! Monks and Brahmans who observe the Precepts, who do good works, permit what is not yet ripe to become fully ripe. What is more, being wise men, they wait patiently for it to become fully ripe. For, Warrior, there is need of monks and Brahmans who observe the Precepts, who do good works, continuing alive.

Warrior, in the same proportion as monks and Brahmans who observe the Precepts, who do good works, remain alive for a long long time, in the same proportion they generate much merit and act for the welfare of many, for the happiness of many, out of tender compassion for the world, for the weal and welfare and happiness of angels and men."

But Pāyāsi the Warrior remained unconvinced. Said he:

We cannot see the soul after death.

"Here, my lord Kassapa, my men capture a brigand, a criminal, and arraign him before me, saying: 'Here, lord, is a brigand, a criminal. Inflict upon him whatever punishment you desire.' And I say to them: 'Well, place this man, alive as ever, in a jar; put the lid on the jar; cover it with a wet skin; seal it with a thick paste of wet clay; lift it up on the oven; start a fire.' 'Very well,' they say to me. In obedience to my command they place that man, alive as ever, in a jar, put the lid on the jar, cover it with a wet skin, seal it with a thick paste of wet clay, lift it up on the oven, start a fire. When we know, 'That man is dead,' then we lift that jar down, break the seal, take off the lid, and look down with bated breath: 'Perhaps we may see his soul coming out!' But no! We do not see his soul coming out."

"Well, Warrior, I will reply by asking you a question on the subject. You may answer it in any way you please."

WE CANNOT SEE THE SOUL DURING LIFE

Warrior, do you not recollect, while taking a siesta, seeing in a dream the delights of the grove, the delights of the woods, the delights of cleared ground, the delights of the lotus-pond?—I do recollect, my lord Kassapa, while taking a siesta, seeing in a dream the delights of the grove, the delights of the woods.—Were people watching you at that time? —Yes.—Did they see your soul coming in or going out?—No, indeed, my lord Kassapa.—So then, Warrior, although you were alive, living persons did not see your soul coming in or going out. How then, after your death, could they be expected to see your soul coming in or going out?

But Pāyāsi the Warrior remained unconvinced. Said he:

The dead are heavier than the living.

"Here, my lord Kassapa, my men capture a brigand, a criminal, and arraign him before me, saying: 'Here, lord, is a brigand, a criminal. Inflict upon him whatever punishment you desire.' And I say to them: 'Well, weigh this man, while yet alive, in the balances; strangle him to death with a bow-string; then weigh him again in the balances.' 'Very well,' they say to me. In obedience to my command they weigh that man, while yet alive, in the balances, strangle him to death with a bow-string, and then weigh him again in the balances. When he is alive, then he is lighter and softer and more pliable. But when he is dead, then he is heavier, more rigid, less pliable."

"Well then, Warrior, I will compose a parable for you."

HEAT MAKES THINGS LIGHT

Suppose, Warrior, a man were to weigh in the balances an iron ball which had been heated all day until it was red-hot, glowing, gleaming, flaring; and suppose, afterwards, he were to weigh in the balances that same iron ball, cold, extinguished. When would that iron ball be lighter, softer, more pliable,—when it was glowing, gleaming, flaring,—or when it was cold, extinguished?

When, my lord Kassapa, that iron ball was connected with heat, was connected with wind, when it was glowing, gleaming, flaring, then it was lighter and softer and more pliable. But when that iron ball was not connected with heat, was not connected with wind, when it was cold, extinguished, then it was heavier, more rigid, less pliable.

"Precisely so, Warrior, when this body is connected with life, and connected with heat, and connected with consciousness, then it is lighter and softer and more pliable.

76

But when this body is not connected with life, is not connected with heat, is not connected with consciousness, then it is heavier, more rigid, less pliable."

But Pāyāsi the Warrior remained unconvinced. Said he:

We cannot see the soul.

"Here, my lord Kassapa, my men capture a brigand, a criminal, and arraign him before me, saying: 'Here, lord, is a brigand, a criminal. Inflict upon him whatever punishment you desire.' And I say to them: 'Well, batter this man,—cuticle and skin and flesh and sinews and bones and marrow,—and deprive him of life.' 'Very well,' they say to me. In obedience to my command they batter that man, —cuticle and skin and flesh and sinews and bones and marrow,—and deprive him of life. When he is half-dead, I say to them: 'Now then, fling this man down on his back. Perhaps we may see his soul coming out!' They fling that man down on his back. But no! We do not see his soul coming out!

"I say to them: 'Now then, fling this man down bent double . . . on one side . . . on the other side . . . ; stand him right side up . . . up side down . . . ; beat him with the hand . . . with clods . . . with a stick . . . with a sword; shake him down . . . shake him together . . . shake him out. Perhaps we may see his soul coming out!' They do so. But no! We do not see his soul coming out!

"Now he has that same organ of sight, the eye; but that organ does not sense these visible objects. He has that same organ of hearing, the ear; but that organ does not sense these sounds. He has that same organ of smell, the nose; but that organ does not sense these odors. He has that same organ of taste, the tongue; but that organ does not sense these flavors. He has that same organ of touch, the body; but that organ does not sense these objects of touch."

"Well then, Warrior, I will compose a parable for you."

VILLAGERS AND TRUMPET

In olden times, Warrior, a certain trumpeter went to a frontier district with his trumpet. He approached a certain village, and having approached, stood in the centre of the village, blew the trumpet three times, set the trumpet on the ground, and sat down on one side.

Now, Warrior, to those frontiersmen occurred the following thought: "What is it that makes that sound,—so charming, so delightful, so intoxicating, so fascinating, so infatuating?" Assembling, they said this to that trumpet-blower: "Sir, what is it that makes that sound,—so charming, so delightful, so intoxicating, so fascinating, so infatuating?" "Friends, it is that trumpet which makes that sound,—so charming, so delightful, so intoxicating, so fascinating, so infatuating."

They flung that trumpet down on its bottom. "Speak, O trumpet! Speak, O trumpet!" But no! That trumpet made not a sound! They flung that trumpet down bent double . . . on one side . . . on the other side . . . ; they stood it right side up . . . up side down . . . ; they beat it with the hand . . . with clods . . . with a stick . . . with a sword . . . ; they shook it down . . . shook it together . . . shook it out. "Speak, O trumpet! Speak, O trumpet!" But no! That trumpet made not a sound!

Then, Warrior, to that trumpet-blower occurred the following thought: "How foolish these frontiersmen are! How can they hope to hear the sound of the trumpet by seeking otherwise than in the right way?" With the frontiersmen watching him, he picked up the trumpet, blew the trumpet three times, and walked off with the trumpet.

Then, Warrior, to those frontiersmen occurred the following thought: "Ah! When this trumpet is connected with a human being, and is connected with exertion, and is connected with wind, then this trumpet makes a sound! But when this trumpet is not connected with a human being, is not connected with exertion, is not connected with wind, then this trumpet makes no sound!"

"Precisely so, Warrior, when this body is connected with life, and is connected with heat, and is connected with consciousness, then it advances and retires and stands and sits and lies down; then it sees visible objects with the eye, and hears sounds with the ear, and smells odors with the nose, and tastes flavors with the tongue, and touches objects of touch with the body, and understands the Doctrine with the mind. But when this body is not connected with life, and is not connected with heat, and is not connected with consciousness, then it does not advance, does not retire, does not sit, does not lie down; then it does not see visible objects with the eye, and does not hear sounds with the ear, and does not smell odors with the nose, and does not taste flavors with the tongue, and does not touch objects of touch with the body, and does not understand the Doctrine with the mind."

But Pāyāsi the Warrior remained unconvinced. Said he:

We cannot see the soul.

"Here, my lord Kassapa, my men capture a brigand, a criminal, and arraign him before me saying: 'Here, lord, is a brigand, a criminal. Inflict upon him whatever punishment you desire.' And I say to them: 'Well, cut this man's cuticle. Perhaps we may see his soul coming out!' They cut that man's cuticle. But no! We do not see that man's soul coming out! I say to them: 'Now then, cut this man's skin . . . flesh . . . sinews . . . bones . . . marrow. Perhaps we may see his soul coming out!' But no! We do not see his soul coming out!"

"Well then, Warrior, I will compose a parable for you."

THE SEARCH FOR FIRE

In olden times, Warrior, a fire-worshipper, a Jaṭila, dwelt in a forest-abode, in a leaf-hut. Now, Warrior, a certain country district rose in revolt. And that multitude spent one night near the hermitage of that fire-worshipper, that Jaṭila, and departed. Now, Warrior, to that fire-worshipper, that Jaṭila, occurred the following thought: "Suppose I were to approach that encampment! Perhaps I may find something of use there!"

Accordingly that fire-worshipper, that Jaṭila, arose betimes and approached that encampment. Having approached, he saw in that encampment, abandoned, a slip of a young boy lying on his back. When he saw him, the following thought

79

occurred to him: "It would ill become me were a human being to die with me looking on. Suppose I were to lead this boy to my hermitage, and to bring him up and feed him and rear him!" Accordingly that fire-worshipper, that Jaṭila, led that boy to his hermitage, and brought him up and fed him and reared him.

When that boy was about ten or twelve years old, that fire-worshipper, that Jaṭila, had occasion to go to the country on some business or other. Now that fire-worshipper, that Jaṭila, said this to that boy: "I desire, my son, to go to the country. Please tend the fire, and do not let it go out on you. Only, if the fire should go out on you,—here is a hatchet, here are sticks of wood, here is a fire-drill,—please kindle the fire and tend it." And having thus instructed that boy, that fire-worshipper, that Jaṭila, went to the country.

Now while that boy was absorbed in play, the fire went out. Thereupon to that boy occurred the following thought: "My father said this to me: 'My son, please tend the fire, and do not let it go out on you. Only, if the fire should go out on you,—here is a hatchet, here are sticks of wood, here is a fire-drill,—please kindle the fire and tend it.' Suppose I were to kindle the fire and tend it!"

Accordingly that boy began to chop up the fire-drill with his hatchet: "Perhaps I may produce fire!" But no! He did not produce fire! He split the fire-drill into two pieces . . . into three pieces . . . into four pieces . . . into five pieces . . . into ten pieces . . . into a hundred pieces. He reduced it to so many bits; having reduced it to so many bits, he pounded them in a mortar; having pounded them in a mortar, he winnowed them in a strong wind: "Perhaps I may produce fire!" But no! He did not produce fire!

Now that fire-worshipper, that Jaṭila, having transacted that business in the country, approached his own hermitage. Having approached, he said this to that boy: "My son, did the fire go out on you?" "Father, while I was absorbed in play here, the fire went out on me." So saying, the boy told his foster-father what he had done.

Then to that fire-worshipper, that Jaṭila, occurred the following thought: "How foolish this boy is! how short-sighted! How could he hope to produce fire by seeking otherwise than in the right way?" With the boy watching him, he picked up a fire-drill, produced fire, and said this to that boy: "This, my son, is the way to produce fire; not, as you, a foolish, short-sighted boy, tried to produce it, by seeking otherwise than in the right way."

"Precisely thus, Warrior, are you, a foolish, short-sighted man, seeking the next world otherwise than in the right way. Renounce, Warrior, this wicked heresy! Renounce, Warrior, this wicked heresy! Let it not be to your disadvantage and sorrow for a long time to come."

Wilful persistence in error.

"No matter how emphatically my lord Kassapa says this, yet, for all that, I cannot bring myself to renounce this wicked heresy. Even King Pasenadi Kosala knows, even kings outside know regarding me: 'Pāyāsi the Warrior holds this doctrine, holds this view: "There is no life after death; there are no living beings reborn without the intervention of parents; there is no fruition, no ripening, of good and evil deeds."' If, my lord Kassapa, I were to renounce this wicked view, there would be those who would say of me: 'How foolish is Pāyāsi the Warrior! how short-sighted! how ready to accept what is hard to accept!' Even with anger will I hold to this view, even with hypocrisy will I hold to this view, even with conceit will I hold to this view."

"Well then, Warrior, I will compose a parable for you. Even by a parable does many a man of intelligence in this world comprehend the meaning of a statement."

TWO CARAVAN-LEADERS

In olden times, Warrior, a great caravan of a thousand carts went from the eastern country to the western country. Wherever it went, very quickly were consumed grass, sticks, water, and pot-herbs. Now over that caravan were two caravan-leaders, one over five hundred carts, one over five hundred carts. And to these caravan-leaders occurred the following thought: "This is a great caravan of a thousand carts. Wherever we go, very quickly are consumed grass, sticks, water, and pot-herbs. Suppose we were to divide this caravan into two caravans of five hundred carts each!" They divided that caravan into two caravans, one of five hundred carts, one of five hundred carts. One caravan-leader only loaded his carts with abundant grass and sticks and water, and started his caravan forward.

Now when he had proceeded a journey of two or three days, that caravan-leader saw coming in the opposite direction in a chariot drawn by asses, a black man with bloodshot eyes, with ungirt quiver, wearing a garland of lilies, his garments wet, the hair of his head wet, the wheels of his chariot smeared with mud. Seeing, he said this: "Whence, sir, do you come?" "From such-and-such a country." "Whither do you intend to go?" "To such-and-such a country." "Evidently, sir, farther on in the wilderness a heavy rain has been in progress." "Yes, indeed, sir. Farther on in the wilderness a heavy rain has been in progress. The roads are drenched with water; abundant are grass and sticks and water. Throw away, sir, the old grass, sticks, and water; with lightly burdened carts go ever so quickly; do not overburden the conveyances."

Now that caravan-leader told his drivers what that man had said, and gave orders as follows: "Throw away the old grass, sticks, and water; with lightly burdened carts start the caravan forward." "Yes, sir," said those drivers to that caravan-leader. And in obedience to his command they threw away the old grass, sticks, and water, and with lightly burdened carts started the caravan forward. Neither in the first stage of the journey, nor in the second, nor in the third, nor in the fourth, nor in the fifth, nor in the sixth, nor in the seventh, did they see grass or sticks or water; they all met destruction and death. And all that were in that caravan, whether men or beasts, did that ogre, that demon, devour, leaving only the bare bones.

When the second caravan-leader knew, "It is now a long time since that caravan started out," he loaded his carts with abundant grass and sticks and water, and started his caravan forward. Now when he had proceeded a journey of two or three days, this caravan-leader saw coming in the opposite direction in a chariot drawn by asses, a black man with blood-shot eyes, with ungirt quiver, wearing a garland of lilies, his garments wet, the hair of his head wet, the wheels of his chariot smeared with mud. Seeing, he said this: "Whence, sir, do you come?" "From such-and-such a country." "Whither do you intend to go?" "To such-and-such a country." "Evidently, sir, farther on in the wilderness a heavy rain has been in progress." "Yes, indeed, sir. Farther on in the wilderness a heavy rain has been in progress. The roads are drenched with water; abundant are grass and sticks and water. Throw away, sir, the old grass, sticks, and water; with lightly burdened carts go ever so quickly; do not overburden the conveyances."

Now that caravan-leader told his drivers what that man had said, adding: "This man surely is no friend of ours, no kinsman or blood-relative. How can we trust him on our journey? On no account must the old grass, sticks, and water, be thrown away. Start the caravan forward, leaving the things just as they are. I will not permit you to throw away the old." "Yes, sir," said those drivers to that caravan-leader. And in obedience to his command they started the caravan forward, leaving the things just as they were. Neither in the first stage of the journey, nor in the second, nor in the third, nor in the fourth, nor in the fifth, nor in the sixth, nor in the seventh, did they see grass or sticks or water; but they saw that caravan in destruction and ruin. And of those that were in that caravan, whether men or beasts, they saw only the bare bones, for they had been eaten by that ogre, by that demon.

Thereupon that caravan-leader addressed his drivers: "This caravan here met destruction and ruin solely through the folly of that foolish caravan-leader who acted as its guide. Now then, throw away those wares in our own caravan which are of little worth, and take those wares in this other caravan which are of great worth." "Yes, sir," said those drivers to that caravan-leader. And in obedience to his command they threw away all those wares in their own caravan which were of little worth, and took those wares in that other caravan which were of great worth. And they passed in safety through that wilderness solely through the wisdom of that wise caravan-leader who acted as their guide.

"Precisely so, Warrior, you, a foolish, short-sighted man, will meet destruction and ruin by seeking the next world otherwise than in the right way, just as did that man in the parable, that caravan-leader. And those who fondly imagine that they must listen to you, that they must put their trust in you, they also will meet destruction and ruin, just as did those drivers. Renounce, Warrior, this wicked heresy! Renounce, Warrior, this wicked heresy! Let it not be to your disadvantage and sorrow for a long time to come."

But Pāyāsi the Warrior remained obstinate. "I cannot bring myself," said he, "to renounce this wicked heresy." "Well then, Warrior, I will compose a parable for you."

DUNG FOR FODDER

In olden times, Warrior, a certain swineherd went from his own village to another village. There he saw much dry dung thrown away. When he saw it, the following thought occurred to him: "Here I have much dry dung thrown away which would make fodder for my pigs. Suppose I were to take the dry dung away from here!" He spread out his upper robe, took much dry dung, wrapped it up in a bundle, put the bundle on his head, and went his way.

When he was half-way home, a great cloud rained out of season. He went on with the load of dung oozing and trickling, smeared with dung to his finger-tips. People saw him going along in this manner and spoke as follows: "Aren't you crazy, sir? aren't you out of your mind? Otherwise how can you be carrying a load of dung, oozing and trickling, smeared with dung to your finger-tips?" "You, sirs, are crazy; you, sirs, are out of your mind. Why, what I am carrying is fodder for my pigs!"

"Warrior, you are just like the man in the parable who carried dung. Renounce, Warrior, this wicked heresy!" "That will I not." "Well then, Warrior, I will compose a parable for you."

TWO DICERS

In olden times, Warrior, two dicers played at dice. The first dicer swallowed every ace. The second dicer saw that dicer swallow every ace. Seeing, he said this to that dicer: "You, sir, have it all your own way. Give me the dice, sir; I must hurry away." "Yes, sir," said that dicer, and handed over the dice to that dicer.

Now that dicer painted the dice with poison, and said this to that dicer: "Come, sir, let us play at dice." "Yes, sir," said that dicer in assent to that dicer.

A second time also those dicers played at dice; a second time also that dicer swallowed every ace. The second dicer saw that dicer swallow for the second time also every ace. Seeing, he said this to that dicer:

> Smeared with the strongest poison
> Was the die the man swallowed, but knew it not.
> Swallow, O swallow, wicked dicer!
> Later it will taste bitter to you.

"Warrior, you are just like the dicer in the parable. Renounce, Warrior, this wicked heresy! Renounce, Warrior, this wicked heresy! Let it not be to your disadvantage and sorrow for a long time to come."

Wilful persistence in error.

"No matter how emphatically my lord Kassapa says this, yet, for all that, I cannot bring myself to renounce this wicked heresy. Even King Pasenadi Kosala knows, even kings outside know regarding me: 'Pāyāsi the Warrior holds this doctrine, holds this view: "There is no life after death; there are no living beings reborn without the intervention of parents; there is no fruition, no ripening, of good and evil deeds." ' If, my lord Kassapa, I were to renounce this wicked view, there would be those who would say of me: 'How foolish is Pāyāsi the Warrior! how short-sighted! how ready to accept what is hard to accept!' Even with anger will I hold to this view, even with hypocrisy will I hold to this view, even with conceit will I hold to this view."

"Well then, Warrior, I will compose a parable for you."

GIVING UP BETTER FOR WORSE

In olden times, Warrior, a certain district rose in revolt. And friend said to friend: "Let's go, sir; let's go to that district; there, perhaps, we may come by some spoils." "Yes, sir," said friend to friend in assent. They went to that country, to some village or other where there was an uproar. There they saw much hemp thrown away. Seeing, friend addressed friend: "Here, sir, is much hemp thrown away. Now then, sir, you pack up a load of hemp, and I'll pack up a load of hemp; we'll both carry off a load of hemp." "Yes, sir," said friend to friend in assent, and packed up a load of hemp.

They both went with their loads of hemp to some village or other where there was an uproar. There they saw much hempen thread thrown away. Seeing, friend addressed friend: "The very thing, sir, for which we should have wanted hemp! Here is much hempen thread thrown away! Now then, sir, you throw away your load of hemp, and I'll throw away my load of hemp; we'll both carry off a load of hempen thread." "This load of hemp I have has been carried a long way and is well tied together. Let me alone! Decide for yourself!" And that friend threw away his load of hemp and took a load of hempen thread.

They went to some village or other where there was an uproar. There they saw many hempen cloths thrown away. Seeing, friend addressed friend: "The very thing, sir, for which we should have wanted hemp or hempen thread! Here are many hempen cloths thrown away! Now then, sir, you throw away your load of hemp, and I'll throw away my load of hempen thread; we'll both carry off a load of hempen cloths." "This load of hemp I have, has been carried a long way and is well tied together. Let me alone! Decide for yourself!" And that friend threw away his load of hempen thread and took a load of hempen cloths.

They went to some village or other where there was an uproar. There they saw an abundance of flax . . . linen thread . . . linen cloths; . . . cotton . . . cotton thread . . . cotton cloths; . . . iron; . . . copper; . . . tin; . . . lead; . . . silver; . . . gold thrown away. Seeing, friend addressed friend: "The very thing, sir, for which we should have wanted hemp or hempen thread or hempen cloths, or flax or linen thread or linen cloths, or cotton or cotton thread or cotton cloths, or iron or copper or tin or lead or silver! Here, sir, is gold in abundance thrown away! Now then, sir, you throw away your load of hemp and I'll throw away my load of silver; we'll both carry off a load of gold." "This load of hemp I have, has been carried a long way and is well tied together. Let me alone! Decide for yourself!" And that friend threw away his load of silver and took a load of gold.

They approached their own village. That friend who went there with a load of hemp, was welcomed neither by mother and father, nor by children and wife, nor by friends and companions. Nor from them did he obtain happiness and satisfaction. But that friend who went there with a load of gold, was welcomed by mother and father, and by children and wife, and by friends and companions. And from them he obtained happiness and satisfaction.

"Warrior, you are just like the man in the parable who carried a load of hemp. Renounce, Warrior, this wicked heresy! Renounce, Warrior, this wicked heresy! Let it not be to your disadvantage and sorrow for a long time to come."

Conversion of the unbeliever.

"Even with your former parables, my lord Kassapa, have I been pleased and delighted. Moreover, I like to

87

hear your picturesque and quick-witted answers. Only I should have realized sooner the importance of identifying myself with you. It is delightful, my lord Kassapa! It is delightful, my lord Kassapa! It is precisely, my lord Kassapa, as if one were to set upright what has been thrown down, or were to reveal what is hidden, or were to point out the way to a bewildered person, or were to carry a lamp into the darkness so that persons with eyes might see things;—precisely so has my lord Kassapa illustrated the Doctrine in manifold ways. Lo! my lord Kassapa, I seek refuge in that Exalted One, Gotama, and in the Doctrine, and in the Congregation of Monks. Let my lord Kassapa keep me, who have sought the Refuges, as his disciple from this day forth, so long as I shall live."

Chapter VI
QUESTIONS OF MILINDA

The non-canonical Pāli work *Milindapañha* (Questions of Milinda), from which numerous selections follow, is a collection of imaginary dialogues between Menander, Greek king of Bactria, 125–95 B.C. (there is some divergence of opinion regarding these dates), and the sage Nāgasena, whose expositions of Buddhist teaching on the non-existence of the soul and Nibbana (Nirvana) are of significance to all interested in Buddhist philosophy. Menander was a well-informed scholar and expert debater who wanted to understand Buddhism, but no one he approached could help him. One day quite by chance he ran into the monk Nāgasena, who was going on his begging round, and he began questioning him. He was impressed with the monk's knowledge, and a meeting was arranged at the Sankheyya Monastery at Sāgal, where the monk was staying. The king arrived in the company of five hundred of his followers, and their dialogue began. At the request of the king it was resumed at his palace, though Nāgasena made it conditional that it be held in the scholastic way (Panditavāda) and not the royal (Rājavāda). The deepest spiritual problem confronting the king was his inability to comprehend how the Buddha could believe in rebirth without at the same time believing in a reincarnating self or ego. The Venerable Nāgasena, masterly at every turn of the dialogue, was able not only to resolve the king's doubts but make a convert of him and his followers. Menander, in his gratitude, built a monastery, the Milinda-vihāra, and handed it over to Nāgasena.

THERE IS NO PERMANENT INDIVIDUALITY

Now King Milinda approached Venerable Nāgasena. Having approached, he greeted Venerable Nāgasena in a friendly manner. Having completed the usual friendly greetings, he sat down on one side. Venerable Nāgasena returned the compliment, thereby delighting the heart of King Milinda. Then King Milinda said this to Venerable Nāgasena: "How is your Reverence known? what is your name, Reverend Sir?"

"As 'Nāgasena,' great king, am I known; 'Nāgasena,' great king, is what my fellow-religious are accustomed to call me. However, although mothers and fathers give such names as 'Nāgasena' or 'Sūrasena' or 'Vīrasena' or 'Sīhasena,' yet, great king, this 'Nāgasena' is only a conventional epithet, designation, appellation, style,—a mere name. For no 'individual' is thereby assumed to exist."

Then King Milinda spoke as follows: "Give ear to me, you five hundred Greeks and you eighty thousand monks! Nāgasena here speaks as follows: 'For no "individual" is thereby assumed to exist.' Is it reasonable to accept this?"

Then King Milinda said this to Venerable Nāgasena: "If, Reverend Nāgasena, an 'individual' is not assumed to exist, who, pray, gives you the Requisites,—robes, alms, lodging, medicines for the relief of the sick? Who enjoys them? Who keeps the Precepts? Who applies himself to the Practice of Meditation? Who realizes the Paths and the Fruits and Nibbāna? Who kills living beings? Who takes what is not given? Who misconducts himself in the matter of the Pleasures of Sense? Who speaks falsehood? Who drinks intoxicants? Who does the five evil deeds which bring immediate retribution? Ergo,—there is no good, there is no evil; there is no one who either does or causes to be done either good or evil deeds; there is no fruition, no ripening, of good and evil deeds. If, Reverend Nāgasena, he that kills you does not exist, then it is also true that he does not take life; it is also true, Reverend Nāgasena, that you have no teacher, no preceptor, no reception into the Order of Monks.

"Now you say: '"Nāgasena" is what my fellow-religious are accustomed to call me.' What is this 'Nāgasena' you speak of? Pray, Reverend Sir, is the hair of the head 'Nāgasena'?" "No indeed, great king." "Is the hair of the body 'Nāgasena'?" "No indeed, great king." "Are the nails, the teeth, the skin, the flesh, the sinews, the bones, the marrow of the bones, the kidneys, the heart, the liver, the peritoneum, the spleen, the lungs, the intestines, the mesentery, the stomach, the faeces, the bile, the phlegm, the pus, the blood, the sweat, the fat, the tears, the serum, the saliva, the mucus of the nose, the synovial fluid, the urine, the grey matter in the skull,—are any or all of these 'Nāgasena'?" "No indeed, great king."

"Pray, Reverend Sir, is Form 'Nāgasena'?" "No indeed, great king." "Is Sensation 'Nāgasena'?" "No indeed, great king." "Is Perception 'Nāgasena'?" "No indeed, great king." "Are the States of Mind 'Nāgasena'?" "No indeed, great king." "Is Consciousness 'Nāgasena'?" "No indeed, great king." "Well, Reverend Sir! Is the sum total of Form, Sensation, Perception, the States of Mind, and Consciousness,—is this 'Nāgasena'?" "No indeed, great king." "Well, Reverend Sir! Is something other than the sum total of Form, Sensation, Perception, the States of Mind, and Consciousness,—is this 'Nāgasena'?" "No indeed, great king." "Reverend Sir, I have asked you every question I can think of, but I cannot discover 'Nāgasena'! Apparently 'Nāgasena' is nothing but a sound! But, Reverend Sir, what is there about all this that is 'Nāgasena'? Reverend Sir, you utter untruth, you utter falsehood, when you say: 'There is no "Nāgasena."'" Then Venerable Nāgasena said this to king Milinda:

CHARIOT

You, great king, are a delicate prince, an exceedingly delicate prince. If you, great king, being the kind of man you are, travel on foot in the middle of the day, when the earth has become heated, when the sand is hot, treading on sharp pebbles and gravel and sand, your feet ache, your body grows weary, your mind is distressed, and a body-consciousness associated with pain arises within you. Tell me,—did you come on foot or in a vehicle?—

Reverend Sir, I do not travel on foot; I came in a chariot.—

If, great king, you came in a chariot, tell me about the chariot. Pray, great king, is the pole the "chariot"?—No indeed, Reverend Sir.

Is the axle the "chariot"?—No indeed, Reverend Sir.

Are the wheels the "chariot"?—No indeed, Reverend Sir.

Is the chariot-body the "chariot"?—No indeed, Reverend Sir.

Is the flagstaff of the chariot the "chariot"?—No indeed, Reverend Sir.

Is the yoke the "chariot"?—No indeed, Reverend Sir.

Are the reins the "chariot"?—No indeed, Reverend Sir.

Is the goad-stick the "chariot"?—No indeed, Reverend Sir.

Well, great king! Is the sum total of pole, axle, wheels, chariot-body, flagstaff, yoke, reins, and goad,—is this the "chariot"?—No indeed, Reverend Sir.

Well, great king! Is something other than the sum total of pole, axle, wheels, chariot-body, flagstaff, yoke, reins, and goad,—is this the "chariot"?—No indeed, Reverend Sir.

Great king, I have asked you every question I can think of, but I cannot discover the "chariot"! Apparently the "chariot" is nothing but a sound! But, great king, what is there about all this that is the "chariot"? Great king, you utter untruth, you utter falsehood, when you say: "There is no 'chariot.'" You, great king, are the foremost king in all the Land of the Rose-apple. Of whom, pray, are you afraid that you utter falsehood?

Give ear to me, you five hundred Greeks and you eighty thousand monks! King Milinda here speaks as follows: "I came in a chariot." But when I say to him: "If, great king, you came in a chariot, tell me about the chariot!" he cannot prove that there is any chariot. Is it reasonable to accept this?

Hearing this, the five hundred Greeks applauded Venerable Nāgasena, and said this to King Milinda: "Now, great king, answer if you can!" Then King Milinda said this to Venerable Nāgasena: "Reverend Nāgasena, I do not utter falsehood. Because of the pole, and because of the axle, and because of the wheels, and because of the chariot-body, and because of the flagstaff, the epithet, designation, appellation, style, name—'chariot'—comes into use."

"Great king, you understand perfectly what a chariot is. And precisely the same thing, is true with reference to me also. Because of the hair of the head, and because of the hair of the body, and because of the nails, and because of the teeth, and because of the skin, and because of the flesh, and because of the sinews, and because of the bones, and because of the marrow of the bones, and because of the kidneys, and because of the heart, and because of the liver, and because of the peritoneum, and because of the spleen, and because of the lungs, and because of the intestines, and because of the mesentery, and because of the stomach, and because of the faeces, and because of the bile, and because of the phlegm, and because of the pus, and because of the blood, and because of the sweat, and because of the fat, and because of the tears, and because of the serum, and because of the saliva, and because of the mucus of the nose, and because of the synovial fluid, and because of the urine, and because of the grey matter in the skull,—and because of Form, and because of Sensation, and because of Perception, and because of the States of Mind, and because of Consciousness,—because of all these, there comes into use the epithet, designation, appellation, style, name,—but name only,—'Nāgasena.' In the highest sense of the word, however, no 'individual' is thereby assumed to exist. Moreover, great king, listen to what the nun Vajirā said in the presence of the Exalted One:

> For just as for an assemblage of parts
> The term "chariot" is employed,
> So, when the Aggregates are present,
> The expression "living being" is employed.

"It is wonderful, Reverend Nāgasena! it is marvelous, Reverend Nāgasena! Brilliant beyond measure, highly illuminating, are the answers you have given to these questions! If the Buddha were standing here, he would give his applause. Well done, well done, Nāgasena! Brilliant beyond measure, highly illuminating, are the answers you have given to these questions!"

THERE IS NO CONTINUOUS PERSONAL IDENTITY

Said the king: "Reverend Nāgasena, is the person who is reborn the same person, or a different person?" Said the Elder: "He is neither the same person nor a different person." "Give me an illustration."

EMBRYO AND CHILD

What do you think about this, great king? You are now big. You were once young, tender, weak, lying on your back. Are you the same person now that you were then?

No indeed, Reverend Sir. He that was young, tender, weak, lying on his back, was one person; I, big as I am now, am a different person.

If this be true, great king, then it must also be true that you never had a mother, that you never had a father, that you never had a teacher, that you never acquired the arts and crafts, that you never took upon yourself the Precepts, that you never acquired a store of merit. Can it possibly be true, great king, that the mother of the embryo in the first stage of development is one person, that the mother of the embryo in the second stage is another, that the mother of the embryo in the third stage is another, that the mother of the embryo in the fourth stage is another? Is the mother of the little child one person, and the mother of the grown man another? Is it one person who acquires the arts and crafts, and another person who has acquired them? Is it one person who does evil deeds, and another person whose hands and feet are cut off?

No indeed, Reverend Sir. But how about you, Reverend Sir? suppose that same question were put to you; what would you have to say to it?

It was I myself, great king, who was once young, tender, weak, lying on my back; it is I myself who am now big. Solely because of dependence on this body, all these are embraced in one.—Give me an illustration.

LAMP AND FLAME

Suppose, great king, some man or other were to light a lamp. Would that lamp burn all night long?—Yes, Reverend Sir, it would burn all night long.

Well, great king, is the flame that burns in the first watch the same as the flame that burns in the middle watch?—No indeed, Reverend Sir.

Is the flame that burns in the middle watch the same as the flame that burns in the last watch?—No indeed, Reverend Sir.

Well, great king, was the lamp one thing in the first watch, something different in the middle watch, and something still different in the last watch?—No indeed, Reverend Sir. The lamp was only the cause of the flame that burned all night long.

"Precisely so, great king, there is an uninterrupted succession of mental and physical states. One state ceases to exist and another comes to exist. The succession is such that there is, as it were, none that precedes, none that follows. Thus it is neither that same person nor yet a different person which goes to the final summation of consciousness." "Give me another illustration."

MILK AND BUTTER

Take the case of sweet milk, great king. Let it stand for a time after it has been drawn, and it will turn into sour milk; from sour milk, it will turn into fresh butter, and from fresh butter into clarified butter. Suppose, great king, a man were to say: "The sweet milk is the same thing as the sour milk, and the sour milk is the same thing as the fresh butter, and

the fresh butter is the same thing as the clarified butter."
Great king, would a man speak correctly who said such a
thing as that?

No indeed, Reverend Sir. The milk is only the cause of
the butter which comes.

"Precisely so, great king, there is an uninterrupted succession of mental and physical states. One state ceases to
exist and another comes to exist. The succession is such
that there is, as it were, none that precedes, none that
follows. Thus it is neither that same person nor yet a different person which goes to the final summation of consciousness."

"You are a clever man, Reverend Nāgasena!"

WHAT, THEN, IS REBORN?

Name-and-Form is reborn.

Said the king: "Reverend Nāgasena, what is reborn?" Said
the Elder: "Name-and-Form, great king, is reborn." "Is
it this same Name-and-Form that is reborn?" "No, great
king, it is not this same Name-and-Form that is reborn.
On the contrary, great king, with one Name-and-Form
Kamma is wrought, a man does good or evil deeds, and by
the power of this Kamma another Name-and-Form is reborn." "If, Reverend Sir, it is not this same Name-and-Form
that is reborn, surely the man must be released from his
evil deeds." Said the Elder: "If he were *not* reborn, he
would be released from his evil deeds; but since, great
king, he *is* reborn, therefore he is *not* released from his
evil deeds." "Give me an illustration."

THEFT OF MANGOES

Great king, it is precisely as if some man or other were
to steal mangoes belonging to a certain man, and the owner
of the mangoes were to catch that thief and were to arraign
him before the king and were to say, "This man, your majesty, stole my mangoes," and the thief were to say, "Your

majesty, I didn't steal this man's mangoes; the mangoes this man planted are one thing, and the mangoes I stole are another; I am not guilty." In point of fact, great king, would not that man be guilty?

Yes, Reverend Sir, he would be guilty.

For what reason?

No matter what that man might say, Reverend Sir, he would not be able to deny that the last mango came from the first, and therefore he would be guilty of the theft of the last mango.

"Precisely so, great king, with one Name-and-Form Kamma is wrought, a man does good or evil deeds, and by the power of this Kamma another Name-and-Form is reborn. Therefore he is not released from his evil deeds." "Give me another illustration."

Great king, it is precisely as if some man were to steal another man's rice . . . sugar-cane . . .

FIRE IN A FIELD

Great king, it is precisely as if some man, in the winter-time, were to light a fire and warm himself and then go away without putting it out, and that fire were to set fire to a certain man's field, and the owner of the field were to catch that man and were to arraign him before the king and were to say, "This man, your majesty, set fire to my field," and the man were to say, "Your majesty, I didn't set fire to this man's field; the fire I failed to put out is one thing, and the fire that set fire to this man's field is another; I am not guilty." In point of fact, great king, would not that man be guilty?

Yes, Reverend Sir, he would be guilty.

For what reason?

No matter what that man might say, Reverend Sir, he would not be able to deny that the last fire came from the first, and therefore he would be guilty of setting the last fire.

LAMP UNDER A THATCH

Great king, it is precisely as if some man or other were to take a lamp and were to climb to the attic of a thatched house and were to eat, and the lamp as it burned were to set fire to the thatch, and the thatch as it burned were to set fire to the house, and the house as it burned were to set fire to the village, and the village-folk were to catch that man and were to say, "Why, Master man, did you set fire to the village?" and the man were to say, "Friends, I didn't set fire to the village; the fire of the lamp by whose light I ate is one thing, but the fire that burned the village is another." Suppose they carried the dispute to you. Whose side, great king, would you take?

The side of the village-folk, Reverend Sir.

Why?

That man might say whatever he would, but all the same, that last fire came straight from the first.

GIRL AND WOMAN

Great king, it is precisely as if some man or other were to choose a young girl to be his wife and were to pay the purchase-money and were to go his way, and after a time that young girl were to become a grown woman, were to attain her majority, and then a second man were to pay the purchase-money and were to marry her, and the first man were to come and say, "But why, Master man, are you carrying off my wife?" and the second man were to say, "I am not carrying off your wife; that young girl of tender years whom you chose to be your wife and for whom you paid the purchase-money is one person; this grown woman who has attained her majority, whom I chose to be my wife and for whom I paid the purchase-money, is another person." Suppose they carried the dispute to you. Whose side, great king, would you take?

The side of the first man, Reverend Sir.

Why?

That man might say whatever he would, but all the same, that grown woman came straight from that young girl.

MILK AND CURDS

Great king, it is precisely as if some man or other were to buy a pot of milk from the hands of a cowherd, and were to place it in the hands of that same cowherd and were to go his way, saying, "To-morrow I'll come and get it," and on that morrow that milk were to turn to curds, and that man were to come and say, "Give me the pot of milk," and the cowherd were to show him the curds, and the man were to say, "I didn't buy curds at your hands; give me the pot of milk!" and the cowherd were to say, "I didn't know your milk had turned to curds!" Suppose they carried the dispute to you. Whose side, great king, would you take?

The side of the cowherd, Reverend Sir.

Why?

That man might say whatever he would, but all the same, those curds came straight from that milk.

"Precisely so, great king, although one Name-and-Form comes to an end at death, and another Name-and-Form comes into existence at rebirth, nevertheless the second comes straight from the first. Therefore that man is not released from his evil deeds."

"You are a clever man, Reverend Nāgasena!"

What is Name and what is Form?

Said the king: "Reverend Nāgasena,—but as for this expression which you employ,—Name-and-Form:—in this complex, what is Name? what is Form?" "Whatever in this complex, great king, is gross and coarse, this is Form; whatever entities in this complex are fine, of the mind, mental, these are Name." "Reverend Nāgasena, why is it that Name, all by itself, is not reborn? or Form, all by it-

99

self?" "Dependent one upon the other, great king, are these entities; they invariably come into existence together." "Give an illustration."

GERM AND EGG

Suppose, great king, a hen had no germ of new life in her. In that case neither would there be any egg. Of these two,—germ and egg,—both are absolutely dependent the one upon the other; they invariably come into existence together.

"Precisely so, great king, if in this complex there were no Name, neither would there be any Form. Of these two,—Name and Form,—both are absolutely dependent the one upon the other; they invariably come into existence together. Thus has Name-and-Form been brought into existence for a long time."

"You are a clever man, Reverend Nāgasena!"

TIME HAS NO BEGINNING

Said the king: "Reverend Nāgasena,—but as for this expression which you employ,—'long time': what do you mean by this word 'time'?" "Past time, great king, future time, present time. . . . And of all this time a starting-point is unknown." . . . "But as for this statement which you make, —'a starting-point is unknown': give an illustration of this."

SEED AND FRUIT

Great king, it is precisely as if a man were to plant a tiny seed in the earth, and from that seed a sprout were to come up and in the course of time were to attain growth, increase, development, and were to yield fruit; and as if, from that fruit, the man were to take a seed and plant again, and from that seed a sprout were to come up and in the course of time were to attain growth, increase, development, and were to yield fruit. Is there any end to this series?

There is not, Reverend Sir.

"Precisely so, great king, is it with time also; of it no starting-point is known." "Give me another illustration."

EGG AND HEN

Great king, it is precisely as if you had an egg from a hen, and a hen from the egg, and an egg from the hen. Is there any end to this series?

There is not, Reverend Sir.

"Precisely so, great king, is it with time also; of it no starting-point is known." "Give me another illustration."

CIRCLE

The Elder drew a circle on the ground and said this to King Milinda:

Great king, is there any end to this circle?

There is not, Reverend Sir.

"Precisely so, great king, is it with time also; of it no starting-point is known." .

"You are a clever man, Reverend Nāgasena!"

OUT OF NOTHING COMES NOTHING

Said King Milinda to the sage Nāgasena: "Reverend Nāgasena, are there any things that exist which come out of things that did not exist?" "There are not, great king, any things that exist which come out of things that did not exist. Only out of things that existed, great king, come things that exist." "Give me an illustration."

TIMBERS AND HOUSE

Well, what do you think, great king? Did this house where you are now sitting come out of things that did not exist?

There is not a single thing here, Reverend Sir, which came out of things that did not exist. Only out of things that existed did it come. For example, Reverend Sir, these timbers existed in the forest, and this clay existed in the earth. Thus, through the effort, through the exertion, of women and men, did this house come to exist.

"Precisely so, great king, there are not any things that exist which come out of things that did not exist. Only out of things that existed, great king, come things that exist." "Illustrate the point further."

SEEDS AND PLANTS

For example, great king, when the different varieties of seed-life and plant-life are placed in the earth, in due course they will attain increase, growth, development, and will yield flowers and fruits. But these plants do not come out of things that did not exist. Only out of things that existed do they come.

CLAY AND VESSELS

For example, great king, a potter takes clay out of the earth and makes various kinds of vessels. But these vessels do not come out of things that did not exist. Only out of things that existed do they come.

LYRE AND SOUND

For example, great king, suppose a lyre had no leaf, had no skin, had no bowl, had no handle, had no neck, had no strings, had no quill, and suppose there were no effort or exertion on the part of a human being,—would any sound come out?

No indeed, Reverend Sir.

On the other hand, great king, if the lyre had a leaf, had a skin, had a bowl, had a handle, had a neck, had strings, had a quill, and if there were effort and exertion on the part of a human being,—a sound would come out?

Yes, Reverend Sir, a sound would come out.

FIRE-DRILL AND FIRE

For example, great king, suppose a fire-drill had no fire-stick, had no fire-stick base, had no fire-stick cord, had no upper fire-stick, had no rag, and suppose there were no effort or exertion on the part of a human being,—could fire be produced?

No indeed, Reverend Sir.

On the other hand, great king, if the fire-drill had a fire-stick, had a fire-stick base, had a fire-stick cord, had an upper fire-stick, had a rag, and if there were effort and exertion on the part of a human being,—fire could be produced?

Yes, Reverend Sir, fire could be produced.

BURNING-GLASS AND FIRE

For example, great king, suppose there were no burning-glass, no heat from the sun, no cow-dung,—could fire be produced?

No indeed, Reverend Sir.

On the other hand, great king, if there were a burning-glass, if there were heat from the sun, if there were cow-dung,—fire could be produced?

Yes, Reverend Sir, fire could be produced.

MIRROR AND REFLECTION

For example, great king, suppose there were no mirror, no light, no face,—would any reflection appear?

No indeed, Reverend Sir.

On the other hand, great king, if there were a mirror, if there were light, if there were a face,—a reflection would appear?

Yes, Reverend Sir, a reflection would appear.

"Precisely so, great king, there are not any things that exist which come out of things that did not exist. Only out of things that existed, great king, come things that exist."

"You are a clever man, Reverend Nāgasena!"

THERE IS NO SOUL

Said the king: "Reverend Nāgasena, do you assume the existence of the soul?" "But, great king, what is this thing you call the 'soul'?" "The living principle within, Reverend Sir, which with the eye sees visible objects, with the ear hears sounds, with the nose smells odors, with the tongue tastes flavors, with the body touches tangible objects, with the mind perceives the Doctrine:—just as we here, sitting in this palace, may look out of whatever window we please,—east, west, north, south,—so also, Reverend Sir, this living principle within looks out of whatever door it pleases." Said the Elder: "Let me tell you, great king, about the Five Doors of the Senses. Hearken to this! give close attention!"

SIX DOORS OF THE SENSES

If there is a living principle within which sees visible objects with the eye, just as we, sitting in this palace, may look out of whatever window we please,—east, west, north, south,—can this living principle within, in like manner, see visible objects equally well with the ear, the nose, the tongue, the body, and the mind? Can it hear sounds equally well with the eye, the nose, the tongue, the body, and the mind? Can it smell odors equally well with the eye, the ear, the tongue, the body, and the mind? Can it taste flavors equally well with the eye, the ear, the nose, the body, and the mind? Can it touch tangible objects equally well with the eye, the ear, the nose, the tongue, and the mind? Can it perceive the Doctrine equally well with the eye, the ear, the nose, the tongue, and the body?

No indeed, Reverend Sir.

But, great king, what you said last does not agree with what you said first, nor does what you said first agree with what you said last.

MEN IN PALACE

But again, great king, take ourselves for example. You and I, sitting in this palace, with these lattice-windows flung open, in broad daylight, with our faces turned outward, see visible objects perfectly. Can this living principle within, also, in like manner, when the doors of the eyes are flung open, in broad daylight, see visible objects perfectly? When the doors of the ears are flung open, when the door of the nose is flung open, when the door of the tongue is flung open, when the door of the body is flung open, in broad daylight, can it hear sounds perfectly, smell odors, taste flavors, touch tangible objects?

No indeed, Reverend Sir.

But, great king, what you said last does not agree with what you said first, nor does what you said first agree with what you said last.

MAN OUTSIDE OF GATEWAY

But again, great king, suppose Dinna here were to go out and stand outside of the gateway. Would you, great king, know: "Dinna here has gone out and stands outside of the gateway"?

Yes, Reverend Sir, I should know.

But again, great king, suppose Dinna here were to come in and stand in front of you. Would you, great king, know: "Dinna here has come in and is standing in front of me"?

Yes, Reverend Sir, I should know.

In just the same way, great king, in case a flavor were placed on the tongue, would this living principle within know whether it was sour or salt or bitter or pungent or astringent or sweet?

Yes, Reverend Sir, it would know.

But after that flavor has passed into the stomach, would the living principle then know whether it was sour or salt or bitter or pungent or astringent or sweet?

No indeed, Reverend Sir.

But, great king, what you said last does not agree with what you said first, nor does what you said first agree with what you said last.

MAN IN TROUGH OF HONEY

Suppose, great king, some man or other were to fetch a hundred pots of honey and were to fill a trough of honey and were to seal some man's lips and were to throw that man into the trough of honey. Great king, would that man know whether he was in honey or not?

No indeed, Reverend Sir.

Why?

Because, Reverend Sir, the honey could not get into his mouth.

But, great king, what you said last does not agree with what you said first, nor does what you said first agree with what you said last.

"I am no match for you in an argument. Be good enough to explain the matter to me."

The Elder enlightened King Milinda with a discourse on Abhidhamma: "Here in this world, great king, because of the eye and because of visible objects arises the sense of sight; simultaneously are produced contact, sensation, perception, thought, focussing of thoughts, vitality, attention. Thus do these physical and mental states originate from a cause, *for there is no soul involved in any of them.* Because of the ear and because of sounds arises the sense of sound; because of the nose and because of odors arises the sense of smell; because of the tongue and because of flavors arises the sense of taste; because of the body and because of tangible objects arises the sense of touch. Because of the mind and because of objects of thought arises mental consciousness; simultaneously are produced contact, sensation, perception, thought, focussing of thoughts, vitality, attention. Thus do these physical and mental states originate from a cause, *for there is no soul involved in any of them.*"

"You are a clever man, Reverend Nāgasena!"

WHY DOES NOT THE FIRE OF HELL DESTROY THE DENIZENS OF HELL?

Because of the Power of Kamma.

Said the king: "Reverend Nāgasena, you Buddhists say: 'Far hotter than any ordinary fire is the Fire of Hell. A tiny stone, cast into any ordinary fire, will smoke for a whole day and not crumble. But a rock as big as a pagoda, cast into the Fire of Hell, will crumble in an instant.' But on the other hand you also say this: 'As for the living beings that are reborn in Hell, no matter how many thousands of years they are tormented therein, they go not to destruction.' That is something I do not believe."

Said the Elder:

EMBRYO OF REPTILES AND BIRDS

What do you think about this, great king? Do not female sharks and crocodiles and tortoises and peacocks and pigeons swallow hard stones and gravel?

Yes, Reverend Sir, they do.

Now these hard substances, once inside of their abdomen, once in their belly, go to destruction; do they not?

Yes, Reverend Sir, they do.

But does the embryo in their belly also go to destruction?

No indeed, Reverend Sir.

For what reason?

I suppose, Reverend Sir, it is because of the Power of Kamma that it does not go to destruction.

"Precisely so, great king, because of the Power of Kamma, the denizens of Hell, no matter how many thousands of years they are tormented in Hell, go not to destruction. Right there are they born, right there do they grow up, right there do they die. Moreover, great king, this was said by the Exalted One: 'He shall not die so long as that Evil Kamma is not exhausted.'"

"Give me another illustration."

EMBRYO OF BEASTS OF PREY

What do you think about this, great king? Do not lionesses and tigresses and leopardesses and bitches eat meat with hard bones in it? . . .

HUMAN EMBRYO

What do you think about this, great king? Do not the delicate princesses of the Greeks and of the Warriors and of the Brahmans and of the householders eat pieces of meat that are hard and tough?

Yes, Reverend Sir, they do.

Now these hard substances, once inside of their abdomen, once in their belly, go to destruction; do they not?

Yes, Reverend Sir, they do.

But does the embryo in their belly also go to destruction?

No indeed, Reverend Sir.

For what reason?

I suppose, Reverend Sir, it is because of the Power of Kamma that it does not go to destruction.

"Precisely so, great king, because of the Power of Kamma, the denizens of Hell, no matter how many thousands of years they are tormented in Hell, go not to destruction. Right there are they born, right there do they grow up, right there do they die. Moreover, great king, this was said by the Exalted One: 'He shall not die so long as that Evil Kamma is not yet exhausted.'"

"You are a clever man, Reverend Nāgasena!"

NIBBĀNA IS UNALLOYED BLISS

"Reverend Nāgasena, is Nibbāna unalloyed bliss, or is it alloyed with pain?" "Nibbāna, great king, is unalloyed bliss; it is not alloyed with pain." "I, Reverend Nāgasena, do not believe that statement: 'Nibbāna is unalloyed bliss.' This, Reverend Nāgasena, is my firm conviction on the subject: 'Nibbāna is alloyed with pain.' Now I have a reason to give for this statement: 'Nibbāna is alloyed with pain.' What is the reason for this?

"Reverend Nāgasena, in the case of all those who seek after Nibbāna, plainly evident are their effort and exertion of body and mind, their self-restraint in standing and walking and sitting and lying and eating, their suppression of sleep, their repression of the Organs of Sense, their renunciation of goods and grain and of dear kinsfolk and friends.

"Now persons in the world who are happy, who are endowed with happiness, all with one accord please and increase their Organs of Sense: the eye with all manner of delightful visible objects which yield pleasurable reflexes; the ear with songs and strains; the nose with odors of flowers, fruits, leaves, bark, roots, essences; the tongue with flavors of hard and soft food and of sippings and drinkings and tastings; the body with contacts with objects both delicate and fine, both soft and mild; the mind by fixing the attention of the thoughts on all manner of delightful objects of thought, both good and evil, both pure and impure.

"But you strike at and strike down, hew at and hew down, obstruct and impede, the increase of eye, ear, nose, tongue, body, and mind. Therefore both the body suffers and the mind suffers. When the body suffers, sensations of bodily pain are experienced; when the mind suffers, sensations of mental pain are experienced. Did not also Māgandiya the wandering ascetic, in railing at the Exalted One, say this: 'A Destroyer of Increase is the monk Gotama'?

This is my reason for saying: 'Nibbāna is alloyed with pain.'"

"No indeed, great king, Nibbāna is not alloyed with pain; Nibbāna is unalloyed bliss. Now, great king, as to your statement that Nibbāna is pain,—this pain is not Nibbāna at all; this is only the beginning of the realization of Nibbāna, this is only the seeking after Nibbāna. Nibbāna, great king, is unalloyed bliss, pure and simple; it is not alloyed with pain. Let me explain what I mean."

BLISS OF SOVEREIGNTY

Great king, do kings enjoy the bliss of sovereignty?—Yes, Reverend Sir, kings enjoy the bliss of sovereignty.

Now, great king, is this bliss of sovereignty alloyed with pain?—No indeed, Reverend Sir.

But, great king, what have you to say to this? When a border-province breaks into insurrection, in order to quell those border-inhabitants, kings go afield with their retinues of ministers and captains and soldiers and servants, permit themselves to be tormented by gnats and mosquitoes, by wind and sun, hurry this way and that over even and uneven ground, wage mighty battles, and risk their lives!

Reverend Nāgasena, this is not the bliss of sovereignty; this is only a preliminary to the quest of the bliss of sovereignty. With pain, Reverend Nāgasena, do kings seek after sovereignty; then they enjoy the bliss of sovereignty. Thus, Reverend Nāgasena, the bliss of sovereignty is not alloyed with pain. Bliss of sovereignty is one thing; pain is quite another.

"Precisely so, great king, Nibbāna is unalloyed bliss . . ."

BLISS OF KNOWLEDGE

Great king, do teachers who know the arts and crafts enjoy the bliss of the arts and crafts?—Yes, Reverend Sir, teachers who know the arts and crafts enjoy the bliss of the arts and crafts.

Now, great king, is this bliss of the arts and crafts alloyed with pain?—No indeed, Reverend Sir.

But, great king, what have you to say to this? They torture their bodies with services to teachers,—by rising to greet, by rising to meet, by fetching water and sweeping houses and presenting toothsticks and water for rinsing the mouth, by accepting remnants of food and shampooing and bathing and dressing the feet, by submission of their own wills, by compliance with the wills of others, by sleeping in discomfort, by eating all kinds of food!

Reverend Nāgasena, this is not the bliss of the arts and crafts; this is only a preliminary to the quest of the arts and crafts. With pain, Reverend Nāgasena, do teachers seek to acquire the arts and crafts; then they enjoy the bliss of the arts and crafts. Thus, Reverend Nāgasena, the bliss of the arts and crafts is not alloyed with pain. The bliss of the arts and crafts is one thing; pain is quite another.

"Precisely so, great king, Nibbāna is unalloyed bliss; it is not alloyed with pain. But those who are seeking after this Nibbāna, torture both body and mind. They restrain themselves in standing and walking and sitting and lying and eating; they suppress sleep; they repress the Organs of Sense; they renounce both body and life. However, having sought Nibbāna with pain, they enjoy a Nibbāna which is unalloyed bliss, just as teachers enjoy the bliss of the arts and crafts. Thus, great king, Nibbāna is unalloyed bliss; it is not alloyed with pain. Pain is one thing; Nibbāna is quite another."

"Good, Reverend Nāgasena! So it is! I agree absolutely!"

NIBBĀNA IS UNLIKE ANYTHING ELSE

"Reverend Nāgasena, you are continually talking about Nibbāna. Now is it possible to make clear the form or figure or age or dimensions of this Nibbāna, either by an illustration or by a reason or by a cause or by a method?"

"Nibbāna, great king, is unlike anything else; it is impossible." "This, Reverend Nāgasena, I cannot admit,—that if Nibbāna really exists, it should be impossible to make known its form or figure or age or dimensions, either by an illustration or by a reason or by a cause or by a method. Tell me why." "Let be, great king; I will tell you why."

UNLIKE ANYTHING ELSE IS THE GREAT OCEAN

Is there, great king, such a thing as the great ocean?—Yes, Reverend Sir, there is such a thing as the great ocean.

If, great king, some man were to ask you: "Great king, how much water is there in the great ocean? And how many living creatures dwell in the great ocean?"—if, great king, some man were to ask you this question, how would you answer him?

If, Reverend Sir, some man were to ask me: "Great king, how much water is there in the great ocean? And how many living creatures dwell in the great ocean?" I, Reverend Sir, should say this to him: "The question you ask, Master man, is a question you have no right to ask; that is no question for anybody to ask; that question must be set aside. The hair-splitters have never gone into the subject of the great ocean. It is impossible to measure the water in the great ocean, or to count the living beings that make their abode there." That is the reply I should give him, Reverend Sir.

But, great king, if the great ocean really exists, why should you give him such a reply as that? Surely you ought to measure and count, and then tell him: "There is so much water in the great ocean, and there are so many living beings dwelling in the great ocean!"

It's impossible, Reverend Sir. That question isn't a fair one.

"Great king, just as, although the great ocean exists, it is impossible to measure the water or to count the living beings that make their abode there, precisely so, great king, although Nibbāna really exists, it is impossible to make clear the form or figure or age or dimensions of Nibbāna, either by an illustration or by a reason or by a cause or by a method. Great king, a person possessed of magical power, possessed of mastery over mind, could estimate the quantity of water in the great ocean and the number of living beings dwelling there; but that person possessed of magical power, possessed of mastery over mind, would never be able to make clear the form or figure or age or dimensions of Nibbāna, either by an illustration or by a reason or by a cause or by a method.

"Yet again, great king, hear one more reason why this is impossible:"

UNLIKE ANYTHING ELSE ARE THE GODS WITHOUT FORM

Are there, great king, among the gods, gods that are called the Formless Gods?—Yes, Reverend Sir, according to sacred lore, there are, among the gods, gods that are called the Formless Gods.

Now, great king, in the case of these Formless Gods, is it possible to make clear their form or figure or age or dimensions, either by an illustration or by a reason or by a cause or by a method?—No indeed, Reverend Sir.

Well then, Reverend Sir, there are no Formless Gods!

Reverend Sir, there are Formless Gods! But it is not possible to make clear their form or figure or age or dimensions, either by an illustration or by a reason or by a cause or by a method.

"Great king, just as, although the Formless Gods are beings that really exist, it is not possible to make clear their form or figure or age or dimensions, either by an illustration or by a reason or by a cause or by a method, precisely so, great king, although Nibbāna really exists, it is not possible to make clear its form or figure or age or dimensions, either by an illustration or by a reason or by a cause or by a method."

Nibbāna, however, has certain qualities.

"Reverend Nāgasena, granted that Nibbāna is unalloyed bliss, and that it is impossible to make clear its form or figure or age or dimensions, either by an illustration or by a reason or by a cause or by a method. But, Reverend Sir,

has Nibbāna any qualities in common with other things,—
something that might serve as an illustration or example?"

"In the matter of form, great king, it has not. But in
the matter of qualities, there are some illustrations and examples which might be employed."

"Good, Reverend Nāgasena! And that I may receive,
even with reference to the qualities of Nibbāna, some
little light on a single point, speak quickly! Quench the
fever in my heart! Subdue it with the cool, sweet breezes
of your words!"

Great king, Nibbāna has one quality in common with the
lotus.

Two qualities of water.

Three qualities of medicine.

Four qualities of the great ocean.

Five qualities of food.

Ten qualities of space.

Three qualities of the wishing-jewel.

Three qualities of red-sandalwood.

Three qualities of the cream of ghee.

Nibbāna has five qualities in common with a mountain-
peak.

ONE QUALITY OF THE LOTUS

Just as the lotus is not polluted by water, so also Nibbāna is
not polluted by any of the Depravities.

TWO QUALITIES OF WATER

Just as water is cool and quenches fever, so also Nibbāna
is cool and quenches every one of the Depravities.

But again further,—water subdues the thirst of the races of
men and animals when they are tired and weary and thirsty
and overcome with the heat. Precisely so Nibbāna subdues
the thirst of Craving for the Pleasures of Sense, of Craving
for Existence, of Craving for Power and Wealth.

THREE QUALITIES OF MEDICINE

Just as medicine is the refuge of living beings oppressed by poison, so also Nibbāna is the refuge of living beings oppressed by the poison of the Depravities.

But again further,—medicine puts an end to bodily ills. Precisely so Nibbāna puts an end to all sufferings.

But again further,—medicine is deathless. Precisely so Nibbāna is the Deathless.

FOUR QUALITIES OF THE GREAT OCEAN

Just as the great ocean is free from any corpses, so also Nibbāna is free from any of the Depravities.

But again further,—the great ocean is vast, boundless, fills not up for all of the streams [that flow into it]. Precisely so Nibbāna is vast, boundless, fills not up for all of the living beings [that pass thereunto].

But again further,—the great ocean is the abode of mighty beings. Precisely so Nibbāna is the abode of mighty beings,—the mighty Saints, in whom there is no stain, in whom the Contaminations are extinct, who have attained unto power, who have become masters of self.

But again further,—the great ocean is all in blossom, as it were, with the flowers of its waves,—mighty, various, unnumbered. Precisely so Nibbāna is all in blossom, as it were, with the Flowers of Purity, Knowledge, and Deliverance,—mighty, various, unnumbered.

FIVE QUALITIES OF FOOD

Just as food is the support of life of all living beings, so also Nibbāna, once realized, is the support of life, for it destroys old age and death.

But again further,—food increases the strength of all living beings. Precisely so Nibbāna, once realized, increases the strength of the Power of Magic of all living beings.

But again further,—food is the source of the beauty of all living beings. Precisely so Nibbāna, once realized, is the source of the beauty of the virtues of all living beings.

But again further,—food relieves the wear and tear to which all living beings are subject. Precisely so Nibbāna, once realized, relieves the wear and tear to which all living beings are subject because of the Depravities, one and all.

But again further,—food dispels the weakness of hunger in all living beings. Precisely so Nibbāna, once realized, dispels the weakness of hunger produced by all manner of sufferings in all living beings.

TEN QUALITIES OF SPACE

Just as space is not produced, does not age, does not suffer death, does not pass out of existence, does not come into existence, cannot be forcibly handled, cannot be carried away by thieves, rests on nothing, is the pathway of birds, presents no obstacles, is endless,—so also Nibbāna is not produced, does not age, does not suffer death, does not pass out of existence, does not come into existence, cannot be forcibly handled, cannot be carried away by thieves, rests on nothing, is the pathway of the Noble, presents no obstacles, is endless.

THREE QUALITIES OF THE WISHING-JEWEL

Just as the wishing-jewel fulfils desires, so also Nibbāna fulfils desires.

But again further,—the wishing-jewel provokes a smile of satisfaction. Precisely so Nibbāna provokes a smile of satisfaction.

But again further,—the wishing-jewel diffuses lustre. Precisely so Nibbāna diffuses lustre.

THREE QUALITIES OF RED-SANDALWOOD

Just as red-sandalwood is difficult to obtain, so also Nibbāna is difficult to obtain.

But again further,—red-sandalwood exhales fragrance which is unequalled. Precisely so Nibbāna exhales fragrance which is unequalled.

But again further,—red-sandalwood is praised by the well-born. Precisely so Nibbāna is praised by the Noble.

THREE QUALITIES OF THE CREAM OF GHEE

Just as the cream of ghee possesses beauty, so also Nibbāna possesses beauty of quality.

But again further,—the cream of ghee possesses fragrance. Precisely so Nibbāna possesses the Fragrance of Morality.

But again further,—the cream of ghee possesses flavor. Precisely so Nibbāna possesses flavor.

FIVE QUALITIES OF A MOUNTAIN-PEAK

Just as a mountain-peak is exceedingly lofty, so also Nibbāna is exceedingly lofty.

But again further,—a mountain-peak is immovable. Precisely so Nibbāna is immovable.

But again further,—a mountain-peak is difficult of ascent. Precisely so Nibbāna is difficult of ascent for the Depravities, one and all.

But again further,—on a mountain-peak seeds, any and all, will not grow. Precisely so, in Nibbāna the Depravities, any and all, will not grow.

But again further,—a mountain-peak is free from cringing and repulsion. Precisely so Nibbāna is free from cringing and repulsion.

"Good, Reverend Nāgasena! It is even so! I agree absolutely!"

NIBBĀNA IS NEITHER PAST NOR FUTURE NOR PRESENT

It is neither produced nor not produced nor to be produced.
Yet it exists, and may be realized.

"Reverend Nāgasena, you Buddhists say: 'Nibbāna is neither past nor future nor present; it is neither produced nor not produced nor to be produced.' With reference to this point, Reverend Nāgasena,—does the person who, by ordering his walk aright, realizes Nibbāna, realize something which has already been produced?—or does he first produce it and then realize it?"

"Whoever, great king, by ordering his walk aright, realizes Nibbāna, neither realizes something which has already been produced, nor first produces and then realizes it. Nevertheless, great king, this element Nibbāna, which whoever orders his walk aright realizes, exists."

"Do not, Reverend Nāgasena, throw light on this question by covering it; throw light on it by uncovering it, by making it manifest. Rouse your will! rouse your effort! pour out on this very point all that you have learned from your training. On this point this people here is bewildered, perplexed, plunged in doubt. Destroy this arrow within!"

"Great king, this element Nibbāna exists,—peaceful, blissful, sublime; and whoever orders his walk aright, whoever, in accordance with the teaching of the Conquerors, through wisdom, grasps the Aggregates, realizes Nibbāna. Great king, just as a pupil, by following the instructions of his teacher, through wisdom, realizes what is to be known, precisely so, great king, a man, by ordering his walk aright, by following the teaching of the Conquerors, by wisdom, realizes Nibbāna.

"But how is Nibbāna to be viewed? By its freedom from trouble, by its freedom from adversity, by its freedom from peril, by its security, by its peace, by its bliss, by its sweetness, by its sublimity, by its purity, by its coolness."

ESCAPE FROM A BON-FIRE

Great king, just as a man burning in a blazing, crackling fire heaped up with many faggots, escaping therefrom with effort, entering a place free from fire, will there experience supreme bliss, precisely so, great king, whoever orders his walk aright, will, by diligent mental effort, realize Nibbāna, Supreme Bliss, from which the torment of the Three-fold Fire is absent.

"Great king, the fire of faggots is to be viewed as the Three-fold Fire; the man in the fire is to be viewed as the man who orders his walk aright; the place free from fire is to be viewed as Nibbāna."

ESCAPE FROM A HEAP OF CORPSES

Or again, great king, just as a man in a heap of fragments of corpses and excrement of snakes and dogs and men, enmeshed in the tangled tangles of corpses, escaping therefrom with effort, entering a place free from corpses, will there experience supreme bliss, precisely so, great king, whoever orders his walk aright, will, by diligent mental effort, realize Nibbāna, Supreme Bliss, from which the torment of the Three-fold Fire is absent.

"Great king, the corpses are to be viewed as the Five Pleasures of Sense; the man among the corpses is to be viewed as the man who orders his walk aright; the place free from corpses is to be viewed as Nibbāna."

ESCAPE FROM PERIL

Or again, great king, just as a man, frightened, trembling, quaking, his thoughts whirling and twirling, escaping from that peril with effort, entering a place that is firm and fast and immovable and free from peril, will there experience supreme bliss, precisely so, great king, whoever orders his walk aright, will, by diligent mental effort, realize Nibbāna, Supreme Bliss, from which the torment of the Three-fold Fire is absent.

"Great king, the peril is to be viewed as the perils which proceed forth, one after another, from Birth, Old Age, Disease, and Death; the man in a fright is to be viewed as the man who orders his walk aright; the place free from peril is to be viewed as Nibbāna."

ESCAPE FROM MUD

Or again, great king, just as a man fallen in a place that is foul and filthy, full of mud and mire, removing that mud and mire with effort, going to a place that is perfectly clean, free from filth, will there experience supreme bliss, precisely so, great king, whoever orders his walk aright, will, by diligent mental effort, realize Nibbāna, from which the filth and mire of the Depravities is absent.

"Great king, the mud is to be viewed as gain and honor and fame; the man in the mud is to be viewed as the man who orders his walk aright; the place that is perfectly clean, free from filth, is to be viewed as Nibbāna."

How does a man "order his walk aright"?

"Now as to the statement: 'A person, by ordering his walk aright, realizes Nibbāna.' What is meant by the expression: 'by ordering his walk aright'?"

"Whoever, great king, orders his walk aright, grasps the course of the Aggregates. Grasping their course, he sees therein Birth, he sees therein Old Age, he sees therein Disease, he sees therein Death. He sees therein nothing that is pleasant, nothing that is agreeable; from the beginning to the middle to the end he sees nothing therein which it is possible for him to lay hold of."

RED-HOT IRON BALL

Great king, just as in the case of a man who, when an iron ball has been heated all day until it blazes and glows and crackles, from the beginning to the middle to the end sees no spot which it is possible for him to lay hold of, precisely so, great king, in the case of a man who grasps the course of the Aggregates;—grasping their course, he sees therein Birth, he sees therein Old Age, he sees therein Disease, he sees therein Death; he sees therein nothing that is pleasant, nothing that is agreeable; from the beginning to the middle to the end he sees nothing which it is possible for him to lay hold of. When he sees that there is nothing which it is possible for him to lay hold of, discontent springs up and abides in his heart, a fever descends upon his body; being without protection, without a refuge, refugeless, he conceives disgust for the Existences.

BON-FIRE

Suppose, great king, a man were to enter a mighty mass of fire of flaming flames; being without protection there, without a refuge, refugeless, he would conceive disgust for the fire. Precisely so, great king, when the man in question sees that there is nothing which it is possible for him to lay hold of, discontent springs up and abides in his heart, a fever descends upon his body; being without protection, without a refuge, refugeless, he conceives disgust for the Existences.

When he sees the perils in the course of the Aggregates, the following thought arises within him: "Red-hot, indeed, is this course of the Aggregates,—flaming and blazing, full of suffering, full of despair! If only one might obtain cessation of the course of the Aggregates,—that were good, that were excellent!—namely, quiescence of all the Aggregates, riddance of all the Conditions of Existence, destruction of Craving, freedom from Lust, Cessation, Nibbāna!" Thus indeed these thoughts of his spring forward to the cessation of the course of the Aggregates, are satisfied, bristle with joy, leap for joy: "I have indeed gained Escape from the Round of Existences!"

TRAVELER WHO HAS LOST HIS WAY

Great king, just as a man traveling in an unfamiliar region who has lost his way, upon seeing a path which will take him out, springs forward thereto, is satisfied, bristles with joy, leaps for joy: "I have gained a path which will take me out!" precisely so, great king, the thoughts of a man who sees the perils in the course of the Aggregates, spring forward to the cessation of the course of the Aggregates, are satisfied, bristle for joy, leap for joy: "I have indeed gained Escape from the Round of Existences!"

To cessation of the course of the Aggregates he battles, seeks, cultivates, broadens, a way. To that end mindfulness abides steadfast in him, to that end vigor abides steadfast in him, to that end joy abides steadfast in him. As he continues mental effort from one point to another, those thoughts of his leap over the course of the Aggregates and descend upon cessation of the course of the Aggregates; then he has reached cessation of the course of the Aggregates.

"This, great king, is what is meant by the statement: 'A person, by ordering his walk aright, realizes Nibbāna.'"
"Good, Reverend Nāgasena! It is just as you say! I agree absolutely!"

NIBBĀNA IS NOT A PLACE

"Reverend Nāgasena, is this region in the East, or in the South, or in the West, or in the North, or above or below or across,—this region where Nibbāna is located?"
"Great king, the region does not exist, either in the East, or in the South, or in the West, or in the North, or above or below or across, where Nibbāna is located."
"If, Reverend Nāgasena, there is no place where Nib-

bāna is located, then there *is* no Nibbāna; and as for those who have realized Nibbāna, their realization also is vain. Let me tell you why I think so:"

FIELDS AND CROPS

Reverend Nāgasena, just as on earth, a field is the place of origin of crops, a flower is the place of origin of odors, a bush is the place of origin of flowers, a tree is the place of origin of fruits, a mine is the place of origin of jewels, insomuch that whoever desires anything, has but to go to the proper place and get it,—precisely so, Reverend Nāgasena, if Nibbāna really exists, it also follows that a place of origin of this Nibbāna must be postulated. But since, Reverend Nāgasena, there is no place of origin of Nibbāna, therefore I say: There is no Nibbāna; and as for those who have realized Nibbāna: Their realization also is vain.

"Great king, there is no place where Nibbāna is located. Nevertheless, this Nibbāna really exists; and a man, by ordering his walk aright, by diligent mental effort, realizes Nibbāna."

FIRE-STICKS AND FIRE

Great king, just as there is such a thing as fire, but no place where it is located,—the fact being that a man, by rubbing two sticks together, produces fire,—so also, great king, there is such a thing as Nibbāna, but no place where it is located,—the fact being that a man, by ordering his walk aright, by diligent mental effort, realizes Nibbāna.

SEVEN JEWELS OF A KING

Or again, great king, just as there are Seven Jewels of a King, to wit, the Jewel of the Wheel of Empire, the Jewel of the Elephant, the Jewel of the Horse, the Jewel of the Gem, the Jewel of the Woman, the Jewel of the Householder, the

Jewel of the Captain,—but no place exists where these Jewels are located,—the fact being that a Prince, by ordering his walk aright, by a right walk, comes by these Jewels,—precisely so, great king, there is such a thing as Nibbāna, but no place where it is located,—the fact being that a man, by ordering his walk aright, by diligent mental effort, realizes Nibbāna.

"Reverend Nāgasena, let it be granted that there is no place where Nibbāna is located. But is there a place where a man must stand to order his walk aright and realize Nibbāna?"

Morality is the Place of Origin of Nibbāna.

"Yes, great king, there *is* a place where a man must stand to order his walk aright and realize Nibbāna."

"But what, Reverend Sir, is the place where a man must stand to order his walk aright and realize Nibbāna?"

"Morality, great king, is the place! Abiding steadfast in Morality, putting forth diligent mental effort,—whether in the land of the Scythians or in the land of the Greeks, whether in China or in Tartary, whether in Alexandria or in Nikumba, whether in Kāsi or in Kosala, whether in Cashmere or in Gandhāra, whether on a mountain-top or in the highest heaven,—no matter where a man may stand, by ordering his walk aright, he realizes Nibbāna."

"Good, Reverend Nāgasena! You have made it plain what Nibbāna is, you have made it plain what the realization of Nibbāna is, you have well described the Power of Morality, you have made it plain how a man orders his walk aright, you have uplifted the Banner of Truth, you have set the Eye of Truth in its socket, you have demonstrated that Right Effort on the part of those who put forth diligent effort is not barren. It is just as you say, most excellent of excellent teachers! I agree absolutely!"

HOW DO WE KNOW THAT THE BUDDHA EVER EXISTED?

Now King Milinda approached Venerable Nāgasena. Having approached, he bowed to Venerable Nāgasena and sat down on one side. Sitting on one side, King Milinda, desiring to know, desiring to hear, desiring to bear in mind, desiring to see the Light of Knowledge, desiring to rend Ignorance asunder, desiring to make the Light of Knowledge rise, desiring to destroy the Darkness of Ignorance, summoning up surpassing courage and energy and mindfulness and intelligence, said this to Venerable Nāgasena:
"Reverend Nāgasena,—but did you ever see the Buddha?"—"No indeed, great king."
"But did your teachers ever see the Buddha?"—"No indeed, great king."
"Reverend Nāgasena, you say you never saw the Buddha, and you say your teachers never saw the Buddha either. Well then, Reverend Nāgasena, the Buddha never existed! for there is nothing here to show that he ever did!"

How do we know that Kings existed of old?
"But, great king, did Kings exist of old,—those who were your predecessors in the line of Kings?"—"Yes, Reverend Sir,—why doubt? Kings did exist of old,—those who were my predecessors in the line of Kings."
"Did you, great king, ever see those Kings of old?"—"No indeed, Reverend Sir."
"But, great king, did those who instructed you,—house-priests, commanders-in-chief, judges, ministers,—did they ever see those Kings of old?"—"No indeed, Reverend Sir."
"But, great king, if you never saw those Kings of old, and if, as you say, your instructors never saw those Kings of old either,—where are those Kings of old?—for there is nothing here to show that those Kings of old ever existed!"

We know that Kings existed of old by what they have left us.
"Visible, Reverend Nāgasena, are the insignia employed

by Kings of old, to wit, the white parasol, the diadem, the slippers, the yak's tail fan, the jeweled sword, and the couches of great price. By these, we may know and believe: 'Kings existed of old.'"

So is it in the case of the Buddha.
"Precisely so, great king, we also, with reference to that Exalted One, may know and believe. There is a reason why we may know and believe: 'That Exalted One existed.' What is the reason? There exist, great king, the insignia employed by that Exalted One, the All-knowing One, the All-seeing One, the All-worthy, the Supremely Enlightened, the Buddha; to wit, the Four Intent Contemplations, the Four Right Exertions, the Four Bases of Magical Power, the Five Sensations, the Five Forces, the Seven Prerequisites of Enlightenment, the Noble Eightfold Path. By these, the world of men and the Worlds of the Gods know and believe: 'That Exalted One existed.' This, great king, is the reason, this is the cause, this is the way, this is the method of inference, by which it is to be known: 'That Exalted One existed.'"

"As for him who ferried a multitude over the Ocean of Rebirth,
Who, by destroying the Constituents of Being, attained Nibbāna,
By inference may it be known: 'That Best of Men existed.'"

"Reverend Nāgasena, give an illustration."

THE BUILDER OF A CITY IS KNOWN BY HIS CITY

Take the case, great king, of the builder of a city. Desiring to create a city, he would first of all look out a spot of ground which was smooth, without elevations, without depressions, free from stones and rocks, immune from attack, faultless, pleasing to the eye. The rough places therein, he would make smooth; stumps and brambles he would clear away. There he would create a city,—resplendent, well-proportioned, divided into parts, with trenches and ramparts thrown up, with strong gates and towers and fortifications,

oad commons and squares and junctions and cross-
, with clean, smooth-surfaced king's highways, with well-
portioned open shops, furnished with groves and gardens
d lakes and lotus-pools and wells, adorned with all manner
of holy places, free from all faults. When that city was complete in every way, he would go to another country. And
after a time that city would become prosperous, flourishing,
plentifully supplied with food, secure, highly prosperous,
happy, free from trouble, immune from attack, the resort of
all sorts and conditions of men. And all sorts and conditions
of men . . . from all parts of the earth . . . coming to that
city to live, and seeing that it was new, well-proportioned, free
from defect, free from fault, pleasing to the eye, would know
by inference: "Skilful indeed was that city-builder who
created this city!"

SO IS THE BUDDHA KNOWN BY HIS CITY OF RIGHTEOUSNESS

Precisely so, great king, that Exalted One, without an
equal, without equals, without a peer, without a similar, not
to be weighed, not to be reckoned, not to be measured, not
to be estimated, whose virtues were immeasurable, who attained the perfection of virtues, whose wisdom was endless,
whose glory was endless, whose vigor was endless, whose
power was endless, who attained the perfection of the Powers of a Buddha,—precisely so that Exalted One conquered
Māra the Evil One and his host, burst asunder the Net of
False Views, put down Ignorance, uplifted Knowledge, up-
held the Torch of Righteousness, attained Omniscience, and
unconquered and unconquerable in the fight, created the City
of Righteousness.

Moreover, great king, the City of Righteousness created
by the Exalted One has Morality for its ramparts, Shame for
its trenches, Knowledge for its battlemented gateway, Vigor
for its towers, Faith for its pillars, Mindfulness for its
gate-keeper, Wisdom for its terraced heights, the Suttantas

for its commons and squares, the Abhidhamma for its junctions and crossroads, the Vinaya for its court of justice, the Earnest Meditations for its street.

Seven Shops of the Buddha.

Moreover, great king, in this City of Righteousness, in the Street of the Earnest Meditations, Seven Shops are open, and these are their names: a Flower-shop, a Perfume-shop, a Fruit-shop, a Medicine-shop, an Herb-shop, an Ambrosia-shop, a Jewel-shop,—and a General shop.

FLOWER-SHOP OF THE BUDDHA

"Reverend Nāgasena, what is the Flower-shop of the Exalted One, the Buddha?"

There exist, great king, proclaimed by the Exalted One, the All-knowing One, the All-seeing One, the All-worthy, the Supremely Enlightened, Subjects of Meditation, duly systematized and classified, as follows: the Ideas of Impermanence, Unreality, Impurity, Disadvantage, Renunciation, Passionlessness, Cessation; the Idea of Dissatisfaction with any and all worlds; the Idea of the Impermanence of the Constituents of Being; Meditation on In- and Out-breathing; Ideas of the Corpses: bloated, purple, festering, fissured, gnawed, scattered, pounded-and-scattered, bloody, wormy, bony; the Ideas of Friendliness, Compassion, Joy, Indifference; Meditation on Death; Meditation on the Body. These, great king, are the Subjects of Meditation, duly systematized and classified, proclaimed by the Exalted One, the Buddha.

With reference to these,—whoever desires to be delivered from Old Age and Death, chooses one or another of these Subjects of Meditation, and by means of this Subject of Meditation obtains deliverance from Lust, Ill-will, Delusion, Pride, False Views; crosses the Ocean of the Round of Existences; stems the Stream of Craving; cleanses himself of the Threefold Stain; destroys all the Contaminations; enters that

Best of Cities, the City of Nibbāna, which is free from stain, free from dust, clean white, free from Birth, free from Old Age, free from Death, which is Bliss, Coolness, Freedom from Peril,—through Sainthood obtains deliverance of the heart.

This, great king, is what is meant by the Flower-shop of the Buddha.

With Kamma as the price, go up unto the shop;
Buy a Subject of Meditation; so obtain deliverance through Deliverance.

PERFUME-SHOP OF THE BUDDHA

"Reverend Nāgasena, what is the Perfume-shop of the Exalted One, the Buddha?"

There exist, great king, proclaimed by the Exalted One, certain Precepts, duly systematized and divided; and anointed with the Perfume of these Precepts, the sons of the Exalted One fume and perfume with the Perfume of the Precepts the world of men and the Worlds of the Gods. They exhale fragrance, they exhale exceeding sweet fragrance, in the principal directions, in the intermediate directions, with the wind, against the wind; they abide ever suffusing them.

Now what are these Precepts, duly systematized and divided? The Precepts of the Refuges, the Five Precepts, the Eight Precepts, the Ten Precepts, the Precepts of Restraint contained in the Book of Confession and included in the Five Recitations thereof.

This, great king, is what is meant by the Perfume-shop of the Buddha. Moreover, great king, this has been said by the Exalted One, god over gods:

The perfume of flowers goes not against the wind,
Nor that of sandal, or of Tagara and Mallikā flowers;
But the perfume of the righteous goes against the wind;
In all directions a good man exhales fragrance.

Above and beyond all varieties of perfume,
Whether of sandal or of lotus
Or of Tagara and Vassikī flowers,
The perfume of virtue is preëminent.

Weak is this perfume, this perfume of Tagara and of
    sandal;
The perfume of the virtuous is the finest that is wafted to
    the gods.

FRUIT-SHOP OF THE BUDDHA

"Reverend Nāgasena, what is the Fruit-shop of the
Exalted One, the Buddha?"

There are Fruits, great king, proclaimed by the Exalted
One, to wit: the Fruit of Conversion, the Fruit of one-
who-will-be-reborn-but-once, the Fruit of one-who-will-be-
reborn-no-more-on-earth, and the Fruit of Sainthood; the
Attainment of the Fruit of Freedom from the Depravities; the Attainment of the Fruit of Freedom from the Marks
of Lust, Ill-will, and Delusion; the Attainment of the Fruit of
Freedom from Inclination thereto. Of these, whichever Fruit
a man desires, he gives Kamma as the price, and buys the
Fruit he wants.

BUYER AND SELLER OF MANGOES

Suppose, great king, some man or other had a mango-tree
which bore fruit continually, and suppose he never shook
down mangoes so long as buyers did not come, but when a
buyer arrived, he took the price and told him this: "Master
man, this mango-tree bears fruit continually; take from it as
much fruit as you want,—immature, or decayed, or hairy,
or unripe, or ripe"; and suppose the buyer, for the price he
had given the seller, if he wanted immature, took immature;
if he wanted decayed, took decayed; if he wanted hairy, took
hairy; if he wanted unripe, took unripe; if he wanted ripe,
took ripe.

Precisely so, great king, whichever Fruit a man desires, he gives Kamma as the price, and buys the Fruit he wants. If he desires the Fruit of Conversion, he receives it; if he desires the Fruit of one-who-will-be-reborn-but-once, he receives it; if he desires the Fruit of one-who-will-be-reborn-no-more-on-earth, he receives it; if he desires the Fruit of Sainthood, he receives it; if he desires the Attainment of the Fruit of Freedom from the Depravities, he receives it; if he desires the Attainment of the Fruit of Freedom from the Marks of Lust, Ill-will, and Delusion, he receives it; if he desires the Attainment of the Fruit of Freedom from Inclination thereto, he receives it.

This, great king, is what is meant by the Fruit-shop of the Buddha.

People give Kamma as the price, and buy the Fruit of the
    Deathless;
Therefore they are in Bliss that have bought the Fruit of
    the Deathless.

MEDICINE-SHOP OF THE BUDDHA

"Reverend Nāgasena, what is the Medicine-shop of the Exalted One, the Buddha?"

There are Medicines, great king, proclaimed by the Exalted One, and with these Medicines that Exalted One frees the world of men and the Worlds of the Gods from the Poison of the Depravities. Now what are these Medicines? Great king, they are the Four Noble Truths proclaimed by the Exalted One; to wit, the Noble Truth regarding Suffering, the Noble Truth regarding the Origin of Suffering, the Noble Truth regarding the Cessation of Suffering, the Noble Truth regarding the Way to the Cessation of Suffering. Now whosoever, longing for Sublime Knowledge, hearken to the Doctrine of the Four Truths, they are delivered from Birth, they are delivered from Old Age, they are delivered from Death, they are delivered from sorrow, lamentation, suffering, dejection, and despair.

This, great king, is what is meant by the Medicine-shop of the Buddha.

Of all the medicines in the world that are antidotes for
poison,
There is none equal to the Medicine of the Doctrine; drink
this, O monks!

HERB-SHOP OF THE BUDDHA

"Reverend Nāgasena, what is the Herb-shop of the Exalted One, the Buddha?"

There are Herbs, great king, proclaimed by the Exalted
One, with which herbs that Exalted One cures both gods and
men; to wit: the Four Earnest Meditations, the Four Right
Exertions, the Four Bases of Magical Power, the Five Sensations, the Five Forces, the Seven Prerequisites of Enlightenment, the Noble Eightfold Path. With these Herbs the
Exalted One purges Wrong Views, purges Wrong Resolution,
purges Wrong Speech, purges Wrong Conduct, purges
Wrong Means of Livelihood, purges Wrong Exertion, purges
Wrong Mindfulness, purges Wrong Concentration; produces vomiting of Desire, produces vomiting of Ill-will,
produces vomiting of Delusion, produces vomiting of Pride,
produces vomiting of False Views, produces vomiting of
Doubt, produces vomiting of Arrogance, produces vomiting
of Sloth-and-Torpor, produces vomiting of Shamelessness and
of Fearlessness of Wrongdoing,—produces vomiting of all the
Depravities.

This, great king, is what is meant by the Herb-shop of
the Buddha.

Of all the herbs that are known in the world, many and
various,
There are none equal to the Herbs of the Doctrine; drink
these, O monks!

They that drink the Herbs of the Doctrine will no more
  grow old and die;
By Concentration and Insight destroying the Constituents
  of Being, they will attain Nibbāna.

AMBROSIA-SHOP OF THE BUDDHA

"Reverend Nāgasena, what is the Ambrosia-shop of the
Exalted One, the Buddha?"

An Ambrosia, great king, has been proclaimed by the Exalted One, and with this Ambrosia that Exalted One sprinkles
the world of men and the Worlds of the Gods; and sprinkled
with this Ambrosia, both gods and men have obtained
deliverance from Birth, Old Age, Disease, Death, and from
sorrow, lamentation, suffering, dejection, and despair. What
is this Ambrosia? It is Meditation on the Body. Moreover, great
king, this has been said by the Exalted One, god over gods:
"Ambrosia, O monks, do they enjoy who enjoy Meditation
on the Body."

This, great king, is what is meant by the Ambrosia-shop of
the Buddha.

Afflicted with disease he saw mankind, and opened an
  Ambrosia-shop.
"With Kamma, monks, come, buy and eat Ambrosia!"

JEWEL-SHOP OF THE BUDDHA

"Reverend Nāgasena, what is the Jewel-shop of the Exalted One, the Buddha?"

Jewels, great king, have been proclaimed by the Exalted
One, and adorned with these Jewels, the sons of the Exalted
One brighten, illuminate, irradiate, the world of men and
the Worlds of the Gods,—shine, shine forth,—diffuse light
above, below, across. What are these Jewels? The Jewel of the
Precepts of Morality, the Jewel of Concentration, the Jewel
of Wisdom, the Jewel of Deliverance, the Jewel of Insight

through Knowledge of Deliverance, the Jewel of the Analytical Powers, the Jewel of the Prerequisites of Enlightenment.

Seven Jewels of the Buddha

JEWEL OF MORALITY

What, great king, is the Jewel of the Precepts of Morality proclaimed by the Exalted One?

It is the Precepts of Restraint contained in the Book of Confession, the Precepts of Restraint of the Organs of Sense, the Precepts regarding Purity of Means of Livelihood, the Precepts relating to the Monastic Requisites, the Lower Precepts, the Middle Precepts, the Higher Precepts, the Precepts regarding the Paths, the Precepts regarding the Fruits.

Moreover, great king, for a man adorned with the Jewel of the Precepts of Morality, all living beings, the world of men, the Worlds of the Gods, the World of Māra, the World of Brahmā, the world of monks and nuns, cherish affection, cherish longing. Moreover, great king, a monk wearing the Jewel of the Precepts of Morality, brightens, brightens exceedingly, the principal directions and the intermediate directions, above and below and across; from the Waveless Hell below to the Highest Heaven above, he abides irradiating light which exceeds, which surpasses, the light of all the jewels that are between. Such, great king, are the Jewels of the Precepts of Morality which are exposed for sale in the Jewel-shop of the Exalted One.

This, great king, is what is meant by the Jewel-shop of the Buddha.

Such are the Precepts in the Shop of the Buddha;
Buy these Jewels with Kamma, and deck yourselves therewith.

JEWEL OF CONCENTRATION

What, great king, is the Jewel of Concentration proclaimed by the Exalted One?

Concentration with which is associated reasoning, with which is associated investigation; Concentration which is devoid of reasoning, with which investigation only is associated; Concentration which is devoid of reasoning, which is devoid of investigation; Concentration on Freedom from the Depravities; Concentration on Freedom from the Marks of Lust, Ill-will, and Delusion; Concentration on Freedom from Inclination thereto.

Moreover, great king, when a monk wears the Jewel of Concentration, thoughts of Lust, thoughts of Ill-will, thoughts of Injury, and the many and various evil thoughts which have their bases in the Depravities of Pride, Arrogance, False Views, and Doubt,—all these, on encountering Concentration, scatter, disperse, fall away, abide not, adhere not.

Precisely, great king, as water on a lotus leaf scatters, disperses, falls away, abides not, adheres not,—why is this? because of the purity of the lotus leaf,—just so, great king, when a monk wears the Jewel of Concentration, thoughts of Lust, thoughts of Ill-will, thoughts of Injury, and the many and various evil thoughts which have their bases in the Depravities of Pride, Arrogance, False Views, and Doubt,—all these, on encountering Concentration, scatter, disperse, fall away, abide not, adhere not. Why is this? Because of the purity of Concentration.

This, great king, is what is meant by the Jewel of Concentration proclaimed by the Exalted One. Such, great king, are the Jewels of Concentration exposed for sale in the Jewel-shop of the Exalted One.

Let a monk wear the Necklace of the Jewels of Concentration,
And the evil thoughts will not spring up,
Nor will the thoughts suffer distraction;
Come, deck yourselves therewith.

JEWEL OF WISDOM

What, great king, is the Jewel of Wisdom proclaimed by the Exalted One? Great king, it is the Wisdom with which the Noble Disciple perceives aright: "This is good;" perceives aright: "That is not good;" perceives aright that this is blameworthy and that is not, that this is low and that is high, that this is dark and that is light, that this resembles dark and light; perceives aright: "This is Suffering;" perceives aright: "This is the Origin of Suffering;" perceives aright: "This is the Cessation of Suffering;" perceives aright: "This is the Path which leads to the Cessation of Suffering."

This, great king, is what is meant by the Jewel of Wisdom proclaimed by the Exalted One.

Let a monk wear the Necklace of the Jewels of Wisdom,
And Existence continues not for long;
Quickly he touches the Deathless,
Nor does he delight in Existence.

JEWEL OF DELIVERANCE

What, great king, is the Jewel of Deliverance proclaimed by the Exalted One? Sainthood, great king, is what is meant by the Jewel of Deliverance; and, great king, a monk who has attained Sainthood is said to wear the Jewel of Deliverance.

Precisely, great king, as a man adorned with ornaments of strings of pearls and gems and gold and coral, his limbs anointed . . . , gaily decked with flowers . . . , surpassing other folk, is resplendent, is resplendent exceedingly, shines down, shines forth, shines all about, gleams, gleams forth, overwhelms, overspreads, with his adornments of garlands and perfumes and jewels,—just so, great king, a monk who has attained Sainthood, who has rid himself of the Contaminations, who wears the Jewel of Deliverance, surpassing, far surpassing, all other monks beginning with those in the lowest grade of attainment and extending to those who have attained Deliverance, is resplendent, is resplendent exceedingly, shines down, shines forth, shines all about, gleams, gleams forth, overwhelms, overspreads, with Deliverance. Why is this? Because, great king, this Adornment is the foremost of all the adornments,—that is to say, the Adornment of Deliverance.

This, great king, is what is meant by the Jewel of Deliverance proclaimed by the Exalted One.

> To one who wears a necklace of gems,
> Housefolk look up as lord;
> But to one who wears the Jewel of Deliverance,
> Both gods and men look up.

JEWEL OF INSIGHT THROUGH KNOWLEDGE OF DELIVERANCE

What, great king, is the Jewel of Insight through Knowledge of Deliverance, proclaimed by the Exalted One? Knowledge through Self-examination, great king, is what is meant by the Jewel of Insight through Knowledge of Deliverance, proclaimed by the Exalted One. For by this Knowledge the Noble Disciple examines the Paths and the Fruits and Nibbāna, the Depravities he has got rid of, and the Depravities which remain.

> That Knowledge by which the Noble know their accomplishments,—
> Strive, O true sons of the Conqueror, to obtain that Jewel of Knowledge!

JEWEL OF THE ANALYTICAL POWERS

What, great king, is the Jewel of the Analytical Powers proclaimed by the Exalted One? Four in number, great king, are the Analytical Powers: Understanding of the Meaning of Words, Understanding of the Doctrine, Grammar and Exegesis, and Readiness in Speaking. Adorned, great king, with these Four Analytical Powers, a monk, no matter what manner of assemblage he approaches, whether it be an assemblage of Warriors or an assemblage of Brahmans or an assemblage of householders or an assemblage of religious, approaches confident, approaches that assemblage untroubled, unafraid, unalarmed, untrembling, with no bristling of the hair of the body.

Precisely, great king, as a warrior, a hero in battle, girded with the Five Weapons, goes into battle: "If enemies shall be far off, I will lay them low with arrows; if they shall be nearer, I will hit them with the javelin; if they shall be nearer yet, I will hit them with the spear; if an enemy shall come to close quarters with me, I will cleave him in twain with my sabre; if he shall grapple with me, I will pierce him through and through with my knife;"—just so, great king, a monk, adorned with the Jewel of the Four Analytical Powers, approaches an assemblage unafraid:

"If any man shall ask me a question involving Understanding of the Meaning of Words, I will tell him the meaning by another meaning; I will tell him the reason by another reason; I will tell him the cause by another cause: I will tell him the way by another way: I will render him free from doubt, I will dispel his perplexity, I will delight him with my handling of the question.

"If any man shall ask me a question involving Understanding of the Doctrine, to him I will explain the Doctrine by another doctrine, the Deathless by ambrosia, the Uncreate by the uncreated, Nibbāna by extinguishment, Freedom from the Depravities by freedom, Freedom from the Marks of Lust, Ill-will, and Delusion, by freedom from marks, Freedom from Inclination thereto by freedom by inclination, Freedom from Lust by freedom from lust: I will render him free from doubt, I will dispel his perplexity, I will delight him with my handling of the question.

"If any man shall ask me a question involving Grammar and Exegesis, to him I will explain one etymology by another etymology, one word by another word, one particle by another particle, one letter by another letter, one assimilation by another assimilation, one consonant by another consonant, one semi-consonant by another semi-consonant, one vowel by another vowel, one accent by another accent, one rule by another rule, one usage by another usage: I will render him free from doubt, I will dispel his perplexity, I will delight him with my handling of the question.

"If any man shall ask me a question involving Readiness in Speaking, to him I will render easy of comprehension one exposition by another exposition, one comparison by another comparison, one characteristic by another characteristic, one quality by another quality: I will render him free from doubt, I will dispel his perplexity, I will delight him with my handling of the question."

This, great king, is what is meant by the Jewel of the Analytical Powers proclaimed by the Exalted One.

Whoever, buying the Analytical Powers, touches them
    with Knowledge,
Unfrightened, unterrified, illuminates the worlds of men
    and gods.

JEWEL OF THE PREREQUISITES OF ENLIGHTENMENT

What, great king, is the Jewel of the Prerequisites of Enlightenment proclaimed by the Exalted One? Seven in number, great king, are these Prerequisites of Enlightenment: Mindfulness, Examination of the Doctrine, Vigor, Joy, Repose, Concentration, Indifference. Adorned, great king, with these Seven Prerequisites of Enlightenment, a monk overcomes all darkness, and brightens, illuminates, and irradiates the world of men and the Worlds of the Gods.

This, great king, is what is meant by the Jewel of the Prerequisites of Enlightenment proclaimed by the Exalted One.

Before a monk wearing the Necklace of the
Jewels of the Prerequisites of Enlightenment,
Both gods and men stand up.
Buy these Jewels with Kamma, and deck yourselves there-
    with.

GENERAL SHOP OF THE BUDDHA

"Reverend Nāgasena, what is the General shop of the Exalted One, the Buddha?"

Great king, the General shop of the Exalted One is the Ninefold Word of the Buddha, relics of his body, relics consisting of things which he used, mounds erected over them, and the Jewel of the Order of Monks. In the General shop, great king, the Exalted One has exposed for sale the Attainments of high birth, wealth, long life, health, beauty, wisdom, worldly glory, heavenly glory, Nibbāna. Whoever desire any one of these Attainments, give Kamma as the price, and buy whatever Attainment they long for. Some buy by taking upon themselves the Precepts, some buy by keeping Fastday; with Kamma as the price, though it be but the merest trifle, they obtain the Attainments, beginning with the lowest and extending to the highest.

Precisely, great king, as in the shop of a shop-keeper, with a very small quantity of sesame and beans or a small quantity of rice and beans as the price, men obtain what they require, beginning with the least and extending to the greatest, just so, great king, in the General shop of the Exalted One, with Kamma as the price, though it be but the merest trifle, men receive the Attainments in return, beginning with the lowest and extending to the highest.

This, great king, is what is meant by the General shop of the Exalted One.

Long life, health, beauty, heaven, high birth,
And the Uncreate, Nibbāna, are in the Conqueror's General shop.
Be it little or much, with Kamma as the price are they obtained.
With Faith as the Price, buy, and be rich, O monks!

THE PURE PRACTICES

Twenty-six similes.

Like the earth are they in properties, for they are a firm footing to those who desire Salvation.

Like water are they, for they wash away all the flecks of the Depravities.

Like fire are they, for they burn the whole forest of the Depravities.

Like wind are they, for they blow away all the dust and flecks of the Depravities.

Like medicine are they, for they cure all the diseases of the Depravities.

Like ambrosia are they, for they counteract all the poisons of the Depravities.

Like a field are they, for therein grow crops of all the virtues of the Religious Life.

Like the wish-fulfiller are they, for they grant all the Attainments prayed for and longed for by those who desire Salvation.

Like a ship are they, for they ferry those who desire Salvation across the Great Ocean of the Round of Existences.

Like a shelter for the frightened are they, for they restore confidence to those who are frightened by Old Age and Death.

Like a mother are they, for they treat kindly those who are oppressed with the sufferings caused by the Depravities.

Like a father are they, for they foster all the virtues of the Religious Life in those who desire to increase in good works.

Like a friend are they, for they break not their word to those who seek after all the virtues of the Religious Life.

Like the lotus are they, for to them adhere not any of the flecks of the Depravities.

Like the four choice kinds of perfumes are they, for they dispel the foul odors of the Depravities.

Like a lofty mountain-peak are they, for they cannot be shaken by the winds of the Eight Conditions of Life.

Like space are they, for they are impalpable, broad, diffused, outspread, mighty.

Like a river are they, for they wash away the flecks of the Depravities.

Like a skilful guide are they, for they conduct those who desire Salvation out of the wilderness of Rebirth, out of the tangle of the forest of the Depravities.

Like a mighty caravan-leader are they, for they enable those who desire Salvation to reach that blessed, most blessed, City of Nibbāna, which is free from all perils, secure, without perils.

Like a well-polished, spotless mirror are they, for they enable those who desire Salvation to see the true nature of the Constituents of Being.

Like a shield are they, for they ward off the clubs and arrows and swords of the Depravities.

Like an umbrella are they, for they ward off the rain of the Depravities, and the heating and scorching of the Three-fold Fire.

Like the moon are they, for they are prayed for and longed for by those who desire Salvation.

Like the sun are they, for they dispel the darkness and gloom of Delusion.

Like the ocean are they, for to those who desire Salvation they are the place of origin of the priceless jewels of the many and various virtues of the Religious Life; and they are not to be measured, not to be reckoned, not to be estimated.

Chapter VII
QUESTIONS WHICH TEND NOT
TO EDIFICATION

This work, which constitutes Sutta 63 of the *Majjhima-nikāya*, illustrates as much as anything in Buddhist literature Gautama's realism and common sense. Māluṅkyāputta, who for some time had been a member of the Sangha (Order of Monks), was much addicted to speculation of the sort leading nowhere. After a particularly bitter bout with his questioning, he resolved that if the Buddha did not offer him satisfactory answers he would leave the Order, and it was in such a state of mind that he went to him. Throughout Buddhist literature there are similar confrontations between the Buddha or his disciples and doubting Thomases, men with whom the Western reader can find it easy to sympathize, yet perhaps in only a very few are there to be found analogies as graphic as that of the man wounded by a poisoned arrow. That which distinguishes the Middle Path is its rationality, and the Buddha insisted that his followers understand not only what it was but what it was not. As is very clear from this dialogue, in any case, he would not permit himself to be trapped into fruitless discussion. The Four Noble Truths and the Noble Eightfold Path were the only answers he offered, and as even the doubters were made to see they were answers enough.

SERMON NUMBER 1

Thus have I heard.

On a certain occasion The Blessed One was dwelling at Sāvatthi in Jetavana monastery in Anāthapiṇḍika's Park. Now it happened to the venerable Māluṅkyāputta, being in seclusion and plunged in meditation, that a consideration presented itself to his mind, as follows:—

"These theories which The Blessed One has left unelucidated, has set aside and rejected,—that the world is eternal, that the world is not eternal, that the world is finite, that the world is infinite, that the soul and the body are identical, that the soul is one thing and the body another, that the saint exists after death, that the saint does not exist after death, that the saint both exists and does not exist after death, that the saint neither exists nor does not exist after death,—these The Blessed One does not elucidate to me. And the fact that The Blessed One does not elucidate them to me does not please me nor suit me. Therefore I will draw near to The Blessed One and inquire of him concerning this matter. If The Blessed One will elucidate to me, either that the world is eternal, or that the world is not eternal, or that the world is finite, or that the world is infinite, or that the soul and the body are identical, or that the soul is one thing and the body another, or that the saint exists after death, or that the saint does not exist after death, or that the saint both exists and does not exist after death, or that the saint neither exists nor does not exist after death, in that case will I lead the religious life under The Blessed One. If The Blessed One will not elucidate to me, either that the world is eternal, or that the world is not eternal, . . . or that the saint neither exists nor does not exist after death, in that case will I abandon religious training and return to the lower life of a layman."

Then the venerable Māluṅkyāputta arose at eventide from his seclusion, and drew near to where The Blessed One was; and having drawn near and greeted The Blessed One, he sat down respectfully at one side. And seated respectfully at one side, the venerable Māluṅkyāputta spoke to The Blessed One as follows:—

"Reverend Sir, it happened to me, as I was just now in seclusion and plunged in meditation, that a consideration presented itself to my mind, as follows: 'These theories which

The Blessed One has left unelucidated, has set aside and rejected,—that the world is eternal, that the world is not eternal, . . . that the saint neither exists nor does not exist after death,—these The Blessed One does not elucidate to me. And the fact that The Blessed One does not elucidate them to me does not please me nor suit me. I will draw near to The Blessed One and inquire of him concerning this matter. If The Blessed One will elucidate to me, either that the world is eternal, or that the world is not eternal, . . . or that the saint neither exists nor does not exist after death, in that case will I lead the religious life under The Blessed One. If The Blessed One will not elucidate to me, either that the world is eternal, or that the world is not eternal, . . . or that the saint neither exists nor does not exist after death, in that case will I abandon religious training and return to the lower life of a layman.'

"If The Blessed One knows that the world is eternal, let The Blessed One elucidate to me that the world is eternal; if The Blessed One knows that the world is not eternal, let The Blessed One elucidate to me that the world is not eternal. If The Blessed One does not know either that the world is eternal or that the world is not eternal, the only upright thing for one who does not know, or who has not that insight, is to say, 'I do not know; I have not that insight.'

"If The Blessed One knows that the world is finite, . . .

"If The Blessed One knows that the soul and the body are identical, . . .

"If The Blessed One knows that the saint exists after death, . . .

"If The Blessed One knows that the saint both exists and does not exist after death, let The Blessed One elucidate to me that the saint both exists and does not exist after death; if The Blessed One knows that the saint neither exists nor does not exist after death, let The Blessed One elucidate to me that the saint neither exists nor does not exist after death. If The Blessed One does not know either that the saint both exists and does not exist after death, or that the saint neither exists nor does not exist after death, the only upright thing for one who does not know, or who has not that insight, is to say, 'I do not know; I have not that insight.'"

"Pray, Māluñkyāputta, did I ever say to you, 'Come, Māluñkyāputta, lead the religious life under me, and I will elucidate to you either that the world is eternal, or that the world is not eternal, . . . or that the saint neither exists nor does not exist after death'?"

"Nay, verily, Reverend Sir."

"Or did you ever say to me, 'Reverend Sir, I will lead the religious life under The Blessed One, on condition that The Blessed One elucidate to me either that the world is eternal, or that the world is not eternal, . . . or that the saint neither exists nor does not exist after death'?"

"Nay, verily, Reverend Sir."

"So you acknowledge, Māluñkyāputta, that I have not said to you, 'Come, Māluñkyāputta, lead the religious life under me and I will elucidate to you either that the world is eternal, or that the world is not eternal, . . . or that the saint neither exists nor does not exist after death;' and again that you have not said to me, 'Reverend Sir, I will lead the religious life under The Blessed One, on condition that The Blessed One elucidate to me either that the world is eternal, or that the world is not eternal, . . . or that the saint neither exists nor does not exist after death.' That being the case, vain man, whom are you so angrily denouncing?

"Māluñkyāputta, any one who should say, 'I will not lead the religious life under The Blessed One until The Blessed One shall elucidate to me either that the world is eternal, or that the world is not eternal, . . . or that the saint neither exists nor does not exist after death;'—that person would die, Māluñkyāputta, before The Tathāgata had ever elucidated this to him.

"It is as if, Māluñkyāputta, a man had been wounded by an arrow thickly smeared with poison, and his friends and companions, his relatives and kinsfolk, were to procure for him a physician or surgeon; and the sick man were to say, 'I will not have this arrow taken out until I have learnt whether the man who wounded me belonged to the warrior caste, or to

the Brahman caste, or to the agricultural caste, or to the
menial caste.'

"Or again he were to say, 'I will not have this arrow taken
out until I have learnt the name of the man who wounded
me, and to what clan he belongs.'

"Or again he were to say, 'I will not have this arrow taken
out until I have learnt whether the man who wounded me
was tall, or short, or of the middle height.'

"Or again he were to say, 'I will not have this arrow
taken out until I have learnt whether the man who wounded
me was black, or dusky, or of a yellow skin.'

"Or again he were to say, 'I will not have this arrow
taken out until I have learnt whether the man who wounded
me was from this or that village, or town, or city.'

"Or again he were to say, 'I will not have this arrow taken
out until I have learnt whether the bow which wounded me
was a cāpa, or a kodaṇḍa.'

"Or again he were to say, 'I will not have this arrow taken
out until I have learnt whether the bow-string which wounded
me was made from swallow-wort, or bamboo, or sinew, or
maruva, or from milk-weed.'

"Or again he were to say, 'I will not have this arrow taken
out until I have learnt whether the shaft which wounded
me was a kaccha or a ropima.'

"Or again he were to say, 'I will not have this arrow taken
out until I have learnt whether the shaft which wounded
me was feathered from the wings of a vulture, or of a heron,
or of a falcon, or of a peacock, or of a sithilahanu.'

"Or again he were to say, 'I will not have this arrow
taken out until I have learnt whether the shaft which
wounded me was wound round with the sinews of an ox, or
of a buffalo, or of a ruru deer, or of a monkey.'

"Or again he were to say, 'I will not have this arrow taken
out until I have learnt whether the arrow which wounded
me was an ordinary arrow, or a claw-headed arrow, or a
vekaṇḍa, or an iron arrow, or a calf-tooth arrow, or a kara-
vīrapatta.' That man would die, Māluṅkyāputta, without
ever having learnt this.

"In exactly the same way, Māluṅkyāputta, any one who should say, 'I will not lead the religious life under The Blessed One until The Blessed One shall elucidate to me either that the world is eternal, or that the world is not eternal, . . . or that the saint neither exists nor does not exist after death;'— that person would die, Māluṅkyāputta, before The Tathāgata had ever elucidated this to him.

"The religious life, Māluṅkyāputta, does not depend on the dogma that the world is eternal; nor does the religious life, Māluṅkyāputta, depend on the dogma that the world is not eternal. Whether the dogma obtain, Māluṅkyāputta, that the world is eternal, or that the world is not eternal, there still remain birth, old age, death, sorrow, lamentation, misery, grief, and despair, for the extinction of which in the present life I am prescribing.

"The religious life, Māluṅkyāputta, does not depend on the dogma that the world is finite; . . .

"The religious life, Māluṅkyāputta, does not depend on the dogma that the soul and the body are identical; . . .

"The religious life, Māluṅkyāputta, does not depend on the dogma that the saint exists after death; . . .

"The religious life, Māluṅkyāputta, does not depend on the dogma that the saint both exists and does not exist after death; nor does the religious life, Māluṅkyāputta, depend on the dogma that the saint neither exists nor does not exist after death. Whether the dogma obtain, Māluṅkyāputta, that the saint both exists and does not exist after death, or that the saint neither exists nor does not exist after death, there still remain birth, old age, death, sorrow, lamentation, misery, grief, and despair, for the extinction of which in the present life I am prescribing.

"Accordingly, Māluṅkyāputta, bear always in mind what it is that I have not elucidated, and what it is that I have elucidated. And what, Māluṅkyāputta, have I not elucidated? I have not elucidated, Māluṅkyāputta, that the world is eternal; I have not elucidated that the world is not eternal; I have not elucidated that the world is finite; I have not elucidated that the world is infinite; I have not elucidated that the soul and the body are identical; I have not elucidated that the soul is one thing and the body another; I have not elucidated that the saint exists after death; I have not elucidated that the saint does not exist after death; I have not elucidated that the saint both exists and does not exist after death; I have not elucidated that the saint neither exists nor does not exist after death. And why, Māluṅkyāputta, have I not elucidated this? Because, Māluṅkyāputta, this profits not, nor has to do with the fundamentals of religion, nor tends to aversion, absence of passion, cessation, quiescence, the supernatural faculties, supreme wisdom, and Nirvana; therefore have I not elucidated it.

"And what, Māluṅkyāputta, have I elucidated? Misery, Māluṅkyāputta, have I elucidated; the origin of misery have I elucidated; the cessation of misery have I elucidated; and the path leading to the cessation of misery have I elucidated. And why, Māluṅkyāputta, have I elucidated this? Because, Māluṅkyāputta, this does profit, has to do with the fundamentals of religion, and tends to aversion, absence of passion, cessation, quiescence, knowledge, supreme wisdom, and Nirvana; therefore have I elucidated it. Accordingly, Māluṅkyāputta, bear always in mind what it is that I have not elucidated, and what it is that I have elucidated."

Thus spake The Blessed One; and, delighted, the venerable Māluṅkyāputta applauded the speech of The Blessed One.

Chapter VIII
BUDDHAGHOSA

Canonical Pāli Buddhist literature, along with the *Questions of Milinda*, is Indian in origin, though preserved in the texts of Ceylon, Burma, and Thailand. The rest of uncanonical Pāli writing is for the most part the work of Sinhalese monks, or of Indians like the fifth-century monk Buddhaghosa. This most illustrious of Buddhist commentators, of a Brahman family of Bodh Gaya, was converted to Buddhism by the monk Mahāsthavira Revata, who strongly encouraged him to continue his study of the philosophy in Ceylon, which had become the center of Buddhist activity. While there Buddhaghosa composed *Vissudhi Magga* (Way of Purity), from which selections follow. He was able in this work not only to touch on virtually all aspects of Buddhism, including its cosmology and time cycles, but he managed to quote freely from the whole of canonical and post-canonical literature. While residing at the Great Monastery of Anurādhapur he wrote other important commentaries as well, including those on the four Nikāyas. Buddhaghosa possessed encyclopaedic knowledge, but what most distinguished him from his fellow commentators, of whom there were many, was his talent as a writer, which is well demonstrated in his rendering of the famous "Story of Kisagotami."

THE COMPOSITION OF THE BODY

The amount of the earthy element in the body of a man of medium size is about a bushel, and consists of an exceedingly fine and impalpable powder. This is prevented from being dispersed and scattered abroad, because it is held together by about half a bushel of the watery element and is preserved by the fiery element and is propped up by the windy element. And thus prevented from being dispersed and scattered abroad, it masquerades in many different disguises, such as the various members and organs of women and men, and gives the body its thinness, thickness, length, shortness, firmness, solidity, etc.

The watery element is of a juicy nature and serves to hold the body together. It is prevented from trickling or flowing away, because it rests in the earthy element and is preserved by the fiery element and is propped up by the windy element. And thus prevented from trickling or flowing away, it gives the body its plumpness or leanness.

The fiery element has heat as its characteristic, and has a vaporous nature, and digests what is eaten and drunk. Resting in the earthy element and held together by the watery element and propped up by the windy element, it cooks the body and gives it its beauty of complexion. And the body thus cooked is kept free from decay.

The windy element is characterized by its activeness and its ability to prop up, and courses through every member of the body. Resting in the earthy element and held together by the watery element and preserved by the fiery element, it props up the body. And it is because the body is thus propped up that it does not fall over, but stands upright. And it is when the body is impelled by the windy element that it performs its four functions of walking, standing, sitting, or lying-down, or draws in and stretches out its arms, or moves its hands and its feet.

Thus does this machine made of the four elements move like a puppet, and deceives all foolish people with its femininity, masculinity, etc.

ON GETTING ANGRY

"My friend, who hast retired from the world and art angry with this man, tell me what it is you are angry with? Are you angry with the hair of the head, or with the hair of the body, or with the nails, etc.? Or are you angry with the earthy element in the hair of the head and the rest? Or are you angry with the watery element, or with the fiery element, or with the windy element in them? What is meant by the venerable N. N. is only the five groups, the six organs of sense, the six objects of sense, and the six sense-consciousnesses. With which of these are you angry? Is it with the form-group? Or is it with the sensation-group, perception-group, predisposition-group, or consciousness-group? Or are you angry with an organ of sense, or an object of sense, or a sense-consciousness?"

For a person who has made the above analysis, there is no hold for anger, any more than there is for a grain of mustard-seed on the point of an awl, or for a painting in the sky.

INANIMATE NATURE

The forms of Nature are forms which have been coming into being since the renovation of the world-cycle and exist without organs of sense or mental faculties outside of ourselves, such as: iron, copper, tin, lead, gold, silver, pearls, gems, cat's-eyes, shells, rocks, coral, rubies, sapphires, earth, stones, mountains, grass, trees, vines, etc. This will be made plain by instancing the bud of an Asoka tree. For the form of an Asoka bud is at first of a delicate red; after the lapse of two or three days, of a deep red; after the lapse of two or three more, of a dull red; then of the color of a tender shoot, then of a mature twig, then of a green leaf, and then of the color of a dark green leaf. In the course of a year from the time of its being the color of a dark green leaf, this form, in the series of forms belonging to its own nature, becomes a yellow leaf, and breaking loose from its stalk falls to the ground. When the meditative priest has grasped all this, he applies the Three Characteristics, as follows:

"The form that was in existence at the time of the delicate red color perished without attaining to the time of the deep red color; the form that was in existence at the time of the deep red color, without attaining to the time of the dull red color; the form that was in existence at the time of the dull red color, without attaining to the time of the tender-shoot color; the form that was in existence at the time of the tender-shoot color, without attaining to the time of the mature-twig color; the form that was in existence at the time of the mature-twig color, without attaining to the time of the green-leaf color; the form that was in existence at the time of the green-leaf color, without attaining to the time of the dark-green-leaf color; the form that was in existence at the time of the dark-green-leaf color, without attaining to the time of the yellow-leaf color; the form that was in existence at the time of the yellow leaf perished without attaining to the time of breaking loose from the stalk and falling to the ground. Therefore is it transitory, evil, and without substantive reality."

Having thus applied the Three Characteristics in this particular instance, he then in the same way reflects on all other forms of Nature.

NAME AND FORM

By "Name" are meant the three Groups beginning with Sensation [*i.e.*, Sensation, Perception, and the Predispositions]; by "Form," the four elements and form derivative from the four elements.

. . .

Name has no power of its own, nor can it go on of its own impulse, either to eat, or to drink, or to utter sounds, or to make a movement. Form also is without power and cannot go on of its own impulse. It has no desire to eat, or to drink, or to utter sounds, or to make a movement. But Form goes on when supported by Name, and Name when supported by Form. When Name has a desire to eat, or to drink, or to utter sounds, or to make a movement, then Form eats, drinks, utters sounds, makes a movement.

To make this matter clear they give the following illustration:

It is as if two men, the one blind from birth and the other a cripple, were desirous of going traveling. And the man blind from birth were to say to the cripple as follows: "See here! I am able to use my legs, but I have no eyes with which to see the rough and the smooth places in the road." And the cripple were to say to the man blind from birth as follows: "See here! I am able to use my eyes, but I have no legs with which to go forward and back." And the man blind from birth, pleased and delighted, were to mount the cripple on his shoulders. And the cripple sitting on the shoulders of the man blind from birth were to direct him, saying, "Leave the left and go to the right; leave the right and go to the left."

Here the man blind from birth is without power of his own, and weak, and cannot go of his own impulse or might. The cripple also is without power of his own, and weak, and cannot go of his own impulse or might. Yet when they mutually support one another it is not impossible for them to go.

In exactly the same way Name is without power of its own, and cannot spring up of its own might, nor perform this or that action. Form also is without power of its own, and cannot spring up of its own might, nor perform this or that action. Yet when they mutually support one another it is not impossible for them to spring up and go on.

• • •

And he knows as follows:

"No heap or collection of material exists for the production of Name and Form; nor are Name and Form sprung

154

from any such heap or collection of material; and when Name
and Form cease, they do not go to any of the cardinal or
intermediate points of the compass; and after Name and
Form have ceased, they do not exist anywhere in the shape
of heaped-up material. But, just as when a lute is played
upon, there is no previous store of sound; and when the
sound comes into existence, it does not come from any such
store; and when it ceases, it does not go to any of the cardinal or intermediate points of the compass; and when it has
ceased, it exists nowhere in a stored-up state; but having
previously been non-existent, it came into existence in dependence on the body and neck of the lute and the exertions of the performer; and having come into existence passes
away: in exactly the same way, all the elements of being,
both those with form and those without, come into existence
after having previously been non-existent; and having come
into existence pass away.

"Strictly speaking, the duration of the life of a living being
is exceedingly brief, lasting only while a thought lasts. Just
as a chariot wheel in rolling rolls only at one point of the tire,
and in resting rests only at one point; in exactly the same
way, the life of a living being lasts only for the period of one
thought. As soon as that thought has ceased, the living being
is said to have ceased. "As it has been said:

"The being of a past moment of thought has lived, but does
not live, nor will it live.

"The being of a future moment of thought will live, but
has not lived, nor does it live.

"The being of the present moment of thought does live,
but has not lived, nor will it live."

IGNORANCE

"Ignorance is non-knowledge of pain, etc. In coming to be
in the world of sense-desire ignorance is the cause of the aggregates of that world, and so in the world of form and the
formless world. In the world of sense-desire the aggregates

are the cause of rebirth-consciousness in that world, and so of the other worlds. In the world of sense-desire rebirth-consciousness is the cause of mind and body, and so in the world of form. In the formless world it is the cause of mind only. In the world of sense-desire mind and body (*nāma-rūpa*, the concrete individual) are the cause of the six organs of sense, in the world of form they are the cause of three organs of sense (sight, hearing, and mind), and in the formless world of one (mind). In the world of sense-desire the six organs of sense are the cause of six-fold contact, in the world of form of three contacts, and in the formless world the mind-organ is the cause of one contact. In the world of sense-desire the six contacts are the cause of the six senses, in the world of form three contacts are likewise the cause of three senses, and in the formless world one is the cause of one sense. In the world of sense-desire the six senses are the cause of six groups of craving, likewise three senses in the world of form and one sense in the formless world. In this and that existence this and that craving is the cause of this and that grasping. Grasping, etc., is the cause of the various forms of coming to be. How? Here one person thinks he will enjoy sense-pleasures, and commits misconduct with body, speech, or mind on account of his grasping at sense-pleasures, and through the fullness of his misconduct he is reborn in a state of unhappiness. There his karma which is the cause of his rebirth is karma-becoming. Rebirth-becoming consists of the khandhas (the five groups constituting the individual) due to his karma. The arising of these groups is birth, their ripening is old age, and their break-up is death. Another person thinks he will enjoy the happiness of heaven, so he practises good conduct, and through the fullness of his good conduct is born in heaven. There his karma is as before. Still another thinks he will enjoy the happiness of the Brahma-world, and through his grasping after sense-desires he practises friendliness, compassion, sympathy, and equanimity, and through the fullness of this practice he is born in the Brahma-world. There his karma is as before. Still another thinks he will enjoy happiness in the formless world . . . and so on as with the explanations based upon the remaining forms of grasping . . .

"Now ignorance and the aggregates form one group; consciousness, mind and body, the six sense-organs, contact, and the senses another; craving, grasping, and becoming another. The first group belongs to past existence, the two middle ones to the present, and the last to the future."

FORTY SUBJECTS OF MEDITATION

The ten devices:

1. Earth device—a circle made of dawn-colored clay, generally a span and four inches in diameter
2. Water device—a bowl of clean water
3. Fire device—a bright flame appearing through a hole
4. Air device—the perception of air shaking and swaying the top of a tree
5. Blue device—a circle of blue cloth or the like
6. Yellow device—a circle of yellow cloth or the like
7. Red device—a circle of red cloth or the like
8. White device—a circle of white cloth or the like
9. Light device—a light falling through a circular hole
10. Space device—a limited space of a prescribed dimension, seen through an opening

The ten impurities:

1. A swollen corpse
2. A discolored, blue-green corpse
3. A corpse full of pus
4. A fissured corpse
5. A corpse mangled by dogs or other animals
6. A corpse with dismembered limbs
7. A corpse with its limbs partly destroyed and scattered
8. A corpse covered here and there with blood
9. A worm-infested corpse
10. A skeleton

The ten recollections are the recollection of:

1. The virtues of the Buddha
2. The merits of the Dhamma
3. The Order of the Holy Disciples of the Buddha
4. The merits of the observance of the precepts
5. The merits of liberality
6. The equality between one's self and the deities in regard to the virtues
7. Death—that is, mindfulness of the fact that everyone is subject to inevitable death
8. The body—that is, mindfulness regarding the body
9. Respiration—that is, mindfulness of respiration
10. Peace of mind—that is, cognition of the attributes of peace of mind

The four sublime states are the development of:

1. Universal love, amity (*metta*)
2. Compassion (*karuna*)
3. The happiness of others
4. Equanimity

The four immaterial stages are the attainment of:

1. Infinite space
2. Infinite consciousness
3. Nothingness
4. Neither perception nor nonperception

The one notion is meditation on the loathsomeness of food. The one analysis is the analysis of the four primary elements.

WORLD-CYCLES

THE FOURTH HIGH POWER

Can call to mind—Can remember by following either the succession of the groups, or the sequence of births and deaths.

For there are six classes of persons who can call to mind
former states of existence: members of other sects, ordinary
disciples, great disciples, chief disciples, Private Buddhas, and
Buddhas. Now members of other sects can call to mind former states of existence for forty world-cycles, and no more.
And why? On account of the weakness of their wisdom. For
their wisdom is weak, as they are unable to define name and
form. Ordinary disciples can call to mind former states of
existence for one hundred or even one thousand world-cycles,
on account of the strength of their wisdom. The eighty great
disciples can call to mind former states of existence for one
hundred thousand world-cycles; the two chief disciples, for
one immensity and one hundred thousand world-cycles; Private Buddhas, for two immensities and one hundred thousand world-cycles, for such is the limit of their earnest wish.
But The Buddhas have their power unlimited.

Members of other sects follow only the succession of the
groups; they cannot leave the consideration of that succession
and follow the sequence of births and deaths, for they are
like blind men, in that they cannot go freely where they
please. Just as the blind cannot walk without a staff, so they
cannot remember if they let go the succession of the groups.
The ordinary disciples can call to mind former states of existence by following either the succession of the groups, or they
can travel along by the sequence of births and deaths. So,
likewise, the eighty great disciples. But the two chief disciples do not need to make use of the succession of the groups;
they behold the death of a person in one existence and his
rebirth in another, and again his death in that existence and
his rebirth in a third. Thus they travel along the sequence of
births and deaths. So, likewise, the Private Buddhas. The
Buddhas, however, do not need to make use of the succession of the groups, nor yet of the sequence of births and
deaths. For any point which they choose to remember,
throughout many times ten million world-cycles, becomes
plain to them, and that in either direction. Thus they contract
many times ten million world-cycles, as one would make an
abridgment in a Pāli text, arriving at the desired point with

the stride of a lion. Just as an arrow shot from the bow of a skilled archer, trained like Sarabhañga to shoot at a hair's breadth, goes straight to the mark, and is not caught in the way by any tree or plant, nor sticks fast, nor misses its aim, so the intellect of The Buddhas is not caught by any intervening birth, nor do they miss their aim, but go straight to the wished-for place.

Now the power possessed by members of other sects to perceive former states of existence resembles the light of a glow-worm; that of the ordinary disciples, the light of a lamp; that of the great disciples, the light of a torch; that of the chief disciples, the light of the morning star; that of the Private Buddhas, the light of the moon; that of The Buddhas resembles the thousand-rayed disk of the autumnal sun.

The power possessed by members of other sects to call to mind former states of existence is like the groping of a blind man with the aid of a stick; that of the ordinary disciples, like walking with the aid of a staff; that of the great disciples, like walking without a staff; that of the chief disciples, like riding in a cart; that of the Private Buddhas, like riding on camel-back; that of The Buddhas, like rolling in a chariot on a great highway.

But our present text concerns itself only with disciples and their power to call to mind former states of existence. Therefore was it I said: "'Can call to mind'—Can remember by following either the succession of the groups, or the sequence of births and deaths."

The priest, then, who tries for the first time to call to mind former states of existence, should choose a time after breakfast when he has returned from his begging-rounds, and is alone and plunged in meditation, and has been absorbed in the four trances in succession. On rising from the fourth trance, the one that leads to the High Powers, he should consider the event which last took place, namely, his sitting down; next the spreading of the mat; the entering of the room; the putting away of bowl and robe; his eating; his leaving the village; his going the rounds of the village for alms; his entering the village for alms; his issuing forth from

the monastery; his paying worship in the courts of the shrine
and of the Bo-tree; his washing the bowl; his taking the bowl;
what he did between his taking the bowl and rinsing his
mouth; what he did at dawn; what he did in the middle
watch of the night; what he did in the first watch of the
night. Thus, in retrograde order, must he consider all that
he did for a whole day and night.

As much as this is plain even to the ordinary mind, but it
is exceedingly plain to one whose mind is in preliminary
concentration. But if there is any one event which is not
plain, then he should again enter upon the trance that leads
to the High Powers, and when he has risen from it, he must
again consider that past event; this will be sufficient to make
it as plain as if he had used a lighted lamp. In this retrograde order must he consider what he did the day before,
the day before that, up to the fifth day, tenth day, half-
month, month, year: and having in the self-same manner
considered the previous ten, twenty years, and so on up to
the time of his conception in this existence, he must then
consider the name and form present at the moment of his
death in the previous existence. For a clever priest is able
at the first trial to penetrate beyond conception, and to take as
his object of thought the name and form present at the moment of his death. But whereas the name and form of the
previous existence utterly ceased, and another one came into
being, therefore that point of time is like thick darkness, and
difficult to be made out by the mind of any stupid person. But even such a one should not despair, and say, "I shall
never be able to penetrate beyond conception, and take as
my object of thought the name and form present at the moment of my death in the last existence," but he should again
and again enter upon the trance that leads to the High
Powers, and each time he rises from it, he should again consider that point of time.

Just as a strong man, in cutting down a mighty tree to be
used in making the peaked roof of a pagoda, if the edge of
his axe become turned in lopping off the branches and twigs,
will not despair of cutting down the tree, but will go to a

blacksmith's shop, and have his axe made sharp, and return, and go on with the cutting; and if the edge of his axe again become turned, he will again have it sharpened, and return, and go on with the cutting; and inasmuch as nothing that he has chopped needs to be chopped again, he will, in no long time, when there is nothing left to chop, fell that mighty tree. In exactly the same way, the priest, rising from the trance that leads to the High Powers, without considering what he has already considered, and considering only the moment of conception, in no long time will penetrate beyond the moment of conception, and take as his object the name and form present at the moment of his death. This matter can be illustrated by the wood-splitter, extractor of hair, and other similes.

Now the knowledge which has for its object the events from the last sitting down to the moment of conception, is not called the knowledge of former existences, but knowledge belonging to preliminary concentration. Some call it knowledge of past time. This knowledge does not concern itself with the realm of form. When, however, the priest, passing beyond the moment of conception, and taking the name and form present at the moment of his death, considers them with his mind; and when, after he has ceased considering them, the four or the five swiftnesses based on the same object hasten on, of which the first three or four, in the manner aforesaid, are called by such names as preliminary etc., and belong to the realm of sensual pleasure, while the last belongs to the realm of form, and is the attainment-thought belonging to the fourth trance; then the knowledge which accompanies that thought is termed the knowledge which calls to mind former states of existence.

His alert attention, having become possessed of this knowledge, *He can call to mind many former states of existence, to wit, one birth, two births, three births, four births, five births, ten births, twenty births, thirty births, forty births, fifty births, one hundred births, one thousand births, one hundred thousand births, many destructions of a world-cycle, many renovations of a world-cycle, many destructions and many renovations of a world-cycle:* "*I lived in such a place, had such a name, was of such a family, of such a caste, had such a maintenance, experienced such happinesses and such miseries, had such a length of life. Then I passed from that existence, and was reborn in such a place. There also I had such a name, was of such a family, of such a caste, had such a maintenance, experienced such happinesses and such miseries, had such a length of life. Then I passed from that existence, and was reborn in this existence.*" *Thus he can call to mind many former states of existence, and can specifically characterize them.*

Here *one birth* is the series of the groups, beginning at the moment of conception and ending at the moment of death, and comprised in one existence. Similarly as respects *two births,* and so on.

As respects, however, *many destructions of a world-cycle etc.*, when a world-cycle is on the wane, that is known as the destruction of a world-cycle; when it is on the increase, that is known as the renovation of a world-cycle. Here destruction includes the continuance of destruction, from being its beginning, and renovation includes the continuance of renovation. Accordingly the four immensities of the following quotation are all included: "There are four immensities, O priests, to a world-cycle. And what are the four? The destruction, continuance of destruction, renovation, and continuance of renovation."

Now there are three destructions: the destruction by water, the destruction by fire, the destruction by wind. And there are three boundaries: the Heaven of the Radiant Gods, the Heaven of the Completely Lustrous Gods, the Heaven of the Richly Rewarded Gods. When a world-cycle is destroyed by fire, it is consumed by fire from the Heaven of the Radiant Gods down. When it is destroyed by water, it is engulfed by water from the Heaven of the Completely Lustrous Gods down. When it is destroyed by wind, it is demolished by wind from the Heaven of the Richly Rewarded Gods down. In lateral expansion it always perishes to the extent of a Buddha's domain.

Now a Buddha's domain is threefold: birth-domain, authority-domain, knowledge-domain. Birth-domain comprises ten thousand worlds; all these quake at various periods in the life of a Tathāgata, as, for instance, when he is conceived. Authority-domain comprises one hundred thousand times ten million worlds; over all of these extends the protective power of the Ratana-Sutta, of the Khandha-Paritta, of the Dhajagga-Paritta, of the Āṭānāṭiya-Paritta, and of the Mora-Paritta. Knowledge-domain is endless and boundless, and the passage which says, "Or as far as he may wish," means that the knowledge of a Tathāgata extends to any place or to any subject he may wish. Of these three Buddha-domains, it is the authority-domain which perishes; but when that perishes, the birth-domain perishes likewise. They perish coincidently, and they exist coincidently. Now the perishing and the existing of a world-cycle are after the following manner:

When a world-cycle perishes by fire, there arises in the beginning a cycle-destroying great cloud, and a great rain falls throughout one hundred thousand times ten million worlds. The people are delighted and overjoyed, and bring forth seed of all kinds and sow; but when the crops have grown just large enough for cow-fodder, the clouds keep up a braying noise, but do not allow a drop to fall; all rain is utterly cut off. Concerning which the following has been said by The Blessed One:

"There comes a time, O priests, when, for many years, for many hundreds of years, for many thousands of years, for many hundreds of thousands of years, the god does not rain."

Those creatures who depend on rain die, and are reborn in the Brahma-world; likewise the divinities who live on flowers and fruits. When thus a long time has elapsed, here and there the ponds of water dry up. Then, one by one, the fishes and turtles also die and are reborn in the Brahma-world; likewise the inhabitants of the hells. But some say the inhabitants of the hells perish with the appearing of the seventh sun.

But it may be said: "Without the trances, there is no being

born in the Brahma-world. Yet some of these beings were overcome by famine, and some were incapable of attaining the trances. How could they be born in that world?" Because of their having attained the trances in the lower heavens.

For when it is known that after the lapse of a hundred thousand years the cycle is to be renewed, the gods called Loka-byūhas, inhabitants of a heaven of sensual pleasure, wander about through the world, with hair let down and flying in the wind, weeping and wiping away their tears with their hands, and with their clothes red and in great disorder. And thus they make announcement:

"Sirs, after the lapse of a hundred thousand years the cycle is to be renewed: this world will be destroyed; also the mighty ocean will dry up; and this broad earth, and Sineru, the monarch of the mountains, will be burnt up and destroyed, —up to the Brahma-world will the destruction of the world extend. Therefore, sirs, cultivate friendliness; cultivate compassion, joy, and indifference; wait on your mothers; wait on your fathers; and honor your elders among your kinsfolk."

When the people and the terrestrial deities hear these words, they, for the most part, become agitated, and their minds soften towards each other, and they cultivate friendliness, and do other meritorious deeds, and are reborn in the world of the gods. There they have heavenly ambrosia for food, and induce the trances by means of the air-kasina. Others, however, are born in the world of the gods by the alternation of the rewards of their good and evil deeds. For there is no being in the round of rebirth but has an alternation of the rewards of his good and evil deeds. Thus do they attain the trances in the world of the gods; and having there attained the trances, all are reborn in the Brahma-world.

When now a long period has elapsed from the cessation of the rains, a second sun appears. Here is to be supplied in full what was said by The Blessed One in the Discourse on the Seven Suns, beginning with the words, "There comes, O priests, a time."

When this second sun has appeared, there is no distinction of day and night; each sun rises when the other sets, and an incessant heat beats upon the world. And whereas the ordinary sun is inhabited by its divinity, no such being is to be found in the cycle-destroying sun. When the ordinary sun shines, clouds and patches of mist fly about in the air. But when the cycle-destroying sun shines, the sky is free from mists and clouds, and as spotless as a mirror, and the water in all streams dries up, except in the case of the five great rivers. After the lapse of another long period, a third sun appears, and the great rivers dry up. After the lapse of another long period, a fourth sun appears, and the sources of the great rivers in the Himalaya Mountains dry up, namely, the seven great lakes, Sīhapapātana, Haṁsapapātana, Kaṇṇamuṇḍaka, Rathakāradaha, Anotattadaha, Chaddantadaha, Kuṇāladaha. After the lapse of another long period, a fifth sun appears, and the mighty ocean gradually dries up, so that not enough water remains to moisten the tip of one's finger. After the lapse of another long period, a sixth sun appears, and the whole world becomes filled with smoke, and saturated with the greasiness of that smoke, and not only this world but a hundred thousand times ten million worlds. After the lapse of another long period, a seventh sun appears, and the whole world breaks into flames; and just as this one, so also a hundred thousand times ten million worlds. All the peaks of Mount Sineru, even those which are hundreds of leagues in height, crumble and disappear in the sky. The flames of fire rise up and envelop the Heaven of the Four Great Kings. Having there burnt up all the mansions of gold, of jewels, and of precious stones, they envelop the Heaven of the Thirty-three. In the same manner they envelop all the heavens to which access is given by the first trance. Having thus burnt up three of the Brahma-heavens, they come to a stop on reaching the Heaven of the Radiant Gods. This fire does not go out as long as anything remains; but after everything has disappeared, it goes out, leaving no ashes, like a fire of clarified butter or sesamum oil. The upper regions of space become one with those below, and wholly dark.

Now after the lapse of another long period, a great cloud arises. And first it rains with a very fine rain, and then the rain pours down in streams which gradually increase from the thickness of a water-lily stalk to that of a staff, of a club, of the trunk of a palmyra-tree. And when this cloud has filled every burnt place throughout a hundred thousand times ten million worlds, it disappears. And then a wind arises, below and on the sides of the water, and rolls it into one mass which is round like a drop on the leaf of a lotus. But how can it press such an immense volume of water into one mass? Because the water offers openings here and there for the wind. After the water has thus been massed together by the wind, it dwindles away, and by degrees descends to a lower level. As the water descends, the Brahma-heavens reappear in their places, and also the four upper heavens of sensual pleasure. When it has descended to its original level on the surface of the earth, mighty winds arise, and they hold the water helplessly in check, as if in a covered vessel. This water is sweet, and as it wastes away, the earth which arises out of it is full of sap, and has a beautiful color, and a fine taste and smell, like the skimmings on the top of thick rice-gruel.

Then beings, who have been living in the Heaven or the Radiant Gods, leave that existence, either on account of having completed their term of life, or on account of the exhaustion of their merit, and are reborn here on earth. They shine with their own light and wander through space. Thereupon, as described in the Discourse on Primitive Ages, they taste that savory earth, are overcome with desire, and fall to eating it ravenously. Then they cease to shine with their own light, and find themselves in darkness. When they perceive this darkness, they become afraid. Thereupon, the sun's disk appears, full fifty leagues in extent, banishing their fears and producing a sense of divine presence. On seeing it, they are delighted and overjoyed, saying, "Now we have light; and whereas it has banished our fears and produced a sense of divine presence [sura-bhāva], therefore let it be called suriya [the sun]." Hence they named it suriya. After the sun has given light throughout the day, it sets. Then they are alarmed again, saying, "The light which we had has perished." Then they think: "It would be well if we had some other light.". Thereupon, as if divining their thoughts, the disk of the moon appears, forty-nine leagues in extent. On seeing it, they are still more delighted and overjoyed, and say, "As if divining our wish [chanda], has it arisen: therefore is it canda [the moon]." And therefore they named it canda. When thus the sun and the moon have appeared, the constellations and the stars arise. From that time on night and day succeed each other, and in due course the months and half-months, seasons and years. Moreover, on the same day with the sun and the moon, Mount Sineru, the mountains which encircle the world, and the Himalaya Mountains reappear. These all appear simultaneously on the day of the full moon of the month Phagguna. And how? Just as when panick-seed porridge is cooking, suddenly bubbles appear and form little hummocks in some places, and leave other places as depressions, while others still are flat; even so the mountains correspond to the little hummocks, and the oceans to the depressions, and the continents to the flat places.

Now after these beings have begun to eat the savory earth, by degrees some become handsome and some ugly. Then the handsome despise the ugly, and as the result of this despising, the savoriness of the earth disappears, and the bitter pappataka plant grows up. In the same manner that also disappears, and the padālatā plant grows up. In the same way that also disappears, and rice grows up without any need of cultivation, free from all husk and red granules, and exposing the sweet-scented naked rice-grain. Then pots appear for the rice, and they place the rice in the pots, and place these pots on the tops of stones. And flames of fire spring up of their own accord, and cook the rice, and it becomes rice-porridge resembling the jasmine flower, and needing the addition of no broth or condiments, but having any desired flavor. Now when these beings eat this material food, the excrements are formed within them, and in order that they may relieve themselves, openings appear in their bodies, and the virility of the man, and the femininity of the woman. Then the woman begins to meditate excessively on the man, and the man on the woman, and as a result of this excessive meditation, the fever of lust springs up, and they have carnal connection. And being tormented by the reproofs of the wise for their low conduct, they build houses for its concealment. And having begun to dwell in houses, after a while they follow the example of some lazy one among themselves, and store up food. From that time on the red granules and the husks envelop the rice-grains, and wherever a crop has been mown down, it does not spring up again. Then these beings come together, and groan aloud, saying, "Alas! wickedness has sprung up among men; for surely we formerly were made of mind." The full account of this is to be supplied from the Discourse on Primitive Ages.

Then they institute boundary lines, and one steals another's share. After reviling the offender two or three times, the third time they beat him with their fists, with clods of earth, with sticks, etc. When thus stealing, reproof, lying, and violence have sprung up among them, they come together, and say, "What if now we elect some one of us, who shall get angry with him who merits anger, reprove him who merits reproof, and banish him who merits banishment. And we will give him in return a share of our rice." When, however, the people of this, our world-cycle came to this decision, our Blessed One, who was at the time a Future Buddha, was of all these beings the handsomest, the most pleasing of appearance, possessing the greatest influence and wisdom, and able to raise up and put down. Then they all came to him, and having gained his assent, they elected him their chief. Thus, inasmuch as he was elected by the multitude, he was called the Great Elect, and as he was lord of the fields [khetta], he was called khattiya [lord, the name for a member of the governing or warrior caste]. And as he pleased [saṁ-rañj-eti from root raj] his fellows by his even justice, he was called rājā [king]. Thus did he acquire these three appellations. A Future Buddha always becomes chief in that position in life which is most highly esteemed by mankind. When thus the association of warriors had been formed, with the Future Buddha at its head, by degrees the Brahmans and the other castes arose.

Now from the cycle-destroying great cloud to the termination of the conflagration constitutes one immensity, and is called the period of destruction. And from the cycle-destroying conflagration to the salutary great rains filling one hundred thousand times ten million worlds is the second immensity, and is called the continuance of destruction. From the salutary great rains to the appearing of the sun and moon is the third immensity, and is called the period of renovation. From the appearing of the sun and moon to the cycle-destroying great cloud is the fourth immensity, and is called the continuance of renovation. These four immensities form one great world-cycle.

This, then, is the order of events in a world-cycle when it perishes by fire.

But when a world-cycle perishes by water, it perishes in the manner above described, where it was said, "There arises in the beginning a cycle-destroying great cloud." But there are the following points of difference:—Instead of the second sun, there arises a cycle-destroying great cloud of salt water. At first it rains with a very fine rain which gradually increases to great torrents which fill one hundred thousand times ten million worlds, and the mountain-peaks of the earth become flooded with saltish water, and hidden from view. And the water is buoyed up on all sides by the wind, and rises upward from the earth until it engulfs the heavens to which access is given by the second trance. Having there flooded three of the Brahma-heavens, it comes to a stop at the Heaven of the Completely Lustrous Gods, and it does not settle as long as anything remains, but everything becomes impregnated with water, and then suddenly settles and disappears. And the upper regions of space become one with those below, and wholly dark. This is all as described above; only in this case the world begins to appear again at the Heaven of the Radiant Gods, and beings leave the Heaven of the Completely Lustrous Gods, and are reborn in the Heaven of the Radiant Gods, or in a lower heaven.

Now from the cycle-destroying great cloud to the termination of the cycle-destroying rain is one immensity; from the termination of the rain to the salutary great rains is the second immensity; from the salutary great rains to the appearing of the sun and moon is the third immensity; and from the appearing of the sun and moon to the cycle-destroying great cloud is the fourth immensity. These four immensities form one great world-cycle.

This is the order of events in a world-cycle when it perishes by water.

When a world-cycle is destroyed by wind, it perishes in the manner above described, where it was said, "There arises in the beginning a cycle-destroying great cloud." But there are the following points of difference:—Instead of the second sun, there arises a wind to destroy the world-cycle. And first it raises a fine dust, and then coarse dust, and then fine sand, and then coarse sand, and then grit, stones, etc., up to boulders as large as the peak of a pagoda, and mighty trees on the hill-tops. These mount from the earth to the zenith, and do not fall again, but are there blown to powder and annihilated. And then by degrees the wind arises from underneath the earth, and turns the ground upside down, and throws it into the sky, and areas of one hundred leagues in extent, two hundred, three hundred, five hundred leagues in extent, crack, and are thrown upwards by the force of the wind, and are blown to powder in the sky and annihilated. And the wind throws up also into the sky the mountains which encircle the earth, and Mount Sineru. These meet together, and are ground to powder and destroyed.

Thus are destroyed all the mansions on earth, and in the skies, also the six heavens of sensual desire, and a hundred thousand times ten million worlds. Worlds clash with worlds, Himalaya Mountains with Himalaya Mountains, and Mount Sinerus with Mount Sinerus, until they have ground each other to powder and have perished. From the earth upward does the wind prevail, until it has embraced all the heavens to which access is given by the third trance. Having there destroyed three of the Brahma-heavens, it comes to a stop at the Heaven of the Richly Rewarded Gods. When it has thus destroyed everything, it perishes. And the upper regions of space become one with those below, and wholly dark. All this is as described above. But now it is the Heaven of the Completely Lustrous Gods which first appears, and beings leave the Heaven of the Richly Rewarded Gods, and are reborn in the Heaven of the Completely Lustrous Gods, or in some lower heaven.

Now from the cycle-destroying great cloud to the termination of the cycle-destroying wind is one immensity; from the termination of the wind to the salutary great cloud is the second immensity; from the salutary great cloud to the appearing of the sun and moon is the third immensity; and from the appearing of the sun and moon to the cycle-destroying great cloud is the fourth immensity. These four immensities form one great world-cycle.

This is the order of events in a world-cycle when it perishes by wind.

Why does the world perish in these particular ways? It is on account of the special wickedness that may be at bottom. For it is in accordance with the wickedness preponderating that the world perishes. When passion preponderates, it perishes by fire; when hatred, it perishes by water.—But some say that when hatred preponderates, it perishes by fire, and that when passion preponderates it perishes by water.—When infatuation preponderates, it perishes by wind.

Now the world, in perishing, perishes seven times in succession by fire, and the eighth time by water; and then again seven times by fire, and the eighth time by water. Thus the world perishes each eighth time by water, until it has perished seven times by water, and then seven more times by fire. Thus have sixty-three world-cycles elapsed. Then the perishing by water is omitted, and wind takes its turn in demolishing the world; and when the Completely Lustrous Gods have reached their full term of existence of sixty-four world-cycles, their heaven also is destroyed.

Now it is of such world-cycles that a priest who can call to mind former existences and former world-cycles, can call to mind many destructions of a world-cycle, and many reno-

vations of a world-cycle, and many destructions and renovations of a world-cycle.

And after what manner?

"I lived in such a place," etc.

THE STORY OF KISAGOTAMI

Kisagotami became in the family way, and when the ten
months were completed, gave birth to a son. When the boy
was able to walk by himself, he died. The young girl, in her
love for it, carried the dead child clasped to her bosom, and
went about from house to house asking if any one would
give her some medicine for it. When the neighbours saw this,
they said, "Is the young girl mad that she carries about on her
breast the dead body of her son!" But a wise man thinking
to himself, "Alas! this Kisagotami does not understand the
law of death, I must comfort her," said to her, "My good girl,
I cannot myself give medicine for it, but I know of a doctor
who can attend to it." The young girl said, "If so, tell me who
it is." The wise man continued, "Gautama can give medicine,
you must go to him."

Kisagotami went to Gautama, and doing homage to him,
said, "Lord and master, do you know any medicine that will
be good for my boy?" Gautama replied, "I know of some."
She asked, "What medicine do you require?" He said, "I
want a handful of mustard seed." The girl promised to procure it for him, but Gautama continued, "I require some
mustard seed taken from a house where no son, husband,
parent, or slave has died." The girl said, "Very good," and
went to ask for some at the different houses, carrying the dead
body of her son astride on her hip. The people said, "Here
is some mustard seed, take it." Then she asked, "In my
friend's house has there died a son, a husband, a parent, or a
slave?" They replied, "Lady, what is this that you say! The living are few, but the dead are many." Then she went to other
houses, but one said, "I have lost a son"; another, "I have
lost my parents"; another, "I have lost my slave." At last, not

being able to find a single house where no one had died, from which to procure the mustard seed, she began to think, "This is a heavy task that I am engaged in. I am not the only one whose son is dead. In the whole of the Savatthi country, everywhere children are dying, parents are dying." Thinking thus, she acquired the law of fear, and putting away her affection for her child, she summoned up resolution, and left the dead body in a forest; then she went to Gautama and paid him homage. He said to her, "Have you procured the handful of mustard seed?" "I have not," she replied; "the people of the village told me, 'The living are few, but the dead are many.'" Gautama said to her, "You thought that you alone had lost a son; the law of death is that among all living creatures there is no permanence." When Gautama had finished preaching the law, Kisagotami was established in the reward of Sotapatti; and all the assembly who heard the law were also established in the reward of Sotapatti.

Some time afterwards, when Kisagotami was one day engaged in the performance of her religious duties, she observed the lights in the houses now shining, now extinguished, and began to reflect, "My state is like these lamps." Gautama, who was then in the Gandhakuti building, sent his sacred appearance to her, which said to her, just as if he himself were preaching, "All living beings resemble the flame of these lamps, one moment lighted, the next extinguished; those only who have arrived at Nirvana are at rest." Kisagotami, on hearing this, reached the stage of a Rahanda possessed of intuitive knowledge.

Chapter IX
SHORT PASSAGES,
CHIEFLY FROM THE NIKĀYAS

The short passages which follow, drawn from a number of sources, chiefly the Nikāyas, in the Tripitaka, form a virtual microcosm of Buddhist philosophy, dealing as they do with metaphysical argument to views on such subjects as the taking of animal life. Here we have parables, brief sermons, and dramatic statement of principles, and as in the confrontation between Gautama and Assalāyana, who was sent to refute him on the subject of caste purity by the Brahmans and recluses, dialogue of great significance. In these passages the Buddha's personality is given further dimension, but above all he reveals himself as the spiritual leader whose mission is to pull men from quicksands of their own making.

MEDITATION AND CONTEMPLATION

Monks, being prudent and thoughtful, make become immeasurable contemplation. Monks, if immeasurable contemplation is made become by the prudent and thoughtful, to each one there accrue five (kinds of) knowledge. What are the five?

This contemplation is ease for the present as well as resulting in ease in the future—this knowledge accrues to each one.

This contemplation is noble, disinterested—this knowledge accrues to each one.

This contemplation is practised by those who are not base men—this knowledge . . .

This contemplation is peaceful, excellent, it is for gaining tranquillity, for reaching one-pointed concentration, it is not of the habit of painful self-denial—this knowledge . . .

This contemplation is one which I, mindful, enter upon; mindful, emerge from—this knowledge accrues to each one.

Monks, being prudent and thoughtful, make become immeasurable contemplation. Monks, if immeasurable contemplation is made become by the prudent and thoughtful, to each one there accrue these five (kinds of) knowledge. (Anguttara-nikāya.)

Monks, I will teach you the making become of the ariyan right contemplation that is five-limbed. Listen carefully, pay attention, and I will speak. What are the five?

Monks, take the case of a monk who, aloof from pleasures of the senses, aloof from wrong states of mind, enters on and abides in the first (stage in) meditation which has analysis and investigation and is the zest and ease that are born of aloofness. He drenches, permeates, fills, pervades this body itself with the zest and ease that are born of aloofness, so that there is not any part of this entire body that is not pervaded by the zest and ease that are born of aloofness.

Monks, as a skilled shampooer or his apprentice, having scattered bath-powder in a bronze vessel, might gradually pour in water so that the shampooing-ball, taking up the moisture, soaking up the moisture, is pervaded inside and out with moisture, although not dripping with it—even so, monks, does a monk drench, permeate, fill and pervade this body itself with the zest and ease that are born of aloofness. This, monks, is the first (way of) making become the five-limbed ariyan right contemplation.

Again, monks, a monk by the allaying of analysis and investigation, being inwardly calmed, the mind become concentrated on one point, without analysis, without investigation, enters on and abides in the second (stage in) meditation that is the zest and ease that are born of contemplation. He drenches, permeates, fills, pervades this body itself . . .

not pervaded by the zest and ease that are born of contemplation.

Monks, as a pool of water having a spring of water, but no inlet for water either on the east side or on the west, or on the north or on the south, and where the (rain-) *deva* does not pour down showers from time to time, yet because cool waters have welled up in that pool of water, that pool of water would be drenched, permeated, filled, pervaded with the cool water, so that no part of the entire pool of water would not be pervaded by the cool water—even so, monks, does a monk drench, permeate, fill and pervade this body itself with the zest and ease that are born of contemplation so that there is not any part of this entire body that is not pervaded by the zest and ease that are born of contemplation.

And again, monks, a monk, by the fading of zest abides indifferent and mindful and circumspect, and he experiences that ease of body by reason of which the noble ones say of him that he is indifferent, mindful, an abider in ease; and he enters on and abides in the third (stage in) meditation. He drenches, permeates, fills, pervades this body itself with an ease that lacks zest, so that there is not any part of this entire body that is not pervaded by ease that lacks zest.

Monks, as in a pond of red lotuses, in a pond of blue lotuses, in a pond of white lotuses, some lotuses in each pond are born in the water, grow up in the water, never rising above the water, but flourishing beneath it, are drenched, permeated, filled, pervaded from root to tip by the cool water so that there is no part of all the red, blue, and white lotuses that is not pervaded by the cool water—even so, monks, does a monk drench, permeate, fill, pervade this body itself with the ease that lacks zest so that there is not any part of that entire body that is not pervaded by the ease that lacks zest.

And again, monks, a monk by getting rid of ease, by getting rid of ill, and by the going down of his former joys and sorrows, enters on and abides in the fourth (stage in) meditation which, being without ease, without ill, is the utter purity of mindfulness that is indifference. As he, having permeated this body itself with a mind that is purified and cleansed, comes to be sitting down there is no part of his entire body that is not permeated by a mind that is purified and cleansed.

As in the case of a man who should be sitting down, having clothed himself including his head with a white cloth, there would be no part of his entire body not pervaded by the white cloth—even so, monks, does a monk, having permeated this body itself with a mind that is purified and cleansed, as he comes to be sitting down there is no part of his entire body that is not permeated by a mind that is purified and cleansed.

And again, monks, a feature for consideration comes to be rightly taken up by a monk, rightly attended to, rightly reflected upon, rightly penetrated by wisdom. It is as if, monks, some one should consider someone else—as one standing might consider one sitting, as one sitting might consider one lying down—even so, monks, does a feature for consideration come to rightly be . . . penetrated by wisdom. This, monks, is the fifth way of making become the five-limbed ariyan right contemplation.

Monks, when a monk has made become and has made much of the five-limbed ariyan right contemplation, he bends his mind for the realization by super-knowledge of whatever state it is that is to be realized by super-knowledge, so that in every case he attains to being a witness in whatever faculty it may be. . . .

(Thus) if he desires: "May I, from being one, become many; from being many, become one . . ." in every case he attains to being a witness in whatever faculty it may be.

If he desires: "May I, by the condition of *deva*-hearing which is purified and surpasses that of men, hear both kinds of sounds—those of *devas* and those of men, and those which are distant and those which are near," in every case he attains to being a witness in whatever faculty it may be.

If he desires: "May I by mind know of other beings, of other men, the minds which are passionate as such, the minds devoid of passion as such, the minds full of hatred as such, the minds devoid of hatred as such, the minds full of stupidity as such, the minds devoid of stupidity as such, the

congested minds as such, the minds devoid of congestion as
such, the diffuse minds as such, the minds devoid of diffuse-
ness as such, the liberal minds as such, the illiberal minds as
such, the inferior minds as such, the not inferior minds as
such, the contemplative minds as such, the uncontemplative
minds as such, the freed minds as such, the unfreed minds
as such," in every case he attains to being a witness in whatever faculty it may be.

If he desires: "May I remember my manifold former
abodes, that is to say: One birth . . . I, deceasing thence
rose up again here," in every case he attains to being a witness
in whatever faculty it may be.

If he desires: "May I see beings with *deva*-sight which is
purified and surpasses that of men . . . these, at the breaking-
up of the body arise in the Happy Bourn, the heaven-world,"
in every case he attains to being a witness in whatever
faculty it may be.

If he desires: "May I, through the destruction of the flux-
ions, having realized here and now by my own super-knowledge the freedom of mind, freedom of wisdom which are
fluxionless—may I abide in them," in every case he attains
to being a witness in whatever faculty it may be. (Anguttara-
nikāya.)

GO NOT BY HEARSAY

Now look you, Kālāmas. Do not be misled by report or
tradition or hearsay. Do not be misled by proficiency in the
Collections, nor by mere logic and inference, nor after considering reasons, nor after reflection on some view and approval of it, nor because it fits becoming, nor because the
recluse (who holds it) is your teacher. But when you know
for yourselves: These things are not good, these things are
faulty, these things are censured by the intelligent, these
things, when performed and undertaken, conduce to loss
and sorrow—then do you reject them. (Anguttara-nikāya.)

RIGHT VIEWS AND HERESIES

There is, Sīha, a way in which one speaking truly of me could say: "The recluse Gotama asserts what ought not to be done, he teaches a doctrine of what ought not to be done and in this he leads disciples." There is, Sīha, a way in which one speaking truly of me could say: "The recluse Gotama asserts what ought to be done, he teaches a doctrine of what ought to be done and in this he leads disciples. . . . The recluse Gotama asserts annihilation, he teaches a doctrine of annihilation and in this he leads disciples. . . . The recluse Gotama is one who detests, he teaches a doctrine of detestation and in this he leads disciples. . . . The recluse Gotama is one who diverts, he teaches a doctrine of diverting and in this he leads disciples. . . . The recluse Gotama is a 'burner up,' he teaches a doctrine of 'burning up' and in this he leads disciples. . . . The recluse Gotama is not destined to another kind of becoming, he teaches a doctrine of no other kind of becoming and in this he leads disciples." There is, Sīha, a way in which one speaking truly of me could say: "The recluse Gotama is confident, he teaches a doctrine of confidence and in this he leads disciples."

And what, Sīha, is the way in which one speaking truly of me could say: "The recluse Gotama is one who asserts what ought not to be done, he teaches a doctrine of what ought not to be done and in this he leads disciples?" Indeed I, Sīha, assert of bad conduct in body, speech and thought that it ought not to be done; I assert of manifold evil and wrong states (of mind) that they ought not to be done. This is the way, Sīha, in which one speaking truly of me could say: "The recluse Gotama asserts what ought not to be done, he teaches a doctrine of what ought not to be done and in this he leads disciples."

And what, Sīha, is the way in which one . . . could say: "The recluse Gotama asserts what ought to be done . . . trains disciples?" Indeed I, Sīha, assert of good conduct in body, speech and thought that it ought to be done; I assert of manifold right states (of mind) that they ought to be done. This is the way. . . .

And what, Sīha, is the way in which one . . . could say: "The recluse Gotama is one who detests, he teaches a doctrine of detestation and in this he leads disciples?" Indeed I, Sīha, detest bad conduct in body, speech and thought. I teach a doctrine of detesting to enter upon manifold evil wrong states (of mind). This is the way. . . .

And what, Sīha, is the way in which one . . . could say: "The recluse Gotama is one who diverts, he teaches a doctrine of diverting and in this he leads disciples?" Indeed I, Sīha, teach a doctrine of diverting passion, hatred, delusion; I teach a doctrine of diverting manifold evil wrong states (of mind). This is the way. . . .

And what, Sīha, is the way in which one . . . could say: "The recluse Gotama is a 'burner up,' he teaches a doctrine of 'burning up' and in this he leads disciples?" Indeed I, Sīha, speak of evil wrong states that are searing: bad conduct in body, speech and thought. He for whom, Sīha, evil wrong states that are searing are destroyed, cut off like a palm-tree at the stump, so utterly done away with that they can come to no future existence—him I call a "burner up". For a Truth-finder, Sīha, evil wrong states that are searing are destroyed, cut off like a palm-tree at the stump, so utterly done away with that they can come to no future existence. This is the way. . . .

And what, Sīha, is the way in which one . . . could say: "The recluse Gotama is not one who is destined for another kind of becoming, he teaches a doctrine of no other kind of becoming and in this he leads disciples"? He for whom, Sīha, future conception in a womb, becoming again and coming forth are destroyed, cut off like a palm-tree at the stump, so utterly done away with that they can come to no future existence—him I call one not destined to another kind of becoming. For a Truth-finder, Sīha, future conception in a womb, becoming again and coming forth are destroyed, cut off like a palm-tree at the stump, so utterly done away with that they can come to no future existence. This is the way. . . .

And what is the way, Sīha, in which one speaking truly of me could say: "The recluse Gotama is one who is confident, he teaches a doctrine of confidence and in this he leads disciples"? Indeed I, Sīha, am confident with the highest confidence, I teach a doctrine of confidence and in this I lead disciples. This is the way, Sīha, in which one speaking truly of me could say: "The recluse Gotama is confident, he teaches a doctrine of confidence and in this he leads disciples." (Vinaya-pitaka and Anguttara-nikāya.)

Monks, these three sectarian folds, although strictly questioned, investigated and discussed by the wise, persist in the traditional (view) of an ought-not-to-be-done. What are the three?

There are, monks, some recluses and brahmans who speak like this and hold this view: "Whatever a man experiences of pleasure or pain or neither, all this is due to something previously done." If they approach me, I ask them if it is true that they have this view, and if they say it is, I speak thus: "Well, then, the venerable ones will become those to make onslaught on creatures, to take what is not given, to lead what is not the Brahma-faring, they will become liars, slanderers, abusive, babblers, covetous, malicious, they will become of wrong view because of something done previously." Monks, to those who fall back on something done previously as the essential reason, there comes to be no desire or exertion connected with the idea that this is to be done or this is not to be done. Thus, if what is to be done and what is not to be done, though actually existing, are incomprehensible, the term recluse cannot be legitimately applied to yourselves, since you dwell muddled in mindfulness, unguarded.

There are, monks, some recluses and brahmans who speak like this and hold this view: "Whatever a man experiences of pleasure or pain or neither, all this is due to creation by an Overlord." If they approach me, . . . I speak thus: "Well, then, the venerable ones will become those to make onslaught on creatures . . . they will become of wrong view because of creation by an Overlord." Monks, to those who fall back on creations by an Overlord as the essential reason, there comes to be no desire or exertion connected with the idea that this is to be done or this is not to be done. Thus, if what is to be done and what is not to be done, although actually existing, are incomprehensible, the term recluse cannot be legitimately applied to yourselves, since you dwell muddled in mindfulness, unguarded.

There are, monks, some recluses and brahmans who speak like this and hold this view: "Whatever a man experiences of pleasure or pain or neither, all this is uncaused, unconditioned." If they approach me, . . . I speak thus: "Well, then, the venerable ones will become those to make onslaught on creatures . . . they will become of wrong view, uncaused, unconditioned." Monks, to those who fall back on no cause, no condition as the essential reason, there comes to be no desire or exertion connected with the idea that this is to be done or this is not to be done. Thus, if what is to be done and what is not to be done, although actually existing, are incomprehensible, the term recluse cannot be legitimately applied to yourselves, since you dwell muddled in mindfulness, unguarded. (Anguttara-nikāya.)

The world, Kaccāyana, is for the most part attached to two (propositions): existence as well as non-existence. If anyone sees, through right wisdom, the arising of the world as it really comes to be—whatever is not existent in the world, that does not come to be. If anyone sees, through right wisdom, the stopping of the world as it really comes to be—whatever is existent in the world, that does not come to be.

Grasping after systems, imprisoned by dogmas for the most part is this world, Kaccāyana. But he who does not go in for this system-grasping, for this mental standpoint, for this dogmatic bias, who does not take it up, does not take his stand upon it, thinking: "It is not my self; it is just ill uprising that uprises, ill being stopped that is stopped"—he neither doubts nor is perplexed; by not depending on others, knowledge herein comes to be his own. To this extent, Kaccāyana, there comes to be right view.

"Everything exists": this, Kaccāyana, is one dead-end. "Everything exists not": this, Kaccāyana, is the other dead-end. Not approaching either of these dead-ends, the Truth-finder teaches *dhamma* by the mean: conditioned by ignorance are the constructions; conditioned by the constructions is consciousness (and so on through the "chain of causation"). Thus there comes to be the uprising of this entire mass of ill. But from the utter fading away and stopping of ignorance, there is the stopping of the constructions; from the stopping of the constructions there is the stopping of consciousness; and so on. Thus there comes to be the stopping of this entire mass of ill. (Samyutta-nikāya.)

"Now, good Gotama, is suffering wrought by oneself?"
"Indeed not, Kassapa."
"But is suffering wrought by another?"
"Indeed not, Kassapa."
"Is suffering wrought by oneself and by another?"
"Indeed not, Kassapa."
"But has the suffering, wrought neither by oneself nor by another, originated by chance?"
"Indeed not, Kassapa."
"Is it, good Gotama, that there is not suffering?"
"It is not, Kassapa, that there is not suffering; for, Kassapa, there is suffering."
"Well, then, the good Gotama does not know suffering, does not see it."
"It is not that I, Kassapa, do not know suffering, do not see it; for I, Kassapa, know suffering, I see it."
"But, good Gotama, to all my questions you have replied: 'Indeed not, Kassapa.' You have said that there is suffering and that you know it and see it. Lord, let the lord explain to me about suffering: lord, let the lord teach me about suffering."

"He who does (a deed), it is he who experiences (its result): this which you, Kassapa, spoke of at the beginning as 'suffering wrought by oneself'—this leads on up to the Eternalist theory. But to say, 'One does, another experiences'—if one is harassed by feeling, and thinks, 'Suffering is wrought by another'—this leads on up to the Annihilationist theory.

"Not approaching either of these dead-ends, the Truth-finder teaches you, Kassapa, *dhamma* by the mean: Conditioned by ignorance are the constructions . . . Thus there comes to be the stopping of this entire mass of ill." (Samyutta-nikāya.)

"Now, lord, what is ageing and dying, and whose is this ageing and dying?"

"Not a fit question," the lord said. "Whatever monk should say this or whatever monk should say: 'Ageing and dying are one thing, but another's is this ageing and dying,' both these (questions) have the same meaning, just the form is different. If a monk has the view that the life-principle and the body are the same, there does not come to be a living of the Brahma-faring. Nor does this come to be if a monk has the view that the life-principle is one thing and the body another. Not approaching either of these dead-ends, the Truth-finder teaches you *dhamma* by the mean: Conditioned by birth are ageing and dying."

[The monks then asked the lord about each of the factors in the "causal chain," and to each question he answered as above, ending by mentioning the appropriate factor in the causal chain.]

"It is indeed, monks, by the utter fading away and stopping of ignorance that distortions, disagreements, scufflings, whatever they may be, that all such props come to be given up, cut off at the root, made like the stump of a palm-tree, so utterly done away with as not liable to come to any future existence." (Samyutta-nikāya.)

Baka the Brahmā is indeed under an illusion if he should say that the impermanent is the same as the permanent, that the evanescent is the same as the everlasting, that the non-eternal is the same as the eternal, that the not-whole is the same as the whole, and that what is liable to pass on is the same as what is not liable to pass on; and if he should say in regard to what is born and ages and dies and passes on and uprises: "But this is not born, does not age, does not die, does not pass on, does not uprise"; and if—there being another further escape—he should say: "There is not another further escape." (Majjhima and Samyutta-nikāyas.)

Whatever recluses and brahmans say that by becoming there is release from becoming, all these, I say, are unreleased from becoming. But whatever recluses and brahmans say that by de-becoming there is an escape from becoming, all these, I say, have not gone out from becoming. (Udāna.)

Just now, brahman, people are ablaze with unlawful lusts, overwhelmed by depraved longings, obsessed by wrong doctrines. This being so, they seize sharp knives and take one another's lives. Thus many men come by their end. Again, on these who are thus ablaze, overwhelmed and obsessed, the rain does not pour down steadily. It is hard to get a meal. The crops are poor, afflicted with mildew, and stunted. Thus many men come by their end. Again, against those who are thus ablaze, overwhelmed, and obsessed, the Yakkhas let loose non-human things. Thereby many men come to their end. This is the reason, this the cause of the apparent loss and decrease of human beings. This is why villages are not villages, little towns are not little towns, towns are not towns, and the country districts are depopulated. (Anguttara-nikāya.)

MARVELS

There are these three marvels. What are the three? The marvel of psychic power, the marvel of thought reading, the marvel of teaching. And what is the marvel of psychic power?

In this case, a monk enjoys various kinds of psychic power in divers ways. From being one he becomes many, from being many he becomes one; manifest or invisible he goes unhindered through a wall, through a rampart, through a mountain as if through air; he plunges into the earth and shoots up again as if in water; he walks upon the water without parting it as if on solid ground; he travels through the air, sitting cross-legged, like a bird on the wing. Even this moon and sun, although of such mighty power and majesty—he handles and strokes them with his hand. Even as far as the Brahma-world he has power in regard to his body. This is called the marvel of psychic power.

And what is the marvel of thought reading? In this case a certain one can declare by means of a sign: "Thus is your mind. Such-and-such is your mind. Thus is your thought." And however much he may tell, it is exactly so and not otherwise. Here again, perhaps a certain one does not tell these things by means of a sign, but does so by hearing a voice from men or from non-human beings or from *devas*— and says: "Thus is your mind. Such-and-such is your mind. Thus is your thought." And however much he may tell, it is exactly so and not otherwise. Here again, perhaps a certain one does not tell these things by means of a sign or on hearing a voice from men or non-human beings or *devas*, but does so (judging) from some sound he has heard, an utterance intelligently made by one who is reasoning intelligently. So hearing, he declares: "Thus is your mind. Such-and-such is your mind. Thus is your thought." And however much he may tell, it is exactly so and not otherwise. Then again, in this case, suppose a certain one does not tell by any of

187

these ways . . . yet perhaps when he has attained contemplation, void of reflection and intelligence, he foreknows, fully
grasping thought with his thought, that: "According as the
mental workings of this man so-and-so are directed, he will
apply his reasoning of mind to this and that object immediately." And however much he may tell, it is exactly
so and not otherwise. This is called the marvel of thought-
reading.

And what is the marvel of teaching? In this case a certain
one teaches thus: "Reason thus and not thus. Apply your
mind thus and not thus. Abandon this state, acquire that
state, and abide in it." This is called the marvel of teaching.
So these are the three marvels. (Anguttara and Dīgha-
nikāyas.)

[But the first two marvels might be challenged thus:]

One of little faith, not believing, might say to one of faith,
believing: "There is, good sir, a charm called Gandhārī. It is
because of this that he exercises various kinds of psychic
power in divers ways: from being one, becoming many and
so on." It is because I see this peril in the marvel of psychic
power that I am distressed by it, that I abhor it, that I
loathe it. Similarly, in regard to the marvel of thought
reading, one of little faith, not believing, might say to one of
faith, believing: "There is, good sir, a charm called the
Jewel: it is because of this that he tells the thoughts of
other beings, of other men, and says: 'Thus is your mind.
Such-and-such is your mind. Thus is your thought.' It is because I see this peril in the marvel of thought reading, that I
am distressed by it, that I abhor it, that I loathe it. (Dīgha-
nikāya.)

Indeed, Ānanda, I do understand how to reach the
Brahma-world by psychic power both in this mind-made body
and in this body of the four great elements. Truth-finders are
marvellous and possessed of marvellous powers, they are
wonderful and possessed of wonderful powers. At a time when

a Truth-finder contemplates body in mind and mind in body, and in the body enters into and abides in the consciousness of ease and buoyancy, at that time his body becomes more buoyant, softer, more workable and more radiant. It is just like an iron ball, which, when it has been heated all day long, becomes lighter, softer, more workable and more radiant. Now, Ānanda, whenever a Truth-finder contemplates body in mind and mind in body, and in the body enters into and abides in the consciousness of ease and buoyancy, it is at that time that the body of the Truth-finder with but little effort rises up from the ground into the air; he enjoys various kinds of psychic power in divers ways: from being one he becomes many; from being many he becomes one; manifest or invisible he goes unhindered through a wall, through a rampart, through a mountain as if through air; he plunges into the earth and shoots up again as if in water; he walks upon the water without parting it as if on solid ground; he travels through the air, sitting cross-legged, like a bird on the wing. Even this moon and son, although of such mighty power and majesty—he handles and strokes them with his hand. Even as far as the Brahma-world he has power with his body. And, Ānanda, just as a tuft of cotton seed or a ball of thistledown, lightly wafted on the wind, with but little effort rises up from the ground into the air, even so at a time when a Truth-finder contemplates body in mind and mind in body, and in the body enters into and abides in the consciousness of ease and buoyancy, it is at that time that the body of the Truth-finder with but little effort rises up from the ground into the air, and he enjoys the various kinds of psychic powers in their divers ways. (Samyutta-nikāya.)

[A great merchant of Rājagaha once had a sandalwood bowl tied up at the top of a bamboo pole; and he said: "Let whatever recluse or brahman who is one perfected and of psychic power get down this bowl, and to him it is given." After the leaders of six of the great heretical sects had tried and failed, the monk Piṇḍola the Bhāradvāja succeeded. The populace of Rājagaha greeted the news of his feat

with clamorous applause. For, having risen above the
ground and taken hold of the bowl, he had circled three
times round Rājagaha, and on the request of the great
merchant came to rest exactly at his dwelling. The lord,
hearing the great noise made by the people, asked Ānanda
the cause of it. He replied:]

"Lord, the venerable Piṇḍola the Bhāradvāja has fetched
down the bowl belonging to the great merchant. That is why
the people are making a great noise, a loud noise." The lord
thereupon rebuked the venerable Piṇḍola, saying:
"It is not suitable, Bhāradvāja, it is not becoming, it is not
fitting, it is not worthy of a recluse, it is not allowable, it is
not to be done. How can you, on account of a miserable
wooden bowl, exhibit a condition of further-men, a wonder
of psychic power to householders? Even as a woman exhibits
a loin-cloth for the sake of a miserable stamped *māsaka*,
even so was exhibited by you to householders, for the sake of
a miserable wooden bowl, a condition of further-men, a wonder of psychic power."
Having rebuked him, the lord addressed the monks, saying:
"Monks, a condition of further-men, a wonder of psychic
power is not to be exhibited to householders. Whoever should
exhibit them, there is an offence of wrong doing. Break,
monks, this wooden bowl; having reduced it to fragments,
give them to the monks as perfume for ointment." (Vinaya-
pitaka.)

CASTE

These, sire, are the four castes: the noble, priestly, merchant, and worker. Of these, two are declared chief: the
noble and the priestly, that is in regard to the way (their
members) are addressed, greeted by standing up and by
palms joined in salutation (of them), and by the way they
are treated. There are these five qualities to be striven after:
faith, health, honesty, output of energy, wisdom. The four

castes may be endowed with the five qualities that are to be striven after, and this would be for them for a long time a blessing and a happiness. As to this I do not say that there is a distinction in striving. It is as if there might be a pair of tamed elephants, horses or steers, well tamed and trained, and another pair not tamed or trained. The first pair would be reckoned as tamed and would attain tamed capacity. The second pair would not. In the same way, it cannot happen that that which can be attained by faith, health, honesty, no trickery, the output of energy and wisdom can be won if there is no faith, poor health, deceit, trickery, inertia and weak wisdom. In the case of the four castes, if (their members) are endowed with the five qualities that are to be striven after, if they should have right striving, I say that in such a case there is not any difference, that is to say in freedom as against freedom. It is as if four men, one taking a dry stick of brushwood, another a dry stick of sāl-wood, the third a dry stick of mango wood, and the fourth a dry stick of fig wood, were each to make a fire and get it to give out heat. Would there be any difference in the fires produced by the different woods as to their flame, hue or brilliance? It is the same with the heat kindled by energy and produced by striving. I do not say that there is any difference in freedom as against freedom. (Majjhima-nikāya.)

[Some recluses and brahmans, having heard it said that the recluse Gotama lays down the purity of the four castes, sent a brahman youth, Assalāyana, to refute him. Assalāyana approached Gotama and said:]

"Good Gotama, brahmans say: Just brahmans form the best caste, other castes are low; only the brahman is a fair caste, other castes are dark; only brahmans are pure, not non-brahmans; only brahmans are own sons of Brahma, born of his mouth, born of Brahma, formed by Brahma, heirs of Brahma. What do you say?"

"But, Assalāyana, brahman women have their periods, conceive, give birth, and give suck. And yet these brahmans, born of women like everyone else, say that only brahmans form the best caste, and so on."

"Although the revered Gotama speaks thus, this is what they think."

"Have you heard that in some of the adjacent districts there are only two 'castes'—masters and slaves, and that (a member of) the master (caste) can become a (member of) the slave (caste), and vice versa?"

"Yes, sir, I have heard that; but although the revered Gotama speaks in this way there are brahmans who think that only brahmans form the best caste, and so on."

"Now, would a noble, suppose he made onslaught on creatures or took what was not given, or behaved badly in regard to the pleasures of the senses, or was a liar or slanderer or of violent speech, or was one who tattles or covets, or was malevolent or held a wrong view—would he, at the breaking-up of the body after dying, arise in The Waste, the Bad Bourn, the Downfall, Hell? And would a merchant? Would a worker? But not a brahman?"

"No, good Gotama. A noble who was like this would arise after dying as you say. So would a brahman, and also a merchant and a worker. Indeed (members of) all four castes who made onslaught on creatures, and so on, would arise in the Waste, the Bad Bourn, the Downfall, Hell. But although the revered Gotama speaks in this way there are Brahmans who think that only brahmans form the best caste . . . and are heirs of Brahma."

"If a brahman refrained from onslaught on creatures, from taking what is not given, from bad behaviour in regard to pleasures of the senses, from lying and slandering and violent speech, from tattling, and did not covet, was benevolent and held a right view—would he at the breaking-up of the body after dying arise in a Good Bourn, a heaven world?—he only, not a noble, not a merchant, not a worker?"

"No, good Gotama. If nobles, brahmans, merchants and workers refrained in all these ways, (members of) all four castes would, at the breaking-up of the body after dying, arise in a Good Bourn, a heaven world. But in spite of what the revered Gotama says, there are brahmans who think that only brahmans form the best caste, and so on."

"Now, what do you think, Assalāyana? Is it only a brahman who, in this district, can make become a heart of love that is peaceable and kindly—not a noble, not a merchant, not a worker?"

"No, good Gotama, (members of) all four castes are able to do this. But in spite of what you say there are brahmans who think that only brahmans form the best caste . . . and are heirs of Brahma."

"What do you think, Assalāyana? Is it only a brahman who, taking a string of bath-balls and powder, having gone to a river, is able to cleanse himself of dust and mud—not a noble, not a merchant, not a worker?"

"No, good Gotama. (Members of) all four castes are able to do this, but in spite of what you say there are brahmans who think that only brahmans form the best caste, and so on."

"Now, suppose that a noble who has been anointed king were to assemble a hundred men of varying origins and were to say to them: 'Come, good sirs, those of you who are from noble, priestly, or royal families, take kindling wood of sāl, or of a sweet-scented tree, or of sandal, or of lotus, light a fire and get it to give out heat.' What do you think, Assalāyana? Would it not be possible for all of these to make a fire and get heat showing flame, hue, and brilliance, no matter which of these woods they used? But if a fire were lit and heat produced by one belonging to a despised family—a trapper, bamboo-plaiter, cartwright, or scavenger family—suppose him to have taken kindling wood from a dog's trough or a pig's trough or from a trough for dyeing or sticks of a castor-oil shrub—would this fire have neither flame nor hue nor brilliance so that it would not be possible for it to serve the purpose of a fire?"

"No, good Gotama. It is possible to make all the fires, in regard to flame, hue, and brilliance, serve the purpose of a fire no matter the member of whatever family it was who lit them and no matter whatever was the kind of wood he used. But in spite of what you say there are brahmans who think that brahmans alone form the best caste . . . and are heirs of Brahma."

"Now, Assalāyana, suppose there were two young brahmans, blood brothers, one skilled (in the Vedas) and having received the (brahmanical) education, the other unskilled and uneducated. To which of these would brahmans offer food first at the time of offering to the departed or of sacrifice or of hospitality to a guest?"

"To the skilled and educated young brahman. For what great result could derive from giving to one who was unskilled and uneducated?"

"But suppose the skilled and educated young brahman was weak in moral habit and given to evil, while the unskilled and uneducated one was of (good) moral habit and given to what is lovely. To which of these would brahmans offer food first?"

"To the unskilled and uneducated one who was of (good) moral habit and given to what is lovely. For what great result could derive from giving to one of weak moral habit and given to evil?"

"First, you, Assalāyana, set off about birth; you went on to mantras, from there you have come round to the purity of the four castes, which is what I am laying down." (Majjhima-nikāya.)

ANIMALS

If a monk were to suffuse with a heart of love the four great snake families, he would not pass away if he were bitten by a snake. I allow you, monks, to suffuse with a heart of love these four great snake families for the warding of self, for the guarding of self, for the protection of self:

> For the Virūpakkhas my love,
> My love for the Erāpathas,
> For the Chabbyāputtas my love,
> And for the Kaṇhāgotamakas,

For the footless my love,
My love for the bipeds,
For the four-footed my love,
My love for those with many feet.
Let not the footless do me harm,
Nor those that have two feet,
Let not the four-footed ones me harm,
Nor those with many feet.
All creatures, all breathers,
All beings and everything—
May they all see luck,
May none come to evil.

     (Anguttara-nikāya and Vinaya-pitaka.)

Do you see that fisherman, monks, who, having slaughtered a haul of fish, is selling fish-nets? I have never seen, monks, nor have I heard of such a fisherman who, as a result of his action, as a result of his mode of living, goes about on an elephant or horse or in a chariot or vehicle, or who feasts at feasts or who lives in the abundance of great wealth. Why is this? It is because he gloats evilly on fish being slaughtered or brought to the slaughter. It is the same with a butcher who kills and sells cattle or sheep or swine or game or forest beasts. It is because he gloats evilly on their being slaughtered or brought to the slaughter that he does not go about on an elephant or . . . live in the abundance of great wealth. Indeed, monks, he who gloats evilly on animals being slaughtered or brought to the slaughter shall become neither one who goes about on an elephant . . . nor one who lives in the abundance of great wealth. But he who gloats evilly on a human being being slaughtered or brought to the slaughter—for this there will be woe and sorrow for him for a long time: at the breaking-up of the body after dying he will arise in the Waste, in the Bad Bourn, in the Downfall, in Niraya Hell. (Anguttara-nikāya.)

In many a figure could I, monks, talk a talk on animal birth, but this is as far as I go; it is not easy to describe in full, monks, so many are the woes of animal birth. (Majjhima-nikāya.)

How can you, foolish men, dig the ground or get someone else to do so? For people think that there are living things in the ground. Whatever monk should dig the ground or get some one else to do so, there is an offence of expiation. (Vinaya-pitaka.)

How can you, foolish men, fell a tree or get some one else to do so? For people think that there are living things in a tree. There is an offence of expiation for destroying vegetable growth. (Vinaya-pitaka.)

Whatever monk should intentionally deprive a breathing thing of life, there is an offence of expiation. (Vinaya-pitaka.)

Whatever monk should make use of water knowing that it contains breathing things, there is an offence of expiation. (Vinaya-pitaka.)

Whatever monk should sprinkle water that he knows to contain breathing things over grass or clay or get someone else to do so, there is an offence of expiation. (Vinaya-pitaka.)

Fish and meat are pure in three respects: if it is not seen, heard, or suspected (to have been killed specially for you). (Vinaya-pitaka.)

If a monk should make use of human flesh, there is a grave offence. A monk should not eat the flesh of elephants, horses, dogs, snakes, lions, tigers, leopards, bears, hyenas (even in times of scarcity). Whoever should eat the flesh of any of these animals, there is an offence of wrong-doing. (Vinaya-pitaka.)

DEEDS AND TRANSMIGRATION

Incalculable, monks, is the beginning of this faring-on. The earliest point is not revealed of the running-on, the faring-on, of beings hindered by ignorance, fettered by craving. If a man, monks, were to prune out the grasses, sticks, boughs, and foliage in this India and should make a pile of them, saying for each: "This is my mother, this my mother's mother," those grasses, sticks, boughs, and foliage would be used up and ended or ever the mothers of that man's mother were come to an end. Or if a man were to make this great earth into clay balls each only the size of a *kola* kernel and were to lay them down, saying: "This is my father, this is my father's father", this great earth would be used up and ended or ever the fathers of that man's father were come to an end. . . .

And which is the greater—the flood of tears shed by you crying and weeping as you run-on, fare-on for this long while, united as you have been with those that are not dear, separated from those that are dear, or the waters in the four seas? The flood of tears shed by you as you have run-on and fared-on is the greater. For many a long day you have experienced the death of mother, of son, of daughter, the ruin of kinsmen, of wealth, the calamity of disease. What is the cause of this? It is that incalculable is the beginning of this faring-on. . . .

Long is an aeon. It is not easy to reckon how long by saying so many years, so many centuries, so many thousand centuries. But it could be told in a parable. Take where the river Ganges has its source and where it reaches the sea. The sand that lies between, that is not easy to count—so many (grains of) sand, so many hundreds, so many thousands, so many hundred thousand grains of sand. More than that are the aeons that have passed and gone by. But it is not easy to count them—so many aeons, so many hundreds, so many thousands, so many hundreds of thousands of aeons. How is this? Incalculable is the beginning of this faring-on. The earli-est point is not revealed of the running-on, the faring-on of beings hindered by ignorance, fettered by craving. . . .

Not an easy thing it is, monks, to find a being who during this long many-a-day has not at one time been a mother, a father, a brother, a sister, a son, a daughter. How is this? Incalculable is the beginning, monks, of this faring-on. The earliest point is not revealed of the running-on, the faring-on of beings hindered by ignorance, fettered by craving. Thus have you, monks, for a long time suffered ill, pain, misery, and the charnel-field has grown. (Samyutta-nikāya.)

This, monks, that we call thought, that we call mind, that we call consciousness, is that to which the uninstructed many-folk cleave; it is that which they stress as "mine," thinking: "This is mine, I am this, this is my Self." It were better, monks, if the uninstructed many-folk were to approach this body, rather than the mind, as Self. Why should this be so? Monks, this body is seen enduring for one year, for two years, three, four, five, ten, twenty, thirty, forty, fifty years, for a hundred years, and even longer. But this, monks, that is called thought and mind and consciousness, this by night and day dissolves as one thing and reappears even as another. As a monkey faring through jungle and wood catches hold of a bough and, having let it go, takes hold of another, even so that which is called thought and mind and conscious-ness, this by night and day dissolves as one thing and re-appears even as another. (Samyutta-nikāya.)

What the monk, remembering his "former habitations" (past lives), remembers is the five stems of grasping, or some one of them; he thinks, "Such-and-such was my body, or feeling, or perception, constructions or consciousness"; and so reflecting, he becomes indifferent to his past bodies, feelings, etc. For all of these are impermanent; and neither of all or any of them can it be said that "It is mine, I am that, or That is my Self." He rejects them all, and grasps no more. (Samyutta-nikāya.)

Do you not see, monks, that steaminess, that murkiness going even to the eastern quarter, to the western quarter, to the northern, to the southern, going aloft, going downwards, going to the intervening points? That, monks, is Māra, the Evil One, searching about for the discriminative consciousness of Godhika, the clansman, and thinking: "Where is the discriminative consciousness of Godhika, the clansman, instated?" But, monks, the clansman Godhika has attained utter nirvana without his discriminative consciousness being (re-) instated.

> He, a seer, possessed of vision,
> A meditator, ever delighting in meditation,
> Given up to it night and day,
> Not desiring life;
> By overcoming the host of death,
> Not having come to again becoming,
> By conquering craving and its root
> "Godhika" has attained utter nirvana.
>
> (Samyutta-nikāya.)

THE WAY

A Truth-finder, monks, one perfected, fully awakened, causes a Way to arise which had not arisen before; he brings about a Way not brought about before; he proclaims a Way not proclaimed before; he is knower of the Way, understander of the Way, skilled in the Way. And now his disciples, monks, are wayfarers who follow after him. This is the distinction, the specific feature which distinguishes a Truth-finder, a perfected one, a fully awakened one, from a monk who is freed by wisdom. (Samyutta and Majjhima-nikāyas.)

Some of my disciples, brahman, being advised thus and instructed thus, succeed in winning nirvana, the ultimate goal; and some do not. . . . (To explain this, I will ask you a

199

question.) You are conversant with the way to Rājagaha?
Well, then, suppose a man were to come to you and say he
wished to go to Rājagaha, and asked you to point out the
way. And suppose you were to say: "This is the way to
Rājagaha: go along it for a short time and then you will see
a village; a little farther on you will see a township, and still
a little farther on you will see Rājagaha with its lovely parks,
woodlands, open spaces, and lakes." But, although advised
and instructed by you in this manner, he might take a wrong
road and turn west. Then a second man might come along,
also wishing to go to Rājagaha and asking you to point out
the way. You would give him instructions, as to the first man;
and advised and instructed by you in this manner, he might
arrive safely at Rājagaha. Now, how is it that with Rājagaha
existing, with the way to Rājagaha existing, and with you
existing as an adviser, the one man, although advised and
instructed by you, might take the wrong road and turn west,
while the other might arrive safely at Rājagaha?

In the same manner, brahman, nirvana exists, the way to
nirvana exists, and I exist as adviser. Yet, although some of
my disciples, being advised and instructed by me, succeed
in winning nirvana, the ultimate goal, some do not. What do
I do in this matter, brahman? Foreteller of the Way, brahman, is a Truth-finder. (Majjhima-nikāya.)

Suppose now, Tissa, there be two men, one unskilled in
the way, the other skilled in the way. And the one who is
unskilled asks the way of the other who is skilled in the way.
And that other replies: "Yes, this is the way, sir. When you
have gone by it for a short time you will see that it divides
into two paths. Leave the left one and take the one to the
right. Go on for a little and you will see a thick forest. Go on
for a little and you will see a great marshy swamp. Go on for
a little and you will see a steep precipice. Go on for a little
and you will see a delightful stretch of level ground."

Such is my parable, Tissa, to show my meaning; and this is
what it means: By the "man who is unskilled in the way"
is meant the many-folk. By the "man who is skilled in the

way" is meant a Truth-finder, a perfected one, a fully awakened one. By "dividing into two paths" is meant a state of
wavering. "The way to the left" means the wrong eightfold
way, namely that of wrong view, wrong concept, wrong
speech, wrong acting, wrong mode of living, wrong exertion,
wrong mindfulness, wrong contemplation. The "way to the
right" is a synonym for the ariyan eightfold Way, namely that
of right view and so on. The "thick forest," Tissa, is a name for
ignorance. The "great marshy swamp" is a name for pleasures of the senses. The "steep precipice" is a synonym for
the turbulence of anger. The "delightful stretch of level
ground" is a name for nirvana.

Be of good cheer, Tissa. I shall exhort (you), I shall help
(you), I shall instruct (you). (Samyutta-nikāya.)

These two dead-ends, monks, should not be followed by
one who has gone forth. Which two? That which is among
sense-pleasures addiction to attractive sense-pleasures, low, of
the villager, of the average man, unariyan, not connected
with the goal; and that which is addiction to tormenting the
self, ill, unariyan, not connected with the goal. Now, monks,
without adopting either of these two dead-ends, there is a
middle course, thoroughly understood by the Truth-finder,
making for vision, making for knowledge, and which conduces to tranquillity, to super-knowledge, to awakening, to
nirvana. And what, monks, is this middle course? It is just
this ariyan eightfold Way, that is to say: right view, right
concept, right speech, right acting, right mode of living, right
exertion, right mindfulness, right contemplation. (Vinaya-
pitaka.)

CROSSING OVER

Monks, I will teach you *dhamma*—the parable of the raft—
for getting across, not for retaining. Listen to it, pay careful
attention, and I will speak. It is like a man, monks, who as he
is going on a journey should see a great stretch of water,

the hither bank with dangers and fears, the farther bank secure and without fears, but there may be neither a boat for crossing over, nor a bridge across for going from the not-beyond to the beyond. It occurs to him that in order to cross over from the perils of this bank to the security of the farther bank, he should fashion a raft out of grass and sticks, branches and foliage, so that he could, striving with his hands and feet and depending on the raft, cross over to the beyond in safety. When he has done this and has crossed over to the beyond, it occurs to him that the raft has been very useful and he wonders if he ought to proceed taking it with him packed on his head or shoulders. What do you think, monks? That the man, in doing this, would be doing what should be done to the raft?

No, lord.

What should that man do, monks, in order to do what should be done to that raft? In this case, monks, that man, when he has crossed over to the beyond and realizes how useful the raft has been to him, may think: "Suppose that I, having beached this raft on dry ground, or having immersed it in the water, should proceed on my journey?" Monks, a man doing this would be doing what should be done to the raft. In this way, monks, I have taught you *dhamma*—the parable of the raft—for getting across, not for retaining. You, monks, by understanding the parable of the raft, must discard even right states of mind and, all the more, wrong states of mind. (Majjhima-nikāya.)

Those who do not live professing disgust for abstinence, not making disgust for abstinence essential, not cleaving to disgust for abstinence—these can become those for crossing the flood. Those who practise purity in body, speech, and thought, those whose way of living is pure—these can become those for knowledge and vision, for the supreme awakening.

It is like a man who wants to cross a river. Taking a sharp axe he would enter a wood. If he should see there a mighty sāl-tree, straight, young, not of crooked growth, he would cut it down at the root. Having done so, he would cut off the top, then he would clear it thoroughly of the branches and foliage. Having done so, he would chip it with axes, then with knives. He would then scrape it with a scraper and smooth it with a ball of stone. Then he would make a boat and would fasten oars and a rudder, and having done so he would get the boat down to the river. Do you think, Sālha, that this man can become one to cross the river?

Yes, lord.

Why is this?

Why, lord, the sāl-tree log is well worked over outside, well cleared out within, it is made into a boat with oars and a rudder fastened to it. This is to be expected of it: the boat will not sink, the man will go safely beyond. (Anguttara-nikāya.)

Monks, a man terrified of four deadly poisonous snakes, terrified of five murderous foes, terrified of a sixth murderer —a housebreaker—terrified of robbers who plunder villages including deserted ones, might rush about here and there. He might see a great stretch of water, the hither shore beset with dangers and fears, the farther shore secure and without fears, but with no boat for crossing over, nor any bridge across for going from the not-beyond to the beyond. Seeing this, he might think: "Suppose that I were to gather grass, sticks, branches and foliage, and, having fashioned a raft, were to go to the beyond in safety, striving with my hands and feet and depending on the raft?" Then, suppose that he does so— crossed over, gone beyond, the brahman stands on dry land.

I have made this simile, monks, to clarify my meaning. This is the meaning here:

The four deadly poisonous snakes, monks,—this is a synonym for the four great elementals: for the earth element, for the water element, for the fire element, for the wind element.

The five murderous foes, monks,—this is a synonym for the five components of grasping: for the component of grasping material shape, for the component of grasping feeling, for the component of grasping perception, for the component of grasping the constructions, for the component of grasping consciousness.

The sixth, the murderous housebreaker, monks,—this is a synonym for the delight of passion.

Deserted village, monks,—this is a synonym for the six subjective (sense-) spheres. A wise, experienced, intelligent person, if he tests one of them by means of the eye, it seems to be empty, it seems to be deserted, it seems to be void. Similarly, if he tests the other (sense-spheres) by means of the nose, the ear, the tongue, the body, the mind, they seem to be empty, deserted, void.

Robbers who plunder villages, monks,—this is a synonym for the six objective (sense-) spheres. The eye, monks, is destroyed in regard to shapes that are delightful and not delightful, the ear in regard to sounds, the nose in regard to smells, the tongue in regard to tastes, the body in regard to touches, the mind is destroyed in regard to mental states that are delightful and not delightful.

The great stretch of water, monks,—this is a synonym for the four floods: for the flood of pleasures of the senses, for the flood of becoming, for the flood of views, for the flood of ignorance.

The hither shore beset by dangers and fears, monks,—this is a synonym for corporeality.

The farther shore, secure and without fears, monks,—this is a synonym for nirvana.

The raft, monks,—this is a synonym for the ariyan eightfold Way, that is to say, right view . . . right contemplation.

Striving with hands and feet, monks,—this is a synonym for stirring up energy.

Crossed over, gone beyond, the brahman stands on dry land, monks,—this is a synonym for a perfected one. (Samyutta-nikāya.)

Onslaught on creatures is the hither shore; abstaining therefrom is the farther shore. Taking what is not given is the hither shore; abstaining therefrom is the farther shore. Wrong conduct as to pleasures of the senses is the hither

shore; abstaining therefrom is the farther shore. Falsehood
. . . spiteful speech . . . bitter speech . . . idle babble . . .
coveting . . . harmfulness . . . these are the hither shore
and abstinence therefrom is the farther shore. Wrong view
is the hither shore, right view is the farther shore. (Anguttara-nikāya.)

RIVERS OF LIFE AND DEATH

It is, monks, as if a man were to be carried along by the
current of a river that looks pleasant and delightful, and as
if a man with vision standing on the bank, having seen him,
should call out: "Now, you, my good man, are being carried
along by the current of a river that looks pleasant and delightful. But farther down there is a pool with waves and
whirlpools, with sharks and demons. When you get there
you will encounter death or pain like unto death." Then that
man, having heard the other's call, should strive against the
current with his hands and feet.

I have made this parable, monks, to clarify the meaning.
This is the meaning here:

The current of a river—this, monks, is a synonym for
craving.

Pleasant and delightful—this, monks, is a synonym for the
six subjective (sense-) spheres.

Pool farther down—this, monks, is a synonym for the five
fetters that bind to this lower world.

With waves—this, monks, is a synonym for the turbulence
of anger.

With whirlpools—this, monks, is a synonym for the five
strands of the pleasures of the senses.

With sharks and demons—this, monks, is a synonym for
womenkind.

Against the current—this, monks, is a synonym for renunciation.

Striving with hands and feet—this, monks, is a synonym for
stirring up energy.

Man with vision standing on the bank—this, monks, is a synonym for a Truth-finder, a perfected one, a wholly awakened one.

> One should eject pain with sense-pleasures,
> Aspiring for future security from bondage;
> Rightly knowing, the heart well freed,
> One may gain freedom in this or that.
> Who's versed in lore, who's lived the Brahma-faring,
> "Gone to world's end," "gone beyond" is called.
>
> (Itivuttaka.)

THE GREAT OCEAN

Monks, there are these eight strange and wonderful things in the great ocean, from constantly having seen which *asuras* delight in the great ocean. What are the eight? The great ocean, monks, deepens gradually, slopes gradually, shelves gradually, with no abruptness like a precipice. And, monks, that the great ocean deepens gradually, slopes gradually, shelves gradually with no abruptness like a precipice—this, monks, is the first strange and wonderful thing in the great ocean from constantly having seen which *asuras* delight in the great ocean.

And again, monks, the great ocean is stable, it does not overflow its margins. And, monks, that the great ocean is stable, that it does not overflow its margins—this, monks, is the second strange and wonderful thing. . . .

And again, monks, the great ocean does not associate with a dead body, a corpse. Whatever dead body, corpse, there may be in the great ocean, that it just quickly forces ashore and pushes on to the dry land. That the great ocean, monks, does not associate with a dead body, a corpse, . . . this, monks, is the third strange and wonderful thing. . . .

And again, monks, all the great rivers, that is to say, the Ganges, the Jumnā, the Aciravatī, the Sarabhū, the Mahī— these, on reaching the great ocean lose their former names and identities and are reckoned simply as the great ocean. That all the great rivers . . . this, monks, is the fourth strange and wonderful thing. . . .

And again, monks, those streams which in the world flow into the great ocean, and those showers from the sky which fall into it—yet is neither the emptiness nor the fullness of the great ocean affected by that. That those streams which in the world . . . this, monks, is the fifth strange and wonderful thing. . . .

And again, monks, the great ocean has one taste, the taste of salt. That the great ocean, monks, has one taste . . . this, monks, is the sixth strange and wonderful thing. . . .

And again, monks, the great ocean has many treasures, divers treasures; these treasures are there, that is to say: pearl, crystal, lapis lazuli, shell, quartz, coral, silver, gold, ruby, cat's-eye. That the great ocean, monks, has many treasures . . . this, monks, is the seventh strange and wonderful thing. . . .

And again, monks, the great ocean is the abode of great beings; these beings are there: the *timis,* the *timangalas,* the *timitimangalas, asuras, nāgas, gandharvas.* There are in the great ocean individualities a hundred *yojanas* long, two hundred, three hundred, four hundred, five hundred *yojanas* long. That the great ocean, monks, is the abode of great beings; that these beings are there: *timis* . . . individualities five hundred *yojanas* long—this, monks, is the eighth strange and wonderful thing from constantly having seen which *asuras* delight in the great ocean. These, monks, are the eight strange and wonderful things in the great ocean from constantly having seen which *asuras* delight in the great ocean.

In exactly the same way, monks, in this *dhamma* and discipline there are eight strange and wonderful things from constantly having seen which monks delight in this *dhamma* and discipline. What are the eight?

Even, monks, as the great ocean deepens gradually, slopes gradually, shelves gradually with no abruptness like a precipice, even so, monks, in this *dhamma* and discipline there is a gradual training, a gradual (doing of) what is to be done, a gradual course, with no abruptness, such as penetration of profound knowledge. And, monks, that in this *dhamma* and discipline there is a . . . gradual course with no abruptness, such as penetration of profound knowledge, this, monks, is the first strange and wonderful thing from constantly having seen which monks delight in this *dhamma* and discipline.

And even, monks, as the great ocean is stable and does not overflow its margins, even so, monks, whatever course of training has been laid down by me for disciples, my disciples will not transgress it even for life's sake. And that, monks, my disciples will not transgress even for life's sake a course of training laid down by me for disciples, this, monks, is the second strange and wonderful thing. . . .

And even, monks, as the great ocean does not associate with a dead body, a corpse, but whatever dead body, corpse, there may be in the great ocean, that it just quickly forces ashore and pushes on to the dry land, even so, monks, whatever individual is of bad moral habit, of depraved character, of impure and suspicious behaviour, of concealed actions, not a recluse although pretending to be one, not a farer of the Brahma-faring although pretending to be one, rotten within, filled with desire, filthy by nature—the Order (of monks) does not live in communion with him, but having assembled quickly suspends him; and although he is sitting in the midst of an Order of monks, yet he is far from the Order and the Order is far from him . . . this, monks, is the third strange and wonderful thing. . . .

And even, monks, as those great rivers, that is to say the Ganges, the Jumnā, the Āciravatī, the Sarabhū, the Mahī, on reaching the great ocean lose their former names and identities and are reckoned simply as the great ocean, even so, monks, (members of) these four castes: noble, brahman, merchant, and worker, having gone forth from home into homelessness in the *dhamma* and discipline proclaimed by the Truth-finder, lose their former names and clans and are reckoned simply as recluses, sons of the Sakyans . . . this, monks, is the fourth strange and wonderful thing. . . .

And even, monks, as those streams which in the world flow

into the great ocean and those showers which fall into it from
the sky, yet neither the emptiness nor the fullness of the great
ocean is affected by that—even so, monks, even if many monks
are attained to utter nirvana in a condition of nirvana with no
residuum remaining, not by that is the emptiness or fullness
of the condition of nirvana affected . . . this, monks, is the
fifth strange and wonderful thing. . . .

, And even, monks, as the great ocean has one taste, the
taste of salt, even so, monks, has this *dhamma* and discipline
one taste, the taste of freedom . . . this, monks, is the sixth
strange and wonderful thing. . . .

And even, monks, as the great ocean has many treasures,
divers treasures; these treasures are there, that is to say:
pearl, crystal, lapis lazuli, shell, quartz, coral, silver, gold,
ruby, cat's-eye—even so, monks, does this *dhamma* and discipline have many treasures, divers treasures; these treasures
are there, that is to say: the four stations of mindfulness,
the four right efforts, the four bases of psychic potency, the
five faculties, the five powers, the seven limbs of awakening,
the ariyan eightfold Way . . . this, monks, is the seventh
strange and wonderful thing. . . .

And even, monks, as the great ocean is the abode of great
beings; these beings are there: *timis* . . . individualities five
hundred *yojanas* long—even so, monks, this *dhamma* and
discipline is the abode of great beings; these beings are there:
the stream-attainer, the one going along to the realization of
the fruit of stream-attainment, the once-returner, the one going along to the realization of the fruit of once-returning; the
non-returner, the one going along to the realization of the
fruit of non-returning, the perfected one, the one going along
to perfection. And that, monks, this *dhamma* and discipline is
the abode of great beings; these beings are there: the stream-
attainer . . . the one going along to perfection . . . this,
monks, is the eighth strange and wonderful thing in this
dhamma and discipline from constantly having seen which
monks delight in this *dhamma* and discipline. These, monks,
are the eight strange and wonderful things in this *dhamma*
and discipline from constantly having seen which monks de-

light in this *dhamma* and discipline. (Vinaya-pitaka, Anguttara-nikāya, and Udāna.)

TRANSCENDENT

A Truth-finder does not say anything that he knows to be not a fact, untrue, not connected with the goal and which is also displeasing and disagreeable to others; he does not say anything that he knows to be a fact, true, but not connected with the goal and also displeasing and disagreeable to others. But if a Truth-finder knows something to be a fact, true, connected with the goal, although it is displeasing and disagreeable to others, then he knows the right time when it may be stated. A Truth-finder does not say anything that is not a fact, untrue, not connected with the goal even if it is pleasing and agreeable to others; and he does not say anything that is a fact, true, but not connected with the goal and which is pleasing and agreeable to others. But if a Truth-finder knows something to be a fact, true, connected with the goal and which is pleasing and agreeable to others, then the Truth-finder knows the right time when it may be stated. What is the reason? A Truth-finder has compassion for beings. (Majjhima-nikāya.)

ON VARIOUS SUBJECTS

"Here, O Bhikkhus, a certain person is not disciplined in body, is not disciplined in morality, is not disciplined in mind, is not disciplined in wisdom, is with little good and less virtue, and lives painfully in consequence of trifles. Even a trivial evil act committed by such a person will lead him to a state of misery.

"Here, O Bhikkhus, a certain person is disciplined in body, is disciplined in morality, is disciplined in mind, is disciplined in wisdom, is with much good, is high souled, and lives without limitation. A similar evil act committed by such a person is expiated in this life itself and not even a small effect manifests itself (after death), not to say a great one.

"It is as if, O Bhikkhus, a man were to put a lump of salt into a small cup of water. What do you think, O Bhikkhus? Would now the small amount of water in this cup become saltish and undrinkable?"

"Yes, Lord."

"And why?"

"Because, Lord, there was very little water in the cup, and so it became saltish and undrinkable by this lump of salt."

"Suppose, O Bhikkhus, a man were to put a lump of salt into the river Ganges. What think you, O Bhikkhus, would now the river Ganges become saltish and undrinkable by the lump of salt?"

"Nay, indeed, Lord."

"And why not?"

"Because, Lord, the mass of water in the river Ganges is great, and so it would not become saltish and undrinkable."

"In exactly the same way, O Bhikkhus, we may have the case of a person who does some slight evil deed which brings him to a state of misery, or again, O Bhikkhus, we may have the case of another person who does the same trivial misdeed, and expiates it in the present life. Not even a small effort manifests itself (after death), not to say of a great one." (Anguttara-nikāya.)

Then there is the story of Sona the young, overenthusiastic monk who through excessive exertion paced up and down meditating until his feet bled without attaining the desired concentration of mind. Having failed in his attempts, he became disheartened and was thinking of leaving the Order. Through his supernatural psychic powers the Buddha became aware of what was passing through Sona's mind. He went where Sona was meditating and told him about the thoughts which had been passing through his mind, and said:

"Now, Sona, were you not a clever musician and skilled lute player formerly, when you were a layman?"

"Yes, Sir."

"Now what do you think, when the strings of your lute become too tight, could you get the right tune, or was it then fit to play?"

"No indeed, Sir."

"Likewise, when the lute strings become too slack, could you get the right tune or was it then fit to play?"

"No indeed, Sir."

"But when the lute strings were neither too tight nor too slack but were keyed to an even pitch then did it give the right tune?"

"Yes indeed, Sir."

"Even so, Sona, too much zeal conduces to restlessness and too much slackness conduces to mental sloth." So saying, the Master admonished the young monk to strike a balance between these two extremes and develop an even tempo of spiritual equilibrium. (Vinaya-pitaka.)

Brethren, for the monk who is a learner not yet come to mastery of mind, but who dwells aspiring for peace from the bond, making it a matter concerning what is outside the self, I see no other single factor so helpful as friendship with the kindly. Brethren, one who is a friend of the kindly abandons the unprofitable and makes the profitable to occur.

> The monk who has a kindly friend, who pays
> Deference and reverence to him, who does
> What friends advise,—if mindful and composed
> Such in due course shall win all fetters' end.

Here, brethren, I discern a certain person with mind at peace to be such because I compass his thoughts with my mind; and, if at this moment this person were to make an end, he would be put just so into the heaven-world according to his deserts. What is the reason for that? His mind at peace. Indeed it is because of a mind at peace, brethren, that in this way certain beings, when body breaks up, after death arise again in the happy bourn, in the heaven-world.

Here seeing a certain one with mind at peace,
The Teacher 'mid the monks set forth this saying:
"If at this time this person were to die,
In the happy bourn he would arise again.
Indeed the mind of him has come to peace.
Thro' peace of mind men reach the happy bourn.
As one lays down what he has taken up,
So such an one, when body breaks up, strong
In wisdom rises up in the heaven-world."

Brethren, if beings knew, as I know, the ripening of sharing gifts, they would not enjoy their use without sharing them,
nor would the taint of stinginess obsess the heart and stay
there. Even if it were their last bit, their last morsel of food,
they would not enjoy its use without sharing it, if there were
any one to receive it. But inasmuch, brethren, as beings do
not know, as I know, the ripening of sharing gifts, therefore
they enjoy their use without sharing them, and the taint of
stinginess obsesses their heart and stays there.

If only beings knew—as said the mighty sage—
The ripening of sharing gifts, how great the fruit thereof,
Putting away the taint of stinginess, with heart
Made pure within, they would bestow in season due
When great the fruit of charity on Aryans.
And giving food as gift to those deserving much
From man-state falling hence givers to heaven go.
And they, to heaven gone, rejoice and there enjoy
In the fullness of their hearts' desire the ripening
Of sharing gifts, the fruit of their unselfishness.

Brethren, whatsoever grounds there be for good works
undertaken with a view to rebirth, all of them are not worth
one sixteenth part of that goodwill which is the heart's release; goodwill alone, which is the heart's release, shines and
burns and flashes forth in surpassing them. Just as, brethren,
the radiance of all the starry bodies is not worth one sixteenth
part of the moon's radiance, but the moon's radiance shines
and burns and flashes forth in surpassing them, even so,

brethren, goodwill . . . flashes forth in surpassing good works undertaken with a view to rebirth.

Just as, brethren, in the last month of the rains, in autumn time, when the sky is opened up and cleared of clouds, the sun, leaping up into the firmament, drives away all darkness from the heavens and shines and burns and flashes forth,— even so, brethren, whatsoever grounds there be for good works . . . goodwill . . . flashes forth in surpassing them.

Just as, brethren, in the night at time of daybreak the star of healing shines and burns and flashes forth, even so, what-soever grounds there be for good works undertaken with a view to rebirth, all of them are not worth one-sixteenth part of that goodwill which is the heart's release. Goodwill, which is the heart's release, alone shines and burns and flashes forth in surpassing them.

Brethren, there are two ethical teachings. . . . What two? "Look at evil as evil" is the first teaching. "Seeing evil as evil, be disgusted therewith, be cleansed of it, be freed of it" is the second teaching. These two teachings of the wayfarer take place one after the other.

> Of the wayfarer, the awakened one,
> Who hath compassion on all things that be,
> Behold the way of speech and teachings twain:
> "Evil behold for what it is, and then
> Conceive disgust for it: with heart made clean
> Of evil, ye shall make an end of ill."

. . . Brethren, there are these three persons found existing in the world. What three? The one who is like a drought, the one who rains locally, and the one who pours down everywhere.

And how, brethren, is a person like a drought?

Herein, brethren, a certain person is not a giver to all alike, no giver of food and drink, clothing and vehicle, flowers, scents and unguents, bed, lodging and lights to recluses and Brahmanas, to wretched and needy beggars. In this way, brethren, a person is like a drought.

And how, brethren, is a person like a local rainfall?

In this case a person is a giver to some, but to others he gives not; be they recluses and Brahmanas or wretched, needy beggars, he is no giver of food and drink . . . lodging and lights. In this way a person is like a local rainfall.

And how, brethren, does a person rain down everywhere?

In this case a certain person gives to all, be they recluses and Brahmanas or wretched, needy beggars; he is a giver of food and drink . . . lodging and lights. In this way a person rains down everywhere.

So these are the three sorts of persons found existing in the world.

Brethren, even if a monk should seize the hem of my garment and walk behind me step for step, yet if he be covetous in his desires, fierce in his longing, malevolent of heart, of mind corrupt, careless and unrestrained, not quieted but scatter-brained and uncontrolled in sense, that monk is far from me and I am far from him. . . .

Brethren, do ye live perfect in virtue, do ye live perfect in the performance of the obligations, restrained with the restraint of the obligations, perfect in the practice of right behaviour; seeing danger in the slightest faults, undertake and train yourselves in the training of the precepts. For him who so lives . . . so restrained . . . who undertakes the training of the precepts, what else remains to be done?

> Whether he walk or stand or rest or lie
> Or stretch his limbs or draw them in again,
> Let him do all these things composedly;
> Above, across, and back again returning—
> Whatever be one's bourn in all the world—
> Let him be one who views the rise-and-fall
> Of all compounded things attentively.
> So dwelling ardent, living a life of peace
> And not elated, but to calmness given,
> For mind's composure doing what is right,
> Ever and always training,—"ever intent"—
> That is the name men give to such a monk.
>
> (Itivuttaka.)

On one occasion a number of disciples went to the Blessed One and said: "Sir, there are living here in Savatthi many wandering hermits and scholars who indulge in constant dispute, some saying that the world is infinite and eternal and others that it is finite and not eternal, some saying that the soul dies with the body and others that it lives on forever, and so forth. What, Sir, would you say concerning them?"

The Blessed One answered: "Brethren, those disputatious fellows are like unto blind men. . . . Once upon a time there was a raja in this region who called to a certain man and said: 'Come thou, good fellow, go and gather together in one place all the men in Savatthi who were born blind.'

" 'Very good, sire,' replied that man, and in obedience to the raja gathered together all the men born blind in Savatthi. And, having done so, he went to the raja and said, 'Sire, all the men born blind in Savatthi are assembled.'

" 'Then, my good man, show the blind men an elephant.'

" 'Very good, sire,' said the man, and did as he was told, and said to them, 'O blind, such as this is an elephant'; and to one man he presented the head of the elephant, to another its ears, to another a tusk, to another the trunk, the foot, back, tail and tuft of the tail, saying to each one that that was the elephant.

"Now, brethren, that man, having thus presented the elephant to the blind men, came to the raja and said, 'Sire, the elephant has been presented to the blind men. Do what is your will.'

"Thereupon, brethren, that raja went up to the blind men and said to each, 'Well, blind men, have you seen the elephant?'

" 'Yes, sire.'

" 'Then tell me, blind men, what sort of thing is an elephant?'

"Thereupon those who had been presented with the head answered, 'Sire, an elephant is like a pot.' And those who had observed an ear only replied, 'An elephant is like a winnowing-basket.' Those who had been presented with a tusk said it was a ploughshare. Those who knew only the trunk said it was a plough; they said the body was a granary; the foot, a pillar; the back, a mortar; the tail, a pestle; the tuft of the tail, just a besom.

"Then they began to quarrel, shouting, 'Yes, it is!' 'No, it is not!' 'An elephant is not that!' 'Yes, it's like that!' and so on, till they came to fisticuffs over the matter.

"Then, brethren, that raja was delighted with the scene.

"Just so are these wanderers holding other views, blind, unseeing, knowing not the profitable, knowing not the unprofitable. They know not dhamma. They know not what is not dhamma. In their ignorance of these things they are by nature quarrelsome, wrangling and disputatious, each maintaining it is thus and thus."

Thereupon the Exalted One at that time, seeing the meaning of it, gave utterance to this verse of uplift:

> O how they cling and wrangle, some who claim
> Of Brahmana and recluse the honoured name!
> For, quarreling, each to his view they cling.
> Such folk see only one side of a thing.

(Udāna.)

Thus have I heard: On a certain occasion the Exalted One was staying near Savatthi in East Park, at the storied house of Visakha, the mother of Migara.

Now at that time the dear and lovely grand-daughter of this Visakha chanced to die, and the woman came with clothes and hair still wet from washing to see the Exalted One. And the Exalted One said to her:

"Why, Visakha! How is it that you come here with clothes and hair still wet at an unseasonable hour?"

"O, sir, my dear and lovely grand-daughter is dead! That is why I come here, with hair and clothes still wet and at an unseasonable hour."

"Visakha, would you like to have as many sons and grandsons as there are men in Savatthi?"

"Yes, sir, I would indeed!"

"But how many men do you suppose die daily in Savatthi?"

"Ten, sir, or maybe nine, or eight. . . . Savatthi is never free from men dying, sir."

"What think you, Visakha? In such case would you ever be without wet hair and clothes?"

"Surely not, sir!" . . .

"Visakha, whoso have a hundred things beloved, they have a hundred sorrows. Whoso have ninety, eighty . . . thirty, twenty things beloved . . . whoso have ten . . . whoso have but one thing beloved, have but one sorrow. Whoso have no one thing beloved, they have no sorrow. Sorrowless are they and passionless. Serene are they, I declare."

> All griefs or lamentations whatso'er
> And divers forms of sorrow in the world,—
> Because of what is dear to these become.
> Thing dear not being, these do not become.
> Happy are they therefore and free from grief
> To whom is naught at all dear in the world.
> Wherefore aspiring for the griefless, sorrowless,
> Make thou in all the world naught dear to thee.
>
> (Udāna.)

Chapter X
RHINOCEROS DISCOURSE

The *Khaggavisana Sutta* (Rhinoceros Discourse), given here, was according to tradition delivered by the Buddha at the request of his favorite disciple, Ānanda. Supposedly it is based on doctrines proclaimed by some of the lesser Buddhas coming before Gautama. Regarding other Buddhas, in the older books of the Pitakas six are mentioned as preceding Gautama, namely Vipassî, Sikhî, Vessabdhû, Kakusandha, Konâgamana and Kassapa; in no passage are more than seven Buddhas mentioned; but later books, such as the *Buddhavamsa* and the introduction to the *Jātaka Book,* describe as many as twenty-five Buddhas, with three extra sometimes mentioned. Gautama's career as a Bodhisattva began in the time of Dîpankara, first of the twenty-five Buddhas, when Gautama was a hermit called Sumedha. The *Khaggavisana Sutta* is especially interesting for the manner in which it presents the supposed position of the Theravada school on such matters as independence, a position disdained by Mahayanists, as has been seen, for its selfishness. The story of Visakha, which concludes the preceding chapter, also points out the folly of making anything dear to one. It should be kept in mind that the rhinoceros-like aloofness recommended by the discourse is meant chiefly for monks still in training, who must avoid attachments representing hindrances to Nirvana.

1. Having abandoned the practising of violence toward all objects, not doing violence to any one of them, let one wish not for children. Why wish for a friend? Let one walk alone like a rhinoceros.

2. There are friendships to one who lives in society; this

our present grief arises from having friendships; observing the evils resulting from friendship, let one walk alone like a rhinoceros.

3. He who is kind toward much-beloved friends loses his own good from his mind becoming partial; observing such danger in friendship, let one walk alone like a rhinoceros.

4. As a spreading bush of bamboo is entangled in various ways so is the longing for children and wives: not clinging to these, even like a bamboo just sprouting forth, let one walk alone like a rhinoceros.

5. As a beast of the forest prowls, free, withersoever he will for pasture, even so let a wise man, observing solitude, walk alone like a rhinoceros.

6. Whilst resting, standing, going, traveling, leave must be obtained by one living in the midst of friends; let one, observing solitude which is not pleasing to others, walk alone like a rhinoceros.

7. If one lives in the midst of company, love of amusement and desire arises; strong attachment for children arises; let therefore one who dislikes separation, which must happen sooner or later from those beloved, walk alone like a rhinoceros.

8. Whoever is possessed of the four Appamannas, and is not opposed to any person, is contented with whatever he gets, endures sufferings and is fearless, let him walk alone like a rhinoceros.

9. Some there are, also difficult to please, even though they be ascetics; on the other hand, there are also some laymen difficult to propitiate; therefore let one, not minding other men's children, walk alone like a rhinoceros.

10. Let a hero abandoning the ways of the world, and also flinging off the bonds of the household, like a Kovilaratree, which has cast off its leaves, walk alone like a rhinoceros.

11. If a wise man secures a wise friend who will act in concert with him, being firmly established in good principles, he will live happily with him, overcoming all afflictions.

12. If a wise man secures not a wise friend who will act in concert with him, being firmly established in good prin-

ciples, let him, like a king who has abandoned the country conquered by him, walk alone like a rhinoceros.

13.   Certainly we praise the acquisition of friendship; but good friends should be admitted into one's company; not obtaining such friends, let one, subsisting on pure food, walk alone like a rhinoceros.

14.   Noticing how even two glittering armlets of gold, though well made by a goldsmith, strike against each other, let one walk alone like a rhinoceros.

15.   Thus, being with a second beside myself, I must either speak too much and be angry with him; observing this danger, for the future, let a man walk alone like a rhinoceros.

16.   Desires are indeed various, sweet and pleasing to the mind; they churn the mind in different ways; observing the distress resulting from desires, let one walk alone like a rhinoceros.

17.   This body is a calamity, an excrescence, a danger, a disease, a dart of sorrow, a fear to me; observing this danger resulting from desires, let one walk alone like a rhinoceros.

18.   There are cold, heat, hunger, thirst, wind, sun, gadflies, snakes; having overcome all these various things, let a man walk alone like a rhinoceros.

19.   As the huge-bodied, white-spotted, noble elephant wanders in the forest, whithersoever he will, deserting his herd, so also let one walk alone like a rhinoceros.

20.   The attaining of even temporary Samadhi (meditation) by any one who is attached to society is impossible; such is the teaching of the kinsman of the Sun; let one, having heard this, walk alone like a rhinoceros.

21.   Thus overcoming those things which injure faith, having attained firmness of mind, and reached the right path, I have indeed arrived at complete knowledge and have nothing left to be known. Let one walk alone like a rhinoceros.

22.   Divested of greediness, deceit, longings, not disparaging others unjustly, in the whole world; released from evil affections and ignorance; desireless, let one walk alone like a rhinoceros.

23. Let one cast away a sinful friend who looks to wicked things, or is established in wicked actions: let the same person associate not with one fond of pleasure, and procrastinating in doing good things. Let him walk alone like a rhinoceros.

24. Let him serve a friend who is very learned, versed in morals, great, and possessed of a quick understanding; having known the real meaning of things, let him remove his doubts and walk alone like a rhinoceros.

25. Indifferent to amusements, lust, and the pleasures of the world; not beautifying oneself, despising ornaments, and speaking the truth, let one walk alone like a rhinoceros.

26. Having abandoned the different kinds of desire, founded on child, wife, father, mother, wealth, corn, relations, let one walk alone like a rhinoceros.

27. Let a wise man, having discovered that such is attachment, that there is in it but little happiness, that it is but insipid, that there is more affliction in it than comfort, that it is a fish-hook, walk alone like a rhinoceros.

28. Having cast off the bonds, like a fish which breaks the net in the water, like a fire that returns not to the spot already burned up, let one walk alone like a rhinoceros.

29. With his eyes looking downward, not moving quickly, with his senses guarded, his mind restrained, not burdened with lust, not burning with desire, let one walk alone like a rhinoceros.

30. Having abandoned the ways of the householder, clothed in yellow robes, like a Parichhatta-tree, which is densely covered with leaves, having given up laymanship, let one walk alone like a rhinoceros.

31. Not being greedy of savory things, not being unsteady, nor maintained by others, begging from house to house without any distinction, not having a mind attached to this or that family, let one walk alone like a rhinoceros.

32. Having cast off the five Nivaranas (evil tendencies) of the mind, having cleared away all the obscurities of the mind, having extinguished the folly of friendship, not allied to anything, let one walk alone like a rhinoceros.

33. Having thrown behind him pleasure and pain, and

first doing away with good and bad intentions, having then secured the middle state, which is pacific and pure, let one walk alone like a rhinoceros.

34. Possessed of courage, persevering in the attainment of Paramattha with a mind not inactive, without living in idleness, resolute in perseverance, endowed with a strong and powerful mind, let one walk alone like a rhinoceros.

35. Looking forward to the extinction of desires, being diligent, not foolish, becoming a good ascetic, endowed with presence of mind, acquainted with justice, observing the rules of the hermits, energetic, let one walk alone like a rhinoceros.

36. Not abandoning the Patisallana meditations, practicing the law daily, remembering the evil consequences of repeated births, let one walk alone like a rhinoceros.

37. Like a lion which fears not noises, unobstructed like the wind whirling through a net, not touching anything like the lotus-leaf untouched by water, let one walk alone like a rhinoceros.

38. As the lion, the king of beasts, powerful from his teeth, lives committing violence and overcoming all, even so let one dwell in hermitages in far-away deserts.

39. In fit time, observe kindness, impartiality, mercy, freedom from sin, and delight at the prosperity of others: unopposed to the whole world, let one walk alone like a rhinoceros.

40. Having abandoned lust, malice, ignorance, having broken the bonds of transmigration, entertaining no fears for the loss of life, let one walk alone like a rhinoceros.

41. Men associate with and serve others for the sake of an object; friends who have no object in view are difficult to obtain. They are wise enough to gain some object for themselves. Men are not pure. Let one walk alone like a rhinoceros.

Chapter XI
THE TEVIGGA SUTTA:
THE BUDDHA AND THE BRAHMANS

As in the confrontation between the Buddha and Assalāyana, presented earlier, we observe in the following, the *Tevigga Sutta*, Gautama arguing against the conception of salvation held by the priests of Brahmanism (Hinduism). He is able to convince the two young Brahmans who have come to question him, Vassettha and Bharadvaga, that since they can have no real knowledge of the God they worship, see him face to face, there is little hope of leading men to union with him. As was his custom, the Buddha did this through the use of analogies. Though he too maintained that union with the Eternal was not only achievable but man's highest purpose, he claimed that it could come about only through a full acceptance of his doctrine, the Noble Eightfold Path to Nirvana.

Then the young brahman, Vasettha, said to the young brahman, Bharadvaga: There is a holy man named Gotama . . . staying in the Mango grove nearby . . . who is of high renown and is even said to be "a fully enlightened One," blessed and worthy, abounding in wisdom and goodness, happy, with knowledge of the world, unsurpassed as a guide to erring mortals, a teacher of gods and men, a blessed Buddha. Come, Bharadvaga, let us go to the place where this Samana Gotama is staying, let us ask him and what he declares let us bear in mind. Very well, assented Bharadvaga.

So these two young brahmans went on to the place where the Blessed One was staying. When they had come there they exchanged with the Blessed One greetings and compliments of friendship and civility and sat down beside him.

When they were thus seated, one spoke up and said to the Blessed One:

"As we were taking exercise, walking up and down, there sprang up a conversation between us as to which was the true path to union with Brahma. . . . Not being able to agree, we decided to refer the dispute to you. . . . Various Brahmans, Gotama, teach various paths to union with Brahma: Is one true and another false, or are all saving paths? . . . Is it like the different roads going toward a village, all of which meet in the center?"

The Blessed One replied: "Vasettha, do you think that all these various paths lead aright?"

"I think so, Gotama."

"Would you be willing to assert that they all lead aright, Vasettha?"

"So I say, Gotama."

"But then, Vasettha, is there a single one of the Brahmans—or of their teachers, their pupils, or their ancestors back to the seventh generation—who has ever seen Brahma face to face?"

"No, indeed, Gotama." . . .

"Well, then, Vasettha, there are the ancient Rishis (*sages*) of the Brahmans; whose words are still chanted, uttered, or composed by the Brahmans of today, and did they ever say: 'We know and have seen where Brahma is, whence Brahma came, wither Brahma goes'?"

"Not so, Gotama." . . .

"And yet, Vasettha, these Brahmans pretend that they can show the path to union with that which they have not seen and which they know not, saying: This is the straight path, this is the direct way, which leads him, who acts according to it, into a state of union with Brahma. Now what think you, Vasettha, does it not follow that the talk of these Brahmans, versed though they be in the Three Vedas, is foolish talk?"

"Yes, Gotama, this being so, it follows that the talk of these Brahmans versed in the Three Vedas is indeed foolish talk."

"Vasettha, it is like a string of blind men clinging to one another, the foremost can not see the way, neither can the middle one, nor the hindmost. Just so, methinks, Vasettha, that the talk of the Brahmans versed in the Three Vedas, is but blind talk. The first sees not, the middle one sees not, the hindmost sees not. The talk, then, of these Brahmans turns out to be ridiculous, mere words, vain and empty. It is as if a man should say, 'How I long for, how I love the most beautiful woman in this land!' And people should ask him, 'Well, good friend! this most beautiful woman in the land whom you thus love and long for, do you know . . . her name, or her family name, whether she is tall or short, dark or of medium complexion, black or fair, or in what village or town or city she dwells?' But when so asked, he should answer, 'I do not know.' And when people should say to him, 'So then, good friend, whom you know not, neither have seen, how do you love and long for her?' And then when so asked, he should answer, 'Nevertheless, I love her.' Now what think you, Vasettha? Would it not turn out that the talk of such a man was foolish talk?"

"In sooth, Gotama, it would be so." . . .

"And just even so, Vasettha, the way to union with Brahma which the Brahmans are proclaiming without having seen Brahma or knowing anything about him, is just as foolish. Is it not so?"

"In sooth, Gotama, it is so." . . .

"Again, Vasettha. If this river Akiravati were full of water even to the brim and overflowing, and a man should come up and want to cross over because he had business on the other side, and he standing on this bank should say, Come hither, O further bank! come over to this side! Now what think you, Vasettha, would the further bank of the river, because of the man's invoking and praying and hoping and praising, come over to this side?"

"Certainly not, Gotama." . . .

"Now, Vasettha, when you have been among Brahmans, listening as they talked among themselves, learners and teachers and those aged and well stricken in years, what have you learned from them and of them? Is Brahma in possession of wives and wealth, or is he not?"

"He is not, Gotama."

"Is his mind full of anger, or is it free from anger?"

"Free from anger, Gotama."

"Is his mind full of malice or free from malice?"

"Free from malice, Gotama."

"Is his mind depraved, or pure?"

"It is pure, Gotama."

"Has he self-mastery, or has he not?"

"He has, Gotama."

"Now what think you, Vasettha? Are the Brahmans in possession of wives and wealth, or are they not?"

"They are, Gotama."

"Have they anger in their hearts?"

"They have, Gotama."

"Do they bear malice, or do they not?"

"They do, Gotama."

"Are they pure in heart or are they not?"

"They are not, Gotama."

"Now you say, Vasettha, that the Brahmans are in possession of wives and wealth, and that Brahma is not. Can there be agreement and likeness between the Brahmans with their wives and property and Brahma who has none of these things?"

"Certainly not, Gotama."

"Very good, Vasettha. But verily, that these Brahmans versed in the Three Vedas, who live married and wealthy should, after death when the body is dissolved, become united with Brahma who has none of these things—such a condition of things is impossible. . . . How can there be concord and likeness between Brahmans and Brahma?"

"There can not be, Gotama." . . .

"So, Vasettha, the Brahmans, versed though they be in the Three Vedas, while they rest in confidence, are really sinking. They think they are crossing over into some happier land, but so sinking they can only arrive at despair. Therefore, the threefold knowledge of the Brahmans in the Vedas is a waterless desert, their knowledge a pathless waste, their knowledge their destruction."

Thereupon the young Brahman Vasettha said to the Blessed One: "It has been told me, Gotama, that you know the way to a state of union with Brahma. Can you teach us?" . . .

"Vasettha, supposing there was a man born in a certain village and who never to this time had left it, and people should ask him the way to this village. Would that man born and brought up there be in any doubt or uncertainty about the way?"

"Certainly not, Gotama. He would be perfectly familiar with every road leading to his native village." . . .

"Even so is it with Tathagata (*Buddha*), when asked about the path which leads to the world of Brahma, there can be neither doubt nor difficulty. For Brahma, the world of Brahma, the path which leadeth to the world of Brahma, I fully know. Yea, I know it even as one who was born there and lives there. . . .

"Know then, Vasettha, that from time to time a Tathagata is born into the world, a fully Enlightened One, blessed and worthy, abounding in wisdom and goodness, happy with knowledge of the worlds, unsurpassed as a guide to erring mortals, a teacher of gods and men, a Blessed Buddha. He thoroughly understands this universe, as though he saw it face to face. . . . The Truth does he proclaim both in its letter and in its spirit, lovely in its origin, lovely in its progress, lovely in its consummation. A higher life doth he make known in all its purity and in all its perfectness. . . .

"Now, Vasettha, how can a man's conduct be good? Herein, O Vasettha, by putting away all unkindness to sentient beings he abstains from destroying life. He lays aside the cudgel and sword and, full of humility and pity, he is compassionate and kind to all creatures that have life. Putting away the desire for things which are not his, he abstains from taking anything that is not freely given him. He has only what has been given him, therewith is he content, and he passes his life in honesty and in purity of heart. Putting away all thoughts of lust, he lives a life of chastity and purity. Putting away all thoughts of deceiving, he abstains from all prevarications; he speaks truthfully, from the truth he never swerves; faithful and trustworthy, he never injures his fellow men by deceit.

"Putting away all judgment of others, he abstains from slander. What he hears he repeats not elsewhere to raise a quarrel; what he hears elsewhere he repeats not here to raise a quarrel. Thus he brings together those who are divided, he encourages those who are friendly; he is a peacemaker, a lover of peace, impassioned for peace, a speaker of words that make for peace. Putting away all bitter thoughts, he abstains from harsh language. Whatever is humane, pleasant to the ear, kindly, reaching to the heart, urbane, acceptable to the people, appreciated by the people—such are the words he speaks. Putting away all foolish thoughts, he abstains from vain conversation. He speaks in season, he speaks truthfully, consistently, wisely, with restraint. He speaks only when it is appropriate for him to speak, words that are profitable, well sustained, well defined, full of wisdom.

"Besides being kind to all animate life, he refrains from injuring insects or even herbs. He takes but one meal a day; abstaining from food at all other times. He abstains from attending dances, concerts and theatrical shows. He abstains from wearing, using or adorning himself with garlands, scents and ointments, he abstains from large and soft beds. He abstains from accumulating silver or gold, from coveting great harvests, herds of cattle; he abstains from the getting of maids and women attendants, slaves either men or women; he abstains from gathering herds of sheep or goats, fowls or swine, elephants, cattle, horses, and mares. He abstains from the getting of fields and lands.

"He refrains from accepting commissions to carry messages, he refrains from all buying and selling, he abstains from the use of all trade deceptions, false weights, alloyed metals, false measures. He abstains from all bribery, cheating, fraud and crooked ways. He refrains from all banditry, killing or maiming, abducting, highway robbery, plundering villages, or obtaining money by threats of violence. These are the kinds of goodness he practices. . . .

"The true ascetic, he who is seeking the way to the Brahma World, lets his mind pervade all quarters of the world with thoughts of Love; first one quarter then the second quarter, then the third quarter and so the fourth quarter. And thus the whole wide world, above, below, around, and everywhere, does he continue to pervade with thoughts of love, far-reaching, beyond measure, all-embracing.

"Just, Vasettha, as a mighty trumpeter makes himself heard—and that without difficulty—in all four directions; even so of all things that have form or life, there is not one that he passes by or leaves aside; he regards them all with mind set free and filled with deep-felt love. Verily, Vasettha, this is the way to a state of union with Brahma. . . .

"Now what think you, Vasettha, will the ascetic be in possession of women and wealth, or will he not?"

"He will not, Gotama."

"Will he be full of anger, or will he be free from anger?"

"He will be free from anger, Gotama."

"Will his mind be full of malice, or free from malice?"

"Free from malice, Gotama."

"Will his mind be lustful or pure?"

"It will be pure, Gotama."

"Will he have self-mastery or will he not?"

"Surely he will, Gotama."

"Vasettha . . . is there then agreement and likeness between such a one and Brahma?"

"There is, Gotama."

"Very good, Vasettha!" . . .

And when the Blessed One had thus spoken, the two young Brahmans, Vasettha and Bharadvaga, addressed the Blessed One, saying:

"Most excellent, Lord, the words of thy mouth are most excellent! It is just as if a man were to set up what was thrown down, or to reveal that which was hidden away, or were to point out the right road to him who has gone astray, or were to bring a lamp into the darkness so that those who have eyes can see: just even so, Lord, the truth has been made known to us by the Blessed One. And we betake ourselves, Lord, to the Blessed One, to the Truth, and to the Brotherhood, as our refuge. May the Blessed One accept us as disciples, as true believers, from this day forth, as long as life shall last."

Chapter XII
MONKS AND LAY FOLLOWERS

The *Vinaya-pitaka*, first of the threefold division of the Tripi-taka, consists mainly of rules and directions governing not only daily life but spiritual development in the Sangha. The first four selections which follow are meant to give some idea of one aspect of the life of Buddhist monks. The first, the *Pātimokkha*, is delivered by the presiding monk at the fortnightly fast-day gatherings, and is self-explanatory, as are the "Moralities" which follow it and to which it in part refers. Next comes the "Concentration Leading to Samādhi (mind control): the Four Trances," then a similar description of the "Eight Stages of Release" resulting from Samādhi. The final selection, from the *Vyaggahapajja* and the *Sigalovada Sutta*, gives Gautama's instructions to the laymen—"Duties of the Lay Followers"—who were also expected to repeat on various occasions the "Three Jewels" or the "Triple Refuge":

> I go to the Buddha for refuge.
> I go to the Doctrine for refuge.
> I go to the Sangha for refuge.

Additionally the laymen were expected to keep the "Five Precepts," namely refraining from killing, stealing, unlawful sexual indulgence, bad speech, and drinking liquor.

THE PĀTIMOKKHA

Let the Assembly, reverend ones, hear me. To-day is the Uposatha of the fifteenth day. If it appears the right time to the Assembly, let the Assembly perform the Uposatha and repeat the Pātimokkha. How is it with regard to the necessary preliminaries for the Assembly? Reverend ones, announce your purity (freedom from disability). I will repeat the Pātimokkha.—We are all listening well and reflecting on it.— He who has incurred a fault should declare it; if there is no fault he should keep silence. Now by your silence, reverend sirs, I shall know that you are pure. Now as there is a reply for each question, so in such a meeting as this it is proclaimed as many as three times. Now should a monk, when it is proclaimed three times, remember a fault that he has committed and not declare it, he is guilty of a conscious falsehood. Now a conscious falsehood, reverend sirs, has been declared by the Lord to be a hindrance (to advance). Therefore a monk who remembers that he had committed a fault, and wishes to be pure, should declare the fault committed, for when declared it will be easy for him (to advance).

The introduction, reverend sirs, has been repeated. So, I ask the reverend ones, are you pure in this matter? A second time I ask, are you pure in this matter? A third time I ask, are you pure in this matter? The reverend ones are pure in this matter, therefore they are silent. Even so I understand it.

THE MORALITIES

He abandons the killing of living things, lays aside the use of a stick or a knife, and full of pity he dwells with compassion for the welfare of all living things.

He abandons the taking of what is not given, takes and expects only what is given, and lives without thieving.

He abandons incontinence and lives apart, avoiding sex intercourse.

He abandons falsehood, and speaks the truth.

He abandons slanderous speech, and does not tell what he has heard in one place to cause dissension elsewhere. He

233

heals divisions and encourages friendships, delighting in concord and speaking what produces it.

He abandons harsh speech, his speech is blameless, pleasant to the ear, reaching the heart, urbane and attractive to the multitude.

He abandons frivolous language, speaks duly and truly and in accordance with the Dhamma and Vinaya. His speech is such as to be remembered, elegant, clear, and to the point.

Then follow a number of rules applying especially to his life as monk.

He abandons injuring seeds or plants.

He eats once at one meal-time, and not at all at night, avoiding unseasonable food.

He abandons the seeing of dancing, singing, music, and shows.

He abandons using and adorning himself with garlands, scents, and unguents.

He abandons the use of a high or big bed.

He abandons the accepting of gold and silver.

The other rules in this section specify the abandoning of various kinds of property, kinds of food (raw grain, raw meat), acting as a go-between, cheating, bribery, fraud, and various acts of violence.

CONCENTRATION LEADING TO SAMĀDHI: THE FOUR TRANCES

When he sees in himself these five hindrances expelled, exultation arises, as he exults joy arises, as his mind feels joy his body becomes serene and feels pleasure, and as it feels pleasure his mind is concentrated. Free from the passions and evil thoughts he attains and abides in the first trance of pleasure with joy, which is accompanied by reasoning and investigation and arises from seclusion. He suffuses, fills, and permeates his body with the pleasure and joy arising from seclusion, and there is nothing in his body untouched by this pleasure and joy arising from seclusion.

Again, with the ceasing of reasoning and investigation, in a state of internal serenity, with his mind fixed on one point, he attains and abides in the second trance of pleasure with joy produced by concentration, without reasoning and investigation. He suffuses, fills, and permeates his body with the pleasure and joy produced by concentration, and there is nothing in his body untouched by it.

Again, with equanimity towards joy and aversion, he abides mindful and conscious, and experiences the pleasure that the noble ones call "dwelling with equanimity, mindful, and happy", and attains and abides in the third trance. He suffuses, fills, and permeates his body with pleasure, without joy, and there is nothing in his body untouched by it.

Again, abandoning pleasure and pain, even before the disappearance of elation and depression he attains and abides in the fourth trance, which is without pain and pleasure, and with the purity of mindfulness and equanimity. He sits permeating his body with mind purified and cleansed, and there is nothing in his body untouched by it.

THE EIGHT STAGES OF RELEASE

1. Possessing form (material shape) he sees forms.
2. Not perceiving forms internally he sees forms.
3. He is intent only on the thought "it is well".
4. Passing entirely beyond perceptions of form, with the disappearance of perceptions of resistance, not attending to perceptions of diversity, (he perceives) "space is infinite", and attains and abides in the stage of the infinity of space.
5. Passing entirely beyond the stage of the infinity of space, (he perceives) "consciousness is infinite", and attains and abides in the stage of the infinity of consciousness.
6. Passing entirely beyond the stage of the infinity of consciousness, (he perceives) "there is nothing", and attains and abides in the stage of nothingness.
7. Passing entirely beyond the stage of nothingness, he

attains and abides in the stage of neither consciousness nor non-consciousness.

8. Passing entirely beyond the stage of neither consciousness nor non-consciousness, he attains and abides in the stage of the cessation of perception and feeling.

DUTIES OF THE LAY FOLLOWERS

Four requisites for earning wealth: dauntless energy in wealth, mindfulness in keeping what is earned, simple living, and keeping company with good people.

Four bad actions to be avoided: killing, stealing, unlawful sexual indulgence, and falsehood.

Four ways of doing injustice to be avoided: doing injustice due to partiality, or due to hatred, or due to fear, or due to ignorance (that is, through deception).

Six things leading to loss of wealth which are to be avoided: addiction to drinking liquor, to walking in the streets at untimely hours, to visiting feasts, to gambling, to bad companions, or to laziness.

Ministry to parents: a child should minister to his parents by supporting them, doing his duties, continuing the family line, acting in such a way as to be worthy of his inheritance, and offering alms in honor of the departed parents.

Ministry of parents to their children: restraining them from the bad, exhorting them to do good, giving them a good education, arranging a suitable marriage in due time, handing over the inheritance to them at the proper time.

Ministry of students to teachers: rising before the teacher, attending to the needs of the teacher, listening attentively, doing personal service to the teacher, and carefully receiving instruction.

Ministry of teachers to students: giving the students the best training, showing them how to grasp things well, teaching them suitable arts and science, introducing them to their friends and companions, keeping them safe in every way.

Ministry of husband to wife: honoring her, avoiding disrespect, being faithful to her, entrusting his treasure to her custody, providing her with garments and ornaments.

Ministry of wife to husband: doing her duties in perfect order, treating the friends and relatives of her husband generously and hospitably, being faithful to him, protecting carefully the treasure entrusted to her, and doing all her duties diligently.

Ministry to friends and companions: showing generosity, speaking courteously, promoting good, treating them with equality, and being truthful to them.

Ministry of friends and companions in return: looking after him when he is careless, safeguarding his property when he is negligent, rendering assistance when he is in trouble, and protecting his children and advancing their welfare.

Ministry to servants and employees: apportioning work to them according to their strength, providing them with food and wages, tending them in sickness, sharing special dainties with them, and giving them rest and holidays at the proper times.

Ministry of servants and employees to their master: rising before him, going to sleep after him, taking only what is given, carrying out his orders promptly and with pleasure, and giving him a good report.

Ministry to members of the Sangha: speaking to them with affection, showing friendliness in deed, thinking of them respectfully, being generous in supplying their wants readily, providing them with their material needs.

Ministry of members of the Sangha to a lay devotee: dissuading him from evil, exhorting him to the good, loving him with a kind heart, teaching him what he has not heard and making clear what he has already heard, pointing out to him the path to a happy state.

Chapter XIII
EMPEROR ASHOKA: THE EDICTS

Ashoka Maurya, who was to become the first great Buddhist patron and ruler of India, succeeded by craft and murder to the throne of Magadha about 270 B.C. Eight years later he conquered Kalinga, modern Orissa, slaughtering 100,000, deporting 150,000, and spreading famine and pestilence which destroyed many more. Then came what must be seen as one of the most astonishing turnabouts in recorded history. Feeling guilt at the spectacle of so much suffering, the Emperor of the whole of India, except for the extreme south, embraced Buddhism. All this, and more, is described in the "Thirteenth Rock Edict" which follows along with other of the Edicts, all of which are concerned with ethical conduct. Establishing goodness through law, Ashoka speaks with firm, almost parental authority in the Edicts, stressing religious tolerance, reverence to the aged and the deserving, such as teachers, the sanctity of animal life (he even prohibited castration), and the cultivation of truthfulness and compassion. Wanting to share the gift of his newly acquired philosophy with others, Ashoka dispatched imperial missionaries to all parts of India, and to Ceylon, Syria, Egypt, Macedonia, etc. Thus it was chiefly through his powerful influence that the doctrine became predominant in Asia. The Edicts were engraved on stone, some on monolithic pillars, and many survive, the finest being the pillar discovered some years ago at Sārnāth on the site of the old deer park at Benares, where the Buddha preached his first sermon.

FROM THE THIRTEENTH ROCK EDICT

When the king, Beloved of the Gods and of Gracious Mien, had been consecrated eight years Kalinga was conquered, 150,000 people were deported, 100,000 were killed, and many times that number died. But after the conquest of Kalinga, the Beloved of the Gods began to follow Righteousness (Dharma), to love Righteousness, and to give instruction in Righteousness. Now the Beloved of the Gods regrets the conquest of Kalinga, for when an independent country is conquered people are killed, they die, or are deported, and that the Beloved of the Gods finds very painful and grievous. And this he finds even more grievous—that all the inhabitants —brāhmans, ascetics, and other sectarians, and householders who are obedient to superiors, parents, and elders, who treat friends, acquaintances, companions, relatives, slaves, and servants with respect, and are firm in their faith—all suffer violence, murder, and separation from their loved ones. Even those who are fortunate enough not to have lost those near and dear to them are afflicted at the misfortunes of friends, acquaintances, companions, and relatives. The participation of all men in common suffering is grievous to the Beloved of the Gods. Moreover there is no land, except that of the Greeks, where groups of brāhmans and ascetics are not found, or where men are not members of one sect or another. So now, even if the number of those killed and captured in the conquest of Kalinga had been a hundred or a thousand times less, it would be grievous to the Beloved of the Gods. The Beloved of the Gods will forgive as far as he can, and he even conciliates the forest tribes of his dominions; but he warns them that there is power even in the remorse of the Beloved of the Gods, and he tells them to reform, lest they be killed.

For all beings the Beloved of the Gods desires security, self-control, calm of mind, and gentleness. The Beloved of the Gods considers that the greatest victory is the victory of

Righteousness; and this he has won here (in India) and even five hundred leagues beyond his frontiers in the realm of the Greek king Antiochus, and beyond Antiochus among the four kings Ptolemy, Antigonus, Magas, and Alexander. Even where the envoys of the Beloved of the Gods have not been sent men hear of the way in which he follows and teaches Righteousness, and they too follow it and will follow it. Thus he achieves a universal conquest, and conquest always gives a feeling of pleasure; yet it is but a slight pleasure, for the Beloved of the Gods only looks on that which concerns the next life as of great importance.

I have had this inscription of Righteousness engraved that all my sons and grandsons may not seek to gain new victories, that in whatever victories they may gain they may prefer forgiveness and light punishment, that they may consider the only [valid] victory the victory of Righteousness, which is of value both in this world and the next, and that all their pleasure may be in Righteousness. . . .

FROM A MINOR ROCK EDICT (MASKI VERSION)

Thus speaks Ashoka, the Beloved of the Gods. For two and a half years I have been an open follower of the Buddha, though at first I did not make much progress. But for more than a year now I have drawn closer to the [Buddhist] Order, and have made much progress. In India the gods who formerly did not mix with men now do so. This is the result of effort, and may be obtained not only by the great, but even by the small, through effort—thus they may even easily win heaven.

Father and mother should be obeyed, teachers should be obeyed; pity . . . should be felt for all creatures. These virtues of Righteousness should be practiced. . . . This is an ancient rule, conducive to long life.

FROM THE SECOND ROCK EDICT

Everywhere in the empire of the Beloved of the Gods, and even beyond his frontiers in the lands of the Cholas, Pāndyas, Satyaputras, Keralaputras, and as far as Ceylon, and in the kingdoms of Antiochus the Greek king and the kings who are his neighbors, the Beloved of the Gods has provided medicines for man and beast. Wherever medicinal plants have not been found they have been sent there and planted. Roots and fruits have also been sent where they did not grow, and have been planted. Wells have been dug along the roads for the use of man and beast.

FROM THE SIXTH ROCK EDICT

I am not satisfied simply with hard work or carrying out the affairs of state, for I consider my work to be the welfare of the whole world, of which hard work and the carrying out of affairs are merely the basis. There is no better deed than to work for the welfare of the whole world, and all my efforts are made that I may clear my debt to all beings. I make them happy here and now that they may attain heaven in the life to come. . . . But it is difficult without great effort.

FROM THE FIRST SEPARATE KALINGA EDICT

By order of the Beloved of the Gods. Addressed to the officers in charge of Tosali. . . . Let us win the affection of all men. All men are my children, and as I wish all welfare and happiness in this world and the next for my own children, so do I wish it for all men. But you do not realize what this entails—here and there an officer may understand in part, but not entirely.

Often a man is imprisoned and tortured unjustly, and then he is liberated for no [apparent] reason. Many other people suffer also [as a result of this injustice]. Therefore it is desirable that you should practice impartiality, but it cannot be attained if you are inclined to habits of jealousy, irritability, harshness, hastiness, obstinacy, laziness, or lassitude. I desire you not to have these habits. The basis of all this is the constant avoidance of irritability and hastiness in your business. . . .

This inscription has been engraved in order that the officials of the city should always see to it that no one is ever imprisoned or tortured without good cause. To ensure this I shall send out every five years on a tour of inspection officers who are not fierce or harsh. . . . The prince at Ujjain shall do the same not more than every three years, and likewise at Taxila.

FROM THE FOURTH PILLAR EDICT

My governors are placed in charge of hundreds of thousands of people. Under my authority they have power to judge and to punish, that they calmly and fearlessly carry out their duties, and that they may bring welfare and happiness to the people of the provinces and be of help to them. They will know what brings joy and what brings sorrow, and, conformably to Righteousness, they will instruct the people of the provinces that they may be happy in this world and the next. . . . And as when one entrusts a child to a skilled nurse one is confident that . . . she will care for it well, so have I appointed my governors for the welfare and happiness of the people. That they may fearlessly carry out their duties I have given them power to judge and to inflict punishment on their own initiative. I wish that there should be uniformity of justice and punishment.

FROM THE EIGHTH ROCK EDICT

In the past kings went out on pleasure trips and indulged in hunting and similar amusements. But the Beloved of the Gods . . . ten years after his consecration set out on the journey to Enlightenment. Now when he goes on tour . . . he interviews and gives gifts to brāhmans and ascetics; he interviews and gives money to the aged; he interviews the people of the provinces, and instructs and questions them on Righteousness; and the pleasure which the Beloved of the Gods derives therefrom is as good as a second revenue.

FROM THE TWELFTH ROCK EDICT

The Beloved of the Gods . . . honors members of all sects, whether ascetics or householders, by gifts and various honors. But he does not consider gifts and honors as important as the furtherance of the essential message of all sects. This essential message varies from sect to sect, but it has one common basis, that one should so control one's tongue as not to honor one's own sect or disparage another's on the wrong occasions; for on certain occasions one should do so only mildly, and indeed on other occasions one should honor other men's sects. By doing this one strengthens one's own sect and helps the others, while by doing otherwise one harms one's own sect and does a disservice to the others. Whoever honors his own sect and disparages another man's, whether from blind loyalty or with the intention of showing his own sect in a favorable light, does his own sect the greatest possible harm. Concord is best, with each hearing and respecting the other's teachings. It is the wish of the Beloved of the Gods that members of all sects should be learned and should teach virtue. . . . Many officials are busied in this matter . . . and the result is the progress of my own sect and the illumination of Righteousness.

FROM THE NINTH ROCK EDICT

People perform various ceremonies, at the marriage of sons and daughters, at the birth of children, when going on a journey . . . or on other occasions. . . . On such occasions women especially perform many ceremonies which are various, futile, and useless. Even when they have to be done [to conform to custom and keep up appearances] such ceremonies are of little use. But the ceremonies of Righteousness are of great profit—these are the good treatment of slaves and servants, respect for elders, self-mastery in one's relations with living beings, gifts to brāhmans and ascetics, and so on. But for their success everyone—fathers, mothers, brothers, masters, friends, acquaintances, and neighbors—must agree—"These are good! These are the ceremonies that we should perform for success in our undertakings . . . and when we have succeeded we will perform them again!" Other ceremonies are of doubtful utility—one may achieve one's end through them or one may not. Moreover they are only of value in this world, while the value of the ceremonies of Righteousness is eternal, for even if one does not achieve one's end in this world one stores up boundless merit in the other, while if one achieves one's end in this world the gain is double.

FROM THE SEVENTH PILLAR EDICT

In the past kings sought to make the people progress in Righteousness, but they did not progress. . . . And I asked myself how I might uplift them through progress in Righteousness. . . . Thus I decided to have them instructed in Righteousness, and to issue ordinances of Righteousness, so that by hearing them the people might conform, advance in the progress of Righteousness, and themselves make great progress. . . . For that purpose many officials are employed among the people to instruct them in Righteousness and to explain it to them. . . .

Moreover I have had banyan trees planted on the roads to give shade to man and beast; I have planted mango groves, and I have had ponds dug and shelters erected along the roads at every eight kos. Everywhere I have had wells dug for the benefit of man and beast. But this benefit is but small, for in many ways the kings of olden time have worked for the welfare of the world; but what I have done has been done that men may conform to Righteousness.

All the good deeds that I have done have been accepted and followed by the people. And so obedience to mother and father, obedience to teachers, respect for the aged, kindliness to brāhmans and ascetics, to the poor and weak, and to slaves and servants, have increased and will continue to increase. . . . And this progress of Righteousness among men has taken place in two manners, by enforcing conformity to Righteousness, and by exhortation. I have enforced the law against killing certain animals and many others, but the greatest progress of Righteousness among men comes from exhortation in favor of noninjury to life and abstention from killing living beings.

I have done this that it may endure . . . as long as the moon and sun, and that my sons and my great-grandsons may support it; for by supporting it they will gain both this world and the next.

Chapter XIV
FROM THE DĪPAVAMSA

The following brief selection from the *Dīpavamsa*, the last
Pāli work to be represented in this volume and one of the
two verse chronicles of Ceylon history, the other being the
Mahāvamsa, concerns the Great Council of seven hundred
monks (Mahāsangīti) which took place at Vaisali one hundred and ten years after the Buddha's death (it was the
second Council, the first having convened at Rajagriha immediately after the Buddha's Nirvana, with the Venerable
Kasyapa presiding). The Great Council was both brought
about by, and contributed to, a schism in the Buddhist Church
and the secession of the Mahāsanghikas which, like the
Sarvāstivādins, were an early school of the Theravada. Parts
of the Mahāsanghika Canon and its other scriptures were to
survive the Muhammadan invasion of India, and such works
as the *Mahāvastu* and the *Lalitavistara* belong to this school.
Asvaghosha, the Sanskrit poet, some of whose work has already been presented and more follows, was a Mahāsanghika.
In a number of ways this school forms a bridge between the
Theravada and the Mahayana, which is why an account of
some of the proceedings at the Council which brought it
into prominence is given at this point.

The monks of the Great Council twisted the teaching round.
They broke up the original scriptures and made a new
  recension,
A chapter put in one place they put in another,
And distorted the sense and the doctrine of the Five
  Nikāyas.

These monks—who knew neither what had been spoken at
 length
Nor what had been spoken in abstract, neither
What was the obvious nor what the higher meaning—
Put things referring to one matter as if they referred to an-
 other,
And destroyed much of the spirit by holding to the shadow
 of the letter.
They partly rejected the Sutta, and the Vinaya so deep,
And made another rival Sutta and Vinaya of their own.
The Parivāra abstract, and the book of the Abhidhamma,
The Paṭisambhidā, the Niddesa, and a portion of the Jātaka,
So much they put aside, and made others in their place.
They rejected the well known rules of nouns and genders too,
Of composition and of literary skill, and put others in their
 place.

Chapter XV
ASVAGHOSHA

We have already seen from Asvaghosha's *Buddha-Karita*, the sole non-Pāli selection in the foregoing (what follows is from the Sanskrit, Tibetan, Chinese, Japanese, and Lao), that this Sanskrit writer would have been considered an important religious poet in any age. He was also a philosopher, and in the *Mahāyāna-sraddha-utpadda* (Awakening of Faith in the Mahayana), a selection from which is given here, he deals with the doctrines of the Tathāgata-garbha and Ālaya-vijñāna after the manner of the Yogāvaracāras and Asanga, who is represented in this volume. This work, which is not known in the Sanskrit original and was translated into the Chinese as late as the sixth century, examines in depth the concept of Suchness, or the "oneness of the totality of things," a doctrine of great significance to Mahayana metaphysics generally but especially to the Sūnyatā philosophy of Nāgārjuna's Mādhyamika school, to be considered later.

THE DOCTRINE OF SUCHNESS

In the one soul we may distinguish two aspects. The one is the soul as suchness, the other is the soul as birth-and-death. Each in itself constitutes all things, and both are so closely interrelated that one cannot be separated from the other.

What is meant by the soul as suchness is the oneness of the totality of things, the great all-including whole, the quintessence of the doctrine. For the essential nature of the soul is uncreate and eternal.

Therefore all things in their fundamental nature are not

nameable or explicable. They cannot be adequately expressed in any form of language. They are without the range of apperception. They are universals. They have no signs of distinction. They possess absolute sameness. They are subject neither to transformation, nor to destruction. They are nothing but the one soul, for which suchness is another designation. Therefore they cannot be fully explained by words or exhausted by reasoning.

In the essence of suchness, there is neither anything which has to be excluded, nor anything which has to be added.

The soul as birth-and-death comes forth (as the law of causation) from the Tathagata's womb. But the immortal (i.e., suchness) and the mortal (i.e., birth-and-death) coincide with each other. Though they are not identical, they are not a duality. Thus when the absolute soul assumes a relative aspect by its self-affirmation it is called the all-conserving mind.

The same mind has a twofold significance as the organizer and the producer of all things.

Again it embraces two principles: (1) enlightenment; (2) non-enlightenment.

Enlightenment is the highest quality of the mind. As it is free from all limiting attributes of subjectivity, it is like unto space, penetrating everywhere, as the unity of all. That is to say, it is the universal Dharmakaya of all Tathagatas.

The multitude of people are said to be lacking in enlightenment, because ignorance prevails there from all eternity, because there is a constant succession of confused subjective states from which they have never been emancipated.

But when they transcend their subjectivity, they can then recognize that all states of mentation, viz., their appearance, presence, change, and disappearance (in the field of consciousness) have no genuine reality. They are neither in a temporal nor in a spatial relation with the one soul, for they are not self-existent.

When you understand this, you also understand that enlightenment in appearance cannot be manufactured, for it is no other thing than enlightenment in its suchness, which is uncreate and must be discovered.

To illustrate: a man who is lost goes astray because he is bent on pursuing a certain direction; and his confusion has no valid foundation other than that he is bent on a certain direction.

It is even the same with all beings. They become unenlightened, foster their subjectivity and go astray, because they are bent on enlightenment.

While the essence of the mind is eternally clean and pure, the influence of ignorance makes possible the existence of a defiled mind. But in spite of the defiled mind, the mind itself is eternal, clear, pure, and not subject to transformation.

When the oneness of the totality of things is not recognized, then ignorance as well as particularization arises, and all phases of the defiled mind are thus developed. But the significance of this doctrine is so extremely deep and unfathomable that it can be fully comprehended by Buddhas and by no others.

When the mind is disturbed, it fails to be a true and adequate knowledge; it fails to be a pure, clean essence; it fails to be eternal, blissful, self-regulating, and pure; it fails to be tranquil. On the contrary, it will become transient, changeable, unfree, and therefore the source of falsity and defilement, while its modifications outnumber the sands of the Ganges. But when there is no disturbance in the essence of the mind, we speak of suchness as being the true, adequate knowledge, and as possessing pure and clean merits that outnumber the sands of the Ganges.

When the mind is disturbed it will strive to become conscious of the existence of an external world and will thus betray the imperfection of its inner condition. But as all infinite merits in fact constitute the one mind which, perfect in itself, has no need of seeking after any external things other than itself, so suchness never fails to actualize all those Buddha-dharmas, that, outnumbering the sands of the Ganges, can be said to be neither identical nor non-identical with the essence of the mind, and that therefore are utterly out of the range of our comprehension. On that account suchness is designated the Tathagata's womb or the Tathagata's Dharmakaya.

The body has infinite forms. The form has infinite attributes. The attribute has infinite excellencies. And the accompanying rewards of Bodhisattvas, that is, the region where they are predestined to be born by their previous karma, also has infinite merits and ornamentations. Manifesting itself everywhere, the body of Bliss is infinite, boundless, limitless, unintermittent in its action, directly coming forth from the mind.

Chapter XVI
FROM THE MAHĀVASTU

The *Mahāvastu* (Book of Great Events), an extremely long work of mixed Sanskrit, is the so-called first book of the *Vinaya-pitaka* of the heretical Lokottaravāda branch of the Mahāsanghikas, already discussed as the school forming a bridge between the Theravada and the Mahayana, which regarded the Buddha as a supernatural being, his career being presented as a series of miracles. There is much in this first- or second-century work (its date is disputed) that is clearly Mahayanist, including a description of the Ten Stations (*bhūmis*) of the Buddha, hymns to him, and so on. I have chosen to represent the *Mahāvastu* rather than the more important *Lalitavistara* (History of the Play of the Buddha), on which Sir Edwin Arnold based his influential poem *The Light of Asia*, because the latter is in the main another Buddha biography. What follows is an account of the conversion of Sāriputra, from the last of the three volumes of the *Mahāvastu.*

So the reverend Upasēna having dressed himself in the morning, having put on his cloak and taken his alms bowl he started out towards Rājagṛha to beg for his food. And the religious Sāriputra caught sight of the reverend Upasēna at a distance coming towards him with a charming way of coming forward and backward, of looking ahead and in back, of extending and withdrawing his arms, of wearing his robes and carrying his bowl as a worthy man who has accomplished his task, with his talents all turned inward, with his spirit meditative, strong, in conformity to the Law, his eyes fixed on the ground at the distance of a yoke before him. And having seen him he felt his soul made completely serene: "In truth the bearing of this monk is attractive; I must absolutely speak to him."

And so the religious Śāriputra approached the reverend Upasēna and, having come close, after having exchanged courteous greetings and a friendly conversation was engaged he remained beside him. Standing beside him the religious Śāriputra said to the reverend Upasēna: "Is your Lordship a master or a disciple?" "I am only a disciple, O reverend." "If it is so, what doctrine does your master teach? What does he preach? And how does he teach his disciples the Law? What do his precepts and his instructions consist in? You must explain it all to me." "I am not learned: it is only of the spirit of the doctrine that I can talk to the reverend." At these words the religious Śāriputra said to the reverend Upasēna:

"It is the spirit which interests me; why attach such importance to the letter?

"It is he who understands the spirit who reaps its benefit,

It is by the spirit that he realizes the price
And we too, after having absorbed
During many days all this collection
Of futile texts and words,
We have each time been previously disappointed."

After these words the reverend Upasēna said to the religious Śāriputra:

"After having shown the phenomena are from a cause the Master indicates its cessation." And then, in truth, the pure and unclouded vision of the Law came to the religious Śāriputra on the spot as he stood there.

And then having understood the Law and rejected the false doctrines, his expectations fulfilled, his doubts dispelled, his thought softened and made active, all his being bending towards Nirvāna, he said to the reverend Upasēna: "Reverend Upasēna, where does your master reside?" "The Master? In the Bamboo Grove, in the field of Kalanda." And having thus spoken the reverend Upasēna continued on his way to the city of Rājagṛha to beg for his food.

The religious Śāriputra went to where the religious Maudgalyāyana was; and the latter saw him coming from a distance with a fresh complexion the color of the lotus and a completely serene morale; and having seen him he said to him: "Fresh and clear is Śāriputra's complexion and his morale is completely serene. Would it be that you have discovered the absence of death and the way leading to it? As a full-blown lotus the material of your robe is fresh and clear and your morale is appeased. Have you somewhere been granted the absence of death, that an aura twice as brilliant radiates from your person?"

"The absence of death, reverend Maudgalyāyana, I have found as well as the way which leads there! He who, say the books, manifests himself as rarely as the flower of the *Ficus glomerata* in the forest, the Buddha, this mass of splendor, He has manifested himself, He, the torch of the world."

At these words the religious Maudgalyāyana said to the religious Śāriputra: "What is the doctrine of the Master? What is his sermon?" To these words Śāriputra answered Maudgalyāyana:

"The phenomena which are born of a cause,
The Predestined One has told of the cause,
He has also told of its cessation:
Such is the doctrine of the Great Sage."

And then, in truth, for the religious Maudgalyāyana, on the spot, such as he stood the pure and unclouded vision of the Law came to him. And then having understood the Law and rejected the false doctrines, his expectations fulfilled, his doubts dismissed, his thought softened, his thought active, and all his propensities seeking Nirvāna, he said to Śāriputra. "Where does the Master reside, O Reverend?" "Reverend, the Master resides in the Bamboo Park, in the field of Kalanda, among a great community of monks, with twelve hundred and fifty monks. Let us go and find the Master in the Bamboo Park after we have invited Sañjayin, and before the Blessed One we shall practice the religious Life." To this Maudgalyāyana said to Śāriputra: "Let us go straight from here to the Bamboo Park; why bother to go and see that false doctor, Sañjayin?" "Not at all, O Reverend Maudgaly-āyana; Sañjayin has not failed us; for it is because of him that we left home."

And so both having gone to the hermitage, they invited Sañjayin, saying: "Let us go to the Blessed One, the great Teacher, to practice the religious life." At these words the religious Sañjayin said to them: "Do not go to the Ascetic Gautama to practice the religious life. I have here five hundred disciples who belong to me: you will guide half of them." "The Law and discipline are well taught by the Blessed One. With him success is in sight and all veils are lifted. We have had enough of waiting in vain for the satisfaction of our aspirations." And so after having invited Sañjayin, they left his hermitage and went towards the Bamboo Park and the five hundred religious went with them while Sañjayin cried out: "It is not one or two or three or four, it is the whole five hundred that Upatiśya takes with him!"

And the Blessed One in the Bamboo Park turned to his monks and said: "Prepare seats, O Monks, for the religious Śāriputra and Maudgalyāyana are coming with a procession of five hundred to practice the religious life near the Pre-destined One. They will be among my disciples the head pair, the fortunate pair; one the leader of those with great intelligence; the other the leader of those with magic powers."

Chapter XVII
MAHAYANA SUTRAS

It is next to impossible even to suggest in an anthology the range and variety of Mahayana sutra literature, selections from which follow, yet an attempt must be made. Though there is no Mahayana canon as such, there are a number of works which are honored by all the sects, foremost among them the late second-century sutra, the *Saddharmapundarīka* (Lotus of the Good Law). In this work the Buddha is a god above all others, and Buddhism thus loses its historical dependency. The sutra is more drama than narrative, a series of dialogues and numerous parables, all of which celebrate the Buddha's glory. It is the chief work of the T'ien-t'ai (Tendai in Japanese), the only surviving Buddhist sect in China, as well as the Japanese Nichiren sect, whose founder, Nichiren, declared it to be the final revelation of truth. Earlier and equally popular sutras deal with *Prajñāpārimitā* (Perfect Wisdom), among them the *Vajracchedikā* (Diamond Cutter) and the *Hridaya* (Heart Sutra), both probably written about 350. Forty-nine of the most authoritative sutras were combined in a collection called *Ratnakūta* (Jewel Peak), among them the *Vimalakīrti*, part of which is given, a work of major importance to Far Eastern Buddhism. There are but fragments available in English of some of the larger sutras like the *Suvarnaprabhāsa* (Golden Splendor), *Samādhirājā* (King of the Concentrations), *Mahāparinirvāna* (Great Decease), and the *Śūrangama* (Japanese for the Chinese classic *Shou ling yen*), a work of Mahayana philosophy. I include a fragment of the *Viçeṣacinta-brahmaparipṛccha*, of which three Chinese translations were made between 265 and 517, and a more substantial selection from

the *Avatamsaka,* which teaches the doctrine of the Absolute
Buddha, the Trikaya, and the Ten Stages of Boddhisattva-
hood, and is of the greatest significance to a number of
sects, including the Zen. The chapter concludes with a discussion of the nature of Nirvana, from the Lankāvatāra Sutra.

A. FROM THE LOTUS OF THE GOOD LAW

1. THE LOST SON

A man parted from his father and went to another city;
and he dwelt there many years. . . . The father grew rich
and the son poor. While the son wandered in all directions
[begging] in order to get food and clothes, the father moved
to another land, where he lived in great luxury, . . . wealthy
from business, money-lending, and trade. In course of time
the son, wandering in search of his living through town and
country, came to the city in which his father dwelled. Now
the poor man's father . . . forever thought of the son whom
he had lost . . . years ago, but he told no one of this, though
he grieved inwardly, and thought: "I am old, and well advanced in years, and though I have great possessions I have
no son. Alas that time should do its work upon me, and that
all this wealth should perish unused! . . . It would be bliss
indeed if my son might enjoy all my wealth!"

Then the poor man, in search of food and clothing, came
to the rich man's home. And the rich man was sitting in
great pomp at the gate of his house, surrounded by a large
throng of attendants, . . . on a splendid throne, with a foot-
stool inlaid with gold and silver, under a wide awning decked
with pearls and flowers and adorned with hanging garlands
of jewels; and he transacted business to the value of mil-
lions of gold pieces, all the while fanned by a fly-whisk.
. . . When he saw him the poor man was terrified . . . and
the hair of his body stood on end, for he thought that he
had happened on a king or on some high officer of state, and
had no business there. "I must go," he thought, "to the poor

quarter of the town, where I'll get food and clothing without trouble. If I stop here they'll seize me and set me to do forced labor, or some other disaster will befall me!" So he quickly ran away. . . .

But the rich man . . . recognized his son as soon as he saw him; and he was full of joy . . . and thought: "This is wonderful! I have found him who shall enjoy my riches. He of whom I thought constantly has come back, now that I am old and full of years!" Then, longing for his son, he sent swift messengers, telling them to go and fetch him quickly. They ran at full speed and overtook him; the poor man trembled with fear, the hair of his body stood on end . . . and he uttered a cry of distress and exclaimed, "I've done you no wrong!" But they dragged him along by force . . . until . . . fearful that he would be killed or beaten, he fainted and fell on the ground. His father in dismay said to the men, "Don't drag him along in that way!" and, without saying more, he sprinkled his face with cold water—for though he knew that the poor man was his son, he realized that his estate was very humble, while his own was very high.

So the householder told no one that the poor man was his son. He ordered one of his servants to tell the poor man that he was free to go where he chose. . . . And the poor man was amazed [that he was allowed to go free], and he went off to the poor quarter of the town in search of food and clothing. Now in order to attract him back the rich man made use of the virtue of "skill in means." He called two men of low caste and of no great dignity and told them: "Go to that poor man . . . and hire him in your own names to do work in my house at double the normal daily wage; and if he asks what work he has to do tell him that he has to help clear away the refuse-dump." So these two men and the poor man cleared the refuse every day . . . in the house of the rich man, and lived in a straw hut nearby. . . . And the rich man saw through a window his son clearing refuse, and was again filled with compassion. So he came down, took off his wreath and jewels and rich clothes, put on dirty garments, covered his body with dust, and, taking a basket in his hand, went up to his son. And he greeted him at a distance and said, "Take this basket and clear away the dust at once!" By this means he managed to speak to his son. [And as time went on he spoke more often to him, and thus he gradually encouraged him. First he urged him to] remain in his service and not take another job, offering him double wages, together with any small extras that he might require, such as the price of a cooking-pot . . . or food and clothes. Then he offered him his own cloak, if he should want it. . . . And at last he said: "You must be cheerful, my good fellow, and think of me as a father . . . for I'm older than you and you've done me good service in clearing away my refuse. As long as you've worked for me you've shown no roguery or guile. . . . I've not noticed one of the vices in you that I've noticed in my other servants! From now on you are like my own son to me!"

Thenceforward the householder called the poor man "son," and the latter felt towards the householder as a son feels towards his father. So the householder, full of longing and love for his son, employed him in clearing away refuse for twenty years. By the end of that time the poor man felt quite at home in the house, and came and went as he chose, though he still lived in the straw hut.

Then the householder fell ill, and felt that the hour of his death was near. So he said to the poor man: "Come, my dear man! I have great riches, . . . and am very sick. I need someone upon whom I can bestow my wealth as a deposit, and you must accept it. From now on you are just as much its owner as I am, but you must not squander it." And the poor man accepted the rich man's wealth, . . . but personally he cared nothing for it, and asked for no share of it, not even the price of a measure of flour. He still lived in the straw hut, and thought of himself as just as poor as before.

Thus the householder proved that his son was frugal, mature, and mentally developed, and that though he knew that he was now wealthy he still remembered his past poverty, and was still . . . humble and meek. . . . So he sent for the poor man again, presented him before a gathering of his relatives, and, in the presence of the king, his officers, and the people of town and country, he said: "Listen, gentlemen! This is my son, whom I begot. . . . To him I leave all my family revenues, and my private wealth he shall have as his own."

2. EXERTION

Thereafter the Bodhisattva Bhaishagyarâga and the Bodhisattva Mahâpratibhâna, with a retinue of twenty hundred thousand Bodhisattvas, spoke before the face of the Lord the following words: Let the Lord be at ease in this respect; we will after the extinction of the Tathâgata expound this Paryâya to (all) creatures, though we are aware, O Lord, that at that period there shall be malign beings, having few roots of goodness, conceited, fond of gain and honour, rooted in unholiness, difficult to tame, deprived of good will, and full of unwillingness. Nevertheless, O Lord, we will at that period read, keep, preach, write, honour, respect, venerate, worship this Sûtra; with sacrifice of body and life, O Lord, we will divulge this Sûtra. Let the Lord be at ease.

Thereupon five hundred monks of the assembly, both such as were under training and such as were not, said to the Lord: We also, O Lord, will exert ourselves to divulge this Dharmaparyâya, though in other worlds. Then all the disciples of the Lord, both such as were under training and such as were not, who had received from the Lord the prediction as to their (future) supreme enlightenment, all the eight thousand monks raised their joined hands towards the Lord and said: Let the Lord be at ease. We also will divulge this Dharmaparyâya, after the complete extinction of the Lord, in the last days, the last period, though in other worlds. For in this Saha-world, O Lord, the creatures are conceited, possessed of few roots of goodness, always vicious in their thoughts, wicked, and naturally perverse.

Then the noble matron Gautamî, the sister of the Lord's mother, along with six hundred nuns, some of them being under training, some being not, rose from her seat, raised the joined hands towards the Lord and remained gazing up to him. Then the Lord addressed the noble matron Gautamî: Why dost thou stand so dejected, gazing up to the Tathâgata? (She replied): I have not been mentioned by the Tathâgata, nor have I received from him a prediction of my destiny to supreme, perfect enlightenment. (He said): But, Gautamî, thou hast received a prediction with the prediction regarding the whole assembly. Indeed, Gautamî, thou shalt from henceforward, before the face of thirty-eight hundred thousand myriads of kotis of Buddhas, be a Bodhisattva and preacher of the law. These six thousand nuns also, partly perfected in discipline, partly not, shall along with others become Bodhisattvas and preachers of the law before the face of the Tathâgatas. Afterwards, when thou shalt have completed the course of a Bodhisattva, thou shalt become, under the name of Sarvasattvapriyadarsana (i.e. lovely to see for all beings), a Tathâgata, an Arhat, &c., endowed with science and conduct, &c. &c. And that Tathâgata Sarvasattvapriyadarsana, O Gautamî, shall give a prediction by regular succession to those six thousand Bodhisattvas concerning their destiny to supreme, perfect enlightenment.

Then the nun Yasodharâ, the mother of Râhula, thought thus: The Lord has not mentioned my name. And the Lord comprehending in his own mind what was going on in the mind of the nun Yasodharâ said to her: I announce to thee, Yasodharâ, I declare to thee: Thou also shalt before the face of ten thousand kotis of Buddhas become a Bodhisattva and preacher of the law, and after regularly completing the course of a Bodhisattva thou shalt become a Tathâgata, named Rasmisatasahasraparipûrnadhvaga, an Arhat, &c., endowed with science and conduct, &c. &c., in the world Bhadra; and the lifetime of that Lord Rasmisatasahasraparipûrnadhvaga shall be unlimited.

When the noble matron Gautamî, the nun, with her suite of six thousand nuns, and Yasodharâ, the nun, with her suite of four thousand nuns, heard from the Lord their future destiny to supreme, perfect enlightenment, they uttered, in wonder and amazement, this stanza:

1. O Lord, thou art the trainer, thou art the leader; thou art the master of the world, including the gods; thou art the giver of comfort, thou who art worshipped by men and gods. Now, indeed, we feel satisfied.

After uttering this stanza the nuns said to the Lord: We also, O Lord, will exert ourselves to divulge this Dharma-paryâya in the last days, though in other worlds.

Thereafter the Lord looked towards the eighty hundred thousand Bodhisattvas who were gifted with magical spells and capable of moving forward the wheel that never rolls back. No sooner were those Bodhisattvas regarded by the Lord than they rose from their seats, raised their joined hands towards the Lord and reflected thus: The Lord invites us to make known the Dharmaparyâya. Agitated by that thought they asked one another: What shall we do, young men of good family, in order that this Dharmaparyâya may in future be made known as the Lord invites us to do? Thereupon those young men of good family, in consequence of their reverence for the Lord and their own pious vow in their pre-vious course, raised a lion's roar before the Lord: We, O Lord, will in future, after the complete extinction of the Lord, go in all directions in order that creatures shall write, keep, meditate, divulge this Dharmaparyâya, by no other's power but the Lord's. And the Lord, staying in another world, shall protect, defend, and guard us.

Then the Bodhisattvas unanimously in a chorus addressed the Lord with the following stanzas:

2. Be at ease, O Lord. After thy complete extinction, in the horrible last period of the world, we will proclaim this sublime Sûtra.

3. We will suffer, patiently endure, O Lord, the injuries, threats, blows and threats with sticks at the hands of foolish men.

4. At that dreadful last epoch men will be malign, crooked, wicked, dull, conceited, fancying to have come to the limit when they have not.

5. 'We do not care but to live in the wilderness and wear

a patched cloth; we lead a frugal life;' so will they speak to the ignorant.

6. And persons greedily attached to enjoyments will preach the law to laymen and be honored as if they possessed the six transcendent qualities.

7. Cruel-minded and wicked men, only occupied with household cares, will enter our retreat in the forest and become our calumniators.

8. The Tîrthikas, themselves bent on profit and honour, will say of us that we are so, and—shame on such monks!—they will preach their own fictions.

9. Prompted by greed of profit and honour they will compose Sûtras of their own invention and then, in the midst of the assembly, accuse us of plagiarism.

10. To kings, princes, king's peers, as well as to Brahmans and commoners, and to monks of other confessions,

11. They will speak evil of us and propagate the Tîrtha-doctrine. We will endure all that out of reverence for the great Seers.

12. And those fools who will not listen to us, shall (sooner or later) become enlightened, and therefore will we forbear to the last.

13. In that dreadful, most terrible period of frightful general revolution will many fiendish monks stand up as our revilers.

14. Out of respect for the Chief of the world we will bear it, however difficult it be; girded with the girdle of forbearance will I proclaim this Sûtra.

15. I do not care for my body or life, O Lord, but as keepers of thine entrusted deposit we care for enlightenment.

16. The Lord himself knows that in the last period there are (to be) wicked monks who do not understand mysterious speech.

17. One will have to bear frowning looks, repeated disavowal (or concealment), expulsion from the monasteries, many and manifold abuses.

18. Yet mindful of the command of the Lord of the world

we will in the last period undauntedly proclaim this Sûtra in the midst of the congregation.

19. We will visit towns and villages everywhere, and transmit to those who care for it thine entrusted deposit, O Lord.

20. O Chief of the world, we will deliver thy message; be at ease then, tranquil and quiet, great Seer.

21. Light of the world, thou knowest the disposition of all who have flocked hither from every direction, (and thou knowest that) we speak a word of truth.

3. DURATION OF LIFE OF THE TATHÂGATA

1. An inconceivable number of thousands of kotis of Æons, never to be measured, is it since I reached superior (or first) enlightenment and never ceased to teach the law.

2. I roused many Bodhisattvas and established them in Buddha-knowledge. I brought myriads of kotis of beings, endless, to full ripeness in many kotis of Æons.

3. I show the place of extinction, I reveal to (all) beings a device to educate them, albeit I do not become extinct at the time, and in this very place continue preaching the law.

4. There I rule myself as well as all beings, I. But men of perverted minds, in their delusion, do not see me standing there.

5. In the opinion that my body is completely extinct, they pay worship, in many ways, to the relics, but me they see not. They feel (however) a certain aspiration by which their mind becomes right.

6. When such upright (or pious), mild, and gentle creatures leave off their bodies, then I assemble the crowd of disciples and show myself here on the Gridhrakûta.

7. And then I speak thus to them, in this very place: I was not completely extinct at that time; it was but a device of mine, monks; repeatedly am I born in the world of the living.

8. Honoured by other beings, I show them my superior

enlightenment, but you would not obey my word, unless the Lord of the world enter Nirvâna.

9. I see how the creatures are afflicted, but I do not show them my proper being. Let them first have an aspiration to see me; then I will reveal to them the true law.

10. Such has always been my firm resolve during an in-conceivable number of thousands of kotis of Æons, and I have not left this Gridhrakûta for other abodes.

11. And when creatures behold this world and imagine that it is burning, even then my Buddha-field is teeming with gods and men.

12. They dispose of manifold amusements, kotis of pleas-ure gardens, palaces, and aerial cars; (this field) is embel-lished by hills of gems and by trees abounding with blos-soms and fruits.

13. And aloft gods are striking musical instruments and pouring a rain of Mandâras by which they are covering me, the disciples and other sages who are striving after enlight-enment.

14. So is my field here, everlastingly; but others fancy that it is burning; in their view this world is most terrific, wretched, replete with number of woes.

15. Ay, many kotis of years they may pass without ever having mentioned my name, the law, or my congregation. That is the fruit of sinful deeds.

16. But when mild and gentle beings are born in this world of men, they immediately see me revealing the law, owing to their good works.

17. I never speak to them of the infinitude of my action. Therefore, I am, properly, existing since long, and yet declare: The Ginas are rare (or precious).

18. Such is the glorious power of my wisdom that knows no limit, and the duration of my life is as long as an endless period; I have acquired it after previously following a due course.

19. Feel no doubt concerning it, O sages, and leave off all uncertainty: the word I here pronounce is really true; my word is never false.

20. For even as that physician skilled in devices, for the sake of his sons whose notions were perverted, said that he had died although he was still alive, and even as no sensible man would charge that physician with falsehood;

21. So am I the father of the world, the Self-born, the Healer, the Protector of all creatures. Knowing them to be perverted, infatuated, and ignorant I teach final rest, myself not being at rest.

22. What reason should I have to continually manifest myself? When men become unbelieving, unwise, ignorant, careless, fond of sensual pleasures, and from thoughtlessness run into misfortune,

23. Then I, who know the course of the world, declare: I am so and so, (and consider): How can I incline them to enlightenment? how can they become partakers of the Buddha-laws?

B.   FROM THE EXPLANATIONS OF VIMALAKĪRTI

At that time, there dwelt in the great city of Vaishālī a wealthy householder named Vimalakīrti. Having done homage to the countless Buddhas of the past, doing many good works, attaining to acquiescence in the Eternal Law, he was a man of wonderful eloquence,

Exercising supernatural powers, obtaining all the magic formulas [dhāranīs], arriving at the state of fearlessness,

Repressing all evil enmities, reaching the gate of profound truth, walking in the way of wisdom,

Acquainted with the necessary means, fulfilling the Great Vows, comprehending the past and the future of the intentions of all beings, understanding also both their strength and weakness of mind,

Ever pure and excellent in the way of the Buddha, remaining loyal to the Mahāyāna,

Deliberating before action, following the conduct of Buddha, great in mind as the ocean,

Praised by all the Buddhas, revered by all the disciples

and all the gods such as a Shakra and the Brahmā Sahāpati ["lord of the world"],

Residing in Vaishālī only for the sake of the necessary means for saving creatures, abundantly rich, ever careful of the poor, pure in self-discipline, obedient to all precepts,

Removing all anger by the practice of patience, removing all sloth by the practice of diligence, removing all distraction of mind by intent meditation, removing all ignorance by fullness of wisdom;

Though he is but a simple layman, yet observing the pure monastic discipline;

Though living at home, yet never desirous of anything;

Though possessing a wife and children, always exercising pure virtues;

Though surrounded by his family, holding aloof from worldly pleasures;

Though using the jeweled ornaments of the world, yet adorned with spiritual splendor;

Though eating and drinking, yet enjoying the flavor of the rapture of meditation;

Though frequenting the gambling house, yet leading the gamblers into the right path;

Though coming in contact with heresy, yet never letting his true faith be impaired;

Though having a profound knowledge of worldly learning, yet ever finding pleasure in things of the spirit as taught by Buddha;

Revered by all as the first among those who were worthy of reverence;

Governing both the old and young as a righteous judge;

Though profiting by all the professions, yet far above being absorbed by them;

Benefiting all beings, going wheresoever he pleases, protecting all beings as a judge with righteousness;

Leading all with the Doctrine of the Mahāyāna when in the seat of discussion;

Ever teaching the young and ignorant when entering the hall of learning;

Manifesting to all the error of passion when in the house of debauchery; persuading all to seek the higher things when at the shop of the wine dealer;

Preaching the Law when among wealthy people as the most honorable of their kind;

Dissuading the rich householders from covetousness when among them as the most honorable of their kind;

Teaching kshatriyas [i.e., nobles] patience when among them as the most honorable of their kind;

Removing arrogance when among brahmans as the most honorable of their kind;

Teaching justice to the great ministers when among them as the most honorable of their kind;

Teaching loyalty and filial piety to the princes when among them as the most honorable of their kind;

Teaching honesty to the ladies of the court when among them as the most honorable of their kind;

Persuading the masses to cherish the virtue of merits when among them as the most honorable of their kind;

Instructing in highest wisdom the Brahmā gods when among them as the most honorable of their kind;

Showing the transient nature of the world to the Shakra gods when among them as the most honorable of their kind;

Protecting all beings when among the guardians as the most honorable of their kind;

—Thus by such countless means Vimalakīrti, the wealthy householder, rendered benefit to all beings.

Now through those means he brought on himself sickness. And there came to inquire after him countless visitors headed by kings, great ministers, wealthy householders, lay-disciples, brahman princes and other high officials. Then Vimalakīrti, taking the opportunity of his sickness, preached to any one who came to him, and said:

"Come, ye gentlemen, the human body is transient, weak, impotent, frail, and mortal; never trustworthy, because it suffers when attacked by disease;

Ye gentlemen, an intelligent man never places his trust in such a thing; it is like a bubble that soon bursts.

It is like a mirage which appears because of a thirsty desire.

It is like a plantain tree which is hollow inside.

It is like a phantom caused by a conjurer.

It is like a dream giving false ideas.

It is like a shadow which is produced by karma.

It is like an echo which is produced by various relations.

It is like a floating cloud which changes and vanishes.

It is like the lightning which instantly comes and goes.

It has no power as the earth has none.

It has no individuality as the fire has none.

It has no durability as the wind has none.

It has no personality as the water has none.

It is not real and the four elements are its house.

It is empty when freed from the false idea of me and mine.

It has no consciousness as there is none in grasses, trees, bricks or stones.

It is impotent as it is revolved by the power of the wind.

It is impure and full of filthiness.

It is false and will be reduced to nothingness, in spite of bathing, clothing, or nourishment.

It is a calamity and subject to a hundred and one diseases.

It is like a dry well threatened by decay.

It is transient and sure to die.

It is like a poisonous snake or a hateful enemy or a deserted village as it is composed of the (five) *skandhas*, the (twelve) *āyatanas* and the (eighteen) *dhātus*.

O ye gentlemen, this body of ours is to be abhorred, and the body of Buddha is to be desired. And why?

The body of Buddha is the body of the law.

It is born of immeasurable virtues and wisdom.

It is born of discipline, meditation, wisdom, emancipation, wisdom of emancipation.

It is born of mercy, compassion, joy, and impartiality.

It is born of charity, discipline, patience, diligence, meditation, emancipation, samādhi, learning, meekness, strength, wisdom, and all the Pāramitās.

It is born of the necessary means.

It is born of the six supernatural powers.

It is born of the threefold intelligence.

It is born of the thirty-seven requisites of enlightenment.

It is born of the concentration and contemplation of mind.

It is born of the ten powers, threefold fearlessness, and the eighteen special faculties.

It is born by uprooting all wicked deeds and by accumulating all good deeds.

It is born of truth.

It is born of temperance.

Of these immeasurable pure virtues is born the body of Tathāgata. Ye gentlemen, if one wishes to obtain the body of Buddha and exterminate the diseases of all beings he should cherish the thought of supreme enlightenment."

Thus Vimalakīrti, the wealthy householder, rightly preached for the profit of those who came to visit him on his bed of sickness and made all these countless thousand people cherish the thought of supreme enlightenment.

C. FROM THE VIÇEṢACINTA-BRAHMA-PARIPṚCCHA SUTRA

Samsâra is Nirvâna, because there is, when viewed from the ultimate nature of the Dharmakâya, nothing going out of, nor coming into, existence, [samsâra being only apparent]: Nirvâna is samsâra, when it is coveted and adhered to.

The essence of all things is in truth free from attachment, attributes, and desires; therefore, they are pure, and, as they are pure, we know that what is the essence of birth and death that is the essence of Nirvâna, and that what is the essence of Nirvâna that is the essence of birth and death (*samsâra*). In other words, Nirvâna is not to be sought outside of this world, which, though transient, is in reality no more than Nirvâna itself. Because it is contrary to our reason to imagine that there is Nirvâna and there is birth and death (*samsâra,*)

and that the one lies outside the pale of the other, and, therefore, that we can attain Nirvâna only after we have annihilated or escaped the world of birth and death. If we are
not hampered by our confused subjectivity, this our worldly
life is an activity of Nirvâna itself.

D. FROM THE AVATAMSAKA SUTRA

"The Dharmakâya, though manifesting itself in the triple
world, is free from impurities and desires. It unfolds itself
here, there, and everywhere responding to the call of karma.
It is not an individual reality, it is not a false existence, but is
universal and pure. It comes from nowhere, it goes to nowhere; it does not assert itself, nor is it subject to annihilation. It is forever serene and eternal. It is the One, devoid
of all determinations. This Body of Dharma has no boundary, no quarters, but is embodied in all bodies. Its freedom
or spontaneity is incomprehensible, its spiritual presence in
things corporeal is incomprehensible. All forms of corporeality
are involved therein, it is able to create all things. Assuming
any concrete material body as required by the nature and
condition of karma, it illuminates all creations. Though it is
the treasure of intelligence, it is void of particularity. There
is no place in the universe where this Body does not prevail.
The universe becomes, but this Body forever remains. It is
free from all opposites and contraries, yet it is working in all
things to lead them to Nirvâna."

"O ye, sons of Buddha! The Tathâgata is not a particular
dharma, nor a particular form of activity, nor has it a particular body, nor does it abide in a particular place, nor is its
work of salvation confined to one particular people. On the
contrary, it involves in itself infinite dharmas, infinite activities, infinite bodies, infinite spaces, and universally works
for the salvation of all things.

"O ye, sons of Buddha! It is like unto space. Space contains in itself all material existences and all the vacuums
that obtain between them. Again, it establishes itself in all

possible quarters, and yet we cannot say of it that it is or it is not in this particular spot, for space has no palpable form. Even so with the Dharmakâya of the Tathâgata. It presents itself in all places, in all directions, in all dharmas, and in all beings; yet the Dharmakâya itself has not been thereby particularised. Because the Body of the Tathâgata has no particular body but manifests itself everywhere and anywhere in response to the nature and condition of things.

"O ye, sons of Buddha! It is like unto space. Space is boundless, comprehends in itself all existence, and yet shows no trace of passion [partiality]. It is even so with the Dharmakâya of the Tathâgata. It illuminates all good works worldly as well as religious, but it betrays no passion or prejudice. Why? Because the Dharmakâya is perfectly free from all passions and prejudices.

"O ye, sons of Buddha! It is like unto the Sun. The benefits conferred by the light of the sun upon all living beings on earth are incalculable: e. g. by dispelling darkness it gives nourishment to all trees, herbs, grains, plants, and grass; it vanquishes humidity; it illuminates ether thereby benefiting all the living beings in air; its rays penetrate into the waters thereby bringing forth the beautiful lotus-flowers into full blossom; it impartially shines on all figures and forms and brings into completion all the works on earth. Why? Because from the sun emanate infinite rays of life-giving light.

"O ye, sons of Buddha! It is even so with the Sun-Body of the Tathâgata which in innumerable ways bestows benefits upon all beings. That is, it benefits us by destroying evils, all good things thus being quickened to growth; it benefits us with its universal illumination which vanquishes the darkness of ignorance harbored in all beings; it benefits us through its great compassionate heart which saves and protects all beings; it benefits us through its great loving heart which delivers all beings from the misery of birth and death; it benefits us by the establishment of a good religion whereby we are all strengthened in our moral activities; it benefits us by giving us a firm belief in the truth which cleanses all our spiritual impurities; it benefits by helping us to under-

stand the doctrine by virtue of which we are not led to dis-
avow the law of causation; it benefits us with a divine vision
which enables us to observe the metempsychosis of all beings; it benefits us by avoiding injurious deeds which may
destroy the stock of merits accumulated by all beings; it
benefits us with an intellectual light which unfolds the mind-
flowers of all beings; it benefits us with an aspiration whereby
we are enlivened to practice all that constitutes Buddhahood.
Why? Because the Sun-Body of the Tathâgata universally
emits the rays of the Light of Intelligence.

"O ye, sons of Buddha! When the day breaks, the rising
sun shines first on the peaks of all the higher mountains, then
on those of high mountains, and finally all over the plains and
fields; but the sunlight itself does not make this thought: I
will shine first on all the highest mountains and then gradually ascending higher and higher shine on the plains and
fields. The reason why one gets the sunlight earlier than another is simply because there is a gradation of height on the
surface of the earth.

"O ye, sons of Buddha! It is even so with the Tathâgata
who is in possession of innumerable and immeasurable suns
of universal intelligence. The innumerable rays of the Light
of Intelligence, emanating everlastingly from the spiritual
Body of the Tathâgata, will first fall on the Bodhisattvas and
Mahâsattvas who are the highest peaks among mankind, then
on the Nidânabuddhas, then on the Çrâvakas, then on those
beings who are endowed with definitely good character, as
they will each according to his own capacity unhesitatingly
embrace the doctrine of deliverance, and finally on all common mortals whose character may be either indefinite or
definitely bad, providing them with those conditions which
will prove beneficial in their future births. But the Light of
Intelligence emanating from the Tathâgata does not make
this thought: 'I will first shine on the Bodhisattvas and then
gradually pass over to all common mortals, etc.' The Light is
universal and illuminates everything without any prejudice,
yet on account of the diversity that obtains among sentient

beings as to their character, aspirations, etc., the Light of Intelligence is diversely perceived by them.

"O ye, sons of Buddha! When the sun rises above the horizon, those people born blind on account of their defective sight, cannot see the light at all, but they are nevertheless benefited by the sunlight, for it gives them just as much as to any other beings all that is necessary for the maintenance of life: it dispels dampness and coldness and makes them feel agreeable, it destroys all the injurious germs that are produced on account of the absence of sunshine, and thus keeps the blind as well as the not-blind comfortable and healthy.

"O ye, sons of Buddha! It is even so with the Sun of Intelligence of the Tathâgata. All those beings whose spiritual vision is blinded by false doctrine, or by the violation of Buddha's precepts, or by ignorance, or by evil influences, never perceive the Light of Intelligence; because they are devoid of faith. But they are nevertheless benefited by the Light; for it disperses indiscriminately for all beings the sufferings arising from the four elements, and gives them physical comforts, for it destroys the root of all passions, prejudices, and pains for unbelievers as well as for believers . . . By virtue of this omnipresent Light of Intelligence, the Bodhisattvas will attain perfect purity and the knowledge of all things, the Nidânabuddhas and Çrâvakas will destroy all passions and desires; mortals poorly endowed and those born blind will be rid of impurities, control the senses, and believe in the four views; and those creatures living in the evil paths of existence such as hell, world of ghosts, and the animal realm, will be freed from their evils and torture and will, after death, be born in the human or celestial world. . . .

"O ye, sons of Buddha! The Light of Dharmakâya is like unto the full moon which has four wondrous attributes: (1) It outdoes in its brilliance all stars and satellites; (2) It shows in its size increase and decrease as observable in the Jambudvîpa; (3) Its reflection is seen in every drop or body of clear water; (4) Whoever is endowed with perfect sight, perceives it vis-a-vis.

"O ye, sons of Buddha! Even so with the Dharmakâya of the Tathâgata, that has four wondrous attributes: (1) It eclipses the stars of the Nidânabuddhas, Çrâvakas, etc.; (2) It shows in its earthly life a certain variation which is due to the different natures of the beings to whom it manifests itself, while the Dharmakâya itself is eternal and shows no increase or decrease in any way; (3) Its reflection is seen in the Bodhi (intelligence) of every pure-hearted sentient being; (4) All who understand the Dharma and obtain deliverance, each according to his own mental calibre, think that they have really recognised in their own way the Tathâgata face to face, while the Dharmakâya itself is not a particular object of understanding, but universally brings all Buddha-works into completion.

"O ye, sons of Buddha! The Dharmakâya is like unto the Great Brahmarâja who governs three thousand chiliocosms. The Râja by a mysterious trick makes himself seen universally by all living beings in his realm and causes them to think that each of them has seen him face to face; but the Râja himself has never divided his own person nor is he in possession of diverse features.

"O ye, sons of Buddha! Even so with the Tathâgata; he has never divided himself into many, nor has he ever assumed diverse features. But all beings, each according to his understanding and strength of faith, recognise the Body of the Tathâgata, while he has never made this thought that he will show himself to such and such particular people and not to others. . . .

"O ye, sons of Buddha! The Dharmakâya is like unto the maniratna in the waters, whose wondrous light transforms everything that comes in contact with it to its own color. The eyes that perceive it become purified. Wherever its illumination reaches, there is a marvelous display of gems of every description, which gives pleasure to all beings to see.

"O ye, sons of Buddha! It is even so with the Dharmakâya of the Tathâgata, which may rightly be called the treasure of treasures, the thesaurus of all merits, and the mine of intelligence. Whoever comes in touch with this light, is all transformed into the same color as that of the Buddha. Whoever sees this light, all obtains the purest eye of Dharma. Whoever comes in touch with this light, rids of poverty and suffering, attains wealth and eminence, enjoys the bliss of the incomparable Bodhi. . . ."

"Having practised all the six virtues of perfection (*pâramitâ*) and innumerable other meritorious deeds, the Bodhisattva reflects in this wise:

"'All the good deeds practised by me are for the benefit of all sentient beings, for their ultimate purification [from sin]. By the merit of these good deeds I pray that all sentient beings be released from the innumerable sufferings suffered by them in their various abodes of existence. By the turning over (*parivarta*) of these deeds I would be a haven for all beings and deliver them from their miserable existences; I would be a great beacon-light to all beings and dispel the darkness of ignorance and make the light of intelligence shine.'

"He reflects again in this wise:

"'All sentient beings are creating evil karma in innumerable ways, and by reason of this karma they suffer innumerable sufferings. They do not recognise the Tathâgata, do not listen to the Good Law, do not pay homage to the congregation of holy men. All these beings carry an innumerable amount of great evil karma and are destined to suffer in innumerable ways. For their sake I will in the midst of the three evil creations suffer all their sufferings and deliver every one of them. Painful as these sufferings are, I will not retreat, I will not be frightened, I will not be negligent, I will not forsake my fellow-beings. Why? Because it is the will [of the Dharmakâya] that all sentient beings should be universally emancipated.'

"He reflects again in this wise:

"'My conduct will be like the sun-god who with his universal illumination seeks not any reward, who ceases not on account of one unrighteous person to make a great display of his magnificent glory, who on account of one unrighteous person abandons not the salvation of all beings. Through the dedication (*parivarta*) of all my merits I would make every one of my fellow-creatures happy and joyous.'"

E. FROM THE LANKĀVATĀRA SUTRA

Then said Mahamati to the Blessed One: Pray tell us about Nirvana?

The Blessed One replied: The term, Nirvana, is used with many different meanings, by different people, but these people may be divided into four groups: There are people who are suffering, or who are afraid of suffering, and who think of Nirvana; there are the philosophers who try to discriminate Nirvana; there are the class of disciples who think of Nirvana in relation to themselves; and, finally there is the Nirvana of the Buddhas.

Those who are suffering or who fear suffering, think of Nirvana as an escape and a recompense. They imagine that Nirvana consists in the future annihilation of the senses and the sense-minds; they are not aware that Universal Mind and Nirvana are One, and that this life-and-death world and Nirvana are not to be separated. These ignorant ones, instead of meditating on the imagelessness of Nirvana, talk of different ways of emancipation. Being ignorant of, or not understanding, the teachings of the Tathagatas, they cling to the notion of Nirvana that is outside what is seen of the mind and, thus, go on rolling themselves along with the wheel of life and death.

As to Nirvanas discriminated by the philosophers: there really are none. Some philosophers conceive Nirvana to be found where the mind-system no more operates owing to the cessation of the elements that make up personality and its world; or is found where there is utter indifference to the objective world and its impermanency. Some conceive Nirvana to be a state where there is no recollection of the past or present, just as when a lamp is extinguished, or when a seed is burnt, or when a fire goes out; because then there is the cessation of all the substrate, which is explained by the philosophers as the non-rising of discrimination. But this is not Nirvana, because Nirvana does not consist in simple annihilation and vacuity.

Again, some philosophers explain deliverance as though it was the mere stopping of discrimination, as when the wind stops blowing, or as when one by self-effort gets rid of the dualistic view of knower and known, or gets rid of the notions of permanency and impermanency; or gets rid of the notions of good and evil; or overcomes passion by means of knowledge;—to them Nirvana is deliverance. Some, seeing in "form" the bearer of pain, are alarmed by the notion of "form" and look for happiness in a world of "no-form." Some conceive that in consideration of individuality and generality recognizable in all things inner and outer, that there is no destruction and that all beings maintain their being for ever and, in this eternality, see Nirvana. Others see the eternality of things in the conception of Nirvana as the absorption of the finite-soul in Supreme Atman; or who see all things as a manifestation of the vital-force of some Supreme Spirit to which all return; and some, who are especially silly, declare that there are two primary things, a primary substance and a primary soul, that react differently upon each other and thus produce all things from the transformations of qualities; some think that the world is born of action and interaction and that no other cause is necessary; others think that Ishvara is the free creator of all things; clinging to these foolish notions, there is no awakening, and they consider Nirvana to consist in the fact that there is no awakening.

Some imagine that Nirvana is where self-nature exists in its own right, unhampered by other self-natures, as the variegated feathers of a peacock, or various precious crystals, or the pointedness of a thorn. Some conceive being to be Nirvana, some non-being, while others conceive that all things and Nirvana are not to be distinguished from one another. Some, thinking that time is the creator and that as the rise of the world depends on time, they conceive that Nirvana consists in the recognition of time as Nirvana. Some think that there will be Nirvana when the "twenty-five" truths are generally accepted, or when the king observes the six virtues, and some religionists think that Nirvana is the attainment of paradise.

These views severally advanced by the philosophers with their various reasonings are not in accord with logic nor are they acceptable to the wise. They all conceive Nirvana dualistically and in some causal connection; by these discriminations philosophers imagine Nirvana, but where there is no rising and no disappearing, how can there be discrimination? Each philosopher relying on his own textbook from which he draws his understanding, sins against the truth, because truth is not where he imagines it to be. The only result is that it sets his mind to wandering about and becoming more confused as Nirvana is not to be found by mental searching, and the more his mind becomes confused the more he confuses other people.

As to the notion of Nirvana as held by disciples and masters who still cling to the notion of an ego-self, and who try to find it by going off by themselves into solitude: their notion of Nirvana is an eternity of bliss like the bliss of the Samadhis— for themselves. They recognise that the world is only a manifestation of mind and that all discriminations are of the mind, and so they forsake social relations and practise various spiritual disciplines and in solitude seek self-realisation of Noble Wisdom by self-effort. They follow the stages to the sixth and attain the bliss of the Samadhis, but as they are still clinging to egoism they do not attain the "turning-about" at the deepest seat of consciousness and, therefore, they are not free from the thinking-mind and the accumulation of its habit-energy. Clinging to the bliss of the Samadhis, they pass to their Nirvana, but it is not the Nirvana of the Tathagatas. They are of those who have "entered the stream"; they must return to this world of life and death.

Then said Mahamati to the Blessed One: When the Bodhisattvas yield up their stock of merit for the emancipation of all beings, they become spiritually one with all animate life; they themselves may be purified, but in others there yet remain unexhausted evil and unmatured karma. Pray tell us, Blessed One, how the Bodhisattvas are given assurance of Nirvana? and what is the Nirvana of the Bodhisattvas?

The Blessed One replied: Mahamati, this assurance is not an assurance of numbers nor logic; it is not the mind that is to be assured but the heart. The Bodhisattva's assurance comes with the unfolding insight that follows passion hindrances cleared away, knowledge hindrance purified, and egolessness clearly perceived and patiently accepted. As the mortal-mind ceases to discriminate, there is no more thirst for life, no more sex-lust, no more thirst for learning, no more thirst for eternal life; with the disappearance of these fourfold thirsts, there is no more accumulation of habit-energy; with no more accumulation of habit-energy the defilements on the face of Universal Mind clear away, and the Bodhisattva attains self-realisation of Noble Wisdom that is the heart's assurance of Nirvana.

There are Bodhisattvas here and in other Buddha-lands, who are sincerely devoted to the Bodhisattva's mission and yet who cannot wholly forget the bliss of the Samadhis and the peace of Nirvana—for themselves. The teaching of Nirvana in which there is no substrate left behind, is revealed according to a hidden meaning for the sake of these disciples who still cling to thoughts of Nirvana for themselves, that they may be inspired to exert themselves in the Bodhisattva's mission of emancipation for all beings. The Transformation-Buddhas teach a doctrine of Nirvana to meet conditions as they find them, and to give encouragement to the timid and selfish. In order to turn their thoughts away from themselves and to encourage them to a deeper compassion and more earnest zeal for others, they are given assurance as to the future by the sustaining power of the Buddhas of Transformation, but not by the Dharmata-Buddha.

The Dharma which establishes the Truth of Noble Wisdom belongs to the realm of the Dharmata-Buddha. To the Bodhisattvas of the seventh and eighth stages, Transcendental Intelligence is revealed by the Dharmata-Buddha and the Path is pointed out to them which they are to follow. In the perfect self-realisation of Noble Wisdom that follows the inconceivable transformation death of the Bodhisattva's individualised will-control, he no longer lives unto himself, but the life that he lives thereafter is the Tathagata's universalised life as manifested in its transformations. In this perfect self-realisation of Noble Wisdom the Bodhisattva realises that for Buddhas there is no Nirvana.

The death of a Buddha, the great Parinirvana, is neither destruction nor death, else would it be birth and continuation. If it were destruction, it would be an effect-producing deed, which it is not. Neither is it vanishing nor an abandonment, neither is it attainment, nor is it of no attainment; neither is it of one significance nor of no significance, for there is no Nirvana for the Buddhas.

The Tathagata's Nirvana is where it is recognised that there is nothing but what is seen of the mind itself; is where, recognising the nature of the self-mind, one no longer cherishes the dualisms of discrimination; is where there is no more thirst nor grasping; is where there is no more attachment to external things. Nirvana is where the thinking-mind with all its discriminations, attachments, aversions and egoism is forever put away; is where logical measures, as they are seen to be inert, are no longer seized upon; is where even the notion of truth is treated with indifference because of its causing bewilderment; is where, getting rid of the four propositions, there is insight into the abode of Reality. Nirvana is where the twofold passions have subsided and the twofold hindrances are cleared away and the twofold egolessness is patiently accepted; is where, by the attainment of the "turning-about" in the deepest seat of consciousness, self-realisation of Noble Wisdom is fully entered into—that is the Nirvana of the Tathagatas.

Nirvana is where the Bodhisattva stages are passed one after another; is where the sustaining power of the Buddhas upholds the Bodhisattvas in the bliss of the Samadhis; is where compassion for others transcends all thoughts of self; is where the Tathagata stage is finally realised.

Nirvana is the realm of Dharmata-Buddha; it is where

the manifestation of Noble Wisdom that is Buddhahood expresses itself in Perfect Love for all; it is where the manifestation of Perfect Love that is Tathagatahood expresses itself in Noble Wisdom for the enlightenment of all;—there, indeed, is Nirvana!

There are two classes of those who may not enter the Nirvana of the Tathagatas: there are those who have abandoned the Bodhisattva ideals, saying, they are not in conformity with the sutras, the codes of morality, nor with emancipation. Then there are the true Bodhisattvas who, on account of their original vows made for the sake of all beings, saying, "So long as they do not attain Nirvana, I will not attain it myself," voluntarily keep themselves out of Nirvana. But no beings are left outside by the will of the Tathagatas; some day each and every one will be influenced by the wisdom and love of the Tathagatas of Transformation to lay up a stock of merit and ascend the stages. But, if they only realised it, they are already in the Tathagata's Nirvana for, in Noble Wisdom, all things are in Nirvana from the beginning.

Chapter XVIII
NĀGĀRJUNA

The late second-century Mahayana dialectician Nāgārjuna, who like Asvaghosha was a Brahman, literally created an age in the history of Buddhist metaphysics. He founded the Mādhyamika school, also known as the Śūnyavāda, of which the *Mādhyamika Çâstra*, a selection from which is given, is the groundwork and a virtual epitome of sutra teaching. The author spent most of his life in South India, at Śrī Parvata or Śrī Śailam, which he made a Buddhist center. About twenty works available in Chinese translation are generally credited to him, of which eighteen are mentioned as definite by Bunyiu Nanjio in his *Catalogue*. I-Tsing tells of observing Indian children memorizing some of his works, and adults making of it a lifelong study. In the *Mādhyamika Çâstra* (Discourse on the Middle Path) Nāgārjuna sets forth the Middle View, clearly answering the objection that if all be void, then the Four Noble Truths, the Order of Monks, and the Buddha himself must be considered unreal. His explanation, briefly: the Buddha speaks of two truths, one in the absolute sense, the other conventional and relative. One who does not see the distinction cannot hope to understand Buddhism. The Mahayana point of view, as advanced by the author, is not that Nirvana is non-existence. Rather it is positive, or positively is, not some state to enter into: one experiences it when ignorance, which obscures and makes impossible real freedom, is overcome. Mahayana non-duality, so important to later Buddhism, culminates in the astonishing paradox that Nirvana is Samsara, or as Nāgārjuna puts it, "This our worldly life is an activity of Nirvana itself, not the slightest distinction exists between them." In addition to selections from his greatest work, there follows an excerpt from his *Bodhicitta*, which gives the Mahayanist notion of Bodhisattvahood, and a passage from one of his commentators, Pingalaka.

FROM THE DISCOURSE ON THE MIDDLE PATH

"Some say that there are seeing, hearing, feeling, etc., because there is something which exists even prior to those [manifestations]. For how could seeing, etc., come from that which does not exist? Therefore, it must be admitted that that being [i. e. soul] existed prior to those [manifestations].

"But [this hypothesis of the prior (*pûrva*) or independent existence of the soul is wrong, because] how could that being be known if it existed prior to seeing, feeling, etc.? If that being could exist without seeing, etc., the latter too could surely exist without that being. But how could a thing which could not be known by any sign exist before it is known? How could *this* exist without *that*, and how could *that* exist without *this*? [Are not all things relative and conditioning one another?]

"If that being called soul could not exist prior to all manifestations such as seeing, etc., how could it exist prior to each of them taken individually?

"If it is the same soul that sees, hears, feels, etc., it must be assumed that the soul exists prior to each of these manifestations. This, however, is not warranted by facts. [Because in that case one must be able to hear with the eyes, see with the ears, as one soul is considered to direct all these diverse faculties at its will.]

"If, on the other hand, the hearer is one, and the seer is another, the feeler must be still another. Then, there will be hearing, seeing, etc., simultaneously,—which leads to the assumption of a plurality of souls. [This too is against experience.]

"Further, the soul does not exist in the element (*bhûta*) on which seeing, hearing, feeling, etc., depend. [To use modern expression, the soul does not exist in the nerves which respond to the external stimuli.]

"If seeing, hearing, feeling, etc., have no soul that exists prior to them, they too have no existence as such. For how could *that* exist without *this*, and *this* without *that?* Subject and object are mutually conditioned. The soul as it is has no independent, individual reality whatever. Therefore, the hypothesis that contends for the existence of an ego-soul prior to, simultaneous with, or posterior to, seeing, etc., is to be abandoned as fruitless, for the ego-soul existeth not." "[Some one may object to the Buddhist doctrine of emptiness, declaring:] If all is void (*çûnya*) and there is neither creation nor destruction, then it must be concluded that even the Fourfold Noble Truth does not exist. If the Fourfold Noble Truth does not exist, the recognition of Suffering, the stoppage of Accumulation, the attainment of Cessation, and the advancement of Discipline,—all must be said to be unrealisable. If they are altogether unrealisable, there cannot be any of the four states of saintliness; and without these states there cannot be anybody who will aspire for them. If there are no wise men, the Sangha is then impossible. Further, as there is no Fourfold Noble Truth, there is no Good Law (*saddharma*); and as there is neither Good Law nor Sangha, the existence of Buddha himself must be an impossibility. Those who talk of emptiness, therefore, must be said to negate the Triple Treasure (*triratna*) altogether. Emptiness not only destroys the law of causation and the general principle of retribution (*phalasadbhâvam*), but utterly annihilates the possibility of a phenomenal world."

"[To this it is to be remarked that]

"Only he is annoyed over such scepticism who understands not the true significance and interpretation of emptiness (*çûnyatâ*).

"The Buddha's teaching rests on the discrimination of two kinds of truth (*satya*): absolute and relative. Those who do not have any adequate knowledge of them are unable to grasp the deep and subtle meaning of Buddhism. [The essence of being, dharmata, is beyond verbal definition or intellectual comprehension, for there is neither birth nor death in it, and it is even like unto Nirvâna. The nature of Suchness, tattva, is fundamentally free from conditionality, it is tranquil, it distances all phenomenal frivolities, it discriminates not, nor is it particularised].

"But if not for relative truth, absolute truth is unattainable, and when absolute truth is not attained, Nirvâna is not to be gained.

"The dull-headed who do not perceive the truth rightfully go to self-destruction, for they are like an awkward magician whose trick entangles himself, or like an unskilled snake-catcher who gets himself hurt. The World-honored One knew well the abstruseness of the Doctrine which is beyond the mental capacity of the multitudes and was inclined not to disclose it before them.

"The objection that Buddhism onesidedly adheres to emptiness and thereby exposes itself to grave errors, entirely misses the mark; for there are no errors in emptiness. Why? Because it is on account of emptiness that all things are at all possible, and without emptiness all things will come to naught. Those who deny emptiness and find fault with it, are like a horseman who forgets that he is on horseback.

"If they think that things exist because of their self-essence (*svabhâva*), [and not because of their emptiness,] they thereby make things come out of causelessness (*ahetupratyaya*), they destroy those relations that exist between the acting and the act and the acted; and they also destroy the conditions that make up the law of birth and death.

"All is declared empty because there is nothing that is not a product of universal causation (*pratyayasamutpâda*). This law of causation, however, is merely provisional, though herein lies the middle path.

"As thus there is not an object (*dharma*) which is not conditioned (*pratîtya*), so there is nothing that is not empty.

"If all is not empty, then there is no death nor birth, and withal disappears the Fourfold Noble Truth.

"How could there be Suffering, if not for the law of causation? Impermanence is suffering. But with self-essence there will be no impermanence. [So long as impermanence is the condition of life, self-essence which is a causeless existence, is out of question.] Suppose Suffering is self-existent, then it could not come from Accumulation, which in turn becomes impossible when emptiness is not admitted. Again, when Suffering is self-existent, then there could be no Cessation, for with the hypothesis of self-essence Cessation becomes a meaningless term. Again, when Suffering is self-existent, then there will be no Path. But as we can actually walk on the Path, the hypothesis of self-essence is to be abandoned.

"If there is neither Suffering nor Cessation, it must be said that the Path leading to the Cessation of Suffering is also non-existent.

"If there is really self-essence, Suffering could not be recognised now, as it had not been recognised, for self-essence as such must remain forever the same. [That is to say, enlightened minds, through the teaching of Buddha, now recognise the existence of Suffering, though they did not recognise it when they were still uninitiated. If things were all in a fixed, self-determining state on account of their self-essence, it would be impossible for those enlightened men to discover what they had never observed before. The recognition of the Fourfold Noble Truth is only possible when this phenomenal world is in a state of constant becoming, that is, when it is empty as it really is.]

"As it is with the recognition of Suffering, so it is with the stoppage of Accumulation, the attainment of Cessation, the realisation of Path as well as with the four states of saintliness.

"If, on account of self-essence, the four states of saintliness were unattainable before, how could they be realised now, still upholding the hypothesis of self-essence? [But we can attain to saintliness as a matter of fact, for there are many holy men who through their spiritual discipline have emerged from their former life of ignorance and darkness. If everything had its own self-essence which makes it impossible to transform from one state to another, how could a person desire to ascend, if he ever so desire, higher and higher on the scale of existence?]

"If there were no four states of saintliness (*catvâri phal-âni*), then there would be no aspirants for it. And if there were no eight wise men (*purusapuñgala*), there could exist no Sangha.

"Again, when there could not be the Fourfold Noble Truth, the Law would be impossible, and without the Sangha and the Law how could the Buddha exist? You might say: 'A Buddha does not exist on account of wisdom (*Bodhi*), nor does wisdom exist on account of the Buddha.' But if a man did not have Buddha-essence [that is, Bodhi] he could not hope to attain to Buddhahood, however strenuously he might exert himself in the ways of Bodhisattva.

"Further, if all is not empty but has self-essence, [i. e. if all is in a fixed, unchangeable state of sameness], how could there be any doing? How could there be good and evil? If you maintain that there is an effect (*phala*) which does not come from a cause good or evil [which is the practical conclusion of the hypothesis of self-essence], then it means that retribution is independent of our deed, good or evil. [But is this justified by our experience?]

"If it must then be admitted that our deed good or evil becomes the cause of retribution, retribution must be said to come from our deed, good or evil; then how could we say there is no emptiness?

"When you negate the doctrine of emptiness, the law of universal causation, you negate the possibility of this phenomenal world. When the doctrine of emptiness is negated, there remains nothing that ought to be done; and a thing is called done which is not yet accomplished; and he is said to be a doer who has not done anything whatever. If there were such a thing as self-essence, the multitudinousness of things must be regarded as uncreated and imperishable and eternally existing which is tantamount to eternal nothingness.

"If there were no emptiness there would be no attainment of what has not yet been attained, nor would there be the annihilation of pain, nor the extinction of all the passions (*sarvakleça*).

"Therefore, it is taught by the Buddha that those who recognise the law of universal causation, recognise the Buddha as well as Suffering, Accumulation, Cessation, and the Path."

FROM THE BODHICITTA

"Thus the essential nature of all Bodhisattvas is a great loving heart (*mahâkarunâcitta*), and all sentient beings constitute the object of its love. Therefore, all the Bodhisattvas do not cling to the blissful taste that is produced by the divers modes of mental tranquilisation (*dhyâna*), do not covet the fruit of their meritorious deeds, which may heighten their own happiness.

"Their spiritual state is higher than that of the Çrâvakas, for they do not leave all sentient beings behind them [as the Çrâvakas do]. They practise altruism, they seek the fruit of Buddha-knowledge [instead of Çrâvaka-knowledge].

"With a great loving heart they look upon the sufferings of all beings, who are diversely tortured in Avici Hell in consequence of their sins—a hell whose limits are infinite and where an endless round of misery is made possible on account of all sorts of karma [committed by sentient creatures]. The Bodhisattvas filled with pity and love desire to suffer themselves for the sake of those miserable beings.

"But they are well acquainted with the truth that all those diverse sufferings causing diverse states of misery are in one sense apparitional and unreal, while in another sense they are not so. They know also that those who have an intellectual insight into the emptiness (*cûnyatâ*) of all existences, thoroughly understand why those rewards of karma are brought forth in such and such ways [through ignorance and infatuation].

"Therefore, all Bodhisattvas, in order to emancipate sentient beings from misery, are inspired with great spiritual energy and mingle themselves in the filth of birth and death. Though thus they make themselves subject to the laws of birth and death, their hearts are free from sins and attachments. They are like unto those immaculate, undefiled lotusflowers which grow out of mire, yet are not contaminated by it.

"Their great hearts of sympathy which constitute the essence of their being never leave suffering creatures behind [in their journey towards enlightenment]. Their spiritual insight is in the emptiness (*cûnyatâ*) of things, but [their work of salvation] is never outside the world of sins and sufferings."

FROM PINGALAKA, A COMMENTATOR ON NĀGĀRJUNA

"The cloth exists on account of the thread; the matting is possible on account of the rattan. If the thread had its own fixed, unchangeable self-essence, it could not be made out of the flax. If the cloth had its own fixed, unchangeable self-essence, it could not be made from the thread. But as in point of fact the cloth comes from the thread and the thread from the flax, it must be said that the thread as well as the cloth had no fixed, unchangeable self-essence. It is just like the relation that obtains between the burning and the burned. They are brought together under certain conditions, and thus there takes place a phenomenon called burning. The burning and the burned, each has no reality of its own. For when one is absent the other is put out of existence. It is so with all things in this world, they are all empty, without self, without absolute existence. They are like the will-o'-the-wisp."

Chapter XIX
ASANGA AND VASUBANDHU, OTHERS

The brothers Asanga and Vasubandhu, of a fourth-century Brahman family of Purusapura in Gandhāra, belonged originally to the Sarvāstivada school. Asanga, who was a disciple of Maitreyanātha, founder of the Yogācāra or Vijñānavāda school, and was to become its most prominent philosopher, induced his younger brother to join it. The Yogācāra, while a Mahayana school, differs in some respects from the Mādhyamika, for it distinguishes not two kinds of truth or knowledge, as in Nāgārjuna, but three, the third being "positive error." If it can be said that the Mādhyamika is agnostic, then the Yogācāra is idealistic, because the latter conceives of a cosmic mind (*ālaya-vijñāna*) which contains all (the phenomenal universe is its expression in eternal evolution) and provides the basis for something very close, in Western terms, to Platonic idealism. The objective world is thought to consist entirely of mind-stuff, and it is illusion, caused by ignorance, which projects an external universe. Asanga's most influential works are the *Mahāyāna-sangraha-çâstra*, the *Prakarama-āryavācā*, the *Yogācāra-bhumi-çâstra* and the *Mahāyāna-sūtrālankāra*, while Vasubandhu's best-known work is the *Abhidharma-kośa*, a virtual encyclopaedia of Buddhist philosophy. Selections from Asanga and Vasubandhu are followed by excerpts from works dealing with, among other things, the nature of Nirvana, by the Mahayana philosophers Sthiramati and Devala.

FROM ASANGA'S MAHĀYĀNA-SANGRAHA-ÇĀSTRA

".(1) All Buddha-dharmas are characterised with eternality, for the Dharmakâya is eternal.

"(2) All Buddha-dharmas are characterised with an extinguishing power, for they extinguish all the obstacles for final emancipation.

"(3) All Buddha-dharmas are characterised with regeneration, for the Nirmânakâya [Body of Transformation] constantly regenerates.

"(4) All Buddha-dharmas are characterised with the power of attainment, for by the attainment [of truth] they subjugate innumerable evil passions as cherished by ignorant beings.

"(5) All Buddha-dharmas are characterised with the desire to gain, ill humor, folly, and all the other passions of vulgar minds, for it is through the Buddha's love that those depraved souls are saved.

"(6) All Buddha-dharmas are characterised with non-attachment and non-defilement, for Suchness which is made perfect by these virtues cannot be defiled by any evil powers.

"(7) All Buddha-dharmas are above attachment and defilement, for though all Buddhas reveal themselves in the world, worldliness cannot defile them."

FROM THE GENERAL TREATISE ON MAHAYANISM
by Asanga and Vasubandhu

"When the Bodhisattvas think of the Dharmakâya, how have they to picture it to themselves?

"Briefly stated, they will think of the Dharmakâya by picturing to themselves its seven characteristics, which constitute the faultless virtues and essential functions of the Kâya. (1) Think of the free, unrivaled, unimpeded activity of the Dharmakâya, which is manifested in all beings; (2) Think of the eternality of all perfect virtues in the Dharmakâya; (3) Think of its absolute freedom from all prejudice, intellectual and affective; (4) Think of those spontaneous activities that uninterruptedly emanate from the will of the Dharmakâya; (5) Think of the inexhaustible wealth, spiritual and physical, stored in the Body of the Dharma; (6) Think of its intellectual purity which has no stain of onesidedness; (7) Think of the earthly works achieved for the salvation of all beings by the Tâthâgatas who are reflexes of the Dharmakâya."

(1) "Would that all the merits I have accumulated in the past as well as in the present be distributed among all sentient beings and make them all aspire after supreme knowledge, and also that this my pranidhâna be constantly growing in strength and sustain me throughout my rebirths.

(2) "Would that, through the merits of my work, I may, wherever I am born, come in the presence of all Buddhas and pay them homage.

(3) "Would that I be allowed all the time to be near Buddhas like shadow following object, and never to be away from them.

(4) "Would that all Buddhas instruct me in religious truths as best suited to my intelligence and let me finally attain the five spiritual powers of the Bodhisattva.

(5) "Would that I be thoroughly conversant with scientific knowledge as well as the first principle of religion and gain an insight into the truth of the Good Law.

(6) "Would that I be able to preach untiringly the truth to all beings, and gladden them, and benefit them, and make them intelligent.

(7) "Would that, through the divine power of the Buddha, I be allowed to travel all over the ten quarters of the world, pay respect to all the Buddhas, listen to their instructions in the Doctrine, and universally benefit all sentient beings.

(8) "Would that, by causing the wheel of immaculate Dharma to revolve, all sentient beings in the ten quarters of the universe who may listen to my teachings or hear my

name, be freed from all passions and awaken in them the Bodhicitta.

(9) "Would that I all the time accompany and protect all sentient beings and remove for them things which are not beneficial to them and give them innumerable blessings, and also that through the sacrifice of my body, life, and possessions I embrace all creatures and thereby practise the Right Doctrine.

(10) "Would that, though practising the Doctrine in person, my heart be free from the consciousness of compulsion and unnaturalness, as all the Bodhisattvas practise the Doctrine in such a way as not practising it yet leaving nothing unpractised; for they have made their pranidhânas for the sake of all sentient beings."

The Bodhicitta or Intelligence-heart is awakened in us (1) by thinking of the Buddhas, (2) by reflecting on the faults of material existence, (3) by observing the deplorable state in which sentient beings are living, and finally (4) by aspiring after those virtues which are acquired by a Tathâgata in the highest enlightenment.

To describe these conditions more definitely:

(1) *By thinking of the Buddhas.* "All Buddhas in the ten quarters, of the past, of the future, and of the present, when first started on their way to enlightenment, were not quite free from passions and sins (*kleça*) any more than we are at present; but they finally succeeded in attaining the highest enlightenment and became the noblest beings.

"All the Buddhas, by strength of their inflexible spiritual energy, were capable of attaining perfect enlightenment. If enlightenment is attainable at all, why should we not attain it?

"All the Buddhas, erecting high the torch of wisdom through the darkness of ignorance and keeping awake an excellent heart, submitted themselves to penance and mortification, and finally emancipated themselves from the bondage of the triple world. Following their steps, we, too, could emancipate ourselves.

"All the Buddhas, the noblest type of mankind, success-
fully crossed the great ocean of birth and death and of passions and sins; why, then, we, being creatures of intelligence,
could also cross the sea of transmigration.

"All the Buddhas manifesting great spiritual power sacri-
ficed the possessions, body, and life, for the attainment of
omniscience (*sarvajñâ*); and we, too, could follow their noble
examples."

(2) *The faults of the material existence.* "This our bodily
existence consisting of the five skandhas and the four mahats
(elements) is a perpetuator of innumerable evil deeds; and
therefore it should be cast aside. This our bodily existence
constantly secretes from its nine orifices filths and impurities
which are truly loathsome; and therefore it should be cast
aside. This our bodily existence, harboring within itself anger,
avarice, and infatuation, and other innumerable evil passions,
consumes a good heart; and therefore it should be destroyed.
This our bodily existence is like a bubble, like a spatter, and
is decaying every minute. It is an undesirable possession and
should be abandoned. This our bodily existence engulfed in
ignorance is creating evil karma all the time, which throws
us into the whirlpool of transmigration through the six gates."

(3) *The miserable conditions of sentient beings which
arouse the sympathy of the Bodhisattvas.* "All sentient beings
are under the bondage of ignorance. Spell-bound by folly
and infatuation, they are suffering the severest pain. Not believing in the law of karma, they are accumulating evils; going astray from the path of righteousness, they are following
false doctrines; sinking deeper in the whirlpool of passions,
they are being drowned in the four waters of sin.

"They are being tortured with all sorts of pain. They are
needlessly haunted by the fear of birth and death and old
age, and do not seek the path of emancipation. Mortified
with grief, anxiety, tribulation, they do not refrain from committing further foul deeds. Clinging to their beloved ones and
being always afraid of separation, they do not understand that
there is no individual reality, that individual existences

are not worth clinging to. Trying to shun enmity, hatred, pain, they cherish more hatred."

(4) *The virtues of the Tathâgata.* "All the Tathâgatas, by virtue of their discipline, have acquired a noble, dignified mien which inspires every beholder with the thought that dispels pain and woe. The Dharmakâya of all the Tathâgatas is immortal and pure and free from evil attachments. All the Tathâgatas are possessed of moral discipline, tranquillity, intelligence, and emancipation. They are not hampered by intellectual prejudices and have become the sanctuary of immaculate virtues. They have the ten bâlas (powers), four abhayas (fearlessness), great compassion, and the three smṛtyupasthânas (contemplations). They are omniscient, and their love for suffering beings knows no bounds and brings all creatures back to the path of righteousness, who have gone astray on account of ignorance."

FROM STHIRAMATI'S DISCOURSE ON THE MAHÂYÂNA-DHARMADHÂTU

"Nirvâna, Dharmakâya, Tathâgata, Tathâgata-garbha, Paramârtha, Buddha, Bodhicitta, or Bhûtatathâtâ,—all these terms signify merely so many different aspects of one and the same reality; and Bodhicitta is the name given to a form of the Dharmakâya or Bhûtatathâtâ as it manifests itself in the human heart, and its perfection, or negatively its liberation from all egoistic impurities, constitutes the state of Nirvana."

"It is free from compulsive activities; it has no beginning, it has no end; it cannot be defiled by impurities, it cannot be obscured by egoistic individualistic prejudices; it is incorporeal, it is the spiritual essence of Buddhas, it is the source of all virtues earthly as well as transcendental; it is constantly becoming, yet its original purity is never lost.

"It may be likened unto the ever-shining sunlight which may temporarily be hidden behind the clouds. All the modes of passion and sin arising from egoism may sometimes darken the light of the Bodhicitta, but the Citta itself forever remains

free from these external impurities. It may again be likened
unto all-comprehending space which remains eternally identical, whatever happenings and changes may occur in things
enveloped therein. When the Bodhicitta manifests itself in a
relative world, it appears to be subject to constant becoming,
but in reality it transcends all determinations, it is above the
reach of birth and death (*samsâra*).

"So long as it remains buried under innumerable sins arising from ignorance and egoism, it is productive of no earthly
or heavenly benefit. Like the lotus-flower whose petals are yet
unfolded, like the gold that is deeply entombed under the
débris of dung and dirt, or like the light of the full moon
eclipsed by Açura; the Bodhicitta, when blindfolded by the
clouds of passion, avarice, ignorance, and folly, does not reveal its intrinsic spiritual worth.

"Destroy at once with your might and main all those en-
tanglements; then like the full-bloomed lotus-flower, like genuine gold purified from dirt and dust, like the moon in a
cloudless sky, like the sun in its full glory, like mother earth
producing all kinds of cereals, like the ocean containing innumerable treasures, the eternal bliss of the Bodhicitta will
be upon all sentient beings. All sentient beings are then emancipated from the misery of ignorance and folly, their hearts
are filled with love and sympathy and free from the clinging
to things worthless.

"However defiled and obscured the Bodhicitta may find
itself in profane hearts, it is essentially the same as that in
all Buddhas. Therefore, says the Muni of Çakya: 'O Çâripu-
tra, the world of sentient beings is not different from the
Dharmakâya; the Dharmakâya is not different from the world
of sentient beings. What constitutes the Dharmakâya is the
world of sentient beings; and what constitutes the world of
sentient beings is the Dharmakâya.'

"As far as the Dharmakâya or the Bodhicitta is concerned,
there is no radical distinction to be made between profane
hearts and the Buddha's heart; yet when observed from the
human standpoint [that is, from the phenomenal side of exist-
ence] the following general classification can be made:

"(1) The heart hopelessly distorted by numberless ego-istic sins and condemned to an eternal transmigration of birth and death which began in the timeless past, is said to be in the state of profanity.

"(2) The heart that, loathing the misery of wandering in birth and death and taking leave of all sinful and depraved conditions, seeks the Bodhi in the ten virtues of perfection (*pâramitâ*) and 84,000 Buddha-dharmas and disciplines itself in all meritorious deeds, is said to be the [spiritual] state of a Bodhisattva.

"(3) The state in which the heart is emancipated from the obscuration of all passions, has distanced all sufferings, has eternally effaced the stain of all sins and corruptions, is pure, purer, and purest, abides in the essence of Dharma, has reached the height from which the states of all sentient beings are surveyed, has attained the consummation of all knowledges, has realised the highest type of manhood, has gained the power of spiritual spontaneity which frees one from attachment and hesitation,—this spiritual state is that of the fully, perfectly enlightened Tathâgata."

FROM DEVALA'S MAHÂPURUṢA

"Those who are afraid of transmigration and seek their own benefits and happiness in final emancipation, are not at all comparable to those Bodhisattvas, who rejoice when they come to assume a material existence once again, for it affords them another opportunity to benefit others. Those who are only capable of feeling their own selfish sufferings may enter into Nirvâna [and not trouble themselves with the sufferings of other creatures like themselves]; but the Bodhisattva who feels in himself all the sufferings of his fellow-beings as his own, how can he bear the thought of leaving others behind while he is on his way to final emancipation, and when he himself is resting in Nirvânic quietude? . . . Nirvâna in truth consists in rejoicing at other's being made happy, and Sam-sâra in not so feeling. He who feels a universal love for his fellow-creatures will rejoice in distributing blessings among them and find his Nirvâna in so doing.

"Suffering really consists in pursuing one's egotistic happiness, while Nirvâna is found in sacrificing one's welfare for the sake of others. People generally think that it is an emancipation when they are released from their own pain, but a man with loving heart finds it in rescuing others from misery.

"With people who are not kindhearted, there is no sin that will not be committed by them. They are called the most wicked whose hearts are not softened at the sight of others' misfortune and suffering.

"When all beings are tortured by avarice, passion, ill humor, infatuation, and folly, and are constantly threatened by the misery of birth and death, disease and decay . . . how can the Bodhisattva live among them and not feel pity for them?

"Of all good virtues, lovingkindness stands foremost. . . . It is the source of all merit. . . . It is the mother of all Buddhas. . . . It induces others to take refuge in the incomparable Bodhi.

"The loving heart of a Bodhisattva is annoyed by one thing, that all beings are constantly tortured and threatened by all sorts of pain."

Chapter XX
SHĀNTIDEVA

Shāntideva, a poet-philosopher of the Mādhyamika school and the last Indian author represented in this volume, lived in the seventh century. He produced two works, *Śiksāsamuccaya* (Student's Compendium) and *Bodhicaryāvatāra* (Way of Enlightenment), the former compiled from over one hundred early Mahayana works, many no longer extant, the latter dealing with rules of discipline for those following the Bodhisattva ideals. Both works stress the superiority of the Bodhisattva to the Theravada Arhat, and are concerned philosophically with the doctrine of the Void (*Sūnyatā*), though in the *Bodhicaryāvatāra* Shāntideva treats the concept of Bodhicitta from an ethical point of view, advancing it as the initial impulse and motive power of the religious life, combining intellectual illumination and unselfish devotion to the good of others. Briefly the Bodhicitta is the essential quality of a Buddha, and in so far as a man possesses the Bodhicitta he is one with all Buddhas. In such terms it is indistinguishable from the Dharmakaya. Regarding the literary quality of the two works mentioned, in the first Shāntideva provides an extensive commentary for each verse, with the result that the work is impersonal, whereas in the second work there is a true ardor, which makes it one of the most poetic expressions of the Bodhisattva ideal, self-dedication to the task of salvation and love for all beings.

SELECTIONS

"I rejoice exceedingly in all creatures' good works that end the sorrows of their evil lot; may the sorrowful find happi-

ness! . . . In reward for this righteousness that I have won
by my works I would fain become a soother of all the sorrows
of all creatures. . . . The Stillness (Nirvāna) lies in surrender of all things, and my spirit is fain for the Stillness; if I
must surrender all, it is best to give it for fellow-creatures.
I yield myself to all living creatures to deal with me as they
list; they may smite or revile me for ever, bestrew me with
dust, play with my body, laugh and wanton; I have given
them my body, why shall I care? Let them make me do whatever works bring them pleasure; but may mishap never befall
any of them by reason of me. . . . May all who slander
me, or do me hurt, or jeer at me, gain a share in Enlightenment. I would be a protector of the unprotected, a guide of
wayfarers, a ship, a dyke, and a bridge for them who seek
the further Shore; a lamp for them who need a lamp, a bed
for them who need a bed, a slave for all beings who need
a slave. . . . I summon to-day the world to the estate of
Enlightenment, and meanwhile to happiness; may gods,
demons, and other beings rejoice in the presence of all the
Saviours!"

"Trees are not disdainful, and ask for no toilsome wooing;
fain would I consort with those sweet companions! Fain would
I dwell in some deserted sanctuary, beneath a tree or in caves,
that I might walk without heed, looking never behind! Fain
would I abide in nature's own spacious and lordless lands, a
homeless wanderer, free of will, my sole wealth a clay bowl,
my cloak profitless to robbers, fearless and careless of my
body. Fain would I go to my home the graveyard, and com-
pare with other skeletons my own frail body! for this my
body will become so foul that the very jackals will not approach it because of its stench. The bony members born
with this corporeal frame will fall asunder from it, much more
so my friends. Alone man is born, alone he dies; no other has
a share in his sorrows. What avail friends, but to bar his
way? As a wayfarer takes a brief lodging, so he that is travelling through the way of existence finds in each birth but
a passing rest. . . .

"Enough then of worldly ways! I follow in the path of the

wise, remembering the Discourse upon Heedfulness, and putting away sloth. To overcome the power of darkness I concentre my thought, drawing the spirit away from vain paths and fixing it straightly upon its stay. . . .

"We deem that there are two verities, the Veiled Truth and the Transcendent reality. The Reality is beyond the range of the understanding; the understanding is called Veiled Truth. . . . Thus there is never either cessation or existence; the universe neither comes to be nor halts in being. Life's courses, if thou regardest them, are like dreams and as the plantain's branches; in reality there is no distinction between those that are at rest and those that are not at rest. Since then the forms of being are empty, what can be gained, and what lost? Who can be honoured or despised, and by whom? Whence should come joy or sorrow? What is sweet, what bitter? What is desire, and where shall this desire in verity be sought? If thou considerest the world of living things, who shall die therein? who shall be born, who is born? who is a kinsman and who a friend, and to whom? Would that my fellow-creatures should understand that all is as the void! . . . righteousness is gathered by looking beyond the Veiled Truth."

The bodhisattva is lonely, with no . . . companion, and he puts on the armor of supreme wisdom. He acts himself, and leaves nothing to others, working with a will steeled with courage and strength. He is strong in his own strength . . . and he resolves thus:

"Whatever all beings should obtain, I will help them to obtain. . . . The virtue of generosity is not my helper—I am the helper of generosity. Nor do the virtues of morality, patience, courage, meditation and wisdom help me—it is I who help them. The perfections of the bodhisattva do not support me—it is I who support them. . . . I alone, standing in this round and adamantine world, must subdue Māra, with all his hosts and chariots, and develop supreme enlightenment with the wisdom of instantaneous insight!" . . .

Just as the rising sun, the child of the gods, is not stopped

302

. . . by all the dust rising from the four continents of the earth . . . or by wreaths of smoke . . . or by rugged mountains, so the bodhisattva, the Great Being, . . . is not deterred from bringing to fruition the root of good, whether by the malice of others, . . . or by their sin or heresy, or by their agitation of mind. . . . He will not lay down his arms of enlightenment because of the corrupt generations of men, nor does he waver in his resolution to save the world because of their wretched quarrels. . . . He does not lose heart on account of their faults. . . .

"All creatures are in pain," he resolves, "all suffer from bad and hindering karma . . . so that they cannot see the Buddhas or hear the Law of Righteousness or know the Order. . . . All that mass of pain and evil karma I take in my own body. . . . I take upon myself the burden of sorrow; I resolve to do so; I endure it all. I do not turn back or run away, I do not tremble . . . I am not afraid . . . nor do I despair. Assuredly I must bear the burdens of all beings . . . for I have resolved to save them all. I must set them all free, I must save the whole world from the forest of birth, old age, disease, and rebirth, from misfortune and sin, from the round of birth and death, from the toils of heresy. . . . For all beings are caught in the net of craving, encompassed by ignorance, held by the desire for existence; they are doomed to destruction, shut in a cage of pain . . . ; they are ignorant, untrustworthy, full of doubts, always at loggerheads one with another, always prone to see evil; they cannot find a refuge in the ocean of existence; they are all on the edge of the gulf of destruction.

"I work to establish the kingdom of perfect wisdom for all beings. I care not at all for my own deliverance. I must save all beings from the torrent of rebirth with the raft of my omniscient mind. I must pull them back from the great precipice. I must free them from all misfortune, ferry them over the stream of rebirth.

"For I have taken upon myself, by my own will, the whole of the pain of all things living. Thus I dare try every abode of pain, in . . . every part of the universe, for I must not

defraud the world of the root of good. I resolve to dwell in
each state of misfortune through countless ages . . . for the
salvation of all beings . . . for it is better that I alone suffer
than that all beings sink to the worlds of misfortune. There
I shall give myself into bondage, to redeem all the world
from the forest of purgatory, from rebirth as beasts, from the
realm of death. I shall bear all grief and pain in my own
body, for the good of all things living. I venture to stand surety
for all beings, speaking the truth, trustworthy, not breaking
my word. I shall not forsake them. . . . I must so bring to
fruition the root of goodness that all beings find the utmost
joy, unheard of joy, the joy of omniscience. I must be their
charioteer, I must be their leader, I must be their torch-
bearer, I must be their guide to safety. . . . I must not
wait for the help of another, nor must I lose my resolution
and leave my tasks to another. I must not turn back in my
efforts to save all beings nor cease to use my merit for the
destruction of all pain. And I must not be satisfied with small
successes."

Chapter XXI
TIBETAN BUDDHISM

The formation of Tantric Buddhism, which originated in
Bengal and entered Tibet in the eighth century, is still very
much a mystery, yet it can safely be assumed that it is a
compound of yoga, nature worship, ritual magic, and perhaps—though this is disputed—Shivaite mysticism. As Mahayana school, Tantric Buddhism is divided into two paths,
Right-hand and Left-hand, the former being philosophical
with elaborate disciplines designed to develop the *Iddhis*
(supernormal psychic powers), as in the Shingon school of
Japan, while the latter is said to stress practices in which
sex is of great importance. Of all branches of Buddhism, the
Tantric has been the most neglected and misunderstood,
chiefly because of the malpractices, real or supposed, origi-
nating mainly from the decadent forms of late Hindu tradition, but also because its scriptures, such as the *Hevajra
Tantra*, selections from which are given, cannot be understood except from the point of view of yogic experience.
Moreover the scriptures are written in a peculiar idiom, a
language of double meanings and secret conventions, accompanied by diagrams and symbols like the *mandala*, or circle
of glory, which represents, among many other things, the
male and female forces held in balance. This language—San-
dhyābhāsā (Twilight Language)—serves as a protection
against the snooping of other sects and the misuse of yogic
practices by the uninitiated, but it was also created because
ordinary language, or so it must have been assumed, is incapable of expressing mystic experience. Regarding the
much discussed, and maligned, sexual element in Tantri-
cism, it might be said that it stands for the process of en-

lightenment: the union of male and female, in which the active element (*upāya*) is male and the passive (*prajñā*) is female, suggests the process of the knower (Buddha) becoming one with his knowledge (*prajñā*). Figural representations of these symbols are not to be looked upon as humans, but as embodiments of the experiences and visions of meditation. The material from the *Hevajra Tantra* is followed by a few sections from, to give its full title, *The Yoga of Knowing the Mind, The Seeing of Reality, Called Self-Liberation*, one of the greatest of Tibetan works. It is attributed to the Guru Padma-Sambhava, who arrived in Tibet from India in A.D. 747 and taught Tantric Buddhism to a people eager for spiritual instruction. Briefly, *The Yoga of Knowing the Mind* proclaims that mind and the world are inseparable, and that one need only look within to discover the truth. Padma-Sambhava founded in Tibet the Nyingma school of Buddhism, which was inspired by the Indian Yogācāra school, already discussed.

THE PERFORMANCE

a. (1) Now we shall further tell of the practice so excellent and supreme, the cause of perfection by means of which one gains the finality of this perfection in Hevajra.

(2–3) The yogin must wear the sacred ear-rings, and the circlet on his head; on his wrists the bracelets, and the girdle round his waist, rings round his ankles, bangles round his arms; he wears the bone-necklace (4) and for his dress a tiger-skin, and his food must be the five ambrosias. He who practises the yoga of Heruka should frequent the five classes. (5) These five classes that are associated together, he conceives of as one, for by him no distinction is made as between one class or many.

(6) Meditation is good if performed at night beneath a lonely tree or in a cemetery, or in the mother's house, or in some unfrequented spot.

(7) When some heat has been developed, if one wishes to

perform this practice and to gain perfection, then upon this course one should proceed. (8–9) Take a girl of the Vajra-family, fair-featured and large-eyed and endowed with youth and beauty, who has been consecrated by oneself and is possessed of a compassionate disposition, and with her the practice should be performed. In the absence of one from the Vajra-family, it should be performed with a girl from the family of one's special divinity, or (if this fails) from some other. Take her then who is now consecrated with the depositing of the seed of enlightenment.

(10) If in joy songs are sung, then let them be the excellent Vajra-songs, and if one dances when joy has arisen, let it be done with release as its object. Then the yogin, self-collected, performs the dance in the place of Hevajra.

(11) Akṣobhya is symbolized by the circlet, Amitābha by the ear-rings, Ratneśa by the necklace, and Vairocana (by the rings) upon the wrists. (12) Amogha is symbolized by the girdle, Wisdom by the *khaṭvāṅga* and Means by the drum, while the yogin represents the Wrathful One himself. (13) Song symbolizes *mantra*, dance symbolizes meditation, and so singing and dancing the yogin always acts. (14) He should always eat herbs and drink water, then old age and death will not harm him and he will always be protected.

(15) Now he, whose nature is ʜŪṂ (viz. Hevajra), should arrange his piled-up hair as a crest and for the performance of the yoga he should wear the skull-tiara, representing the five buddhas. (16) Making pieces of skull five inches long, he should secure them to the crest. He should wear the two-stranded cord of hair, that symbolizes Wisdom and Means, the ashes and the sacred thread of hair; (17) the sound of the drum is his invocation, and the *khaṭvāṅga* of Wisdom is his meditation. It is this that is intoned and meditated in the practice of Vajra and Skull.

b. (18) He should abandon desire and folly, fear and anger, and any sense of shame. He should forgo sleep and uproot the notion of a self, and then the practice may be performed, there is no doubt. (19) Only when he has made an offering of his own body, should he commence the practice. Nor should he make this gift with the consideration of who is worthy and who is not. (20–21) Enjoying food and drink he should take it as it comes, making no distinction between that which is liked or disliked, eatable or uneatable, drinkable or undrinkable. Nor should he ever wonder whether a thing is suitable or unsuitable.

(22) Even when he has attained to *siddhi* and is resplendent in his perfect knowledge, a disciple respectfully greets his master, if he wishes to avoid the *Avīci* Hell.

(23) Free from learning and ceremony and any cause of shame, the yogin wanders, filled with great compassion in his possession of a nature that is common to all beings. (24) He has passed beyond oblations, renunciation, and austerities, and is freed from *mantra* and meditation. Released from all the conventions of meditation, the yogin performs the practice.

(25) Whatever demon should appear before him, even though it be the peer of Indra, he would have no fear, for he wanders like a lion.

(26) For the good of all beings, his drink is always compassion, for the yogin who delights in the drink of yoga, becomes drunk with no other drink.

CONSECRATION

a. (1) Now I shall expound the ordering of the *maṇḍala*, by means of which a pupil is consecrated, and of the rite too I shall speak.

(2) First the yogin, himself the essence of the god, should purify the site, and having zealously prepared the requisite protection, he should then inscribe the *maṇḍala*. (3) In a garden or in a lonely spot or in a *bodhisattva*'s house or in the centre of the *maṇḍala*-hall one should lay out the *maṇḍala* supreme, (4) using the sacred writing-colours, or secondly powder made from the five gems, or else the grains of rice and so on. (5) With these the *maṇḍala* should be made, in size three cubits plus three inches. The celestial spell who

comes of the Five Families, should be placed there, (6) or whatsoever sixteen-year-old girl is found. A *yoginī* is resorted to, so long as she possesses *śukra*. (7) One binds the face of the *prājñā* and likewise of the *upāya*, and the product of the service rendered one drops into the pupil's mouth. (8) In that very act the Flavour of Sameness should be placed within the pupil's range.

b. From self-experiencing comes this knowledge, which is free from ideas of self and other; (9) like the sky it is pure and void, the essence supreme of non-existence and existence, a mingling of Wisdom and Means, a mingling of passion and absence of passion. (10) It is the life of living things, it is the Unchanging One Supreme; it is all-pervading, abiding in all embodied things. (11) It is the stuff the world is made of, and in it existence and non-existence have their origin. (12) It is all other things that there are: the universal consciousness, the primeval man, *Iśvara, ātman, jīva, sattva, kāla, pudgala.* It is the essential nature of all existing things and illusory in its forms.

(13) First is just Joy,
     Secondly is Joy Supreme,
     Thirdly is the Joy of Cessation,
     Fourth is the Joy Innate.

(14) The first Joy is of this world, the second Joy is of this world, the third Joy is of this world, but the Innate exists not in these three.

(15) Hearing this, all the buddhas, Vajragarbha and the rest, were seized with the greatest astonishment and fell senseless to the ground.

(16) Then the Lord Hevajra whose form comprises all the Buddhas, said these words for the arousing of Vajragarbha, and which were a wondrous cure for their astonishment.

(17) 'Neither passion nor absence of passion is found there, nor yet a middle state. Because of its freedom from all three the Innate is called perfect enlightenment. (18) The essence

of all things and yet free of all things, one may mark it at the beginning of Cessation, but from those other three Joys it is free. (19) At first it appears as cloud, but with realization arisen it appears as *māyā;* then it suddenly appears as sleep with no distinction between sleep and the waking state. (20) The yogin of the Great Symbol gains fulfilment in that which is no fulfilment, for its characteristic is the very absence of any characteristic.'

c. Then the Master spoke of the *maṇḍala,* blazing (21) and brilliant, square with four portals, adorned with garlands and chains and variously coloured streamers, equipped with eight columns (22) and *vajra*-threads, decorated with flowers of different hues, with incense, lamps, and scents, and provided with the eight vessels. (23) These last have branches in them, and their necks are covered with cloth and encircled with the five kinds of gem. To the east one should place the Vessel of Victory. (24) With a fair new thread, well-fastened and of right measurement, the master should bind it round, for it represents the chosen divinity. (25) He should repeat one hundred thousand times the *mantra* of the central divinity, and ten thousand times that of the other components. With the *mantra* quoted above he should purify the site, (26) but first he should present an offering accompanied by the *mantra:* OM A-kāro, &c. He should perform the rite of protection just as prescribed, for as for meditation so it is here. (27) The consecrations which are taught, he should give correctly in his *maṇḍala,* and worship and supplication should be made as ordained.

(28) He should draw the unblemished twofold circle of Gaurī and her companions. In the east he should draw a knife, and continue likewise to the south and west (29) and north, to south-east, south-west, north-west, north-east, even as it is prescribed, and likewise to nadir and zenith.

(30) Then the master should enter the *maṇḍala* as two-armed Hevajra, and assuming the majestic bearing of Vajra-sattva, he should adopt the *ālīḍha* posture. (31) He is washed and purified and perfumed, and adorned with the various

adornments. ʜūṃ ʜūṃ he cries majestically, ʜɪ ʜɪ he cries to terrify.

d. (32) Then the essence is declared, pure and consisting in knowledge, where there is not the slightest difference between *saṃsāra* and *nirvāṇa*.

(33) Nothing is mentally produced in the highest bliss,
　　　and no one produces it,
　　There is no bodily form, neither object nor subject,
　　Neither flesh nor blood, neither dung nor urine,
　　No sickness, no delusion, no purification,

(34) No passion, no wrath, no delusion, no envy,
　　No malignity, no conceit of self, no visible object,
　　Nothing mentally produced and no producer,
　　No friend is there, no enemy,
　　Calm is the Innate and undifferentiated.

e. (35) Then Vajragarbha said: 'How does bodily form consisting of the five elements come about, for in the beginning it is essentially pure and lacks any proper nature?'

(36) Then said the Adamantine Lord, rejoicer of the *ḍākinīs:* 'Calm it is in its proper nature and abiding in all bodily form.'

(37) Vajragarbha then said: 'But how, Lord, should the group of *skandhas* come about?'

(38) The Lord replied: 'At the union of *vajra* and lotus, earth arises there from that contact with the quality of hardness. (39) From the flow of *śukra* water arises, and fire from the friction. Wind comes from the motion, (40) and space corresponds to the bliss. Because it is involved with these five, bliss is not the final essence, for bliss consists in the elements. (41) The Innate is proclaimed as that which arises in spontaneity. The Innate is called self-nature, the single unity of all phenomenal forms.

(42) The *yogin* is Means and Compassion, and the *yoginī* Wisdom and Voidness for she is deprived of causation. The thought of enlightenment is the undivided unity of Compassion and Voidness.

(43) There is no recitation of *mantras*, no austerities, no oblations, no *maṇḍala*, and none of its components.

This is the recitation of *mantras,* the austerities and oblations, this is the *maṇḍala* and its components.

This in short consists of unity of thought.

THE YOGA OF THE NIRVĀṆIC PATH

There being no thing upon which to meditate, no meditation is there whatsoever.

There being no thing to go astray, no going astray is there, if one be guided by memory.

Without meditating, without going astray, look into the True State, wherein self-cognition, self-knowledge, self-illumination shine resplendently. These, so shining, are called 'The *Bodhisattvic* Mind'.

In the Realm of Wisdom, transcendent over all meditation, naturally illuminative, where there is no going astray, the vacuous concepts, the self-liberation, and the primordial Voidness are of the *Dharma-Kāya*.

Without realization of this, the Goal of the *Nirvāṇic* Path is unattainable.

Simultaneously with its realization the *Vajra-Sattva* state is realized.

These teachings are exhaustive of all knowledge, exceedingly deep, and immeasurable.

Although they are to be contemplated in a variety of ways, to this Mind of self-cognition and self-originated Wisdom, there are no two such things as contemplation and contemplator.

When exhaustively contemplated, these teachings merge in at-one-ment with the scholarly seeker who has sought them, although the seeker himself when sought cannot be found.

Thereupon is attained the goal of the seeking, and also the end of the search itself.

Then, nothing more is there to be sought; nor is there need to seek anything.

This beginningless, vacuous, unconfused Clear Wisdom of self-cognition is the very same as that set forth in the Doctrine of the Great Perfection.

Although there are no two such things as knowing and not knowing, there are profound and innumerable sorts of meditation; and surpassingly excellent it is in the end to know one's mind.

There being no two such things as object of meditation and meditator, if by those who practise or do not practise meditation the meditator of meditation be sought and not found, thereupon the goal of the meditation is reached and also the end of the meditation itself.

There being no two such things as meditation and object of meditation, there is no need to fall under the sway of deeply obscuring Ignorance; for, as the result of meditation upon the unmodified quiescence of mind, the non-created Wisdom instantaneously shines forth clearly.

Although there is an innumerable variety of profound practices, to one's mind in its true state they are non-existent; for there are no two such things as existence and non-existence.

There being no two such things as practice and practitioner, if by those who practise or do not practise the practitioner of practice be sought and not found, thereupon the goal of the practice is reached and also the end of the practice itself.

Inasmuch as from eternity there is nothing whatsoever to be practised, there is no need to fall under the sway of errant propensities.

The non-created, self-radiant Wisdom here set forth, being actionless, immaculate, transcendent over acceptance or rejection, is itself the perfect practice.

FROM THE YOGA OF KNOWING THE MIND

Although there are no two such things as pure and impure, there is an innumerable variety of fruits of *yoga*, all of which, to one's mind in its True State, are the conscious content of the non-created *Tri-Kāya.*

There being no two such things as action and performer of action, if one seeks the performer of action and no performer of action be found anywhere, thereupon the goal of all fruit-obtaining is reached and also the final consummation itself.

There being no other method whatsoever of obtaining the fruit, there is no need to fall under the sway of the dualities of accepting and rejecting, trusting and distrusting these teachings.

Realization of the self-radiant and self-born Wisdom, as the manifestation of the *Tri-Kāya* in the self-cognizing mind, is the very fruit of attaining the Perfect *Nirvāṇa.*

THE EXPLANATION OF THE NAMES GIVEN
TO THIS WISDOM

This Wisdom delivers one from the eternally transitory Eight Aims.

Inasmuch as it does not fall under the sway of any extreme, it is called 'The Middle Path'.

It is called 'Wisdom' because of its unbroken continuity of memory.

Being the essence of the vacuity of mind, it is called 'The Essence of the Buddhas'.

If the significance of these teachings were known by all beings, surpassingly excellent would it be.

Therefore, these teachings are called 'The Means of Attaining the Other Shore of Wisdom [or The Transcendental Wisdom]'.

To Them who have passed away into *Nirvāṇa,* this Mind is both beginningless and endless; therefore is it called 'The Great Symbol'.

Inasmuch as this Mind, by being known and by not being known, becomes the foundation of all the joys of *Nirvāṇa* and of all the sorrows of the *Sangsāra,* it is called 'The All-Foundation'.

The impatient, ordinary person when dwelling in his fleshly body calls this very clear Wisdom 'common intelligence'.

Regardless of whatever elegant and varied names be given to this Wisdom as the result of thorough study, what Wisdom other than it, as here revealed, can one really desire?

To desire more than this Wisdom is to be like one who seeks an elephant by following its footprints when the elephant itself has been found.

THE YOGA OF THE THATNESS

Quite impossible is it, even though one seek throughout the Three Regions, to find the Buddha elsewhere than in the mind.

Although he that is ignorant of this may seek externally or outside the mind to know himself, how is it possible to find oneself when seeking others rather than oneself?

He that thus seeks to know himself is like a fool giving a performance in the midst of a crowd and forgetting who he is and then seeking everywhere to find himself.

This simile also applies to one's erring in other ways.

Unless one knows or sees the natural state of substances [or things] and recognizes the Light in the mind, release from the *Sangsāra* is unattainable.

Unless one sees the Buddha in one's mind, *Nirvāṇa* is obscured.

Although the Wisdom of *Nirvāṇa* and the Ignorance of the *Sangsāra* illusorily appear to be two things, they cannot truly be differentiated.

It is an error to conceive them otherwise than as one.

Erring and non-erring are, intrinsically, also a unity.

By not taking the mind to be naturally a duality, and allowing it, as the primordial consciousness, to abide in its own place, beings attain deliverance.

The error of doing otherwise than this arises not from Ignorance in the mind itself, but from not having sought to know the Thatness.

Seek within thine own self-illuminated, self-originated

315

mind whence, firstly, all such concepts arise, secondly, where they exist, and, lastly, whither they vanish.

This realization is likened to that of a crow which, although already in possession of a pond, flies off elsewhere to quench its thirst, and finding no other drinking-place returns to the one pond.

Similarly, the radiance which emanates from the One Mind, by emanating from one's own mind, emancipates the mind.

The One Mind, omniscient, vacuous, immaculate, eternally, the Unobscured Voidness, void of quality as the sky, self-originated Wisdom, shining clearly, imperishable, is Itself the Thatness.

The whole visible Universe also symbolizes the One Mind.

By knowing the All-Consciousness in one's mind, one knows it to be as void of quality as the sky.

Although the sky may be taken provisionally as an illustration of the unpredictable Thatness, it is only symbolically so.

Inasmuch as the vacuity of all visible things is to be recognized as merely analogous to the apparent vacuity of the sky, devoid of mind, content, and form, the knowing of the mind does not depend on the sky-symbol.

Therefore, not straying from the Path, remain in that very state of the Voidness.

Chapter XXII
I-TSING

As I-Tsing, the Chinese monk and traveler, says in this selection from his *A Record of Buddhist Practices,* he began waiting on his Buddhist teachers after his seventh year. He was admitted into the Order at fourteen, and though he had formed the idea of traveling to India much earlier, it was not to be carried out till his thirty-seventh year (671). He was away for twenty-five years, and traveled to more than thirty countries. After his return to China he translated fifty-six works out of around four hundred he brought back, and only death (at the age of seventy-nine in 713) brought an end to this great labor. His voyage took him to a number of sacred spots, including Bodh Gaya, and he spent ten years at Nalanda, learning from the Doctors of the Law and collecting scriptures. So as to be able to translate these eventually, he spent four years at the center of Sanskrit learning Śrī-vijaya, and after returning to China briefly in search of collaborators, he spent another five years there. In addition to the work represented here, I-Tsing wrote *Memoirs of the Eminent Monks Who Went in Search of the Law in the Western Countries* (there is a French translation by Chavannes), a succession of rather sad stories about pilgrims who, like himself, suffered greatly in their quest of the Law. China's T'ang dynasty produced no figure more impressive than I-Tsing, and in this account of his experiences with his two teachers, we not only see him at his best but learn much of significance about relations between masters and disciples during Buddhism's shift eastward, which he helped bring about.

SUCH ACTIONS WERE NOT PRACTISED BY THE VIRTUOUS OF OLD

Now as to my teachers, my Upâdhyâya (i.e. teacher in reading) was the venerable Shan-yü (a Chinese priest), and my Karmâkârya (i.e. teacher in discipline) was Hui-hsi, Master of Dhyâna (i.e. meditation). After the seventh year of my age I had the opportunity of waiting on them. Both of them were teachers of great virtue who lived in the monastery Shên-t'ung, built (A.D. 396) by the Dhyâna-master, (Sêng-) Lang, a sage of the Chin-yü Valley of T'ai Shan. Shan-yü was a native of Teh Chou, and Hui-hsi, of Pei Chou. Both thought that the solitary forest life, though good for one's self, had little power to benefit others, and came to P'ing-lin, where, according to rule, they took up their abode in the temple of 'Earth-Cave' (T'u-k'u), overlooking the clear stream named 'Stooping Tiger.' The temple is situated about forty Chinese miles west of the capital of Ch'i Chou (in Shan-tung).

They were in the habit of preparing an unlimited store of food, by which means they could freely supply the people or make offerings to the Buddhas. Whatever gifts they received, they gave away freely and willingly. It may be said of them that their Four Vows (Pranidhâna) were limitless as heaven and earth, and the salvation they preached to the people by the Four Elements of Popularity (Saṅgraha-vastu) was very liberal, and those who were saved by them were innumerable as the sand or dust. They dutifully built temples wherein to live, and did many meritorious deeds. Now I shall briefly state the seven virtues of my Upâdhyâya, Shan-yü.

1. THE WIDE LEARNING OF MY TEACHER

Besides his deep insight into the Tripitaka, he was well read in very many authors. He was equally learned in both Confucianism and Buddhism, and skilled in all the six arts of the Confucian school. He was well versed in the

Sciences of Astronomy, Geography, and Mathematics, the Arts of Divination, and the Knowledge of the Calendar; thus he could explore the secret of anything, had he cared to do so. How vast in him was the Ocean of Wisdom, with its ever-flowing tide! How brilliant was his garden of literature, with its ever-blooming flowers! The works of his own production, the pronouncing dictionary of the Tripitaka, and several word-books have been handed down to later generations. He used to say, 'There is no character *in* Chinese which I do not know' (more lit. 'It is not a character, if I do not know it').

2. THE IMMENSE ABILITY OF MY TEACHER

My teacher was skilled in writing according to the styles of the 'Seal Character,' Chuan and Chou, and also the styles of Chung and Chang. He had a good ear for the musical notes of string- and wind-instruments, as in the case of Tzŭ Ch'i, who could tell whether *the lute of Yü Po-ya* expressed a peak or a stream. He could use the axe as skilfully as the artisan Shih removes a (little bit of) mud like a (fly's) wing. Thus it may be said of him that a wise man is not a mere utensil (as we should say, 'he is not a one-stringed instrument').

3. MY TEACHER'S INTELLIGENCE

When my teacher was studying the Sûtra of the Great Decease (Mahâparinirvâna-sûtra), he read it through in one day. When he re-read the same for the first time he finished the whole in four months, carefully testing the hidden doctrine contained in it, and earnestly searching for its deep meaning. In educating a little boy he was in the habit of beginning with half a character; one cannot imagine his having occasion to grasp his sword (on account of anger with his pupil). He would instruct a man of great ability as if he were filling a perfect vessel, and the instructed would have the benefit of being beautified by precious gems. Some time ago, when people had become destitute of principle dur-

ing the last period of the Sui dynasty (A.D. 589–617), my
teacher removed to the town of Yang in consequence of the
disturbance. Many priests agreed, when they saw him there,
that he was but a fool, as he was plain and rustic in personal
appearance. They compelled the newcomer to read the
Sûtra of the Great Decease, and ordered two under-teachers
to see it done sentence by sentence. His tone was grave and
sorrowful as he raised his voice in reading. From sunrise till
afternoon all the three cases of the Sûtra were read through.
There was no one amongst those present who did not praise
and congratulate him, and they bade him rest, greatly com-
mending his wonderful powers. People know this incident full
well, and this is not merely my own eulogy.

4. THE LIBERALITY OF MY TEACHER

Here is an instance of his bargaining. Whatever price
one demands, that he gives. Be the article dear or cheap, he
does not mind, and never beats down the price. If some
balance be due to him and the debtor bring the sum, he will
not receive it at all. Men of his time considered him a man
of unsurpassed generosity.

5. THE LOVING-KINDNESS OF MY TEACHER

With him honesty had a greater weight than riches. He
followed the practice of a Bodhisattva; when one begged
from him, he never refused. His constant wish was to give
away three small coins every day. Once during a cold winter
month there came a travelling priest named Tao-an, who had
walked a long way, braving a heavy snowstorm, and his feet
were bitterly frozen. He was obliged to stay in the village for
a few days; his swollen feet were wounded and covered with
sores. The villagers conveyed him in a carriage to the monastery where my teacher dwelt. As soon as the latter came out
to the gate and saw the poor man's feet, without regard to
himself he bound up the sores with his own garment. The
garment was one newly-made and worn that day for the first

time. The bystanders would have hindered him, saying that he had better get an old garment so that he should not stain the new one. In reply he said: 'When rendering help in a case of bitter suffering, what time have we to make use of anything but what is at hand.' All those who saw or heard of this action praised him much. Although such a deed is not in itself very difficult to accomplish, nevertheless its like is not often practised.

6. MY TEACHER'S DEVOTION TO WORK

My teacher read through all the eight classes of the Pragñâpâramitâsûtra a hundred times, and read the same again and again when he afterwards perused the whole of the Tripitaka.

As regards the practice of the meritorious deeds necessary for entrance into the Pure Land (Sukhâvati), he used to exert himself day and night, purifying the ground where the images of the Buddhas were kept, and where the priests abode. He was rarely seen idle during his life. He generally walked bare-footed, fearing lest he should injure any insects. Training his thought and directing his heart, as he did, he was hardly ever seen inactive and remiss. The stands of incense dusted and cleaned by him were beautiful, like the lotus-flowers of Sukhâvati that unfolded for the sake of the nine classes of the saved beings. The sight of the hall of the Sûtras, decked and adorned by him, was something like the sky above the Vulture Peak, showering down the Four Flowers.

One could not but praise his religious merit when one saw his work in the sanctuary. He was personally never conscious of getting tired; he expected the end of his life to be the end of his work. His leisure from reading he devoted to the worship of the Buddha Amitâyus (= Amitâbha). The four signs of dignity were never wanting in him. The sun's shadow never fell upon him idle (i.e. 'he never wasted a minute of time marked by the sun's course'). The smallest grains of sand, when accumulated, would fill up heaven and earth. The deeds which make up salvation are of various kinds.

One year before his death, he collected all his own writings and other books in his possession, and heaping them up into a great pile, he tore them up and made them into mortar to be used (as material) for the two statues of the Vagra, which were then in preparation. His pupils came forward and remonstrated with him, saying: 'Our Honoured Master, if it be necessary to use papers, let us use blank papers instead.' The Master replied: 'I have long been entirely taken up with this literature, by which I have been led astray. Ought I to-day to allow it to mislead others? If I do, it is as bad as causing one to swallow a deadly poison or leading one into a dangerous path. That would never do. A priest may lose sight of his proper function if he attain too great success in secular work. The permission to do both is given by the Buddha to men of superior talent only, but *indulgence* in any but one's proper avocation will lead to great error. What one does not wish to have oneself, must not be given to others.' On hearing this, the pupils retired, saying: 'It is well.' But the important books, such as Shuo-wên and other lexicons, were given to the pupils. He then taught them, saying: 'When you have done a rough study of the Chinese classics and history, and acquired a vague knowledge of the characters, you should turn your attention to the Excellent Buddhist Canon. You must not let this snare prove too great an attraction.' Previous to his death he told his pupils that he was certainly going to leave this world after three days; that he should die while holding a broom, and his remains were to be left in the marshy wilderness. Early in the morning on the third day he walked by the clear stream, and sitting down quietly under a white willow-tree which stood desolate, near to the green waving reeds, he passed away holding a broom in his hand. One of his pupils, the Dhyâna-master, Hui-li by name, went to see his teacher there early that very morning. But what is it? The latter is silent. The pupil drew near and touched the master's body with his hands. He felt warmth still proceeding from the master's head, but the hands and feet were already cold. Then weeping, he called together all the distant friends. When all had assembled, the priests grieved and wept so much that the sad scene might be compared with the red river pouring out its stream of blood on the earth; his lay-followers also sobbed and cried, so that the confused crowd might be compared to the gems on the precious mountain broken to pieces. Sad it is that the tree of Bodhi should wither so soon; it is also piteous that the vessel of the Law should sink so suddenly. He was buried in the west garden of his monastery. He was sixty-three years of age. What he left behind him after his death consisted of only three garments, a pair of slippers and shoes, and the bed-clothes which he was using.

When my teacher died, I was twelve years old. The great elephant (i.e. 'great teacher') having departed, I was destitute of my refuge.

Laying aside my study of secular literature, I devoted myself to the Sacred (Buddhist) Canon. In my fourteenth year I was admitted to the Order, and it was in my eighteenth year that I formed the intention of travelling to India, which was not, however, realised till my thirty-seventh year. On my departure, I went to my late master's tomb to worship, and to take leave. At that time, seared foliage of the trees around had already grown so as to half embrace the tomb, and wild grasses filled the graveyard. Though the spirit world is hidden from us, nevertheless I paid him all honour just as if he had been present. While turning round and glancing in every direction, I related my intention of travelling. I invoked his spiritual aid, and expressed my wish to requite the great benefits conferred on me by that benign personage (lit. 'face').

The Dhyâna-master, Hui-hsi, my second teacher, exclusively devoted himself to the study of the Vinaya. His mind was clear and calm. He never neglected the devotional exer-

cises which were to be performed, six times day and night.
He was never tired of teaching from morning till night the
four classes of the devotees (Bhikshu, -nî, Upâsaka, and
Upâsikâ). It may be said of him that even in time of confusion
he is quite free from alarm, nay, that he is more peaceful and
quiet; and no one, be he priest or layman, has ever found
him partial.

The Saddharmapundarîka was his favourite book; he
read it once a day for more than sixty years; thus the perusal
amounted to twenty thousand times. Although he happened
to live during the troublous times of the last period of the Sui
dynasty (A.D. 589–617), and to wander here and there
guided by fate alone, yet he never relinquished his determined idea (of reading). He possessed the six organs of
sense in perfection, and the four elements of a healthy body.
He never had any illness during the sixty years of his life.
Whenever he began to recite the Sûtras near the stream,
there appeared an auspicious bird which came and alighted
in a corner of the hall. While he was reciting, the bird also
cried as if it were influenced by his voice, and as if listening to him. He was ever good in disposition, and well acquainted with musical notes. He was especially skilled in
writing the running hand, and also the 'clerk's style.' He was
never weary of guiding and instructing. Although he did not
care much for the study of secular books, yet he was naturally gifted and well versed in them. Both his Gâthâ on the
six Pâramitâs and the words of prayer composed by him were
written on the lamp-stands of the Temple of the Earth-
cave. Afterwards when he was engaged in copying the Saddharmapundarîka (the 'Lotus of the Good Law') he compared the styles of the famous handwritings (of old), and
chose the best of all (in copying). Breathing out the impure
air, and keeping scents in his mouth, he was in the habit of
purifying himself by washing and bathing. Suddenly there
once appeared miraculously on this Sûtra a relic of the Buddha. When the copy of the Sûtra was finished, the title on
each scroll was impressed in golden letters, which were
beautiful by the side of the silver hooks of the scroll. He

324

deposited them in the jewelled cases, which, being in themselves bright, added to the brilliancy of the gemmed rollers.
The then ruling emperor came to T'ai Shan, and hearing the
news, asked the owner to present the copy to the imperial
household, to be used in worship.

These two teachers of mine, Shan-yü and Hui-hsi, were
the successors of the former sage, (Sêng-) Lang the Dhyâna-
master.

Lang the Dhyâna-master was born in the time of the two
dynasties of Ch'in, and was celebrated beyond all the five
classes of people. He received offerings from all quarters;
he in person visited the gate of every almsgiver. He taught
men according to circumstance and ability. His deeds were
suited to the needs of the devotees. The exercise, however,
of his personal influence was far above the worldly affairs. The
temple of Shên-t'ung (i.e. 'Miraculous Power') was named
thus after him. His religious character was beyond our understanding. Full information is given in his separate biography
(Liang-kao-sêng-ch'uan).

At that time the rulers respected Buddhism, and people
were devotional (about A.D. 350–417).

When they were intending to build this temple, on entering the forest they heard a tiger roaring near the northern
stream of T'ai Shan. On emerging from it they again heard a
horse neighing in the southern valley of the mountain. The
water in the Heavenly Well, though constantly drawn, never
decreased, and the grains in the Celestial Granary, though
perpetually taken out, did not diminish in quantity. The man
himself has long disappeared, but the influence left behind
him is not yet lost. These two teachers of mine, and another
resident priest, the venerable Dhyâna-master, Ming-teh,
were well versed in the Vinaya doctrine and fully acquainted
with the purport of the Sûtras. As instructors of the disciples
they severely prohibited the practice of such things as burning one's fingers or destroying one's body by fire, which were
never taught by the Buddha. I myself received instruction
from these teachers in person, and did not get my information
from a hearsay statement. You should also carefully examine

the above points of the sages of old, and give your attention to the teaching of the ancients.

From the time that the white horse was unbridled till the dark elephant was saddled, Kâsyapamâtaṅga and Dharmaraksha, illumining the world by their rays (of wisdom), became as it were the sun and moon of the Divine Land (China), and K'ang-sêng-hui and Fà-hien, by virtue of their example, became the ford and bridge to the Celestial Treasure House (India). Tao-an and Hui-yen were stooping like tigers on the south of the rivers Yang-tze and Han; Hsiu and Li were flying high like falcons on the north of the rivers Hwang and Chi.

Successors in the Order were found regularly and continuously; thus the wave of wisdom has been perpetuated uncorrupted. Devout laymen praised and appreciated the unceasing fragrance of the Law. We have never heard that any of those teachers allowed the practice of burning one's fingers.

Nor have we ever seen the burning of one's body permitted by them. The mirror of the Law is before our eyes, and the wise should carefully learn therefrom.

The Dhyâna-master, Hui-hsi, used, in the stillness of the evening, to sympathise with me in my boyhood, and comforted me with many a kind word. Sometimes his talk was about the (frailty of) yellow leaves (i.e. about impermanence), so that he might divert me from my intense longing for my mother.

Sometimes he spoke to me telling me of the habit of young crows, and urging that I should strive to repay the great love with which I had been brought up. Sometimes he said: 'You must arduously strive to promote the prosperity of the Three Jewels, so that they may not cease to exist; nor should you indulge in the study of secular literature to such an extent as to render your life useless.' Even when I had reached the age of ten years, I could only listen to his instruction; I was not yet able to fathom his meaning. Every morning at the fifth watch I went to his room to ask what to do. Each time the master showed his affection by patting me with his hand as lovingly as a kind mother fondles her child. When-

ever he had any nice food, he used to give me the most delicate portion. If I asked him for anything, I was never disappointed. My Upâdhyâya, Shan-yü, was a strict father to me,
while the Dhyâna-master, Hui-hsi, was a tender mother.
Thus our relations were almost as perfect as though we
had been kinsmen.

When I reached the age of Ordination, Hui-hsi became
my Upâdhyâya. Once after I had sworn to the Precepts, when
he was taking the air on a fine night, suddenly as he was
burning incense, my master, overcome by emotion, thus instructed me: 'It is long since the Great Sage attained Nirvâna, and now his teaching is becoming misinterpreted. Many
are those who wish to bow to the Precepts, yet few are they
who observe them. You must abstain with firm resolve from
the important things prohibited, and not transgress the first
group (meaning the Pârâgika-offences). If you are guilty of
any of the other transgressions, it is I who will suffer in hell
on account of you. Besides, you ought not to do such hurtful
things as to burn your fingers or destroy your body with
fire.' On the same day that the Holy Precepts had been
graciously imparted to me, I was thus instructed and happily
favoured with his pity.

Since that time I have made such a strenuous effort that
whenever I found myself liable to fail, I feared greatly that I
had already committed an offence, however small it might
be. I devoted myself to the study of the Vinaya for five
years.

I could fathom the depth of the comments composed by
Fâ-li, the Vinaya teacher, and explain accurately the principles
treated by another Vinaya teacher, Tao-hsüan, in his works.
As soon as I had become acquainted with the Vinaya rules
(lit. 'observance and transgression'), my teacher ordered me
to deliver one lecture on this subject.

While I was attending his lecture on the Greater Sûtra, I
went round begging food, having only one meal, and sat up all
night, without lying down.

The forest monastery where we lived was very distant from
the village, but I never neglected this practice. Whenever I

think of the kind instruction of my great teacher my tears overflow.—I do not know whence they come.

We see that, when a Bodhisattva wishes in pity to save those who are suffering, he is willing to throw himself even into the blazing flame of a great fire, and, when a philanthropist thinks of looking after a child of poverty he watches even the narrow entrance of a small house. This is no mistake. I received all instruction personally from him, and I did not learn from him by hearsay. One day he graciously said to me: 'At present I do not lack those who wait on me, and you should no longer remain with me, for it hinders your study.' Then I departed from him, with a metal staff in my hand, for Eastern Wei, where I devoted myself to the study of the Abhidharma(-saṅgîti) and the Samparigrahasâstra. From thence I went to the Western Capital (Si-an Fu), carrying a satchel on my back, and there I studied diligently the Kosa and the Vidyâmâtrasiddhi. On my departure for India I returned from this capital to my native place. I sought advice from my great teacher Hui-hsi, saying: 'Venerable Sir, I am intending to take a long journey; for, if I witness that with which I have hitherto not been acquainted, there must accrue to me great advantage. But you are already advanced in age, so that I cannot carry out my intention without consulting you.' My teacher thus answered me: 'This is a great opportunity for you which will not occur twice. (I assure you) I am much delighted to hear of your intention so wisely formed (lit. "I am aroused by your righteous reasons"). Why should I indulge any longer my personal affection?

'If I live long enough (to see you return), it will be my joy to witness you transmitting the Light. Go without hesitation; do not look back upon things left behind. I certainly approve of your pilgrimage to the holy places. Moreover it is a most important duty to strive for the prosperity of Religion. Rest clear from doubt.'

Thus not only was my intention graciously approved, but now I had his command, which I could not in any case disobey.

At last I embarked from the coast of Kwang-chou (Can-

ton), in the eleventh month in the second year of the Hsien
Hêng period (A.D. 671), and sailed for the Southern Sea.
Thus I could journey from country to country, and so could
go to India for pilgrimage. On the eighth day in the second
month in the fourth year of the Hsien Hêng period (A.D.
673), I arrived at Tâmralipti, which is a port on the coast
of Eastern India. In the fifth month I resumed my journey
westwards, (while) finding companions here and there.
Then I went to the Nâlanda monastery and to the Diamond
Seat, and thus at last visited all the holy places. Then I
retraced the course of my journey and arrived at Srîbhoga.

It may be said of him that he was a great, good, and wise
teacher, who perfected the Brahmakarya (religious student-
ship), and mastered the true teaching of the Purushadamya-
sârathi (Tamer of the human steed, i.e. the Buddha). Nor
do we err in speaking thus. In fact he became the typical
man of the period, satisfying the needs of the world and
guiding the life of mankind.

I was brought up and instructed by him personally until I
reached manhood. Coming across this raft in the ocean of
existence I advanced one day's voyage (nearer to the shore).
I was fortunate enough to discover the Ford of Life in association with these two teachers. Good actions or charity, however insignificant, are generally praised in songs and music
by the people. How much more then should such great wisdom and benevolence as that of my teachers be eulogised in
poem or composition!

My poem is as follows:—

'My loving father and mother! You protected me in the
past ages. You brought and entrusted me in my boyhood to
the care of these intelligent teachers. You did this, suppress-
ing your love and grief, while I was still a helpless child.
Whilst taking lessons, I practised from time to time what I
had learnt. I rooted my character in the soil of good admonitions and rules. The two teachers were to me as sun and
moon giving light. Their virtues may be compared to those
of the Yin and Yang (i.e. "the positive and negative principles that pervade nature"). The point of my sword of wis-

dom was sharpened by them. And by them also my body of
the Law was nourished. They were never tired in their personal instruction. Sometimes they taught me throughout the
whole night, taking no sleep; sometimes for the whole day,
without any food. The most gifted man looks often as if he
is possessed of no special talent, and yet such a man's wisdom is too deep to be gauged by us. Such men were my
teachers.

'Light disappeared from the Mount T'ai (his two teachers
left T'ai Shan, see the beginning of this chapter). Virtue was
hidden in the riverside of Ch'i (the two teachers came to Ch'i,
and settled there; one died in Ch'i). The sea of wisdom was
in them vast, and stretched far. The grove of meditation
flourished luxuriantly. Their styles of composition were very
elegant; their power of mental abstraction very wonderful.
"Grind, but you cannot reduce the mass. Dye, but you cannot
make it black." On the eve of his departure from this world,
my teacher (Shan-yü) showed a strange sign. A curious example was manifested when the bird listened to a man's
reading. While I was still young, one (Shan-yü) passed away,
leaving the other (Hui-hsi) behind. Whatever meritorious
deeds I may have accomplished, I offer as masses for the
deceased. To one I would repay after his death the benefits
conferred on me during his lifetime. To the other may I be
able to requite his kindness in his lifetime, though I be
far separated from him. May we meet each other some day
in order that we may prolong our happiness.

'May I receive their instruction at each successive birth, in
order to secure Final Liberation. I hope that my charity may
increase to a mountain-height by the practice of righteousness.

'Deep as the depth of a lake be my pure and calm meditation. Let me look for the first meeting under the Tree of
the Dragon Flower, when I hear the deep rippling voice of
the Buddha Maitreya. Passing through the four modes of
birth, I would desire to perfect my mind, and thus fulfil the
three long Kalpas (ages) required for Buddhahood.'

Fearing lest my readers should think my statement about the literary power of my teacher groundless, I shall give a specimen of his style. Once on the fifteenth day of the second month (this day was kept up as the day of Nirvâna), priests and laymen crowded to the South Hill—where (Sêng-) Lang the Dhyâna-master resided (T'ai Shan). They visited the strange objects of the 'Heavenly Well' and 'Celestial Granary,' and worshipped at the holy niche and the sacred temple. There they performed a grand ceremony of worship and alms-giving. About this time all the literary men in the dominion of the king of Ch'i assembled there, each having oceans of writings and mountains of literature at his command. They were all vying for distinction, and boasting of their excellent character.

It was proposed that they should compose a poem celebrating the statue of the deceased Lang and his temple, and they unanimously put my teacher Hui-hsi forward to compose the same. He accepted the offer without hesitation.

It seemed just as if the flowing stream had stirred up its waves and helped him while he was writing on the walls. He did not stop for a moment, but continued writing with fluent pen. He finished without delay the composition, which needed no addition or correction.

His poem was as follows:—

'In great brightness shone the Sage of old.
Far and wide as the ocean was his excellent counsel spread.
A lonely valley was his resort, and here was his residence.
Good fortune smiled upon him to no purpose.
Vast and desolate are the mountains and rivers through
    eternity.
Men and generations pass away with the passing ages.
Spiritual knowledge alone can fathom the problem of non-
    existence.
What else do we see but the picture of the old Sage left
    behind?'

Having seen this poem of my teacher, the whole assembly of literary men were of one mind in greatly admiring it.

Some deposited their pens on a branch of a pine-tree, whilst others threw their inkpots down the side of a rock. They said: 'Si Shih (name of a woman whose beauty was regarded as ideal) has shown her face; how can Mu Mo (name of an ugly woman who served the Yellow Emperor) make her appearance?' There were many clever men present, but none was able to compete with the rhymes. The rest of my teacher's works are separately collected.

I, I-tsing, respectfully send greeting to all the venerable friends of the Great Chou, with whom I used to hold light conversation (Vâhya-kathâ) or discuss the sacred Law (Dharma-kathâ), with some of whom I made acquaintance when I was young, while others became bosom friends in middle age; the more gifted of these became spiritual teachers, but many insignificant men were among them. In the forty chapters of the present work I have treated only of important matters, and what I have recorded is customary at the present time among the teachers and pupils of India. My record rests distinctly on the words of the Buddha, and is not evolved from my own mind. Our life passes swiftly like a rapid river. We cannot prognosticate in the morning what will happen in the evening. Thus fearing lest I may not be able to see you and state these things to you in person, I send the record and present it to you before my return. Whenever you have time to spare, pray study the matter recorded in the book, and thus you may approach my heart. All that I state is in accordance with the Āryamûlasarvâstivâdanikâya (School) and no other.

Again I address you in rhyme as follows:—

'The good doctrine of our master have I respectfully recorded.
Oh, that great and gracious counsel!
All rests on the noble teaching of the Buddha;
I cannot say that my humble intellect has sought it out.
I may not have any chance of a personal meeting with you.
Thus I send on my record to you beforehand.

I shall be happy if you find this work worth keeping.

Let it even accompany you in your carriage.

Let the word of a humble man even such as myself be accepted.

Following in the footprints of sages of a hundred past generations,

I sow the beautiful seed for thousands of years to come.

My real hope and wish is to represent the Vulture Peak in the Small Rooms of my friends, and to build a second Râgagriha City in the Divine Land of China.'

Chapter XXIII
PLATFORM SCRIPTURE
OF THE SIXTH PATRIARCH

No work in the history of Chinese Ch'an Buddhism (Zen in Japanese) has had greater impact than *The Platform Scripture of the Sixth Patriarch*, which is believed to be based on a lecture by the Sixth Patriarch, Hui-neng, 683–713, recorded dy his disciple Fa-hai (the translation is of a text discovered in the Tun-huang caves, one older and much shorter than the traditional version). In spite of the fact that its source is disputed (Hui Shih, for example, believes it to be the work of an eighth-century follower of Shen-hui, 670–762, another disciple of the Patriarch and the monk chiefly responsible for paving the way for his succession), it is accepted as scripture by all branches of the Zen sect in Japan, and Hui-neng, who was a native of Hsin-chou in South China, is second in importance only to Bodhidharma, First Patriarch, the Indian monk who established the Ch'an school in China in 526 (variant: 520). Hui-neng's story and the essence of his teaching are rather fully presented in the scripture, and it only remains to mention that he lived in seclusion for some years after being handed "the robe and the Law," and only when he was thirty-nine, in 676, did he begin to preach. Through his influence the Southern School of Ch'an, which stressed complete and instantaneous enlightenment, triumphed over the Northern, and the subsequent history of the sect is primarily that of the Southern School, which in addition to its insistence on sudden enlightenment developed iconoclastic attitudes toward the Buddhas and the Bodhisattvas and disregarded scriptures and rituals. In the years following Hui-neng and Shen-hui there was a succession of famous

334

Ch'an masters who established different branches of the sect in the T'ang dynasty, notably the masters Lin-chi and Ts'ao-Tung. Essentially Ch'an is an intuitive method of spiritual training whose aim is the discovery of the reality within, which can be described as the fundamental unity in all that makes up the world. This reality is the Buddha-nature or, as in all Mahayana systems, the Void.

Monk Hung-jen [601–675] asked Hui-neng: "Whence have you come to pay homage to me? What do you want from me?"

Hui-neng answered: "Your disciple is from Lingnan ["South of the Mountains Ranges," in the region of the present Canton]. A citizen of Hsin-chou, I have come a great distance to pay homage, without seeking anything except the Law of the Buddha."

The Great Master reproved him, saying: "You are from Lingnan and, furthermore, you are a barbarian. How can you become a Buddha?"

Hui-neng answered: "Although people are distinguished as northerners and southerners, there is neither north nor south in Buddha-nature. In physical body, the barbarian and the monk are different. But what is the difference in their Buddha-nature?"

The Great Master intended to argue with him further, but, seeing people around, said nothing. Hui-neng was ordered to attend to duties among the rest. It happened that one monk went away to travel. Thereupon Hui-neng was ordered to pound rice, which he did for eight months.

One day the Fifth Patriarch [Hung-jen] suddenly called all his pupils to come to him. As they assembled, he said: "Let me say this to you. Life and death are serious matters. You people are engaged all day in making offerings [to the Buddha], going after blessings and rewards only, and you make no effort to achieve freedom from the bitter sea of life and death. Your self-nature seems to be obscured. How can blessings save you? Go to your rooms and examine yourselves. He who is enlightened use his perfect vision of self-nature and write me a verse. When I look at his verse, if it reveals deep understanding, I shall give him the robe and the Law and make him the Sixth Patriarch. Hurry, hurry!"

At midnight Shen-hsiu, holding a candle, wrote a verse on the wall of the south corridor, without anyone knowing about it, which said:

> Our body is the tree of Perfect Wisdom,
> And our mind is a bright mirror.
> At all times diligently wipe them,
> So that they will be free from dust.

The Fifth Patriarch said: "The verse you wrote shows some but not all understanding. You have arrived at the front of the door but you have not yet entered it. Ordinary people, by practicing in accordance with your verse, will not degenerate. But it will be futile to seek the Supreme Perfect Wisdom while holding to such a view. One must enter the door and see his self-nature. Go away and come back after one or two days of thought. If you have entered the door and seen your self-nature, I shall give you the robe and the Law."

Shen-hsiu went away and for several days could not produce another verse.

Hui-neng also wrote a verse . . . which says:

> The tree of Perfect Wisdom is originally no tree.
> Nor has the bright mirror any frame.
> Buddha-nature is forever clear and pure.
> Where is there any dust?

Another verse:

> The mind is the tree of Perfect Wisdom.
> The body is the clear mirror.
> The clear mirror is originally clear and pure.
> Where has it been affected by any dust?

Monks in the hall were all surprised at these verses. Hui-neng, however, went back to the rice-pounding room. The

Fifth Patriarch suddenly realized that Hui-neng was the one
of good knowledge but was afraid lest the rest learn it. He
therefore told them: "This will not do." The Fifth Patriarch
waited till midnight, called Hui-neng to come to the hall,
and expounded the *Diamond Sūtra*. As soon as Hui-neng heard
this, he understood. That night the Law was imparted to
him without anyone knowing it, and thus the Law and the
robe [emblematic] of Sudden Enlightenment were transmitted to him. "You are now the Sixth Patriarch," said the
Fifth Patriarch to Hui-neng, "The robe is the testimony of
transmission from generation to generation. As to the Law, it is
to be transmitted from mind to mind. Let people achieve
understanding through their own effort."

The Fifth Patriarch told Hui-neng: "From the very beginning, the transmission of the Law has been as delicate
as a hanging thread of silk. If you remain here, some one
might harm you. You had better leave quickly."

[Hui-neng, having returned South, said]: I came and stayed
in this place [Canton] and have not been free from perse-
cution by government officials, Taoists, and common folk.
The doctrine has been transmitted down from past sages;
it is not my own idea. Those who wish to hear the teachings
of the past sages should purify their hearts. Having heard
them, they should first free themselves from their delusions
and then attain enlightenment."

Great Master Hui-neng declared: "Good friends, perfection is inherent in all people. It is only because of the delusions of the mind that they cannot attain enlightenment by
themselves. They must ask the help of the enlightened and
be shown the way to see their own nature. Good friends,
as soon as one is enlightened, he will achieve Perfect Wisdom."

"Good friends, in my system, meditation and wisdom are
the bases. First of all, do not be deceived that the two are
different. They are one reality and not two. Meditation is the
substance (*t'i*) of wisdom and wisdom is the function (*yung*)
of meditation. As soon as wisdom is achieved, meditation is
included in it, and as soon as meditation is attained, wisdom is
included in it. Good friends, the meaning here is that medi-

tation and wisdom are identified. A follower after the Way should not think wisdom follows meditation or vice versa or that the two are different. To hold such a view would imply that the dharmas possess two different characters. To those whose words are good but whose hearts are not good, meditation and wisdom are not identified. But to those whose hearts and words are both good and for whom the internal and external are one, meditation and wisdom are identified. Self-enlightenment and practice do not consist in argument. If one concerns himself about whether [meditation or wisdom] comes first, he is deluded. Unless one is freed from the consideration of victory or defeat, he will produce the [imagining of] dharmas and the self, and cannot be free from the characters [of birth, stagnation, deterioration, and extinction]."

"Good friends, there is no distinction between sudden enlightenment and gradual enlightenment in the Law, except that some people are intelligent and others stupid. Those who are ignorant realize the truth gradually, while the enlightened ones attain it suddenly. But if they know their own minds and see their own nature, then there will be no difference in their enlightenment. Without enlightenment, they will be forever bound in transmigration."

"Good friends, in my system, from the very beginning, whether in the sudden enlightenment or gradual enlightenment tradition, absence of thought has been instituted as the main doctrine, absence of phenomena as the substance, and nonattachment as the foundation. What is meant by absence of phenomena? Absence of phenomena means to be free from phenomena when in contact with them. Absence of thought means not to be carried away by thought in the process of thought. Nonattachment is man's original nature. [In its ordinary process], thought moves forward without a halt; past, present, and future thoughts continue as an unbroken stream. But if we can cut off this stream by an instant of thought, the Dharma-Body will be separated from the physical body, and at no time will a single thought be attached to any dharma. If one single instant of thought is attached to anything, then every thought will be attached. That will be bondage. But if in regard to all dharmas, no thought is attached to anything, that means freedom. This is the reason why nonattachment is taken as the foundation.

"Good friends, to be free from all phenomena means absence of phenomena. Only if we can be free from phenomena will the reality of nature be pure. This is the reason why absence of phenomena is taken as the substance.

"Absence of thought means not to be defiled by external objects. It is to free our thoughts from external objects and not to allow dharmas to cause our thoughts to rise. If one stops thinking about things and wipes out all thought, then as thought is terminated once and for all, there will be no more rebirth. Take this seriously, followers of the Path. It is bad enough for a man to be deceived himself through not knowing the meaning of the Law. How much worse is it to encourage others to be deceived! Not only does he fail to realize that he is deceived, but he also blasphemes against the scripture and the Law. This is the reason why absence of thought is instituted as the doctrine.

"All this is because people who are deceived have thoughts about sense-objects. With such thoughts, pervasive views arise, and all sorts of defilements and erroneous thoughts are produced from them.

"However, the school instituted absence of thought as the doctrine. When people are free from [erroneous] views, no thought will arise. If there are no thoughts, there will not even be 'absence of thought.' Absence means absence of what? Thought means thought of what? Absence means freedom from duality and all defilements. Thought means thought of Thusness and self-nature. True Thusness is the substance of thought and thought is the function of True Thusness. It is the self-nature that gives rise to thought. [Therefore] in spite of the functioning of seeing, hearing, sensing, and knowing, the self-nature is not defiled by the many sense-objects and always remains as it truly is. As the *Vimalakīrti Scripture* says: 'Externally it skillfully differentiates the various dharma-characters and internally it abides firmly in the First Principle.'"

"Good friends, in this system sitting in meditation is at bottom neither attached to the mind nor attached to purity, and there is neither speech nor motion. Suppose it should be attached to the mind. The mind is at bottom an imagination. Since imagination is the same as illusion, there is nothing to be attached to. Suppose it were attached to purity, man's nature is originally pure. It is only because of erroneous thought that True Thusness is obscured. Our original nature is pure as long as it is free from erroneous thought. If one does not realize that his own nature is originally pure and makes up his mind to attach himself to purity, he is creating an imaginary purity. Such purity does not exist. Hence we know that what is to be attached to is imaginary."

"This being the case, in this system, what is meant by sitting in meditation? To sit means to obtain absolute freedom and not to allow any thought to be caused by external objects. To meditate means to realize the imperturbability of one's original nature. What is meant by meditation and calmness? Meditation means to be free from all phenomena and calmness means to be internally unperturbed. If one is externally attached to phenomena, the inner mind will at once be disturbed, but if one is externally free from phenomena, the inner nature will not be perturbed. The original nature is by itself pure and calm. It is only because of causal conditions that it comes into contact with external objects, and the contact leads to perturbation. There will be calmness when one is free from external objects and is not perturbed. Meditation is achieved when one is externally free from phenomena and calmness is achieved when one is internally unperturbed. Meditation and calmness mean that externally meditation is attained and internally calmness is achieved."

"All scriptures and writings of the Mahāyāna and Hīnayāna schools as well as the twelve sections of the Canon were provided for man. It is because man possesses the nature of wisdom that these were instituted. If there were no man, there would not have been any dharmas. We know, therefore, that dharmas exist because of man and there are all these scriptures because there are people to preach them.

"Among men some are wise and others stupid. The stupid are inferior people, whereas the wise ones are superior. The ignorant consult the wise and the wise explain the Law to them and enable them to understand. When the ignorant understand, they will no longer be different from the wise. Hence we know that without enlightenment, a Buddha is no different from all living beings, and with enlightenment, all living beings are the same as a Buddha. Hence we know that all dharmas are immanent in one's person. Why not seek in one's own mind the sudden realization of the original nature of True Thusness?"

The Great Master said to Chi-ch'eng [pupil of Shen-hsiu]: "I hear that your teacher in his teaching transmits only the doctrine of discipline, calmness, and wisdom. Please tell me his explanation of these teachings."

Chi-ch'eng said: "The Reverend Shen-hsiu said that discipline is to refrain from all evil actions, wisdom is to practice all good deeds, and calmness is to purify one's own mind. These are called discipline, calmness, and wisdom. This is his explanation. I wonder what your views are."

Patriarch Hui-neng answered: "His theory is wonderful, but my views are different."

Chi-ch'eng asked: "How different?"

Hui-neng answered: "Some people realize [the Law] more quickly and others more slowly."

Chi-ch'eng then asked the Patriarch to explain his views on discipline, calmness, and wisdom. The Great Master said: "Please listen to me. In my view, freeing the mind from all wrong is the discipline of our original nature. Freeing the mind from all disturbances is the calmness of our original nature. And freeing the mind from all delusions is the wisdom of our original nature."

Master Hui-neng continued: "Your teacher's teaching of discipline, calmness, and wisdom is to help wise men of the inferior type but mine is to help superior people. When one realizes his original nature, then discipline, calmness, and wisdom need not be instituted."

Chi-ch'eng said: "Great Master, please explain why they need not be instituted."

The Great Master said: "The original nature has no wrong, no disturbance, no delusion. If in every instant of thought we introspect our minds with Perfect Wisdom, and if it is always free from dharmas and their appearances, what is the need of instituting these things? The original nature is realized suddenly, not gradually step by step. Therefore there is no need of instituting them."

Chi-ch'eng bowed, decided not to leave Ts'ao-li Mountain, but immediately became a pupil and always stayed close by the Master.

Chapter XXIV
ZEN POEMS

What follows is a selection of Zen Buddhist poems written by Japanese masters from the thirteenth century to the present. The poems are so suggestive in themselves that explication is rarely necessary; furthermore, the poets rarely theorized about the poems they would write from time to time, and for good reason: to them poetry was not, as so often in the West, an art to be cultivated but a means by which an attempt at the nearly inexpressible could be made. Though certain of the poems are called *satori* (enlightenment) and others death poems, in a sense all Zen poetry deals with momentous experience. There are, in other words, no finger exercises, and though some of the poems may seem comparatively light, there is not one that is not totally in earnest, fully inspired. Indeed when you consider the Zennist's traditional goal, the all-or-nothing quality of his striving after illumination, this is scarcely to be wondered at. The Zen state of mind has been described as "one in which the individual identifies with an object without any sense of restraint," as in this poem by Bunan:

> The moon's the same old moon,
> The flowers exactly as they were,
> Yet I've become the thingness
> Of all the things I see!

Zen poetry is highly symbolic, and the moon here is a common symbol. It should be remembered, in relation to the use of such symbols, that Zen is a Mahayana school, and that the Zennist searches, always within himself, for the in-

343

divisible moon reflected not only on the sea but on each dew drop. To discover this, the Dharmakaya, in all things is for the Zennist to discover his own Buddha-nature. Perhaps most Zen poems, whether designated as such or not, are satori poems, which are composed immediately after an awakening and are presented to a master for approval. Daito's poem is typical:

> At last I've broken Unmon's barrier!
> There's exit everywhere—east, west; north, south.
> In at morning, out at evening; neither host nor guest.
> My every step stirs up a little breeze.

And here is a satori poem by Eichu:

> My eyes eavesdrop on their lashes!
> I'm finished with the ordinary!
> What use has halter, bridle
> To one who's shaken off contrivance?

Traditionally death poems are written or dictated by Zennists right before death. The author looks back on his life and, in a few highly compressed lines, expresses his state of mind at the inevitable hour. The following are among the best known:

Fumon

> Magnificent! Magnificent!
> No-one knows the final word.
> The ocean bed's aflame,
> Out of the void leap wooden lambs.

Kukoku

> Riding this wooden upside-down horse,
> I'm about to gallop through the void.
> Would you seek to trace me?
> Ha! Try catching the tempest in a net.

Zen Poems

Zekkai

The void has collapsed upon the earth,
Stars, burning, shoot across Iron Mountain.
Turning a somersault, I brush past.

The void, mentioned in all three of these death poems, is
the great Penetralium of Zen. The mind, it is thought, is a
void in which objects are stripped of their objectivity and
reduced to their essence. In the death poem which follows,
by Bokuo, there is an important Zen symbol, the ox, which
here serves as an object of discipline:

For seventy-two years
I've kept the ox well under.
Today, the plum in bloom again,
I let him wander in the snow.

Bokuo, in his calm acceptance of death, proves himself a true
Zen-man. Though satori and death figure heavily in Zen
poetry, most of the poems deal with nature and man's place
in it. Simply put, the Buddha-nature is by no means peculiar to man. It is discoverable in all that exists, animate or
inanimate. Perhaps in this poem by Ryokan the Zen spirit
is perfectly caught:

Without a jot of ambition left
I let my nature flow where it will.
There are ten days of rice in my bag
And, by the hearth, a bundle of firewood.
Who prattles of illusion or nirvana?
Forgetting the equal dusts of name and fortune,
Listening to the night rain on the roof of my hut,
I sit at ease, both legs stretched out.

DOGEN (1200–1253, Soto)

The Western Patriarch's doctrine is transplanted!
I fish by moonlight, till on cloudy days.
Clean, clean! Not a worldly mote falls with the snow
As, cross-legged in this mountain hut, I sit the evening
    through.

DOGEN, *WAKA*

Coming, going, the waterfowl
Leaves not a trace,
Nor does it need a guide.

A waka on "The mind must operate without abiding anywhere" (from the *Diamond Sutra*).

DOGEN

This slowly drifting cloud is pitiful;
What dreamwalkers men become.
Awakened, I hear the one true thing—
Black rain on the roof of Fukakusa Temple.

MUSO (1275–1351, Rinzai)

Many times the mountains have turned from green to yellow—
So much for the capricious earth!
Dust in your eyes, the triple world is narrow;
Nothing on the mind, your chair is wide enough.

MUSO, *SATORI POEM*

Vainly I dug for a perfect sky,
Piling a barrier all around.
Then one black night, lifting a heavy
Tile, I crushed the skeletal void!

DAITO (1282–1337, Rinzai), *DEATH POEM*

To slice through Buddhas, Patriarchs
I grip my polished sword.
One glance at my mastery,
The void bites its tusks!

GETSUDO (1285–1361, Rinzai), *SATORI POEM*

I moved across the Dharma-nature,
The earth was buoyant, marvelous.
That very night, whipping its iron horse,
The void galloped into Cloud Street.

DAICHI (1290–1366, Soto)

Thoughts arise endlessly,
There's a span to every life.
One hundred years, thirty-six thousand days:
The spring through, the butterfly dreams.

JAKUSHITSU (1290–1367, Rinzai)

Refreshing, the wind against the waterfall
As the moon hangs, a lantern, on the peak
And the bamboo window glows. In old age mountains
Are more beautiful than ever. My resolve:
That these bones be purified by rocks.

CHIKUSEN (1292–1348, Soto)

He's part of all, yet all's transcended;
Solely for convenience he's known as master.
Who dares say he's found him?
In this rackety town I train disciples.

BETSUGEN (1294–1364, Rinzai)

All night long I think of life's labyrinth—
Impossible to visit the tenants of Hades.
The authoritarian attempt to palm a horse off as deer
Was laughable. As was the thrust at
The charmed life of the dragon. Contemptible!
It's in the dark that eyes probe earth and heaven,
In dream that the tormented seek present, past.
Enough! The mountain moon fills the window.
The lonely fall through, the garden rang with cricket song.

The authoritarian attempt . . . refers to the Chinese classic
Shiki, in which Choko presents a horse to the Emperor, claiming
it is a deer. The Emperor's courtiers, obsequious to Choko, do not
dispute his claim.

As was the thrust at . . . refers to Soshi (Chuantzu): Shu
spent three years acquiring the skill to kill dragons, but of course
this did him no good.

JUO (1296–1380, Rinzai)

Beyond the snatch of time, my daily life.
I scorn the State, unhitch the universe.
Denying cause and effect, like the noon sky,
My up-down career: Buddhas nor Patriarchs can convey it.

SHUTAKU (1308–1388, Rinzai)

For all these years, my certain Zen:
Neither I nor the world exist.
The sutras neat within the box,
My cane hooked upon the wall,
I lie at peace in moonlight
Or, hearing water plashing on the rock,
Sit up: none can purchase pleasure such as this:
Spangled across the step-moss, a million coins!

Mind set free in the Dharma-realm,
I sit at the moon-filled window
Watching the mountains with my ears,
Hearing the stream with open eyes.
Each molecule preaches perfect law,
Each moment chants true sutra:
The most fleeting thought is timeless,
A single hair's enough to stir the sea.

RYUSHU (1308–1388, Rinzai)

Why bother with the world?
Let others go gray, bustling east, west.
In this mountain temple, lying half-in,
Half-out, I'm removed from joy and sorrow.

SHUNOKU (1311–1388, Rinzai)

After the spring song, "Vast emptiness, no holiness,"
Comes the song of snow-wind along the Yangtze River.
Late at night I too play the noteless flute of Shorin,
Piercing the mountains with its sound, the river.

Vast emptiness, no holiness. Bodhidharma's reply to the question put by Butei, Emperor of Ryo, "What is the primary principle of Buddhism?" (Cf. the first koan of *Hekiganroku*.)
Shorin. Name of the temple where Bodhidharma, on finding that Butei was not a true Zennist, sat in Zen for nine years. To reach the temple, he had to cross the Yangtze River.

TESSHU (14th century, Rinzai)

How heal the phantom body of its phantom ill,
Which started in the womb?
Unless you pluck a medicine from the Bodhi-tree,
The sense of karma will destroy you.

TSUGEN (1322–1391, Soto)

Not a mote in the light above,
Soul itself cannot offer such a view.
Though dawn's not come, the cock is calling:
The phoenix, flower in beak, welcomes spring.

GUCHU (1323–1409, Rinzai)

Men without rank, excrement spatulas,
Come together, perfuming earth and heaven.
How well they get along in temple calm
As, minds empty, they reach for light.

Excrement spatulas. To a monk's question, "What is the Buddha?", Unmon replied, "An excrement spatula." (Cf. the twenty-first koan of *Mumonkan.*)

MUMON (1323–1390, Rinzai)

Life: a cloud crossing the peak.
Death: the moon sailing.
Oh just once admit the truth
Of noumenon, phenomenon,
And you're a donkey-tying pole!

A donkey-tying pole. Often used in Zen writing, meaning a trifle.

GIDO (1325–1388, Rinzai): *INSCRIPTION OVER HIS DOOR*

He who holds that nothingness
Is formless, flowers are visions,
Let him enter boldly!

REIZAN (–1411, Rinzai)

The myriad differences resolved by sitting, all doors opened.
In this still place I follow my nature, be what it may.
From the one hundred flowers I wander freely,
The soaring cliff—my hall of meditation
(With the moon emerged, my mind is motionless).
Sitting on this frosty seat, no further dream of fame.
The forest, the mountain follow their ancient ways,
And through the long spring day, not even the shadow of a
    bird.

MYOYU (1333–1393, Soto), *SATORI POEM*

Defying the power of speech, the Law Commission on Mount
    Vulture!
Kasyapa's smile told the beyond-telling.
What's there to reveal in that perfect all-suchness?
Look up! the moon-mind glows unsmirched.

HAKUGAI (1343–1414, Rinzai), *SATORI POEM*

Last year in a lovely temple in Hirosawa,
This year among the rocks of Nikko,
All's the same to me:
Clapping hands, the peaks roar at the blue!

World of the Buddha

NANEI (1363–1438, Rinzai)

Splitting the void in half,
Making smithereens of earth,
I watch inching toward
The river, the cloud-drawn moon.

KODO (1370–1433, Rinzai)

Serving the Shogun in the capital,
Stained by worldly dust, I found no peace.
Now, straw hat pulled down, I follow the river:
How fresh the sight of gulls across the sand!

IKKYU (1394–1481, Rinzai)

After ten years in the red-light district,
How solitary a spell in the mountains.
I can see clouds a thousand miles away,
Hear ancient music in the pines.

VOID IN FORM

When, just as they are,
White dewdrops gather
On scarlet maple leaves,
Regard the scarlet beads!

A waka on "Void in Form" (from *The Heart Sutra*).

FORM IN VOID

The tree is stripped,
All color, fragrance gone,
Yet already on the bough,
Uncaring spring!

A waka on "Form in Void" (from *The Heart Sutra*).

GENKO (–1505, Soto)

Unaware of illusion or enlightenment,
From this stone I watch the mountains, hear the stream.
A three-day rain has cleansed the earth,
A roar of thunder split the sky.
Ever serene are linked phenomena,
And though the mind's alert, it's but an ash heap.
Chilly, bleak as the dusk I move through,
I return, a basket brimmed with peaches on my arm.

SAISHO (–1506, Rinzai): *ON JOSHU'S NOTHINGNESS*

Earth, mountains, rivers—hidden in this nothingness.
In this nothingness—earth, mountains, rivers revealed.
Spring flowers, winter snows:
There's no being nor non-being, nor denial itself.

YUISHUN (–1544, Soto), *SATORI POEM*

Why, it's but the motion of eyes and brows!
And here I've been seeking it far and wide.
Awakened at last, I find the moon
Above the pines, the river surging high.

TAKUAN (1573–1645, Rinzai), *WAKA*

Though night after night
The moon is stream-reflected,
Try to find where it has touched,
Point even to a shadow.

A waka on "The willow is green, the rose is red."

GUDO (1579–1661, Rinzai)

It's not nature that upholds utility.
Look! even the rootless tree is swelled
With bloom, not red nor white, but lovely all the same.
How many can boast so fine a springtide?

KARASUMARU-MITSUHIRO (1579–1638, Rinzai)

Beware of gnawing the ideogram of nothingness:
Your teeth will crack. Swallow it whole, and you've a treasure
Beyond the hope of Buddha and the Mind. The east breeze
Fondles the horse's ears: how sweet the smell of plum.

UNGO (1580–1659, Rinzai)

Whirled by the three passions, one's eyes go blind;
Closed to the world of things, they see again.
In this way I live: straw-hatted, staff in hand,
I move illimitably, through earth, through heaven.

DAIGU (1584–1669, Rinzai)

Here none think of wealth or fame,
All talk of right and wrong is quelled:
In autumn I rake the leaf-banked stream,
In spring attend the nightingale.

Who dares approach the lion's
Mountain cave? Cold, robust,
A Zen-man through and through,
I let the spring breeze enter at the gate.

MANAN (1591–1654, Soto)

Unfettered at last, a traveling monk,
I pass the old Zen barrier.
Mine is a traceless stream-and-cloud life.
Of those mountains, which shall be my home?

FUGAI (17th century, Soto)

Only the Zen-man knows tranquillity:
The world-consuming flame can't reach this valley.
Under a breezy limb, the windows of
The flesh shut firm, I dream, wake, dream.

BUNAN (1602–1676, Rinzai), *WAKA*

When you're both alive and dead,
Thoroughly dead to yourself,
How superb
The smallest pleasure!

MANZAN (1635–1714, Rinzai)

One minute of sitting, one inch of Buddha.
Like lightning all thoughts come and pass.
Just once look into your mind-depths:
Nothing else has ever been.

TOKUO (1649–1709, Rinzai)

The town's aflame with summer heat,
But Mount Koma is steeped in snow.
Such is a Zen-man's daily life—
The lotus survives all earthly fire.

355

HAKUIN (1685–1768, Rinzai)

Past, present, future: unattainable,
Yet clear as the moteless sky.
Late at night the stool's cold as iron,
But the moonlit window smells of plum.

•

Priceless is one's incantation,
Turning a red-hot iron ball to butter oil.
Heaven? Purgatory? Hell?
Snowflakes fallen on the hearth fire.

•

How lacking in permanence the minds of the sentient—
They are the consummate nirvana of all Buddhas.
A wooden hen, egg in mouth, straddles the coffin.
An earthenware horse breaks like wind for satori-land.

•

You no sooner attain the great void
Than body and mind are lost together.
Heaven and Hell—a straw.
The Buddha-realm, Pandemonium—shambles.
Listen: a nightingale strains her voice, serenading the snow.
Look: a tortoise wearing a sword climbs the lampstand.
Should you desire the great tranquillity,
Prepare to sweat white beads.

SENGAI (1750–1837, Rinzai): *ON BASHO'S "FROG"*

Under the cloudy cliff, near the temple door,
Between dusky spring plants on the pond,
A frog jumps in the water, plop!
Startled, the poet drops his brush.

Basho's haiku on the frog is one of the most famous ever written. Here is Harold G. Henderson's translation (*An Introduction to Haiku*. Doubleday Anchor):

Old pond—
and a frog-jump-in
water-sound.

KOSEN (1808–1893, Rinzai), *SATORI POEM*

A blind horse trotting up an icy ledge—
Such is the poet. Once disburdened
Of those frog-in-the-well illusions,
The sutra-store's a lamp against the sun.

TANZAN (1819–1892, Soto)

Madness, the way they gallop off to foreign shores!
Turning to the One Mind, I find my Buddhahood,
Above self and others, beyond coming and going.
This will remain when all else is gone.

KANDO (1825–1904, Rinzai)

It's as if our heads were on fire, the way
We apply ourselves to perfection of That.
The future but a twinkle, beat yourself,
Persist: the greatest effort's not enough.

SHINKICHI TAKAHASHI (1901–   , Rinzai)

THE POSITION OF THE SPARROW

The sparrow has cut the day in half:
Afternoons—yesterday's, the day after tomorrow's—
Layer the white wall.
Those of last year, and next year's too,
Are dyed into the wall—see them?—
And should the wall come down,
Why, those afternoons will remain,
Glimmering, just as they are, through time.

(That was a colorless realm where,
Nevertheless, most any color could well up.)

Just as the swan becomes a crow,
So everything improves—everything:
No evil *can* persist, and as to things,
Why, nothing is unchangeable.
The squirrel, for instance, is on the tray,
Buffalos lumber through African brush,
The snail wends along the wall,
Leaving a silver trail.
The sparrow's bill grips a pomegranate seed:
Just anything can resemble a lens, or a squirrel

Because the whole is part, there's not a whole,
Anywhere, that is not part.
And all those happenings a billion years ago,
Are happening now, all around us: time.
Indeed this morning the sparrow hopped about
In that nebulous whirlpool
A million light years hence.

And since the morning is void,
Anything can be. Since mornings
A billion years from now are nothingness,
We can behold them.
The sparrow stirs,
The universe moves slightly.

THE PEACH

A little girl under a peach tree,
Whose blossoms fall into the entrails
Of the earth.

There you stand, but a mountain may be there
Instead; it is not unlikely that the earth
May be yourself.

You step against a plate of iron and half
Your face is turned to iron. I will smash
Flesh and bone

And suck the cracked peach. She went up the mountain
To hide her breasts in the snowy ravine.
Women's legs

Are more or less alike. The leaves of the peach tree
Stretch across the sea to the end of
The continent.

The sea was at the little girl's beck and call.
I will cross the sea like a hairy
Caterpillar

And catch the odor of your body.

HORSE

Young girls bloom like flowers.
Unharnessed, a horse trots
Round its driver who
Grasps it by a rope.

Far off a horse is going round and round
In a square plot.

Not miserable, not cheerful either,
The bay horse is prancing,
Shaking its head, throwing up its legs
By turn: it is not running.

But there are no spectators
In what looks like an amphitheater.

White cherry blossoms fall like snowflakes
In the wind. All at once,
Houses, people vanish, into silence.
Nothing moves. Streetcars, buses, are held back
Silently. Quiet, everything.
All visible things become this nothingness.

The horse's bones—beautiful in their gray sheen.

A horse is going round and round,
Dancing now, with *joie de vivre*,
Under the cliff of death.

QUAILS

It is the grass that moves, not the quails.
Weary of embraces, she thought of
Committing her body to the flame.

When I shut my eyes, I hear far and wide
The air of the Ice Age stirring.
When I open them, a rocket passes over a meteor.

A quail's egg is complete in itself,
Leaving not room enough for a dagger's point.
All the phenomena in the universe: myself.

Quails are supported by the universe
(I wonder if that means subsisting by God).
A quail has seized God by the neck

With its black bill, because there is no
God greater than a quail.
(Peter, Christ, Judas: a quail.)

A quail's egg: idle philosophy in solution.
(There is no wife better than a quail.)
I dropped a quail's egg into a cup for buckwheat noodles,

And made havoc of the Democratic Constitution.
Split chopsticks stuck in the back, a quail husband
Will deliver dishes on a bicycle, anywhere.

The light yellow legs go up the hill of Golgotha.
Those quails who stood on the rock, became the rock!
The nightfall is quiet, but inside the congealed exuviae

Numberless insects zigzag, on parade.

MASCOT

Somebody is breathing inside me—
Birds, the very earth.

The ocean's in my chest. Walking,
I always throw myself down.

Newssheets, a puppy were dancing in the wind—
Trucks rushed by,

Empty trucks stout enough to carry the earth
On their puncture-proof tires.

The instant I raised my hand to wave,
I was nowhere.

The puppy was sprawled out on its belly,
Run over—again, again.

You're a badger, I'll bet, posing as a mascot
With that moonlit tie

And, sticking from your pocket, night's flower.

STITCHES

My wife is always knitting, knitting:
Not that I watch her,
Not that I know what she thinks.

(Awake till dawn
I drowned in your eyes—
I must be dead:
Perhaps it's the mind that stirs.)

With that bamboo needle
She knits all space, piece by piece,
Hastily hauling time in.

Brass-cold, exhausted,
She drops into bed and,
Breathing calmly, falls asleep.

Her dream must be deepening,
Her knitting coming loose.

FISH

I hold a newspaper, reading.
Suddenly my hands become cow ears,
Then turn into Pusan, the South Korean port.

Lying on a mat
Spread on the bankside stones,
I fell asleep.
But a willow leaf, breeze-stirred,
Brushed my ear.
I remained just as I was,
Near the murmurous water.

When young there was a girl
Who became a fish for me.
Whenever I wanted fish
Broiled in salt, I'd summon her.
She'd get down on her stomach
To be sun-cooked on the stones.
And she was always ready!

Alas, she no longer comes to me.
An old benighted drake,
I hobble homeward.
But look, my drake feet become horse hoofs!
Now they drop off
And, stretching marvelously,
Become the tracks of the Tokaido Railway Line.

Chapter XXV
ZEN SERMONS

Zen Buddhist sermons are unlike those of any other religion, whatever the sect of the master—Rinzai, which stresses sudden enlightenment, Soto, which maintains that gradually perfected meditation is the same as enlightenment, or Obaku, which has more in common with Rinzai, practicing *zazen* (formal meditation) and employing *koan* (problem for meditation), though the *Nembutsu* (invocation of the Buddha Amida) is also engaged in by this sect. The purpose of the Zen sermon is less to guide toward what is vaguely thought to be the ethical life than to point directly at the experience of enlightenment, for it is assumed by the masters that those listening to them are morally upright, and that what they desire is an awakening which will result in a new way of viewing themselves in the world. In spite of the similarity in the masters' aims, however, their sermons are as individual as they themselves are—Bankei-Eitaku's are a good example. The historical continuity of the sermon literature is possibly due to the fact that when compared with other Buddhist schools, Zen has been able to absorb shifts and upheavals, in politics and culture, which normally bring about changes in religion and philosophy. Most of the sermons which follow, while not expounding doctrine as such, are philosophical, as is almost always true of Mahayana literature, and it may surprise the reader to find ideas advanced which are very contemporary in feeling.

DOGEN (1200–1253, Soto)

ON LIFE AND DEATH

"Since there is Buddhahood in both life and death," says Kassan, "neither exists." Jozan says, "Since there is no Buddhahood in life or death, one is not led astray by either." So go the sayings of the enlightened masters, and he who wishes to free himself of the life-and-death bondage must grasp their seemingly contradictory sense.

To seek Buddhahood outside of life and death is to ride north to reach Southern Etsu or face south to glimpse the North Star. Not only are you traveling the wrong way on the road to emancipation, you are increasing the links in your karma-chain. To find release you must begin to regard life and death as identical to nirvana, neither loathing the former nor coveting the latter.

It is fallacious to think that you simply move from birth to death. Birth, from the Buddhist point of view, is a temporary point between the preceding and the succeeding; hence it can be called birthlessness. The same holds for death and deathlessness. In life there is nothing more than life, in death nothing more than death: we are being born and are dying at every moment.

Now, to conduct: in life identify yourself with life, at death with death. Abstain from yielding and craving. Life and death constitute the very being of Buddha. Thus, should you renounce life and death, you will lose; and you can expect no more if you cling to either. You must neither loathe, then, nor covet, neither think nor speak of these things. Forgetting body and mind, by placing them together in Buddha's hands and letting him lead you on, you will without design or effort gain freedom, attain Buddhahood.

There is an easy road to Buddhahood: avoid evil, do nothing about life-and-death, be merciful to all sentient things, respect superiors and sympathize with inferiors, have neither likes nor dislikes, and dismiss idle thoughts and worries. Only then will you become a Buddha.

MUSO (1275–1351, Rinzai)

DREAM DIALOGUE

A: When we see suffering we are moved to pity. Why is such sympathy rejected as mercy arising from attachment? Furthermore, if you look upon all sentient beings as nothing more than phantoms, how can you pity them?

B: Well, let's take beggars as an example. They can be divided into two classes: those who, born of beggar parents, have always been in a lowly position, and those who, born of noble parents, have later sunk in fortune. Naturally you are likely to pity the latter more. Now, the same applies to the Bodhisattva's mercy. All sentient beings are essentially Buddhas, without the marks of life and death, yet sooner or later they are deluded into thinking of life and death, they dream. The Mahayana Bodhisattva is therefore as much moved by the suffering of other sentient beings as by that of beggars of well-to-do parents. In this he is unlike the Hinayana Bodhisattva who, in considering that all beings are caught up in life and death, shows mercy arising from attachment.

A: Just as a drunkard is not aware of his state, so he who has yielded to Mara's [Devil] temptation is unaware of the fact. Thus he is unable to release himself. How can one resist Mara?

B: Fearing Mara, you are possessed by him. Nagarjuna writes, "If you have mind, you are caught in the Mara-net; without mind, you need not fear it." An old master said, "There are none of Mara's hindrances outside the mind: no mind, no Mara." Master Doju, you'll remember, conquered Mara by neither hearing nor seeing.

To cling to Buddhahood is to be in the Mara-realm; to forget Mara is to be in the Buddha-realm. A true Zennist is

neither attached to the Buddha-realm nor fearful of Mara,
then, and with fortitude, with no thought of gain, will remain
in this state. Also, of course, you must make a vow before
Buddha's image. The Perfect Enlightenment Sutra says,
"Those living in a corrupt age must make this great vow of
purification: May we attain Buddha's perfect enlightenment
and, not ruled by non-Buddhists, Sravakas, and Pratyeka-
Buddhas [those who gain enlightenment for their own sal-
vation], but under good instruction, surmount obstacles one
by one and enter the sanctified place of enlightenment."
Aided by this great vow, even a tyro will not be won over
to devils and heretics throughout his successive lives. Supported by Buddhas and devas, all impediments removed,
such a man will reach the never-receding state of tranquillity.

A: Even if he trains strictly, in accordance with the deep
doctrines, it is possible that a beginner be misled. Indeed
some masters discourage doctrinal studies while insisting on
discipline pure and simple. How would you justify this standpoint?

B: Well, can one who has learned something about medicine cure himself of a serious illness? No. He must go to
another for treatment and, without inquiring how it was com-
pounded, take the medicine given him. The same is true of
Zen discipline. If the seeker after the fundamental self, which
is the aim of satori, tries to learn different doctrines and then,
acting upon what he has learned, sets about training himself,
he is probably doomed to ignorance. The doctrines are so
numerous, life so short. At the end of his life he will see all
the books and their learning as a heap of trash; dazed, he
will be forced by karma along the cycle of rebirth. That is
why Zen masters give you but a word or two, and these are
not meant to provide a moral lesson but serve as a direct in-
dex of your fundamental self. Dull-witted students may not
be able to understand the master's words at once, but if they
continue to masticate them as a koan beyond the reach of
intellect and sensibility, they will sooner or later rid themselves of the most persistent illusion. Suddenly it will be gone
to the four winds.

A: Should one cast off worldly feelings—anger, joy, etc.—before applying himself to the examination of the Truth?

B: All humans, because they are able to profit by the Buddha's Law, are fortunate: it is the greatest rarity in the world. Nothing is less to be relied on than life, the inbreathing, the outbreathing. Knowing it for what it is, you must not yield to worldly feelings nor neglect your study of Zen. But suppose an emotion of that kind is felt. Well, you must examine it minutely, just as it has risen. In this way your feelings can actually help you in your training. But the less-than-serious students must be taught differently: they must be helped in the task of alleviation, which does not mean, of course, that they should be told to eliminate all emotion before undertaking Zen discipline. The one important thing is the awakening and, once it has been attained, the ordinary man is a man of satori, however many emotions he retains.

Even when an emotion is felt, you must not give up probing. As you well know, the most religious are often forgetful of eating and sleeping, for even while doing these things they are scrutinizing themselves without obstacle. Though this is not exactly what the less religious are advised to do, they too should of course continue in self-examination. An ancient said, "While walking, examine the walking; while sitting, the sitting, etc." The same holds true of joy and sorrow. An excellent admonition, that, and one likely to lead to an awakening.

A: There is disagreement about the importance of koan, some considering it all-important; others, paltry. What is your view of the matter?

B: It all depends on the master, the koan being but an expedient. There is no fixed rule about its use. A master once asked his pupil, "Are you in full accord with your koan?" When student and koan are as one, there is neither examined nor examiner. To one advanced as far as that, your question is meaningless. The less advanced, however, may properly do the koan exercise. The master alone, of course, can determine the outcome. Anyone without insight who simply reads the words of the old masters and then proceeds to teach his own hidebound opinions behaves in a most dangerous way.

An ancient censured just such an instructor as binding others to a Hinayanistic view of entity.

MEIHO (1277–1350, Soto)

ZAZEN

Zen-sitting is the way of perfect tranquillity: inwardly not a shadow of perception, outwardly not a shade of difference between phenomena. Identified with yourself, you no longer think, nor do you seek enlightenment of the mind or disburdenment of illusions. You are a flying bird with no mind to twitter, a mountain unconscious of the others rising around it.

Zen-sitting has nothing to do with the doctrine of "teaching, practice, and elucidation" or with the exercise of "commandments, contemplation, and wisdom." You are like a fish with no particular design of remaining in the sea. Nor do you bother with sutras or ideas. To control and pacify the mind is the concern of lesser men: Sravakas, Pratyeka-Buddhas, and Hinayanists. Still less can you hold an idea of Buddha and Dharma. If you attempt to do so, if you train improperly, you are like one who, intending to voyage west, moves east. You must not stray.

Also you must guard yourself against the easy conceptions of good and evil: your sole concern should be to examine yourself continually, asking who is above either. You must remember too that the unsullied essence of life has nothing to do with whether one is priest or layman, man or woman. Your Buddha-nature, consummate as the full moon, is represented by your position as you sit in Zen. The exquisite Way of Buddhas is not the One or Two, being or non-being. What diversifies it is the limitations of its students, who can be divided into three classes—superior, average, inferior.

The superior student is unaware of the coming into the world of Buddhas or of the transmission of the non-transmittable by them: he eats when hungry, sleeps when sleepy.

Nor does he regard the world as himself. Neither is he attached to enlightenment or illusion. Taking things as they come, he sits in the proper manner, making no idle distinctions.

The average student discards all business and ignores the external, giving himself over to self-examination with every breath. He may probe into a koan, which he puts mentally on the tip of his nose, finding in this way that his "original face" (fundamental being) is beyond life and death, and that the Buddha-nature of all is not dependent on the discriminating intellect but is the unconscious consciousness, the incomprehensible understanding: in short, that it is clear and distinct for all ages and is alone apparent in its entirety throughout the universe.

The inferior student must disconnect himself from all that is external, thus liberating himself from the duality of good and evil. The mind, just as it is, is the origin of all Buddhas. In zazen his legs are crossed so that his Buddha-nature will not be led off by evil thoughts, his hands are linked so that they will not take up sutras or implements, his mouth is shut so that he refrains from preaching a word of *dharma* or uttering blasphemies, his eyes are half shut so that he does not distinguish between objects, his ears are closed to the world so that he will not hear talk of vice and virtue, his nose is as if dead so that he will not smell good or bad. Since his body has nothing on which to lean, he is indifferent to likes and dislikes. He negates neither being nor non-being. He sits like Buddha on the pedestal, and though distorted ideas may arise from him, they do so idly and are ephemeral, constituting no sin, like reflections in a mirror, leaving no trace.

The five, the eight, the two hundred and fifty commandments, the three thousand monastic regulations, the eight hundred duties of the Bodhisattva, the Buddha-nature and the Bodhisattvahood, and the Wheel of Dharma—all are comprised in Zen-sitting and emerge from it. Of all good works, zazen comes first, for the merit of only one step into it surpasses that of erecting a thousand temples. Even a moment of sitting will enable you to free yourself from life and death, and your Buddha-nature will appear of itself. Then all you do, perceive, think becomes part of the miraculous Tathata-suchness (true nature, thusness).

Let it be thus remembered that tyros and advanced students, learned and ignorant, all without exception should practice zazen.

RYOHO (1305–1384, Rinzai)

ON EMPTINESS

1. The Buddhas of all times and places preach the empty dharma with their empty bodies, so as to enable empty beings to realize equally empty Buddhahood. For this reason the Buddha declared, "Even if there is something excelling nirvana, it is an empty dream."

If anyone in the reality of "suchness" can understand the dharma of dreamy emptiness and examine and practice it, he will through the dharma of reality conquer self and cherish mercy. In this way he will be able to invent a discipline and devices for what is called "The Way of Purity and Universal Emancipation." If, however, he lingers in this view, he will not be able to attain the proper mental state of the Zen-man.

What is the one phrase (Ryoho lifted his staff before going on) that will lead you to the proper state? Well, say it! (Ryoho's staff came down with a thump.) Don't sleep, and you won't dream!

2. All things being empty, so is the mind. As the mind is empty, all is. My mind is not divisible: all is contained in my every thought, which appears as enlightenment to the wise, illusion to the stupid. Yet enlightenment and illusion are one. Do away with both, but don't remain "in between" either. In this way you will be emptiness itself, which, stainless and devoid of the interrelationship of things, transcends realization. In this way the true Zen priest commonly conducts himself.

SHOZAN (1579–1655, Rinzai)

NIO-ZEN

1. A man said to the master, "Of course, I never think of death." To which the master responded, "That's all very well, but you'll not get very far in Zen, I'm afraid. As for myself, well, I train in Zen in detestation of death and in hope of deathlessness, and I am resolved to carry on in this way, from life to life, until I realize my aim. That you do not think of death shows that you are not a man of enlightenment, because you are incapable of knowing your master, whatever there is in you that uses the six sense organs."

2. In studying Zen you should take Buddha images for models, but that of Tathagata (the Buddha in his corporeal manifestation) does not suit the beginner, because the Tathagata type of zazen is beyond him. Rather model yourself on images of Nio [Vajrapani: literally "Diamond Deity," an indomitable guardian of Buddhism of ferocious mien] and Fudo, both of which are symbolic of discipline. This is apparent from the fact that Nios stand in temple gates, and Fudo is the first of the thirteen Buddhas. Without spirit and vigor you'll be passion's slave. Like these deities, have a dauntless mind.

Unfortunately Buddhism has declined, going from bad to worse, with the result that most are milksops, critically lacking in vigor. Only the valorous can train properly, the ignorant being mild and sanctimonious, mistaken in the belief that such is the way of Buddhist practice. Then there are the madmen who go about trumpeting their attainment of satori —a bagatelle. Myself, I'm a stranger to sanctimoniousness and satorishness, my sole aim being to conquer all with a vivacious mind. Sharing the vitality of Nio and Fudo, exterminate all of your evil karma and passions. (Here the master paused, eyes set, hands clenched, teeth gnashing.) Guard yourself closely, and nothing will be able to interfere. Only bravery will carry you through. We'll have no part of weaklings here! Be wide awake, and attain the vigor of living Zen.

3. The master once gave the following instructions to a samurai: "You had better practice zazen while busily occupied. The samurai's zazen must be the sort that will support him in the midst of battle, when he is threatened by guns and spears. After all, what use can the tranquilizing type of sitting be on the battlefield? You should foster the Nio spirit above all. All worldly arts are cultivated through Zen-sitting. The military arts especially cannot be practiced with a feeble spirit. (So saying, the master pretended to draw a sword.) Zazen must be virile, yet the warrior upholds it only in battle; no sooner does he sheathe his sword than he's off guard again. The Buddhist, on the other hand, always maintains vigor. Never is he a loser. The more he ripens in discipline, the more adept he becomes in everything, from the recitation of a text to tapping a hand drum in Noh. Perfect in all virtues, he can fit in anywhere."

4. A priest asked the master, "Are not your works such as *Fumotokusawake* based on a notion of relative reality?"

"Of course," said the master. "But you know the common man's mind is without exception one of relative reality. And how can you undergo Zen training without such a mind? Many masters nowadays lapse into notions of nothingness, leading their followers astray. They reside complacently in what they call original vacuity, which is the relative reality you speak of. Generally speaking, if you seek satori with your mind, you will leave behind the notion of being. However, if you cling with your no-mind to original vacuity, you cannot hope to succeed. Honen (1133–1212), founder of the Jodo [Pure Land] sect, for example, invoked Amitabha Buddha not with the no-mind but with the mind. And if you try to picture the Pure Land as really existing and repeat Amitabha's name, you will gain the virtue of no-mind. On the other hand, those who now pose as exponents of the primary void, and reject Zen discipline as something concerned with relative being, are merely accumulating evil karma.

5. A birdcatcher: "We have always been birdcatchers.

If we give up, we'll starve. While following this trade, is it possible for me to attain Buddhahood?"

Master: "The mind falls into hell, not the body. Each time you kill a bird, grasp your mind and kill it also. In this way you can attain Buddhahood."

6. The master cheered up an eighteen-year-old monk on the point of death by saying: "However long one lives, life goes on unchanging. You are lucky if you can discard the body, a thing of filth and suffering, even a single day earlier than others. In any case, you'll be free of life's bondage. I have lived to this old age without having seen one new thing. You may think Master Dogen a free man, but not so. He fell short of Lord Buddha's enlightenment, which is beyond the power of all of us. You know, many have failed in achieving their ends, not you alone. Even a long life can be flat, after all. The best thing is to cast the foul body aside as soon as possible. I promise to follow you soon."

On hearing the master's words, the monk passed away in the proper frame of mind.

MANZAN (1635–1714, Soto)

LETTER TO ZISSAN

[Zissan: a monk's name, suggesting "real practice."]

Like training, satori must be true. If one holds that there is something to practice and realize, one is a follower of the false religion of entity based on affirmation. If, on the other hand, one asserts that there is nothing to practice or realize, one is still not above the four types of differentiation and the one hundred forms of negation: one is an adherent of the equally false religion of nothingness, founded on negation. And this is the shadowy product of the dichotomous intellect, holding no truth.

First of all, I ask you to look upon the world's riches as a dunghill, upon the most beautiful men and women as stinking corpses, upon the highest honors and reputation as an echo, upon the most malicious calumny as the cawing of a crow. Regard yourself as a fan in winter, the universe as a straw dog.

This accomplished, train wholeheartedly. Then, and then only, will you awaken. If you dare claim to have undergone real training and attained enlightenment without having gone through all this, you are nothing but a liar and are bound for hell. Bear all I have said in mind—practice truly.

1. If you desire the attainment of satori, ask yourself this question: Who hears sound? As described in the Surangama-samadhi, that is Avalokitesvara's faith in the hearer. Since there is such a hearer in you, all of you hear sounds. You may say that it is the ear that hears, yet the ear is but a mechanism. If it could hear by itself, then the dead could hear our prayers for them. Inside you, then, is a hearer.

Now, this is the way to apply yourself: whether or not you hear anything, keep asking who the hearer is. Doubt, scrutinize, paying no attention to fancies or ideas. Strain every nerve without expecting anything to happen, without willing satori. Doubt, doubt, doubt. If even one idea arises, your doubt is not sufficiently strong, and you must question yourself more intensely. Scrutinize the hearer in yourself, who is beyond your power or vision.

Master Bassui says, "When at wits' end and unable to think another thought, you are applying yourself properly." Thus do not look around, but devote yourself utterly to doubting self-examination until you forget where you are or even that you live. This may lead you to feel completely at sea. Yet you must persist in the search for the hearer, sweating, like a dead man, until you are unconscious, a lump of great doubt. But look! That lump will suddenly break up and out of it will leap the angel of the awakening, the great satori consciousness. It is as if one awoke from the deepest dream, literally returned to life.

2. In Zen practice a variety of supernatural phenomena may be experienced. For example, you may see ghostly faces, demons, Buddhas, flowers, or you may feel your body becoming like that of a woman, or even purified into a state of

non-existence. If this happens, your "doubt in practice" is still inadequate, for if in perfect doubt you will not have such illusions. Indeed it is only when you are not alert that you meet with them. Do not shrink from them, nor prize them. Just doubt and examine yourself all the more thoroughly.

3. Zen practitioners must accept the fact that while in meditation they are likely to suffer one or more of the three maladies: *kon, san,* and *chin. Kon* is sleepiness and *san* instability, both of which are too well known for comment. *Chin,* on the other hand, is a grave malady and always leads to unhappy results. It is a state in which one is free from sleepiness and instability, and all mentalization ceases. One feels gay, immaculate; one can go on in zazen for hours on end. One has a feeling that all things are equal, neither existent nor non-existent, right nor wrong. Those possessed by chin regard it as satori—a most dangerous delusion. If you were to remain in this state, you would go far astray. At such times, in fact, you must have the greatest doubt.

BANKEI-EITAKU (1622–1693, Rinzai)

THE ZEN OF BIRTHLESSNESS

1.

How lucky you are these days! When I was young there wasn't a good master to be found. At least I couldn't uncover one. But the truth is I was rather simple when young, and made one blunder after another. And the fruitless efforts! I don't suppose I'll ever forget those days, if only because they were so painful. That's why I come here every day. I want to teach you how to avoid the blunders I made. How lucky you are these days!

I'm going to tell you about some of my mistakes, and I know you're clever enough—every one of you—to learn from what I say. If by chance one of you should be led astray by my example, the sin will be unpardonable. That must be avoided at all costs. Indeed it was only after great hesitation that I decided to tell you of my experiences. Remember then, you can learn from me without imitating.

My parents came here from the island of Shikoku, and it was right here [the province of Harima in Hyogo Prefecture] that I was born. My father was a lordless samurai and a Confucian scholar as well, but he died when I was a child and I was brought up by my mother. She was to tell me later that I was boss of all the children in the neighborhood (which led me to do a lot of mischief) and that roughly from my third year I began to loathe death, so much so in fact that when I cried all she had to do was mimic a corpse, or even say "death," and I'd stop crying and become good.

When yet a small boy I became interested in Confucianism, which in those days was very popular. One day while reading *Great Learning* [a classic of Chinese philosophy] I came upon the sentence, "The path of the Great Learning lies in clarifying illustrious virtue." This was completely beyond me, and I wondered about illustrious virtue for days on end, asking teacher after teacher, but to no avail. Finally one of them took me aside and said, "Go to a Zen priest. They know all about difficult things of this kind. All we do, day in, day out, is explain the meaning of the Chinese characters and, of course, lecture a bit. We know nothing about your 'illustrious virtue,' I'm afraid. Go ask a Zen priest, I tell you."

I'd have been happy to follow his advice, but there were no Zen priests around at the time. One of the chief motives for my wanting to know about illustrious virtue was that I felt duty bound to teach my mother the path of the Great Learning before she died. I kept going to hear all the Confucian and Buddhist lectures, and would return to her with the wisdom that had been imparted to me, but, alas, my questions remained unanswered.

One day I remembered a certain Zen master and went to him full of expectation. At once I asked him about illustrious virtue. He looked at me gravely and said that to understand I would have to sit in Zen meditation. Soon I would be able to grasp it. Well, I lost no time. Often I would go into the mountains and sit in Zen without taking a morsel for a week, or I would go to a rocky place and, choosing the sharpest rock, meditate for days on end, taking no food, until I toppled over. The results? Exhaustion, a shrunken stomach, and an increased desire to go on.

I returned to my village and entered a hermitage, where sleeping in an upright position and living arduously, I gave myself up to the old spiritual exercise of repeating the name of Amitabha. The results? More exhaustion, and huge painful sores on my bottom. It was impossible for me to sit in comfort, but in those days I was pretty tough. Nevertheless to ease the pain, I had to place layers of soft paper under me, which as they lost their effectiveness had constantly to be replaced. Sometimes I was forced to use cotton, so atrocious was the pain.

I knew I was overdoing it, of course, and finally I became seriously ill. Soon I was bringing up blood, lumps the size of a thumb end. One day I spat on the wall and watched fascinated as the lump of blood rolled down. I was in bad shape, I can tell you. On the advice of friends I engaged a servant to nurse me. Once for seven days running I could eat nothing but a gruel of thin rice. I felt my time was up and kept saying to myself, "No help for it. Soon I'll die without obtaining my old desire."

Suddenly, while at the very depths, it struck me like a thunderbolt that *I had never been born,* and that my birthlessness could settle any and every matter. This seemed to be my satori, the awakening I had been waiting for. I realized then that because I'd been ignorant of this simple truth, I'd suffered needlessly.

I began to feel better, and my appetite returned. I called my servant over and said, "I want a big bowl of rice. Right now." He looked puzzled, for he'd been expecting me to keel over; then he set about in a flurry to prepare the meal. In fact he made it so quickly, and in such a state, that the rice was only half-done and stiff. But I ate three bowls and, I can assure you, it didn't disagree with me. Daily my health improved, and soon I was able to accomplish the greatest desire of my life: I was able to get my mother to see the truth, the secret of birthlessness, before she died.

What I wanted now was the "certification" of my satori. My teacher of Confucianism mentioned a Zen priest by the name of Gudo in the province of Mino who would be able to say whether my experience was genuine. I went to Mino in search of him, but unfortunately he had left a few days before for Tokyo. Not wanting the journey to be a waste of time, I called on some Zen priests of Mino and asked if they would aid me. Immediately they complied by giving me their idea of true Zen. I listened carefully, then said, "Please pardon my impudence, but I want to say something. Your opinions are good as far as they go, but frankly you don't go deep enough. At any rate, I'm not satisfied."

At this their spokesman, who had impressed me as an honest and humble man, said, "You're right, I'm afraid. All we do is merely memorize the sutras and some of the Zen writings, then repeat them like parrots to anyone who will listen. I'm afraid none of us has experienced satori, in spite of knowing that a man who has not done so will never hit the mark. We really envy you."

I thanked them and returned home where I kept to myself most of the time and observed how teachable men were, and I weighed the manner in which I could best help them. One day I chanced to learn that a Zen master, Doja, had come to Nagasaki from China. He would be just the man to be my witness, I thought, and straightway I went to him and told him of my awakening, which had enabled me to virtually transcend life and death. He assured me that I had experienced the real thing and ended up by congratulating me. Naturally I was very pleased, and very grateful to him.

Now it was my turn to begin helping others, and I have been doing just that ever since. That's why I come here to talk to you. It is my desire to bear witness to your satori. You must feel that you are favored. Come forward and let me know if you have had an awakening, and those of you who haven't had the experience, listen carefully to my words. It's in each of you to utterly change your life!

The birthless Buddha-mind can cut any and every knot.
You see, the Buddhas of the past, present and future, and all
successive patriarchs should be thought of as mere names for
what has been born. From the viewpoint of birthlessness,
they are of little significance. To live in a state of non-birth
is to attain Buddhahood; it is to keep your whereabouts
unknown not only to people but even to Buddhas and patriarchs. A blessed state. From the moment you have begun
to realize this fact, you are a living Buddha, and need make
no further efforts on your *tatami* mats.

Once you begin to understand this you will be unerring
in your judgment of others. These days my eye never sizes
up a man incorrectly, and each of you possesses the birthless
eye. That's why we call our sect the True-eye as well as the
Buddha-mind sect. You must not consider yourselves enlightened Buddhas, of course, until you are able to see into
others' minds with your birthless eyes. I suppose you may
think what I say doubtful, but the moment you have awakened you'll be able to penetrate the minds of others. To prepare you for this is my greatest desire.

I never lie. I could not deceive you. The doctrine of birthlessness died out long ago in China and Japan, but it's now
being revived—by me. When you have fully settled in the
immaculate Buddha-mind of non-birth, nothing will deceive
you, no one will be able to persuade you a crow is a heron.
When you've achieved the final enlightenment, you'll be sure
of the truth at all times. Nothing, I repeat, no one, will be
able to deceive you.

When as a young bonze I began preaching birthlessness
there wasn't anyone around who could understand. They were
frightened, and they must have thought me a heretic, as bad
as a Roman Catholic. Not a single person dared approach me.
But gradually they began to see their mistake, and today
all you have to do is look around you to see how many come
to me. Why, I've hardly any time for myself! Everything in
its season, I guess.

In the forty years I've lived here I've instructed many like
yourselves, and I've no hesitation in claiming that some of

these people are as good in every way as the Zen masters themselves.

2

The mind begotten by and given to each of us by our parents is none other than the Buddha-mind, birthless and immaculate, sufficient to manage all that life throws up to us. A proof: suppose at this very instant, while you face me listening, a crow caws and a sparrow twitters somewhere behind you. Without any intention on your part of distinguishing between these sounds, you hear each distinctly. In so doing you are hearing with the birthless mind, which is yours for all eternity.

Well, we are to be in this mind from now on, and our sect will be known as the Buddha-mind sect. To consider, once again, my example of a moment ago, if any of you feel you heard the crow and the sparrow intentionally, you are deluding yourselves, for you are listening to me, not to what goes on behind you. In spite of this there are moments when you hear such sounds distinctly, when you hear with the Buddha-mind of non-birth. This nobody here can deny. All of you are living Buddhas, because the birthless mind which you possess is the beginning and the basis of all.

Now, if the Buddha-mind is birthless, it is necessarily immortal, for how can what has never been born perish? You've all encountered the phrase "birthless and imperishable" in the sutras, but until now you've not had the slightest proof of its truth. Indeed I suppose like most people you've memorized this phrase while being ignorant of birthlessness.

When I was twenty-five I realized that non-birth is all-sufficient to life, and since then, for forty years, I've been proving it to people just like you. I was the first to preach this greatest truth of life. I ask you, have any of you priests heard anyone else teach this truth before me? Of course not.

3

A certain priest once said to me, "You teach the same thing over and over again. Wouldn't it be a good idea, just

for the sake of variety, to tell some of those old and interesting stories illustrative of Buddhist life?"

I may be nothing more than an old dunce, and I suppose
it might help some if I did tell stories of that kind, but I've
a strong hunch that such preaching poisons the mind. No, I
would never carry on in so harmful a way. Indeed I make it
a rule not to give even the words of Buddha himself, let
alone the Zen patriarchs.

To attain the truth today all one needs is self-criticism.
There's no need to talk about Buddhism and Zen. Why, there's
not a single straying person among you: all of you have the
Buddha-mind. If one of you thinks himself astray, let him
come forward and show me in what way. I repeat: there's
no such man here.

However, suppose on returning home you were to see one
of your children or a servant doing something offensive, and
at once you got yourself involved, went astray, turning the
Buddha-mind into a demon's, so to speak. But remember, until
that moment you were secure in the birthless Buddha-mind.
Only at that moment, only then were you deluded.

Don't get involved! Don't get involved with anyone, whoever he happens to be; rather by ridding yourself of the
need for others (which really is a form of self-love) remain
in the Buddha-mind. Then you will never stray, then you
will be a living Buddha for all time.

4

PRIEST: I was born with a quick temper and, in spite of
my master's constant admonitions, I haven't been able to rid
myself of it. I know it's a vice, but, as I said, I was born with
it. Can you help me?

BANKEI: My, what an interesting thing you were born with!
Tell me, is your temper quick at this very moment? If so,
show me right off, and I'll cure you of it.

PRIEST: But I don't have it at this moment.

BANKEI: Then you weren't born with it. If you were, you'd
have it at all times. You lose your temper as occasion arises.
Else where can this hot temper possibly be? Your mistake is

one of self-love, which makes you concern yourself with others and insists that you have your own way. To say you were born a hothead is to tax your parents with something that is no fault of theirs. From them you received the Buddha-mind, nothing else.

This is equally true of other types of illusion. If you don't fabricate illusions, none will disturb you. Certainly you were born with none. Only your selfishness and deplorable mental habits bring them into being. Yet you think of them as inborn, and in everything you do, you continue to stray. To appreciate the pricelessness of the Buddha-mind, and to steer clear of illusion, is the one path to satori and Buddhahood.

It is essential that you not yield to quick temper, for to yield and then to try to cure it is to double the burden. Mark well how you stand. Indeed you're in a rather fortunate position, for once rid of hot temper, it will be easy for you to strip yourself of other illusions. Remain firmly in the self-sufficient Buddha-mind of non-birth.

My advice, then, is that you accustom yourself to remaining in a state of non-birth. Try it for thirty days, and you'll be incapable of straying from it: you'll live in the Buddha-mind for the rest of your life. Be reborn this very day! You can be if you give your ear to me, and forget as so much rubbish all your preconceptions. Indeed at my one word of exhortation, you can gain satori.

5

Hearing Bankei talk in this way, a layman from the province of Izumo said, "If your teaching is right, one should be able to feel at ease in the Buddha-mind at all times, but frankly it all seems a bit weightless."

BANKEI: By no means! Those who make light of the Buddha-mind transform it when angry into a demon's, into a hungry ghost's when greedy, into an animal's when acting stupidly. I tell you my teaching is far from frivolous! Nothing can be so weighty as the Buddha-mind. But perhaps you feel that to remain in it is too tough a job? If so, listen and try to grasp the meaning of what I say. Stop piling up evil deeds, stop being a demon, a hungry ghost, an animal. Keep your distance from those things that transform you in that way, and you'll attain the Buddha-mind once and for all. Don't you see?

LAYMAN: I do, and I am convinced.

6

PRIEST: When you are successful in making me think of my birthlessness, I find myself feeling idle all day.

BANKEI: One in the Buddha-mind is far from idle. When you are not in it, when you sell it, so to speak, for worthless things you happen to be attached to, then you are being idle.

The priest remained silent.

BANKEI: Remain in non-birth, and you will never be idle.

7

PRIEST: Once in the Buddha-mind, I am absent-minded.

BANKEI: Well, suppose you are absent-minded as you say. If someone pricked you in the back with a gimlet, would you feel the pain?

PRIEST: Naturally!

BANKEI: Then you are not absent-minded. Feeling the pain, your mind would show itself to be alert. Follow my exhortation: remain in the Buddha-mind.

8

PRIEST: I often find myself straying from the Buddha-mind. Perhaps it's that I haven't yet seen the truth. Please help me.

BANKEI: The parent-begotten birthless mind is possessed by all, and none truly strays from it if he is aware of doing so. It is that you turn the Buddha-mind into something else. I repeat: aware of the Buddha-mind, you cannot have strayed. Understand? Even in the deepest sleep you're not away from it.

Whether here or at home, remain just as you are now, listening to my exhortation, and you'll feel firmly in the Buddha-mind. It's only when you're greedy or selfish that you feel yourself astray. Remember this: there isn't a sinful person who was born that way. Take the case of the thief. He wasn't born that way. Perhaps when a child he happened to have a sinful idea, acted upon it, and let the habit develop of itself. When apprehended and questioned he will of course speak of an inborn tendency. Nonsense! Show him he's wrong, and he will give up stealing, and in so doing he can immediately attain the everlasting Buddha-mind.

In my home town there lived a pickpocket who was so skillful he could tell at a glance how much money was being carried by someone approaching. When finally nabbed and imprisoned for a few years, he started to change his ways, and when set free he became a sculptor of Buddhist images. He died a holy death, praying to Amitabha for eternal salvation. This shows what a man who repents past conduct is capable of. I tell you no one is born to sin. It's all a question of will.

9

LAYMAN: Though I undertake Zen discipline, I often find myself lazy, weary of the whole thing, unable to advance.

BANKEI: Once in the Buddha-mind there's no need to advance, nor is it possible to recede. Once in birthlessness, to attempt to advance is to recede from the state of non-birth. A man secure in this state need not bother himself with such things: he's above them.

10

LAYMAN: They say you're able to read minds. Is that true?

BANKEI: No such thing happens in our sect. Even if one of us should possess supernatural powers, being in the birthless Buddha-mind he would not use it. I suppose you think I have such powers because I'm always commenting on your personal affairs, but really I'm no different from you. In the Buddha-mind all have the same gifts, for all puzzles are solved by it, all problems overcome. Non-birth is really a very practical doctrine. By criticizing, the master hopes to instruct: that's the long and short of it. And that's why I'm always being so personal. Oh, we're very down-to-earth here!

11

PRIEST: For a long time now I've been trying to understand the story of Hyakujo and the Fox (The second koan in *Mumonkan,* which concerns a monk who had been transformed into a fox because of his denial of cause-and-effect, and who was enlightened by the master Hyakujo's affirmation of it.), but it's beyond me—probably because I haven't involved myself in wholehearted contemplation. Please enlighten me.

BANKEI: We shouldn't concern ourselves with such old wives' tales. The trouble is you're still ignorant of the Buddha-mind which, birthless and immaculate, unties any and every knot.

12

PRIEST (on hearing Bankei chasten the priest of the foregoing): Do you mean to say all the old Zen-men's words and questions are useless?

BANKEI: The old masters' answers were given on the spot to questions asked them, but those questions and their given answers should not concern us. Of course, I'm in no position to say what use they have, but one thing I know: once in the Buddha-mind, one need not fret over them. All your attention is given to irrelevant matters; you stray. Most dangerous!

13

The Buddha-mind in each of you is immaculate. All you've done is reflected in it, but if you bother about one such reflection, you're certain to stray. Your thoughts don't lie deep enough—they rise from the shallows of your mind.

Remember that all you see and hear is reflected in the Buddha-mind and influenced by what was previously seen and heard. Needless to say, thoughts aren't entities. So if you permit them to rise, reflect themselves, or cease altogether as they're prone to do, and if you don't worry about them, you'll never stray. In this way let one hundred, nay, one thousand thoughts arise, and it's as if not one has arisen. You will remain undisturbed.

14

PRIESTESSES OF THE VINAYA SCHOOL [a sect of Buddhism that emphasizes formal monastic rules]: Can we enter nirvana by simply observing the priestess' two hundred and fifty commandments?

BANKEI: One who doesn't drink wine need not be told he shouldn't. Questions of omission or commission apply only to bad priests and priestesses. If the Vinaya sect makes a merit of obeying commandments, it's merely admitting the presence of sinful members. Stay in the Buddha-mind of nonbirth, and such considerations will prove unnecessary.

15

BANKEI: The bell rings, but you hear the sound before it rings. The mind that is aware of the bell before it rings is the Buddha-mind. If however you hear the bell and then say it is a bell, you are merely naming what's been born, a thing of minor importance.

16

The only thing I tell my people is to stay in the Buddha-mind. There are no regulations, no formal discipline. Nevertheless they have agreed among themselves to sit in Zen for a period of two incense sticks [an hour or so] daily. All right, let them. But they should understand that the birthless Buddha-mind has absolutely nothing to do with sitting with an incense stick burning in front of you. If one keeps in the Buddha-mind without straying, there's no further satori to seek. Whether asleep or awake, one is a living Buddha. Zazen means only one thing—sitting tranquilly in the Buddha-mind. But really, you know, one's everyday life, in its entirety, should be thought of as a kind of sitting in Zen. Even during one's formal sitting, one may leave one's seat to attend to something. In my temple, at least, such things are allowed. Indeed it's sometimes advisable to walk in Zen for one incense stick's burning, and sit in Zen for the other. A natural thing, after all. One can't sleep all day, so one rises. One can't talk all day, so one engages in zazen. There are no binding rules here.

Most masters these days use devices (koan, etc.) to teach, and they seem to value these devices above all else—they can't get to the truth directly. They're little more than blind fools! Another bit of their stupidity is to hold that, according to Zen, unless one has a doubt he proceeds to smash, he's good for nothing. Of course, all this forces people to have doubts. No, they never teach the importance of staying in the birthless Buddha-mind. They would make of it a lump of doubt. A very serious mistake.

Chapter XXVI
ZEN ANECDOTES

Once a tyro asked a Zen master, "Master, what is the First Principle?" Without hesitation the master replied, "If I were to tell you, it would become the Second Principle." Such anecdotes—and they are legion—are chiefly responsible for Zen Buddhism's appeal to those not normally interested in philosophy, and the best of them share with the best jokes of a certain type a degree of compactness, point, and wisdom to be found only in the finest writing. Yet Zen anecdotes are meant to do far more than cause laughter: for the most part they are based on dramatic confrontations, during *dokusan* (meeting between master and disciple), whose purpose is to jerk the unenlightened disciple from a state of hebetude and make it possible for him to experience *satori*, see into his true being. Many of the anecdotes are very old, drawn from works like the ancient collection of stories with commentaries, *Hekiganroku* (Blue Cliff Record), another Chinese book, the early thirteenth-century *Mu-mon-kan* (Barrier Without Gate), and the late thirteenth-century Japanese work *Shaseki-shu* (Stone and Sand Collection). Some anecdotes are quite serious in tone, their purpose being to illustrate important Mahayana attitudes (number ten in the following selection is a good example), but for the most part they are farcical, illogical in development, and highly paradoxical. Whether the purpose of a story is to amuse, shock, or edify, or do all three at the same time, like this one, which is greatly condensed, it speaks for itself: Two monks, one old, one young, came to a muddy ford where a beautiful girl was deliberating whether to cross. The elder monk grabbed her and, without a word, carried her across. As they continued on their way the younger, astonished at the sight of his companion touching a woman, kept chattering about it, until at last the elder monk exclaimed, "What! Are you still carrying that girl? I put her down as soon as we crossed the ford."

1

When Ninagawa-Shinzaemon, linked-verse poet and Zen devotee, heard that Ikkyu (1394–1481, Rinzai), abbot of the famous Daitokuji in Murasakino (violet field) of Kyoto, was a remarkable master, he desired to become his disciple. He called on Ikkyu and the following dialogue took place at the temple entrance:

IKKYU: Who are you?
NINAGAWA: A devotee of Buddhism.
IKKYU: You are from?
NINAGAWA: Your region.
IKKYU: Ah. And what's happening there these days?
NINAGAWA: The crows caw, the sparrows twitter.
IKKYU: And where do you think you are now?
NINAGAWA: In a field dyed violet.
IKKYU: Why?
NINAGAWA: Miscanthus, morning glories, safflowers, chrysanthemums, asters.
IKKYU: And after they're gone?
NINAGAWA: It's Miyagino (field known for its autumn flowering).
IKKYU: What happens in the field?
NINAGAWA: The stream flows through, the wind sweeps over.

Amazed at Ninagawa's Zen-like speech, Ikkyu led him to his room and served him tea. Then he spoke the following impromptu verse:

> I want to serve
> You delicacies.
> Alas! the Zen sect
> Can offer nothing.

At which the visitor replied:

> The mind which treats me
> To nothing is the original void—
> A delicacy of delicacies.

Deeply moved, the master said, "My son, you have learned much."

2

One day the Lord Mihara ordered a painter to do a picture for him, and a few weeks later the artist brought him a picture of a wild goose. As soon as his eyes fell on the painting, the lord cried out, "Wild geese fly side by side. Your picture is symbolic of revolt!"

The lord's attendants, frightened out of their wits, sought out Motsugai (1795–1867, Soto), a formidable Zen master, who, besides being a favorite of the lord, was a man of great strength and talent. He was nicknamed Fist Bonze because he could punch a hole in a board, and he was also a good lancer and an expert horseman. But more important to the lord's attendants, he was very wise and skilled with the pen.

Motsugai hastened to Lord Mihara and, casting but a glance at the picture, wrote the following over the painted bird:

> The first wild goose!
> Another and another and another
> In endless succession.

Lord Mihara's good humor was restored, and both the artist and Motsugai were generously rewarded.

3

Kato-Dewanokami-Yasuoki, lord of Osu in the province of Iyo, was passionate about the military arts. One day the great master Bankei called on him and, as they sat face to face, the young lord grasped his spear and made as if to pierce Bankei. But the master silently flicked its head aside with his rosary and said, "No good. You're too worked up."

Years later Yasuoki, who had become a great spearsman, spoke of Bankei as the one who had taught him most about the art.

4

Date-Jitoku, a fine waka poet and a retainer of Lord Tokugawa, wanted to master Zen, and with this in mind made an appointment to see Ekkei, abbot of Shokokuji in Kyoto and one widely known for his rigorous training methods. Jitoku was ambitious and went to the master full of hopes for the interview. As soon as he entered Ekkei's room, however, even before being able to utter a word, he received a blow.

He was, of course, astonished, but as it is a strict rule of Zen to do or say nothing unless asked by the master, he withdrew silently. He had never been so mortified. No one had ever dared strike him before, not even his lord. He went at once to Dokuon, who was to succeed Ekkei as abbot, and told him that he planned to challenge the rude and daring master to a duel.

"Can't you see that the master was being kind to you?" said Dokuon. "Exert yourself in zazen, and you'll discover for yourself what his treatment of you means."

For three days and nights Jitoku engaged in desperate contemplation, then, suddenly, he experienced an ecstatic awakening. This, his satori, was approved by Ekkei.

Jitoku called on Dokuon again and after thanking him for the advice said, "If it hadn't been for your wisdom, I would never have had so transfiguring an experience. As for the master, well, his blow was far from hard enough."

5

Kanzan (1277–1360, Rinzai), the National Teacher, gave Fujiwara-Fujifusa the koan "Original Perfection." For many days Fujifusa sat in Zen. When he finally had an intuition, he composed the following:

Once possessed of the mind that has always been,
Forever I'll benefit men and devas both.
The benignity of the Buddha and Patriarchs can hardly be
  repaid.
Why should I be reborn as horse or donkey?

When he called on Kanzan with the poem, this dialogue
took place:

KANZAN: Where's the mind?
FUJIFUSA: It fills the great void.
KANZAN: With what will you benefit men and devas?
FUJIFUSA: I shall saunter along the stream, or sit down
to watch the gathering clouds.
KANZAN: Just how do you intend repaying the Buddha
and Patriarchs?
FUJIFUSA: The sky's over my head, the earth under my
feet.
KANZAN: All right, but why shouldn't you be reborn as
horse or donkey?

At this Fujifusa got to his feet and bowed.
"Good!" Kanzan said with a loud laugh. "You've gained
perfect satori."

6

Ken-O and his disciple Menzan (1683–1769, Soto) were
eating a melon together. Suddenly the master asked, "Tell
me, where does all this sweetness come from?"
"Why," Menzan quickly swallowed and answered, "it's a
product of cause and effect."
"Bah! That's cold logic!"
"Well," Menzan said, "from where then?"
"From that very 'where' itself, that's where."

7

There was to be a big party at the house of the Chief
Minister of the Kuroda Clan of Hakata, and both Kamei-

Shoyo, the famous Confucian scholar, and the master Sengai
(1750–1837, Rinzai) were invited. The host informed Sengai
that the great teacher would be present, implying that the
master, who was indifferent to worldly matters, would have
to come dressed for the occasion.

On the appointed day Sengai entered the mansion wearing
a costume of white, violet, and gold. His rosary was of
amethyst and he even carried a ceremony-fan. Followed by
his disciples, he crossed the room in great dignity.

Of course, the sight of Sengai's getup was hateful to Shoyo,
and he couldn't restrain himself from calling out, "Master,
why did you come dressed as a fine lady?"

At this the other guests held their breath.

Sengai smiled and, moving straight up to Shoyo, whacked
him on the head with his fan, and said, "Why, it was to give
birth to this fine gentleman."

8

A wealthy man invited Sengai to a housewarming and,
after serving him a fine meal, asked him to write a poem in
honor of the occasion. Sengai quickly wrote down the first
half of a waka, which made the host, who had been hovering
over his shoulder, extremely angry. It read:

> The house is surrounded
> By the gods of poverty.

Ignoring the host and the guests, who on being informed
of what he had written looked daggers at him, Sengai smoked
his pipe in silence. Suddenly he grasped his brush and completed the poem with these lines:

> How can the deities of good luck
> Ever leave it?

When the host and the guests read these lines there was
great rejoicing, and all praised Sengai warmly.

393

9

The master Fugai (1779–1847, Soto), a fine painter and a successor to Motsugai, the famous Fist Bonze, was considered very wise and generous, yet he was most severe, both to himself and his disciples. He went to a mountain cave to sit in Zen, and when hungry would come to the village for scraps.

One day a monk called Bundo, attracted by Fugai's austerities, called at the cave and asked the master whether he could spend the night. The master seemed happy to put him up, and next morning prepared rice gruel for him, but not having an extra bowl, he went out and returned with a skull found lying near a tomb. He filled it with gruel and offered it to Bundo. The guest refused to touch it, and stared at Fugai as if he thought him mad. At this Fugai became furious and drove him from the cave with blows. "Fool!" he shouted after him, "how can you, with your worldly notions of filth and purity, think yourself a Buddhist?"

Some months later the master Tetsugyu visited him and told him frankly that he thought it a great pity that he had so completely forsaken the world.

Fugai laughed loudly and said, "Oh, it's easy enough to forsake the world and become a bonze. The difficult thing is then to become a true Buddhist."

It is told that Fugai met his end in an extraordinary manner. Feeling his last day had come, he quickly had a hole dug and, standing in it with great dignity, had himself covered with earth.

10

Sato-Kaiseki was very much disturbed by the implications of Copernicus' heliocentric theory, which, of course, was inconsistent with the old Buddhist cosmology in which Mount Sumeru occupies the center of the universe. He reasoned that if the Buddhist view of the cosmos were proved false, the triple world and the twenty-five forms of existence would be reduced to nonsense, resulting in the negation of Buddhism itself. Immediately he set about writing a book in defense of the Mount Sumeru position, sparing himself no effort as a champion of Buddhism.

When he had finished the work, he took it at once to Master Ekido and presented it to him triumphantly. After leafing through only the first few pages, however, the master thrust the book back and, shaking his head, said, "How stupid! Don't you realize that the basic aim of Buddhism is to shatter the triple world and the twenty-five forms of existence? Why stick to such utterly worthless things and treasure Mount Sumeru? Blockhead!"

Dumfounded, Kaiseki shoved the book under his arm and went quickly home.

11

Gasan (1853–1900, Rinzai), a distinguished master of the important Tenryuji Temple of Kyoto, was very fond of saké, which made him like many other Zen priests. He would say: "One *go* of saké and I'm vivacious, five *go* and I'm mild as a spring day, one *sho* (ten *go*) and the wintry moon is high in the sky, the carp leaps from the deep pond."

Once after being treated to drink in downtown Kyoto he returned to the temple in the evening almost helplessly drunk. As it was time for *dokusan*, the monks were overjoyed, for they expected the master, who always made dokusan a bitter trial for them, to be lenient for once.

When one by one they entered Gasan's room, however, they found him sitting more solemn than ever, eyes glaring at the doorway.

12

Muso (1275–1351, Rinzai), the National Teacher and one of the most illustrious masters of his day, left the capital in the company of a disciple for a distant province. On reaching the Tenryu river they had to wait for an hour before boarding the ferry; just as it was about to leave the shore, a drunken samurai ran up and leapt into the packed boat, nearly swamping it. He tottered wildly as the small craft made its

way across the river and, fearing for the safety of the pas-
sengers, the ferryman begged him to stand quietly.

"We're like sardines in here!" the samurai said gruffly.
Then, pointing to Muso, "Why not toss out the bonze?"

"Please be patient," Muso said. "We'll reach the other
side soon."

"What!" bawled the samurai. "Me be patient? Listen here,
if you don't jump off this thing and start swimming, I
swear I'll drown you!"

The master's continued calm so infuriated the samurai
that he struck Muso's head with his iron fan, drawing blood.
Muso's disciple had had enough by this time and, as he was
a powerful man, wanted to challenge the samurai on the spot.
"I can't permit him to go on living after this," he said to the
master.

"Why get so worked up over a trifle?" Muso said with a
smile. "It's exactly in matters of this kind that the bonze's
training proves itself. Patience, you must remember, is more
than just a word." He then recited an extempore waka:

> The beater and the beaten:
> Mere players of a game
> Ephemeral as a dream.

When the boat reached shore and Muso and his disciple
got off, the samurai ran up and prostrated himself at the
master's feet. Then and there he became a disciple of the
master.

13

One winter day a masterless samurai came to Eisai's (1141–
1215, Rinzai) temple and made an appeal. "I'm poor and
sick," he said, "and my family's dying of hunger. Please help
us, master."

Eisai, whose life, dependent as he was on widows' mites,
was extremely austere, had nothing whatsoever to give the
man. He was about to send him off when he remembered the
image of Yakushi-Buddha in the hall. Going up to it, he tore

off its halo and gave it to the samurai. "Sell this," he said, "it should tide you over."

The bewildered but desperate samurai took the halo and left.

"But, master," cried one of Eisai's disciples, "it's a sacrilege! How could you have been so reckless?"

"Reckless? Bah! Have you never heard how the Chinese master Tanka (—834) burned a wooden image of the Buddha to warm himself? Surely what I've done isn't half as bad, is it? I've merely put the Buddha's mind, which is full of love and mercy, to use, so to speak. Indeed if he himself had heard that poor samurai, he'd have cut off a limb for him!"

14

Hakuju (1836– , Obaku), who had played the principal role in resuscitating, in the Meiji era, the Obaku sect, served as a distinguished lecturer at the Tendai Sect College. One hot summer afternoon as he lectured with customary zeal on the Chinese classics he noticed that a few of the students were dozing off. He stopped lecturing in midsentence and said, "It is hot, isn't it? Can't blame you for going to sleep. Mind if I join you?"

With this, Hakuju shut his textbook, and leaning well back in his chair fell asleep. The class was dumfounded, and those who had been dozing were wakened by his snores. All sat straight up in their seats and waited for the master to awaken.

15

After six months of instructing the Regent Hojo-Tokiyori in Zen, Dogen left Kamakura for his temple in Echizen, having declined to take over the temple the grateful Tokiyori had built for him. Thus he lived up to his motto that priests should have little or nothing to do with the powerful.

Soon after, one of his followers who had remained behind on business returned with a title to three thousand *kan* of land in Echizen, the gift of Tokiyori. Jubilantly he showed the title around to his fellow monks, then, full of expectation, presented it with a low bow to Dogen.

The master glanced at the title and handed it back with a scowl. "How sordid!" he said. "You know I don't preach for gain of any kind. Else why shouldn't I have accepted that fine temple in Kamakura? Those like yourself who curry favor with the great befoul the path of Buddhas and patriarchs. Your sort stains all you touch—leave this temple at once."

The monk remained speechless before Dogen, who suddenly rose and, snatching off the monk's robe, drove him away. And that wasn't all: the master had the part of the floor where the monk had sat in Zen cut away and the earth below it dug to a depth of six feet.

16

During three years of severe training under the great master Gizan, Koshu (1841–1907, Rinzai) was unable to gain satori. At the beginning of a special seven-day session of discipline, he thought his chance had finally come. He climbed the tower of the temple gate and, going up to the Arhat images, made this vow: "Either I realize my dreams up here, or they'll find my dead body at the foot of the tower!"

He went without food or sleep, giving himself up to constant zazen, often crying out in his torment things like, "What was my karma that in spite of all these efforts I can't grasp the Way?"

At last Koshu admitted his failure and, determined to make an end of it, advanced to the railing and slowly lifted a leg over it. At that very instant he had an awakening. Overjoyed, he rushed down the stairs and through the rain to Gizan's room.

"Bravo!" cried the master before Koshu had a chance to speak. "You've finally had your day!"

17

Tanzan (1819–1892, Soto), a rare master, once officiated as *indoshi* (leader) at a funeral. Facing the coffin, he formally made a great circle in the air with a firebrand. And now all the attendants awaited the customary splendid phrases. But the master's mouth was clamped shut.

Then while the attendants stared in amazement the rays of the setting sun fell directly on the master's bald head, seeming to scorch it. "Hot!" Tanzan said. "Hot! Oh hot!" He then made a slight bow to the coffin and returned to his place.

Needless to say, the attendants remained puzzled long after the coffin had been settled in the earth.

18

Ex-Emperor: Gudo, what happens to the man of enlightenment and the man of illusion after death?
Gudo (1579–1661, Rinzai): How should I know, sir?
Ex-Emperor: Why, because you're a master!
Gudo: Yes, sir, but no dead one!

19

When wolves were discovered in the village near Master Shoju's (1642–1721, Rinzai) temple, he entered the graveyard nightly for all of one week and sat in Zen. Strangely enough, that put a stop to the wolves' prowling. Overjoyed, the villagers asked him to describe the secret rites he had performed.

"I didn't have to resort to such things," he said, "nor could I have done so. While I was in zazen a number of wolves gathered around me, licking the tip of my nose, sniffing my windpipe. They did all sorts of silly things. But because I remained in the right state of mind, I wasn't bitten. As I keep preaching to you, the proper state of mind will make it possible for you to be free in life and death, invulnerable to fire and water. Even wolves are powerless against it. I simply tried to practice what I preach."

20

After gaining satori, Tenkei (1648–1735, Soto) went to see Master Tesshin. The master said, trying him, "I've been waiting for you a long time—what took you so long?"

"On the contrary," retorted Tenkei. "Why were you so late in seeing me?"

"My, you're talkative!"

"Try and stop me!"

Tesshin smiled and said no more.

21

While drinking tea with his disciple Tetsumon, Zenkoku (1670–1742, Soto) said, "The monk must be unfettered in life and death."

Seeing an opportunity to begin *mondo* (Zen questioning), Tetsumon said, "What is life?"

Zenkoku held out his hands.

"What is death?"

Zenkoku joined his hands at his chest [a Chinese salutation].

"That may be your Zen," Tetsumon said, "but it isn't mine."

Now it was the master's turn. "What is life?" he said.

Tetsumon joined his hands at his chest.

"What is death?"

Tetsumon held out his hands.

"Ha!" Zenkoku said. "But you're not very firm, are you?"

Tetsumon smiled triumphantly, got to his feet, and strode out of the room.

But it was long after that Tetsumon, regretting his hauteur, realized perfect satori.

Chapter XXVII
THE SIN XAI

This volume began with a few Jātaka tales, and so as to
bring things full circle and at the same time represent, however inadequately, one aspect of the very rich Southeast
Asian Buddhist literature, it concludes with what is essentially another, a condensed version of Pang Kham's Laotian
epic, the *Sin Xai*. To quote from the translator's introductory
notes, "Stripped to its essentials, the *Sin Xai* still remains a
Jātaka. Its basic story is that of a Bodhisattva, an earlier heroic
incarnation of a Buddha, passing through one of the stages on
his way toward enlightenment. Its main protagonists are the
Bodhisattva-hero, Sin Xai, and Mara, the 'Evil One,' here
represented in both superhuman and human form by Koum
Phan and the five younger princes respectively. In his strug-
gles with the Evil One, the Bodhisattva-hero is assisted by
Providence, represented by Pra-in (Sanscrit: Indra). The
meaning of the poem revolves around the twin doctrines of
Karma and Rebirth. Essentially it is still a parable concerning
the nature of suffering, and the steps which must be taken
in order to achieve its cessation." The history of Buddhism in
Laos is rather typical of Southeast Asian countries. Around
the eighth or ninth century A.D. both Laos and Siam (Thailand) formed part of, and were strongly influenced by the
religious conditions in Cambodia, Hinduism and Buddhism
existing side by side. About the middle of the thirteenth
century the Thais became masters of Siam and Laos, and
under their influence Theravada Buddhism and the Pāli
language, along with the Tripitaka, became dominant forces
throughout the region. Possibly because of their similarity to
native animistic stories, the Jātakas have always been popular

in Laos, and there are special collections to be found there, of which one, containing twenty-seven tales not found elsewhere, is peculiar to the country.

THE SIN XAI, AFTER THE LAO OF PANG KHAM

BOOK ONE

1. In the time when the years of Our Lord Buddha were accomplished, and the world was alive with light, there was, off a distant coast, an island, called Pèng Chane. There, among its great trees, glittered 10,000 granaries, warehouses of ivory and jade and fine linen; and high on its soft red hills rode marvelous palaces, with wind in all their sails, and delicate houses shaped like bells, inhabited by a race of dancers.

2. The ruler of this country, the Phaya Koutsālat, was much in love with gods and men. He practiced the Instructions of the Blessed, and on every eighth day observed the Ten Precepts of the Lord Buddha. At ease in his skin, in his peaceable kingdom, the Phaya, richer than any wishes, desired for nothing more than that which he had already. Each morning, his ministers assembled to discuss the affairs of the state; the merchants crowded the public squares with their goods, and the brown rivers with their gilded boats; and, in the evenings, the bird-calls of flutes and cymbals summoned the yellow monks to prayer.

3. One joy for the Phaya surpassed all others, and this was his only sister, the Nang Soumountha; for she was surely the surest love of his life, sweeter to him than the wild plum that grows only in the wind's places, in the mountain's high weather. With her, the Phaya divided the whole of his kingdom; and these two had no secrets from one another.

4. At this same time, in Anōlat, a country remoter than any star, there lived a solitary Nhak, whose name was Koum Phan, and who was one of the wisest of all the Nhak. Although Koum Phan lived like a king, surrounded by his sub-

jects and servants, in truth he lived alone, entirely to himself. Each morning he would sit mourning on his doorstep for the Unknown who was to be the darling, and the despair of his life. Because of his talents, her face was always before him. He would look into her eyes, which for him were not merely mirrors, but rooms and landscapes, in which he could see the beginning and the end; and he could tell there also how and when her days would be accomplished. With one green finger, Koum Phan wrote her name in the sand, where it bloomed like a garden: *Nang Soumounthal*

5. Then, one day, Koum Phan, knowing that the time had come for certain things to be concluded, sat back against his doorstep, and let himself be overcome with passion, and by his obscure arts came to Pèng Chane. There, beaked and gorgeously feathered, like a great bird of prey, he took Soumountha, and ravished her in front of all the people, and carried her away tucked under one wing. And all the birds, beasts, trees that for her grace and beauty did her accord were struck dumb after weeping. And the sounds of outrage clattered louder than the wind in the trees.

6. Muses! And you, gods and demigods of the four horizons, come now to my aid in this telling of the despair of the Phaya, Koutsālat, bereft of his beloved sister.

7. As he watched the Nhak sail up, and into the enormous East, beating his burning wings, life for Koutsālat ceased to have meaning. His island, that had been for him the original garden, turned wilderness, and bitter. The fruit rotted in the orchards. In the vineyards, the wine soured in the skins of the grapes. His house was as empty as his heart.

8. And so Koutsālat turned his back to his people, and gave up his throne to his first wife, and put on the yellow robes of a monk, and set out by himself to look for his sister.

9. The journey was long, the sea full of storms and wonders, the sky shipwrecked on strange beaches, the coasts bleached white as bone, the jungles burned into autumn, the roads unknown and difficult, the rice-paddies barren, the villages conjured whole out of the rock in desperation, the cities full of strangers. For three long years, Koutsālat walked

through the world, looking neither to the right nor to the left, but straight ahead, at some distant thing.

10. Until, in one burning summer, he came to a pagoda at the end of the road, and stopped walking. Behind the pagoda, which was already crumbling, the jungle was an impenetrable wall of green all the way to the horizon. Here, he had been told, was the final boundary of the world permitted to men. He could go no farther. He had come to the end, and had found nothing. He lay at the edge of the road and slept.

11. When Koutsālat awoke, it was morning. The world was all in sun's color, but for him it was the ultimate color of despair. Even the trees were in mourning. And in mourning also the seven sisters who came then out of the ruined pagoda with their arms full of alms: rice in brass bowls, prawns steamed in dry water, wheat-cakes and wild honey. Koutsālat, who had come from the beginning to the end, and who had found nothing in all that distance, looked now at the seven sisters standing before him, each more beautiful than the next, and fell instantly and completely in love.

12. As he looked into the seven faces dazzling in all their youth before him, a dream struck him. The whole world turned around him. The world was a wheel and he was its axis. That which had been white became black, and black became white. For Koutsālat, the end became the beginning; for he knew now the way to his beloved Soumountha.

13. With all haste, the Phaya returned to his kingdom. And the jungle bloomed on either side of the road, with strange flowers. The bees made constant ceremony in their courts of honey, and the elephant walked out with the tiger. Serpents with gold scales slithered across his path to make an omen. A peacock glittered on a hillside; its thousand eyes spoke a thousand colors; and, once, he thought he saw a rainbow wrap its tail around a mountain.

14. And so the Phaya, Koutsālat, came again to Pèng Chane, and presented himself to his first wife, who had been regent in his absence. And he took off his monk's robes, and put on the dress of a king. From his high throne, he directed his first wife to summon his ministers and chief

priests and all his other wives before him. When these had been assembled, the Phaya spoke to them from the throne, and said he would take the seven sisters from the ruined pagoda at the world's end to wife; and that from these he would be given a son, of great courage, surpassing in beauty, wiser than the wisest men in his kingdom. And he told them that this son would succeed where he had failed, and would find the Nang Soumountha, and wrest her from Koum Phan, and return her to Pèng Chane from the winged house of the Nhak.

15. And so it was. Messengers set out at once with trains of gifts: tapestries woven of sunlight, cages of topaz and ruby birds, boxes of sandalwood containing jewels, sweet bruised fruits, intricate perfumes, medallions of hammered gold and copper, amulets and talismans. And the messengers were received with good welcome at the pagoda at the end of the world. And the seven sisters returned with them to Pèng Chane, where they were married to the Phaya Koutsālat with much festivity and general rejoicing.

16. The seven sisters, now queens, with seven identical thrones, sat on either side of the Phaya their husband, and were waited upon by all of the Phaya's other wives, as their handmaidens. In the mornings, at noon and at evening, at first, middle and last light, the seven queens made offerings, and appealed to all the known and unknown gods that they might be blessed with the son desired by the Phaya; for they knew that Koutsālat would surely elevate to the highest position whichever of them should give him his desire. And, each day, the Phaya lay with each of the seven in turn, that this might be accomplished.

17. Two queens, the Nang Chantha and the Nang Là, were almost at once visited with favorable dreams; but in their zeal they must have managed to arouse the jealousy of heaven, for the court astrologers in unison predicted that these two queens would bring forth monsters. And indeed, after her time, the Nang Chantha was delivered of twins: a boy spiraled and soft as a snail, and a boy whose head was like an elephant's, with gold tusks. So too, in her turn, the Nang

Là delivered up into the world a magnificent gold-skinned boy, already fully armed with bow and arrows. And these names were given them: Sang Thong, or "Golden Snail"; Sihālat, which means "Elephant"; and Sin Xai, which means "He Who Will Triumph by His Virtues."

18. Immediately after these strange births, the country was visited with a number of disasters. Houses toppled like falling trees at the least breath of wind. Everywhere men and beasts were struck down by sudden lightning. A blight killed the rice still in its seed; and even the ships at sea took fire in their sails, and were lost, with all their hands and cargoes. Still full of love for his other five wives, all of whom by this time were heavy with children, Koutsālat ordered the immediate exile of the Nang Chantha and the Nang Là. And so they departed into grief, with their monstrous children in their arms, followed by the sorrow and compassion of all the people.

19. For several years, the two exiled queens wandered in the wilderness with their children: over mountains and down into valleys; at night slept cold under thin starlight; in the mornings woke to the shrieking of monkeys and gibbons; fed on dry husks and wild spices, nutmeg and cinnamon, bitter roots and the remains of birds and beasts murdered and left by the roadside. Years passed, and were forgotten, as they had been forgotten by their husband, and his people.

20. Finally, in desperation, the two queens prayed on their bony knees like two skeletons to Pra-In, All-Powerful, King of the Old Gods. For themselves, they asked nothing but death and an end to their suffering, and for their children only the barest subsistence. And Pra-In by his mercy heard them, and with one flick of his wrist created before them an astonishment, a wonder: a marvelous palace, with its roof in the trees and its foundations cut in deep rock; and with this legend inscribed over the doorway: "This is the house set apart for the sons of God."

BOOK TWO

1. Years passed, and in the secret heart of the forest the three strange brothers grew up into strength and beauty, waxing with each successive weather more graceful and more intelligent.

2. By the time they had reached their ninth year, the twins, Sihālat and Sang Thong, were already in their different ways as superior to anyone their age as most men are to monkeys; and, excellent as these two were, their half-brother, Sin Xai, was even more. Almost from the beginning he had been without equal anywhere in the world; and now, in his ninth year, standing in his golden skin, anyone could tell he was likely to outdazzle even the sun.

3. When Sin Xai slept, the world slept with him, wrapped in leaves. When he walked, whole landscapes and lithe countries moved like a music under his skin; and when he ran, it was like a summer wind in the trees. And yet, although he stood a full measure taller than either of his brothers, although his hair was blacker, his teeth whiter, and his skin the true color of gold, they were not jealous. For how could they envy him whose eyes opened like a book of light wherein all who looked must read, not his, but their own histories intensified, so that to read there was to become, in some part, a god?

4. One day, in the middle of his ninth summer, Sin Xai came to his mother where she sat dreaming under a jackfruit tree, and demanded of her the bow and arrows with which he had come, armed, into his life. In spite of his youth, he drew the great bow without difficulty, and aimed it at the sky. The bow twanged at his touch with a sound like all the bowstrings in the world singing together; so that, out of the sky's heart, where the sun rode silently, remotely on its own mysterious business, there were premonitions of thunder.

5. When the arrow sailed up, it did not stop until it had outdistanced the very air, and penetrated into the heart of the sky, which is also the country of great birds, the divine Khout.

The king of this country, the Phaya Simphali, had many years before given himself, with all of his subjects and possessions, entirely into the service of God. So, now, when the golden arrow tumbled down at his feet, like a thunderbolt returned to its source, he recognized it immediately; and at once gathered together all of his people to witness and pay homage to the sign of the All-Powerful, Pra-In, King of the clear air, best and greatest of gods.

6. And so it was that the nations of birds, led by the Phaya Simphali on his white wings, came again after long absence to the world of men. Beating down out of the sky, they descended in all their winged flocks and phantoms on the exiles' palace in the forest, and came to Sin Xai where he still stood with his bow in his hands, and knelt before him, and offered their services to help sweeten his exile.

7. Again, years passed, and the three brothers continued to grow in their gifts and talents, and in their love and admiration for each other. With the aid of the Khout, they made friends of all the inhabitants of the forest, and even became acquainted with those most remote and inaccessible of all creatures: the spirits of the river, of the wild springs and waterfalls, and those who live only in caves, and those who inhabit the smoke on the top of the mountains.

8. During all this time, in Pèng Chane, the Phaya Koutsālat never ceased to think of his beloved sister, the Nang Soumountha, and of her ravisher, the Nhak Koum Phan. When the sons of his remaining five queens from the pagoda at the end of the world had reached their thirteenth year, Koutsālat cou'd contain his impatience no longer. Summoning his five sons before him, he spoke to them severely from his high throne, and reminded them of the reason for their existence. He spoke of the long years already wasted on the wheel of becoming, and commanded them to begin their preparations immediately to find Soumountha and destroy Koum Phan. So, reluctantly, the five young princes gave up the soft employments and jeweled pastimes of the court, and ventured forth from Pèng Chane, already despairing; for who

that was merely human could be expected to accomplish such a mission?

9. For three months, the princes wandered in the endless forests on the mainland. Finally, at their wits' end, their soft limbs ripped to tatters, their bodies shrunken from lack of food and water, their long perfumed hair tangled with briars, trapped in vines, they could go no farther. Even the foot-falls of padding beasts in the thickets all around could not arouse them. They lay on their faces where they had fallen in the sharp grass, and slept.

10. When they awoke, it was evening. All around them the shadows growing longer rustled and swayed like danc-ers; or, taking the sudden shape of a beast or a bird, lum-bered or darted under the thick-leaved trees. Then, still half-asleep, they thought they heard voices in the distance, barely heard under the wind's singing. Rousing themselves with great difficulty, they set out again, without a word, towards the distant sound. This grew steadily louder as they stumbled through the vines, until suddenly they could hear it quite clearly: a choir of wings, a palaver of beaks and talons. Then, as strangely as it had begun, the sound stopped. De-spairing, the five princes made one last effort. Plunging through the green wall before them, they came into the middle of a clearing, cut, as if from stone, out of the forest's heart.

11. So, for the first time in any of their lives, all the sons of Koutsālat out of the pagoda at the world's end were brought together. Standing before their older brother, Sin Xai, who was sitting on a fallen tree, flanked by Sihālat and Sang Thong and surrounded by the shadowy Khout, the five princes were at first struck dumb with wonder. But Pra-In, who still guides men's destinies, whispered his name in their ears; and so the princes knelt before him, and greeted him as brother and peer, and recounted to him their history.

12. After listening to their story, Sin Xai gave good wel-come to his brothers, and saw that their needs were attended to, and set aside a day for festivity and general rejoicing in the palace at the secret heart of the forest. But, now that

he had learned the true reason for his existence, Sin Xai was impatient to be on his way. In spite of the protests of his mother and his aunt, therefore, by dawn on the third day after the young princes' arrival all eight brothers were already deep in the thickest part of the jungle, following the path which Sin Xai knew from a dream must finally lead them to the winged house of the Nhak.

13. Some hours later, turning a bend in the path, the brothers came suddenly upon a huge serpent, from whose open mouth ripe flames flickered dizzily, barring the way. At this, the five younger princes were terrified, and turned to run away; but Sin Xai stood taller than ever, and put his hands on his brothers' shoulders to reassure them. Taking up his great bow, he loosed against the serpent one of his golden arrows, which flew like a homing bird directly into that gaping mouthful of fires, and smashed the giant head into fragments. From these, however, seven new heads sprouted immediately, each spitting fire and belching smoke. Again Sin Xai drew his bow, and this time, with a rain of arrows, severed all seven heads entirely from the serpent's body. When the heads rolled on the ground, Sihālat jumped forward, and with his ivory tusks cut them into a hundred pieces. And so, at last, the serpent, although it still burned like all the fires in hell, was rendered impotent, incapable of any new and perhaps even more spectacular growth.

14. Their first battle won, the eight brothers continued on their way, pushing ever deeper into the forest. At night, the five younger princes slept always in the biggest tree they could find, while Sin Xai, who by this time had forgotten even the need for sleep, so completely had his quest been put upon him, paced impatiently up and down under them—until, at first light, after a meal of wild berries and honey, the journey was once again resumed.

15. After several days of this travel, the brothers came suddenly out of the trees and onto a shore where the path ended before a sea that was fully nine miles wide and so deep that there was no blue or green in its color, but only an impenetrable black, like that on the underside of a poison-leaf, or a

young bat's wing. Again, the five princes lost heart, and protested that they could go no farther; and again Sin Xai reassured them. For how, he said, can any true god's son abandon in mid-course a task which he has undertaken?

16. For three days and nights the brothers camped on the beach, staring at the black sea before them, unable to think of a way to cross it and so continue their journey. Then, on the morning of the fourth day, Sin Xai went off alone to speak to Sang Thong where he lay resting, curled under a fallen tree. Very soon after this, Sang Thong came down to the sea's edge, and, rearranging his strange body into the shape of a boat, launched himself onto the black water. Immediately, Sin Xai embarked in his brother, and commanded the others to follow; but by this time the five princes were so terrified they could not be persuaded to move. With great reluctance, therefore, Sin Xai left the five fearful princes to await his return; and with them, as guardian, he left also his beloved half-brother and sharer of his exile, Sihālat.

17. On the black sea's farther shore, even the sand was black, and the jungle extended, more black than green, without any discernible path or opening, as far as the two brothers could see. From its depths, muted echoes continually sounded, though no wind stirred the heavy leaves. Surely, Sin Xai told himself, here must originate the lost calls of Thanis, and that dark music to which all men must come, in the end. And still he did not lose heart, but followed steadily behind Sang Thong, who, once again in his own true shape, pushed onward, felling trees, to cut a road through the jungle.

18. Towards the distant mountains slowly turning gold in the falling light, between the roots of strange trees, under the swarms of birds and insects that shot as silently as arrows through the heavy air and buried themselves like nails in whatever they could find, Sin Xai followed the road his brother cut. More and more, as he moved along the edge of the world, and up into horizon, into the heart's own country, he was possessed of a strange melancholy. For how could

these paths, which seemed so brief and tenuous to the eye, come to any certain end?

19. In this state, bemused, hardly knowing or caring where the road led, Sin Xai walked steadily on. With the aid of his brother, who said nothing, but who was always there, just ahead, he crossed seven seas, each wider by nine miles than the one before it. And always the dangers increased with every halt he made. And then it began to seem to him that some action, some obscure but spectacular event, was always just about to begin; so that it was not here and now through which he walked, but a dissolving world of memories, knee-deep in dreams: of Nhaks and demons whose eyes spun like cartwheels and who dined sweetest on human flesh; of wind-spirits and creatures of the upper slopes, snow-blind and striped like tigers; of the burning mad-women of the desert; of the great bone-litter plains, and the tribes of elephants whose trumpeting made the hills shake and whose footprints were small valleys; of the leaf-eyed women who lived in trees and whose hands were brambles; of the Kinari, winged and clawfooted, sailing out of sleep, speaking his name.

20. At last and so suddenly that for a time it seemed he must still be walking in his sleep, pursued by its inhabitants, Sin Xai and Sang Thong crossed the last sea, which was 63 miles wide and surely deeper than the sky; and so entered the kingdom of Koum Phan.

BOOK THREE

1. For seven days and seven nights, Sin Xai lay where he had fallen on the shore of the last sea, and slept. Then, on the morning of the eighth day, he awoke, to find his brother, Sang Thong, whose reserves of energy seemed as inexhaustible as the springs of his heart, still watching patiently beside him. Without speaking, Sang Thong turned and started up the sea-slope behind them. There, as sheer as a wall in the early light, barring the way, a mountain rose up out of the sand to lose itself in cloud somewhere high overhead.

This, Sin Xai knew without doubting, must be Anōlat. And so they had come, at last, to the country of Koum Phan.

2. As he stood up, and took his great bow in his hand, and walked slowly up the sea-slope to the foot of the mountain, Sin Xai thought that surely his long sleep must have begun some finer change in him; for, with each step, another of the shadowy denizens of his dreams departed, as suddenly and unaccountably as they had come; and even when he stood at the top of the sea-slope, and looked up at the endless mass of rock hanging in the air above him, he was not afraid. Without a pause or backward glance, he mounted astride his brother's back, and together they rode slowly up the face of the cliff.

3. For two days and the night between, Sin Xai and Sang Thong continued to climb. All around them on the face of the cliff stone-lizards scuttled and waved their tongues; and as they rode higher, up into the true country of cloud, where the light ran like water, colonies of eagles launched threats of beak and talon from their nests between the stones.

4. Finally, on the evening of the third day, towards sunset, the two brothers rode up and over the final rim of the cliff, to see, glittering before them in the dying light, a palace, constructed more of air than of earth, holding the sunset like colors in a glass: the winged house of the Nhak!

5. Still without stopping, Sin Xai and Sang Thong rode on, straight for the great carved doors which stood wide open before them. Once inside, they found themselves in an enormous hall, whose walls and ceiling receded backward like horizons, without any perceptible end or beginning. The hall was empty, but everywhere its walls were pierced with doors; and everywhere there were more doors behind them: rooms within rooms in endless succession, and all of them empty of anyone or anything but the last light of the sun.

6. In such a place as this, any ordinary man would have been terrified, lost before he began; but Sin Xai knew that he and his brother could always find their way out again, by simply retracing the glistening snail-track left behind by Sang Thong. And so they went on, ever deeper into the laby-

rinth of rooms and passages, stairways and towers and cellars, until up and down and left and right were only words whispered to children, with no certain meaning; and direction itself ceased to matter: north, east, south and west dissolving one into another, spinning out endlessly in the silver trail behind them.

7. Until, rounding a final corner somewhere high in a tower or deep underground or perhaps halfway between, at what seemed close to the heart of the maze, the brothers came to a single, small doorway, framed in light and elaborately carved; and so found what they had come for.

8. On a high bed in a bamboo cage at the exact center of the room, sat a princess, the cracks and crumples of age beginning to show faintly through her formal mask of rice-powder and jeweled colors, wrapped in silks and gold brocades and surrounded by whistling birds: jackdaws and yellow canaries, parakeets and nightingales, birds of paradise and birds of mourning. As the brothers came riding into the room, the princess did not move, but only stared in astonishment at this strange spectacle; and all the birds took to the air at once, beating their blazing wings against the walls of the cage and screeching loudly.

9. Muses! Gods of air and water, of earth and of ashes, come once again to my aid now in this telling of the joy of the Nang, Soumountha, wrested after so many years from the winged house of the Nhak.

10. As she listened to Sin Xai's account of his adventures, of her brother the Phaya's love for her that was so constant it could reach across bottomless seas and climb a hundred mountains to find her, Soumountha looked at the room outside her bamboo cage, and felt her mask of rice-powder and jeweled colors beginning to crack; and saw that, even here, even now, the world still repeated itself in perpetual blossom; and she saw also that the air had never really stopped singing during all the years of her imprisonment.

11. And so, in this way, the prophecy of Koutsālat was accomplished. Leaving the bamboo cage shattered behind them from one touch of his great bow, Sin Xai climbed with

Soumountha onto Sang Thong's broad back; and they rode
among whistling birds back through all the thousand rooms
and passages, following the snail-track to the great hall and
so out into a morning world flooded with sunlight.

12. After hiding the Nang safely in a grotto just over the
edge of the cliff, Sin Xai and Sang Thong returned to the
palace; for they knew they could not hope to run quickly
enough to escape the wrath of the Nhak, which would surely
shake the sky itself when Koum Phan returned home to find
Soumountha gone. And so it was. No sooner had they come
again to the entrance to the palace than there before them,
huger and greener than any tree, stood the ravisher, Koum
Phan, King of all the Nhak. Immediately, a sorcery jumped
out of his eye, and a dream struck the two brothers. Behind
them, the palace burst into flame; and Koum Phan held a
hurricane in each fist. To Sin Xai, fixed in the sudden spell, all
the half-remembered shadows of his sleep returned, hands
and feet clawed like parrots, clutching many knives. But then
he shook his head, shedding the spell as a tree sheds leaves,
and drew his great bow, and laughed derisively up at Koum
Phan; and so the battle commenced.

13. Out of the burning palace poured endless swarms of
the Nhak, with ripped and bloody tongues lolling, and fire
blossoming at ears, eyes and mouths. When they saw Sin
Xai, they were greatly astonished, and laughed to themselves
at the spectacle of such a child, scarcely out of his cradle,
daring to offer them battle. Then they hurled themselves into
the air, and transformed themselves into all sorts of curious
beasts, but neither Sin Xai nor Sang Thong were afraid. The
brothers stood firm in the face of the attack, and their calm was
equalled only by their courage. Sin Xai drew his great bow
without ceasing, sending arrow after arrow into the shrieking
horde; and Sang Thong was everywhere at once, spinning
like a ball, murderous and insatiable, welcoming each new
attack like a fond lover.

14. Despite the great toll the brothers took, however, so
that the dead lay heaped high all about them, they were only
two against a host which seemed to multiply rather than

diminish with its dead. Then, when finally it seemed that they must surely be overcome, buried under the sheer weight of uncountable numbers of the Nhak, they heard, high above the noise of the battle, a sound as of all the birds in the world singing together. For a moment the fighting ceased, as everyone peered up at the sky in amazement and wonder. In the sudden silence the singing grew steadily louder—until, plummeting down out of the sun, beaks and talons flashing, there came a great company of the Khout, led by the Phaya Simphali on his huge white wings. Falling on the Nhak like hawks on snakes, the Khout slashed and ripped and tore without ceasing, until all the terrible captains of the Nhak were struck down. Finally, Koum Phan himself, using the dead for stepping-stones, came down to meet the golden arrow kept especially for him; and with him fell the last defense of his kingdom.

15. When the brothers had expressed their gratitude and said their farewells to the Khout, who flew off the way they had come, into the eye of the sun, they returned to the grotto where they had left Soumountha; and the three of them made their way back down the cliff. Then, at the request of the Nang, they set off in a new direction: towards the kingdom of water, of the Naga, in order to liberate Soumountha's daughter, the Nang Chanh, who some years before had been given in marriage by Koum Phan to the Phaya Lounvālat, ruler of that country.

16. As they walked, low fields and paddies shimmered all around them. Occasional clumps of young bamboo moved languidly, as though from slow currents underwater; and from their branches strange animals, half snake and half bird, with blue-green and silver scales and fine-webbed wings, called softly to them as they passed. Except for these, however, they saw nothing and no one in all the liquid flat distances around them. Until, after they had been walking for the better part of a day, the watery mists began to thin; and in the sudden wet sunlight they saw before them the river and the water palace of Lounvālat, Lord of the Naga.

17. Because the Phaya, Lounvālat, was a great king, who

ruled with justice and propriety over all that country of water
which lies between the mountains and the sea, he welcomed
Soumountha, the mother of his queen, and his queen's cousins,
Sin Xai and Sang Thong, with great ceremony; and provided
them with every comfort, and gave them the freedom of his
country. When he learned that they had come to take the
Nang Chanh from him, however, his temper turned; for the
Nang was his greatest treasure, worth more to him than all
the fine gold and flocks and jade ornaments he possessed; and
he knew he could not part from her and continue to live.

18. Since the Phaya had been kind to them, and had had
them to dine at his own high table, Sin Xai and Sang Thong
did not wish to do him any harm; but Soumountha was
adamant, and refused to return to Pèng Chane without her
beloved daughter. And she berated Sin Xai in front of his
brother for not immediately using his god's gifts to secure
the release of the Nang Chanh, and accused him of having
turned coward, and would not stop from weeping.

19. At last, in desperation, Sin Xai gave in to his aunt's
beseeching, and concocted a ruse by which he hoped to gain
possession of the Nang Chanh without having to engage in
open warfare with his host. That night, after supper, sitting
at the high table with Lounvālat and his chief ministers and
courtiers, Sin Xai challenged the Phaya, as a jest, to a drinking contest, which was accepted amidst much joking and
general amusement. For many hours, the beakers and flagons
were kept continually full to overflowing, and the wine ran
like green sap, singing loudly in the veins of the Phaya and
all that company. Finally, in the early hours, with his courtiers
and ministers drunk and asleep all around him, and only Sin
Xai left to still match him, draught for draught, Lounvālat began to nod drowsily, and his eyes glazed, and he too fell asleep
with his head in his arms. Immediately thereafter, Sin Xai,
staggering under the weight of the wine, came to where the
Nang Chanh lay sleeping in another part of the palace. Dis-
regarding her protests, for she was much in love with the
Phaya, the young lord of the Wheel took her to where
Soumountha and Sang Thong waited outside the palace.

And immediately they all rode off on Sang Thong's back, away from the sleeping palace of the Naga, back towards the place where they had left Sihālat and the five younger princes waiting on the farther shore of the black sea.

20. The following morning, when Lounvālat awoke from his drunken sleep and found his guests departed, and with them his beloved Chanh, he was consumed with despair. Although he immediately sent off soldiers in pursuit, he knew beforehand that they would be unsuccessful; for who were they to overcome the hero of Anōlat, conqueror of the Nhak, favored of Pra-In? And indeed, when they returned, they were empty-handed. And a shadow came with them, and moved across the country of water. And the jewels of the Naga, which were the lights of their eyes, began to go out, one by one. And the drowned gold lost its lustre. And very soon thereafter, as the watch-fires steamed on the water, and the brown fog arose, announcing disaster, the Phaya, alone in his room, fell into a melancholy which no amusements could assuage; and thence into a strange sickness, from which not even the most famous of his astrologers or physicians were able to rouse him.

BOOK FOUR

1. During all this time, on the farther shore of the dead-black sea, the five younger sons of Koutsālat grew steadily fatter and sleeker on the wild grapes and game which Sihālat provided for them out of the forest's abundance. Although they did not look forward to the return of Sin Xai, for whom, in their jealousy, they secretly wished only death or disaster, the idle weeks of waiting made them long for anything that should break the monotony. And so they became increasingly more impatient with the world and one another, and spent their time bickering or sulking; and for amusement they took to spitting out insults and imprecations like grape seeds in every direction.

2. So, now, when Sin Xai and the two Nangs, Soumountha and Chanh, came riding in Sang Thong out of the sea, they

were met with much excitement and rejoicing; and the cele-
brations lasted far into the night on the farther shore of the
dead-black sea.

3. In a very short time, however, the five younger princes
realized that when they should come again to Pèng Chane,
Sin Xai would be hero indeed, crowned with vines and flowers, and idolized by all the people; while they would be lucky
if they were only scorned and laughed at. And so they began
to plot and scheme among themselves, searching for some
means of taking for themselves the triumph that was their
brother's by right. And their secrets bubbled blackly up inside
them, and spilled out onto the ground, like swamp water. And
they put on claws in their minds.

4. Very soon after this, the five younger princes, setting off
to bathe by themselves in a river they knew of nearby, in
the mountains, invited Sin Xai to accompany them. He accepted the invitation gladly, and Sihālat and Sang Thong also
went with them. There, in the warm brown shallows, the
eight brothers splashed and laughed at their games, playing
Touch and Tag-me, and pretending they were fish grown
too large for their homes.

5. Suddenly, in the midst of these games, the five younger
brothers hoisted Sin Xai onto their shoulders; and laughing
and singing a hero's song they carried him out of the river
and up onto a precipice that ran along its other side. There,
while Sihālat and Sang Thong were looking in another
direction, squirting themselves and sporting like two curious
beasts in the water, the five treacherous princes caught Sin
Xai fast by his golden wrists and ankles; and before he knew
what they were about hurled him like a stone over the edge
of the cliff.

6. As Sin Xai vanished from sight into the cool shadows
that lapped at the edge of the cliff, the five princes cried
aloud, and tore their hair, and hugely wept, beating their
fists against the stones and calling on high heaven to witness
the terror of a hero's death.

7. And thus it was that Sihālat, rushing from the river, was
persuaded of his brother's death by the tumult of his other

brothers' grief; and by so doing lost the power of his elephant's eyes, that once made midnight morning, and cut
through solid rock. Despair struck him blind. Black midnight
bit his tongue. The shadow opened its mouth, and the dark
swallowed him.

8. Although Sang Thong also was at first stricken with
grief at the disaster that had befallen them, being calmer
by nature, his first thought was to comfort Sihālat. Being
also possessed of more faith than many, as well as an inclination towards silence (which is only the other side of truth),
he began to question the five princes closely in the midst of
their lamenting.

9. Sang Thong's calm and rationality touched his brother
Sihālat strongly; so that he came out from the shadows and
saw that, whatever had happened, the sun still shone, the
leaves still sang, and the water still ran warm in the brown
shallows. And Sang Thong spoke to Sihālat then, and said
he did not believe that Sin Xai was dead; for how could
such an ordinary thing as death happen to one who walked in
light, sheltered by the white parasol of God? And so the two
brothers, Sihālat and Sang Thong, their faith restored, set off
in search of their beloved brother.

10. Immediately after the departure of Sihālat and Sang
Thong, the five princes, elated, alight with the delight of evil
accomplished, returned to the place where Soumountha and
Chanh awaited their return. There they recounted to them
the circumstances of the unhappy accident of which, they
said, their beloved brother, Sin Xai, had been victim. When
the two women finally ran out of tears, and their wailing
had turned to wondering what should, alas, befall them,
now that their protector was dead, the princes urged that
they should all leave immediately for Pèng Chane; for
what, they said, would be accomplished by waiting longer,
since not even an important god could restore green life to
the dead?

11. Before she would consent to go, however, the Nang
Soumountha insisted that she be taken to the place where
the hero had fallen, that she might offer up prayers and sup-

plications for his deliverance. And when they took her,
she stood for a long time on the edge of the cliff, looking
down into emptiness. And as she left she placed two objects
sacred to the old gods under a cairn of stones on the cliff: a
royal turban woven of gold and silver threads, and an ancient loin-cloth of gold leather, that had belonged to a god in
the days of the world's youth. By these tokens, the princess
said, would the hero of Anōlat make himself known, when he
should come again into his life.

12. During the journey back to Pèng Chane, which was
long and lost, and whose most constant companions were
terror and the death of hope, the five princes, borne up by
the remembrance of evil, played upon the frayed strings of
the women, pretending astonishment at their laments for a
dead hero—who, they said, had never existed except in the
country of madness and diseased imagination. Were the
princesses so loath to return to their rightful and beloved
lord, they said, that they wished to abandon all true memory
of the means by which their deliverance had been secured?

13. And so, in this way, the journey was accomplished.
Despite the dark, light at the end of the road finally opened.
And the Nang Soumountha was returned at last to Pèng
Chane from the winged house of the Nhak. And the wind-bells
rang for joy in all the houses perched on stilts on the hills
overlooking the city. Even the trees looked like dancers. And
the Phaya, Koutsālat, in the midst of his age, came into
blossom.

14. Leading all the general rejoicing, at the center of every
celebration, the five princes were regaled with gifts and
honors. They were made to tell their heroic tales over and
over again, and crowned with iron crowns. No one tired of
staring at them as they sat in fabulous state beside the
Phaya their father. Despite the penalties, there was speculation in every house as to which of them should succeed to the
throne when the Phaya went at last, as he must, to his
fathers; and even the aristocrats fought with each other like
wild animals over the princes' least relic, from the hem of a
skirt to a morsel of gold-dust from one of their collars.

15. After the excitement had somewhat abated, and Soumountha was finally left alone for a time with her brother, she recounted to him for the first time the true history of her rescue from the Nhak, and of the events leading to the death of his lost son, Sin Xai. Koutsālat, however, had already been warned by the five princes that this might transpire; and had been told that Soumountha's suffering at the hands of Koum Phan, and later, during the terrible return journey through the wilderness, had almost certainly affected the balance of her mind; and that this had served to infect the mind of her daughter also. And so, although out of his great love he made every effort to comfort and calm her, he would not believe her story, and would take no action against his five hero sons.

16. Some time after this, an unknown merchant was brought before the Phaya as he sat in his judging seat in the room of thrones, with the Nang Soumountha beside him. And when the Phaya commanded the merchant to present his suit, he bowed without speaking, and drew forth from a satchel that he had with him two objects; and he came up to the throne and put them down at the Phaya's feet, and drew back without speaking. And Soumountha, seeing them, cried out and said, *Behold, the god is come again into his own country.* And Koutsālat saw before him the royal turban and the loin-cloth of a god which Soumountha had left in the cairn on the cliff-edge. And he knew the truth. And he rose to seek the merchant, but he had vanished.

17. Now the anger of the Phaya was greatly aroused; and he was terrible, and splendid. And he caused the brazen trumpets to be sounded, and the drums of strong hide. And he summoned his ministers, and chief priests, and all his wives before him, and commanded that his five sons be stripped of their iron crowns and honors and brought in chains to him, that he might pass judgement. And he instructed his bowmen to loose their strings. When the five princes were brought to him, as he had commanded, he showed them the god's relics and asked if they knew them. And they did. And they fell on their faces before him. And the bowmen took up their

strings and dispatched them there, in the room of thrones to which they had aspired. And the joy of Soumountha was terrible, and splendid.

18. Immediately after these events, the Phaya, at the head of a great train, with Soumountha by his side and his bowmen before him, set off from Pèng Chane in search of his lost son. As he went, the people came out in crowds to salute him. Everywhere he was bombarded with flowers. The trees bowed low as he passed, and dropped their leaves to make a path before him. And even the wildest animals of the jungle, elephant and snake and tiger, stood by the side of the path and paid him homage.

19. Because of his courage and justice, long suffering led him to wisdom. And Pra-In, out of his mercy, set an omen to guide him: a dazzling white crane with yellow beak and wings tipped with fire, sign of the All-Powerful, King of the Gods. And Koutsālat, following the crane, came in procession to the palace at the secret heart of the forest. And there he found Sin Xai, restored to life by Pra-In, his golden body sheathed in a great light and blazing as with a thousand thousand jewels. On either side, bathed in the light, sat Sang Thong and Sihālat; and at his feet knelt his mother, the Nang Là, and his aunt, the Nang Chantha. And the Phaya raised up the wives he had abandoned, and who thereby had come to greatness, and himself knelt at his son's feet and asked for his blessing. And during all this time the Khout never stopped singing.

20. And so it was that Sin Xai, heaven-hero, keeper of his father's promise, king and magician, splendid as a young god in the world's morning, returned at last to his own country. And they put on him the royal turban of gold and silver threads, and the loin-cloth of gold leather, that had belonged to a god. And it was fitting, for he had shown without doubt that he had the true blood of God in him.